STACK AND SWAY

STACK
AND SWAY

*The New Science of
Jury Consulting*

NEIL J. KRESSEL
AND **DORIT F. KRESSEL**

Westview
PRESS

A Member of the Perseus Books Group

Copyright © 2004 by Westview Press, A Member of the Perseus Books Group

Published in the United States of America by Westview Press, A Member of the Perseus Books Group, 5500 Central Avenue, Boulder, Colorado 80301–2877, and in the United Kingdom by Westview Press, 12 Hid's Copse Road, Cumnor Hill, Oxford OX2 9JJ.

Find us on the world wide web at www.westviewpress.com

Westview Press books are available at special discounts for bulk purchases in the United States by corporations, institutions, and other organizations. For more information, please contact the Special Markets Department at the Perseus Books Group, 11 Cambridge Center, Cambridge, MA 02142, or call (617) 252–5298, (800) 255-1514 or email special.markets@perseusbooks.com.

A Cataloging-in-Publication data record for this book is available from the Library of Congress.
ISBN 0-8133-4241-4

The paper used in this publication meets the requirements of the American National Standard for Permanence of Paper for Printed Library Materials Z39.48–1984.

10 9 8 7 6 5 4 3 2 1

In memory of

Morris Kressel
(1912–2000)

Warren Fuchs
(1922–1988)

CONTENTS

1

AMERICA'S WAGER ON THE JURY

THE GREAT NEW ORLEANS
RAIL YARD FIRE

IF YOU DO NOT RECALL the Great New Orleans Rail Yard Fire of 1987,
you are not alone. Nobody died and, in contrast to most other disasters,
few people—if any—suffered serious injuries. Property damage was minimal. In the wee hours of September 9, a railcar leaked its volatile cargo of
butadiene, a petroleum product used to make synthetic rubber backings
for carpets. The tanker had been parked since 7:35 P.M. on tracks in the
lower-middle-class section of Gentilly, not far from the historic French
Quarter. Butadiene fumes spread across the neighborhood until they
reached the pilot light of an outdoor gas-fired water heater. At about 2:00
A.M., the chemical ignited and, before the fire burned out thirty-six hours
later, several thousand people had been temporarily evacuated from their
homes. It soon became clear why the unfortunate incident had occurred.
Phillips Petroleum, owner of the railcar until a year earlier, had installed a
rubber gasket on the tanker instead of the appropriate asbestos one. Unfortunately, from the perspective of those contemplating a lawsuit,
Phillips stood immune from any punitive damages under Louisiana law.[1]

Nonetheless, a large number of Gentilly residents sought compensation
for their inconvenience and suffering. They filed a class-action lawsuit
against nine defendants including CSX Transportation, a deep-pocketed
corporation that owned the tracks beneath the leaky tanker. Other defendants included the company that arranged the shipment, the one that

moved the railcar into the neighborhood, and the one that loaded it with butadiene. In the opinion of the National Transportation Safety Board, CSX bore no responsibility for the accident.

The jury that eventually heard the class-action suit apparently disagreed. It slammed the corporate giant with $2.5 billion in punitive damages. Nearly $1 billion more was added for the other defendants, bringing the total punitive sum to a whopping $3.4 billion.

The Louisiana Supreme Court quickly blocked the verdict from taking effect until the injuries sustained by all 8,000 plaintiffs could be evaluated. Later, the trial court reduced CSX's tab from $2.5 billion to $850 million, finding that the jury's verdict shocked the conscience "for reasons too numerous to cite."[2]

Still, many observers are left wondering how the jury could have arrived at its verdict in the first place. After all, even the plaintiffs' lawyers agreed that no medical evidence established conclusively that the fire had caused the plaintiffs' alleged symptoms (complaints ranging from irritated eyes to lung damage). Several years earlier, Union Carbide had paid what, in contrast, seems like a piddling sum—$470 million—for its more central role in the 1984 Bhopal, India, chemical disaster, an incident that resulted in more than 3,000 deaths and caused injuries to more than 200,000 people.[3] How could jurors in New Orleans have arrived at more than seven times that figure for a fire that resulted in, at most, relatively minor injuries?

Lawyers for the Gentilly residents had apparently hit on the perfect argument: environmental racism. They suggested that tankers containing highly inflammable and poisonous chemicals had deliberately been stored in poor, predominantly black neighborhoods where residents had little money or political clout. Sidney Barthelemy, the mayor of New Orleans at the time of the fire, gave testimony in support of this position. During the trial, he reported that the railroad had formerly parked its tankers in the French Quarter. City officials persuaded them to relocate the cars and believed that the new location would be a nonresidential area. He also told the jury that he was forced to shout and curse at CSX officials during the fire because the company initially had refused to assume responsibility and help out. After the verdict, Wendell Gauthier, one of the plaintiffs' lawyers, voiced the emotion behind the jury's decision: "These scoundrels, they took the position that there's nobody back there worth caring about, they're all black, they're all poor and nobody cares about them. If it was your family out there, would you feel the verdict was outrageous?"[4]

All twelve jurors were black. They voted 11-1 to hold CSX accountable. The one dissenting juror, Lula Ladmirault, a sixty-year-old day-care center employee, complained: "None of the people were sick—had any long-term illness. [For] most of them, the biggest thing [they experienced] was fear and fright. . . . The punishment should fit the crime, that's the way I feel. To me, it was just a bunch of people being greedy— a bunch of lawyers and people being greedy."[5]

But the other jurors disagreed with her. Nearly all thought that the defendants should have taken greater precautions to protect people living in the area. Juror Kimbra Whitney was persuaded that the defendants had not shown adequate regard for the safety and comfort of Gentilly's residents.[6] Alvin Parker, a fifty-six-year-old cab driver, gave reporters his view on why the tankers were stored in Gentilly: "I would think [the company's motivation] was racial because it was a black neighborhood."[7] About half of the jurors shared his belief.

The jury wanted to send a message to the large corporations, and they believed they had to make the award large enough to sting. McKinley Day, a retired chief petty officer in the navy, said, "We felt if we hit them [with] a good, big whop, they'll do something—they'll stop parking those toxic chemical cars in the residential areas." If jurors had awarded only a few million dollars, he argued, "They'd just say, 'We got that. We can pay that out of petty cash and forget about it.'" Day supported the large award even though he, like some of the other jurors, did not go along with the racism argument.[8]

Discussing the New Orleans award, a *Wall Street Journal* editorial objected that each similar case "encourages fee-hungry plaintiff's lawyers to chase crazier and crazier cases, and it encourages companies to settle, no matter how outrageous the claim, if only to avoid having to play Russian roulette in court".[9] And the editorial writers at *The Times-Picayune* (New Orleans) worried that "the message that is . . . likely to stick unfortunately is that Louisiana is a risky place to do business."[10] Srill, McKinley

Day might simply be on target regarding what it takes to change the policies of large corporations. Plainly, this case was not entirely about race. And had a few more jurors shared the attitudes and perceptions of Lula Ladmirault, the outcome might have been much different.

Whatever its final disposition, the CSX case demonstrates the tremendous power vested by the United States in a jury of common citizens and, for that matter, in each individual citizen sitting on that jury. That power, for better or worse, constitutes one of the cornerstones of the American judicial system.

It is a power that frequently makes attorneys and their clients tremble.

IMPROVING THE ODDS IN COURT

Attorney John Kidd was not about to take any unnecessary chances. His client's case did not resemble the CSX lawsuit in any of its particulars, and he had no reason to expect a hostile jury. But his client, the defendant in a patent infringement case, could still lose—and lose big. Six hundred million dollars lay on the line. This case was not apt to arouse the same passions as one stemming from a careless chemical fire in a poor neighborhood. But, as always, success would depend largely on how a group of more or less disinterested people would react to his carefully crafted and elegantly presented arguments.[11]

No stranger to big-money cases, Kidd is a partner and top litigator in the New York office of the prestigious firm of Clifford Chance Rogers & Wells. A big man, probably in his sixties, he comes across as somewhat jovial, with a hint of a smile on his face. Indeed, this smile figured prominently in one of his early encounters with Phil Anthony and Decision-Quest, the jury consulting firm he regularly engages. In Anthony's research conducted during the mid-1980s, a few mock jurors had expressed annoyance with Kidd, saying he seemed too nonchalant and smiled too much. Kidd explains, "I happen to have a natural smile curve to my face, and I never thought about it, nor did anybody else. But what was happening was that jurors thought that I wasn't serious enough about the case. . . . I tried to get, I don't know how to express that on tape, more of a glum face, I guess. I don't know how successful it was but I, ever since then, for the last fifteen years . . . I've had more of a glum-looking face. I try not to look too happy. It all came out of this research." Later he amends his self-description: "Not glum—solemn-looking."[12] Kidd, of course, knows that details like this often have no consequence for the outcome of a case. But one can never be too certain, and he values his relationship with Anthony, in part because of the consultant's ability to identify such details.

DecisionQuest is probably the biggest trial consulting company in the nation, possessing some of the oldest lineage in the field. Whether it is the best, of course, is open to debate, for in this profession everyone claims primacy for one reason or another. Still, few (if any) firms have handled as many cases as DecisionQuest. And Kidd knows that they have probed, scrutinized, and prognosticated about juries for hundreds of intellectual property cases alone. But he does not need to be sold. He is a believer.

By one count, this was going to be the twenty-second time that Anthony's firm had conducted a focus group, mock trial, or other study in connection with this one patent infringement case. By another count, this would be the thirtieth time. DecisionQuest had started working on the case about a year earlier. Some of the early studies were informal. There had been quickie focus groups and half-day sessions, but this was the big event—a full-blown mock trial intended to last four or five days.

The grand ballroom of the Hyatt hotel had been partitioned into several rooms, one of which was designated the courtroom. A retired judge presided over the proceedings. As in a real courthouse, he sat somewhat higher than the other participants. An American flag adorned the room, lending solemnity to the occasion. There were also various pieces of audiovisual equipment, as are often found in modern, high-tech courtrooms. If participants in a mock trial are to act—and react—as they would in a real trial, consultants must re-create the scene as realistically as possible.

There is no point in winning a mock trial. The goal is to learn everything you can about what sells your case and what sells your opponent's case. Lawyers acting the part of opposing counsel feel extra pressure to get it right, to present all of the opposition's strongest arguments with genuine enthusiasm—and without ever tipping their secret preference to the mock jurors.

"If I'm going to do this and I'm going to spend all this god-damned money, we're going to do it the right way," Kidd explains. "The more real you make it, the better your results are. If you cut corners, if you do it halfway, you're going to get a halfway result. What we do is create a real courtroom, a real courtroom atmosphere. We act as if it *is* the courtroom. And that's the only way. Then, often, the results have some legitimacy."[13]

Preparation for the event took about six weeks. Seventy mock jurors took part in the trial. As they listened to attorneys and evidence, they transmitted their level of agreement with what was being said from a special handheld device. Every minute or so they would push buttons on a keypad numbered zero to nine, with nine indicating the greatest agreement. A monitor in a nearby observation room displayed their input as five graphs superimposed over video images fed from the courtroom. Each graph meant something different. The top line commanded the most attention; this graph represented the combined views of the so-called "plaintiff" jurors—those presumed to support the opposing side's perspective. These people were most important to the defense because they were the ones who had to be convinced. Later, when the jurors were divided into groups to deliberate, attorneys and consultants could observe their reactions to every facet of the case. Which arguments did they like? Which events evoked the strongest responses? The consultants had divided them into six groups, each designed to resemble a jury that would be representative of the venue where the case would be tried. Every word uttered as the jurors pored over the evidence was videotaped so the trial team could revisit the results again and again as they crafted and tailored their presentation. Each subsequent study incorporated information gleaned assiduously from prior research.

Anthony explains: "What clients hire us to do is to help them systematically prepare the case at all levels. . . . [In this case] we've investigated everything from case theories to what kind of witnesses to select and how to use them and what they ought to focus on in their testimony. We've designed all the demonstrative exhibits. It's a complete systematic approach."[14] Jury consultants are best known to the public for their guidance in selecting juries, and Anthony often assists with that. But his contribution to a case, he maintains, goes way beyond picking panel members. And the other services his firm provides, especially the development of case strategy, can exert far more impact on a verdict.

Trial consultants often come with six-figure price tags, and seven figures are not unheard of. What do clients purchase for such hefty sums? In the case described here, Anthony reports that when DecisionQuest first began conducting juror studies, panel members were voting 80 percent to 20 percent against his client. According to Anthony, at this stage in the project, similar jurors were running 65 percent to 35 percent *in favor*. Still, these figures are not the result of scientifically controlled and independently reviewed evaluation research. There is no way of knowing the extent to which they are contaminated by self-interest, self-deception, and other factors.

Would Anthony's client win his case? Perhaps. Maybe the case was unwinnable, no matter what, or maybe the case was winnable even without a pricey consultant. With such high stakes, the other side was probably conducting its own jury studies, and it was possible that the consultants would neutralize each other's impact. Maybe, by doing a little bit more, DecisionQuest could learn something decisive that the other side overlooked. This is why Kidd placed his bet on a trial consultant in the first place and why the consulting industry exists. Consultants clearly benefit from the arrangement. Lawyers and their clients also may benefit.

But what about our system of justice?

THE AMERICAN JURY UNDER ASSAULT

Perhaps no principle of American justice has been more valued than the right to trial by an impartial jury. Yet during the past decade, many Americans—inside and outside the legal profession—have voiced concern that the constitutional guarantee of an objective and fair jury may be little more than an unrealized, and even unrealizable, myth. In the eyes of an increasing number of Americans, *who* serves on the jury matters at least as much as what the jurors see and hear at trial. One critic of the jury system harshly complains, "No one in his senses would entrust an important decision in his life—where to live, what job to apply for, whether to have an operation, what shares to buy—to a random sample of twelve people, and yet we place our system of criminal justice in their uncertain hands. In some districts, no doubt, the jurors are above average, but in others they are stupid, feckless, illiterate, and felonious in thought and undetected deed."[15] And many observers have come to see wisdom rather than hyperbole in the famous admonition attributed to defense attorney Clarence Darrow: "Never forget, almost every case has been won or lost when the jury is sworn."[16]

More than a few would go farther, agreeing with Albert Osborn—a quirky but insightful critic of the jury system—who lamented in 1937 that ". . . the most important work of certain attorneys in all criminal cases, as well as in many civil cases, is not the presentation of evidence, but the finding in advance of only one or two jurors of the kind they desire. In many . . . trials, it is not twelve men who defeat justice but only one or two men."[17] Objecting that the jury system invites decisionmaking by those ill-suited to the task, Osborn argued,

> In considering the various qualifications for jury duty it is necessary to give attention to more than the amount of the education of the candidates. . . . The degree of general intelligence and the amount of common sense and experience in practical affairs also are important elements in the qualifications of the juror. . . . When a jury is selected from a panel taken from a community after twenty classes of its busiest and best qualified citizens are first excluded, and then from a particular jury panel after many of the most intelligent and experienced candidates have been intentionally 'excused,' by peremptory challenges, by the attorney against the fact in a civil case, or by the attorney for a guilty defendant in a criminal case, it is safe to say that the jury as finally made up includes some thirteen-year-old minds.[18]

Although Osborn's frank and roughly stated elitism strikes a dissonant chord on contemporary ears, his complaint gets to the heart of what many current critics have in mind when they criticize jury verdicts. Similar objections have been heard more frequently in recent years. For example, New York State Supreme Court Judge Harold Rothwax argued that a defense attorney typically "will seek jurors who will not or cannot intelligently evaluate evidence. He will want gullible, manipulable, emotional, suggestible jurors—and through our system of selection he will get them."[19]

For most critics, this loss of confidence in jury objectivity (and the jury selection system) is tinged with sadness and regret. It is, above all, a reaction to a series of recent and controversial cases that the public has witnessed in heretofore unprecedented detail. The list of trials for which the jury has drawn criticism includes the William Kennedy Smith rape case, the first Menendez brothers murder trial, the Lemrick Nelson (Crown Heights) trial, the trials of the Los Angeles officers accused of brutalizing Rodney King, the case against Damian Williams and others for assaulting Reginald Denny, the civil and criminal trials of O.J. Simpson, the Louise Woodward (nanny) trial, the $3.4 billion New Orleans fire verdict, the McDonalds' hot coffee case, and many others.

There is nothing new about divisive and dramatic trials. Throughout American history, and particularly during the twentieth century, certain cases have captured the public imagination and polarized the nation. Jury verdicts in such cases please some observers and enrage others. But in the past, those who did not attend courthouse proceedings at least had to acknowledge jurors' far greater familiarity with the evidence and the testimony. These days, cameras in the courtroom, Court TV, and televised posttrial interviews with jurors combine to deprive the jury system of some of its purported sanctity and inherent mystique.

Now, American citizens can hear and observe evidence that previously had been presented only to the judge, jury, and a handful of participants and observers. We see attorneys fomenting confusion and stoking the flames of bigotry. We listen to jurors explaining their reasoning once a case has ended. As a result, whatever biases and incompetencies jurors possess become harder to ignore, and the jury's role as arbiter of truth has come under assault.

The most frequent charge is that jury deliberations are unduly influenced by the demographic background of the jurors. Justice and law require cases to be decided objectively—on the evidence and nothing more. The concern is that such factors as the race, gender, ethnicity, age, wealth, and marital status of jurors may prejudice them beyond repair. The personality, beliefs, and intelligence of jurors are also portrayed as sources of bias that may lead to unjust verdicts. Jury reformers have suggested several alternatives to the contemporary jury system, some calling for highly qualified "blue-ribbon" juries to decide complex civil cases, others seeking to eliminate juries altogether and vest power entirely in the hands of judges. Still others have called for panels of trained, "professional" jurors guided closely by judges. The United States, they note, is the only major democracy that places so much legal clout in the fists of the common citizen. It seems only reasonable to question whether the typical juror is up to the task.

The courts, after all, demand much of jurors. Plucked from job, family, and social support, the panel member is expected to show complete impartiality, or what the U.S. Supreme Court has called a "mental attitude of appropriate indifference."[20] Although the courts have suggested various tests for determining when someone meets this standard, the basic goal is for jurors to approach cases free of bias or, at least, with a willingness to suppress whatever biases they may possess. They are also expected to share the agendas of the legal system and—most important—to follow all relevant laws, even when they disagree. Jurors are instructed to stick to this high standard, even while highly trained and clever lawyers take home paychecks for doing whatever they can to arouse emotion and prejudice.

If jurors somehow manage to steer clear of these impediments, they must then complete a formidable intellectual task in an atmosphere that is often emotionally charged, sifting through and dissecting a large body of evidence, testimony, and argument to determine the facts. This may involve detecting dishonesty and prevarication in those who are highly skilled in such matters. Even the very brightest and most perceptive of jurors—those who succeed at many other complex assignments in life—face an additional handicap, for they must apply their information-processing capabilities in a context that almost invariably is new. Once the panel member has arrived at an accurate understanding of the case, he or she may have to stand up to less capable or less scrupulous members of the jury panel. Sometimes, pressures to decide the case one way or another can emanate from the community outside the courtroom as well. A juror's failure at any step might result in a serious miscarriage of justice.

Even though exceptional people can and will carry out their civic duty in accordance with the system's high expectations, it is implausible that all panels will meet this burden. When one juror has veto power, as is often the case, individual limitations become limitations of the jury as a whole. Thus, in evaluating our justice system, we might ask not whether juries ever fail but rather how often, to what extent, and with what consequences.

Some observers, like Harvard scholar Henry Louis Gates Jr., suggest that it is a mistake "to think that the citizen jury was ever meant to be the most efficient and reliable possible means of determining guilt or innocence."[21] One might acknowledge the inferiority of the jury as a means of unearthing truth yet still defend the institution on other grounds. For example, historically, one purpose of the jury was to serve as a protection against unjust intrusions of governmental tyranny into the lives of everyday people. The jury system also ensures that laws remain marginally comprehensible to the average person. Although hard to imagine, the nation's laws might be even more impenetrable had they been written solely for lawyers and judges who would never need to translate them for a panel of jurors. And many have defended the jury system as a school for democracy and a manifestation of self-government. But all of these arguments for the jury system seem hollow if juries cannot deliver just verdicts regularly.

The jury, as many writers have observed, is a profoundly democratic institution. Professor Jeffrey Abramson, a passionate defender of the jury system, calls the jury's democratic gamble "striking in comparison with the hedged bet that most of our institutions of representative democracy make on the people."[22] Whatever role the public plays by voting, contributing, marching, or petitioning, most key decisions are made by a small elite of political leaders. With the jury, this is not so. In the jury room, democracy is most direct and, one would expect, most subject to whatever strengths and weaknesses the common person possesses.

Those weaknesses include ignorance and apathy. Dozens of studies by political scientists have documented the abysmally low level of information the public brings to bear on major policy issues and the simplistic strategies the average citizen uses to make political decisions.[23] In a nation where elections often turn on margins of two or three percentage points, 17 percent of the adult public remains unaware of the right to trial by jury. Forty-eight percent do not know that there are two U.S. senators from their home state.[24] Approximately one voter in five arrives at a choice in a presidential election with virtually no knowledge or concern about candidates' stands on any issues at all.[25]

Despite this bad news, many political scientists agree with W. Russell Neuman, who speaks of the "paradox of mass politics."[26] The general public, according to Neuman, is disturbingly uninformed, yet somehow an articulate public voice is heard by policymakers. One might paraphrase the dilemma he raises by asking how is it that a public that conforms so poorly to the high-minded expectations of the founding fathers has managed to play its role so well in a functioning democratic government? Somehow, it has succeeded, or at least partly succeeded, against all plausibility. And when a panel of jurors attempts to decide a case, they are in some ways the epitome of the direct government of the people. Perhaps, to the extent that the jury system functions at all well, we are presented with what might be dubbed the "paradox of the American jury." From this perspective, the key question is not why juries sometimes fail to produce justice but rather why they often succeed.

Put simply, America's wager on the jury is indeed a hedged bet. The judge in a jury trial has the power to exercise strict control over courtroom proceedings, enforcing carefully defined rules of evidence that are designed to limit the information jurors receive. Certain facts may be logically relevant and psychologically revealing, yet advocates must treat them as legally irrelevant. Lawyers cannot present arguments that might be deemed spurious or prejudicial. Jurors are instructed on what sorts of reasoning processes are permissible and how to conduct themselves during deliberations. When judges disagree with jury verdicts, they have means of limiting and overturning them. For most decisions (except criminal acquittals), a complex appeals process further reins in the power of the jury.

But the most significant opportunity to harness the power of the jury and ensure the integrity of the jury's deliberations is voir dire, that is, the process of jury selection during which the court and the attorneys determine who may serve on the jury. During voir dire, individual jurors are removed from the panel of prospective jurors through a question-and-answer process intended to identify those considered unsuited to serve due to their prior knowledge of the case or the parties, their predisposition or bias concerning the case or the parties, and other reasons.

Prospective jurors may be stricken from the panel either for cause or on the basis of a peremptory challenge. A *challenge for cause* is used to remove a potential juror where there is a clear reason to be concerned about the juror's ability to be objective and fair—for example, the prospective juror has an existing relationship with one of the parties. In contrast, the *peremptory challenge* (or *peremptory strike*) gives lawyers the opportunity to eliminate prospective jurors without articulating a reason. Traditionally, they could do so for no reason at all or even for a discriminatory reason, such as the juror's race However, abuses of the peremptory challenge led in 1986 to the U.S. Supreme Court's landmark ruling in *Batson v. Kentucky*, which made it illegal (although, practically speaking, not impossible) for prosecutors to strike jurors on the basis of race.[27] Subsequent decisions in the 1990s expanded the reach of *Batson* to further limit the peremptory challenge, prohibiting race-based challenges by defense counsel and in civil cases, as well as challenges based on gender.[28] At present, the peremptory challenge, in its somewhat restricted form, remains a fixture in the jury selection process.

In principle, the challenge for cause and the peremptory challenge together enable judges and attorneys to assemble jury panels that will be fair and impartial and deliver just verdicts. During voir dire, the judge can continue to eliminate jurors for cause until he or she is satisfied that the final panel will be unbiased. When functioning as intended, the challenge for cause thus serves as a powerful hedge against juries running amok. The peremptory challenge, too, can serve a constructive purpose, enabling attorneys—even on the basis of a mere hunch—to remove jurors believed to be predisposed against their side. But the peremptory strike is also the mechanism by which some attorneys attempt, in Osborn's words, to find one or two jurors of the kind they desire—the kind who will defeat justice.

THE RISE OF TRIAL CONSULTANTS

Since the early 1970s, a field sometimes called "jury science" has emerged to help attorneys stack and sway the jury, promising to take much of the guesswork out of voir dire. Drawing on a variety of techniques—many of them originally developed for the market research industry—trial consultants advise lawyers on which jurors to select and how to influence them once they have been seated.

Much of this work aims at a simple objective: to construct profiles of the most desirable and the least desirable jurors. The profiles then guide lawyers' questions during voir dire. Commonly, prospective jurors' answers enable attorneys and their consultants to make classifications on the basis of desirability, often rating jurors on a scale from one to five. As much as possible, lawyers try to have the least sympathetic panelists removed by the court for cause by demonstrating to the judge that these individuals cannot consider the evidence fairly. If attorneys are unable to show obvious bias, consultants guide them in selecting a certain number of jurors to exclude with peremptory strikes. If all goes according to plan, the jury consultant's assistance results in selection of the most sympathetic jury possible, given the constraints of the jury pool and the adversarial system.

Jury consultants also assist lawyers in other ways, providing specific insights into the jurors whom they must convince during the trial and suggesting a panoply of tactics by which to sway jurors. And with the help of consultants, lawyers can test-drive their arguments during focus groups and mock trials, as in John Kidd's patent infringement case.

The 1980 federal antitrust trial involving the telecommunications giant AT&T illustrates an early and particularly consequential use of mock juries. At trial, a panel of jurors listened as MCI's lawyers accused AT&T of monopolistic practices. The plaintiff's attorneys had pretested their arguments with several groups of people paid for the purpose. One mock jury had heard the MCI lawyers mention lost profits totaling $100 million, and those panelists subsequently decided to award exactly that amount. Using a different mock jury on another night, MCI's lawyers did not request any particular figure, leaving the calculation entirely in the hands of the paid participants; that group of mock jurors awarded *$900 million.* On the basis of this startling research result, MCI's attorneys devised strategies for jury selection and case presentation that ultimately produced a jury award of $600 million. Antitrust awards are automatically tripled for punitive purposes; in total, AT&T was hit with a $1.8 billion tab (although on appeal that amount was judged excessive, and a second jury reduced it substantially).[29]

Each year, jury consultants expand the services they provide. A recent directory of the American Society of Trial Consultants (ASTC) enumerates a lengthy list, including jury selection and voir dire guidance, witness preparation, courtroom observation, trial simulations, focus groups, posttrial juror interviews, change of venue studies, presentation of visual aids, and a number of other methods that can enhance an attorney's presentation strategy.[30] In addition, many consultants will devise, refine, or test a lawyer's case strategy, tactics, opening statements, closing arguments, and appellate advocacy.

What are we to make of this new industry? Some have denounced it as a form of high-tech jury-rigging, declaring it no more acceptable than cruder means of jury tampering. The thinking is that if such techniques become widespread they might just foreshadow the end of trial by jury as we know it. Others see jury profiling as one more addition to the widening gap between the haves and have-nots in the legal system. Now, they reason, those who can afford the best lawyers can also purchase the best juries.

At the other end of the spectrum, advocates for jury consulting note that prejudiced jurors rarely broadcast their biases in open court. New jury consulting techniques can, they suggest, make a constructive contribution to the objectivity of American juries by increasing the accuracy with which unfair jurors are rooted out. Sophisticated profiling methods will inevitably decrease lawyers' reliance on gross racial and ethnic stereotypes. Fewer jurors will draw suspicion solely on the basis of their demographics.

One thing is certain: If trial consulting really works to the extent advertised by its proponents as well as its foes, it promises to remake the American justice system. In the twenty-five years since its birth, the trial consulting industry has grown at a steady, but not feverish, pace. Now, according to many consultants, business is better than ever, and the field stands ready to expand into new domains. At the same time, a number of critics have urged the all-out prohibition of systematic juror profiling, and some have called for a measure that would have a similar effect: the abolition of peremptory strikes during voir dire. Other commentators suggest that all parties to a case should be able to examine any data collected by jury experts, and still others propose state funding to make the resources available to indigent defendants.

Before these policy issues can be addressed, it is prudent to ask whether jury profiling techniques really work. Several major consulting firms have claimed success rates of 90 percent when their services are used, and others maintain that they are able to predict jury outcomes in an even higher percentage of cases when they construct profiles.[31] Needless to say, however, a consultant's self-promotion always deserves skepticism: One can never be sure how much a jury profile contributes to trial outcome. Those who can afford top consultants can also afford the best lawyers. Attorneys, for their part, seem to straddle the fence concerning the importance of jury consultants. Some denounce the techniques as voodoo, but few forego them in the biggest trials when money is available and the stakes are high.

Trial consultants are surely changing the ways in which we seek justice in the United States. But whether these changes will prove catastrophic, superficial, or somewhere between those extremes is a crucial question to which Americans have devoted little attention. Fortunately, a handful of social scientists have begun to accumulate data addressing this vital matter.[32]

IS JUSTICE SERVED?

Jury consultants already dominate big-money civil cases. They frequently play key roles in those criminal cases with the highest visibility and greatest implications for public policy. The field has been expanding and powerful evidence suggests that it will continue to do so. In the past few years, low-cost options have brought trial consulting technology within the reach of many who previously deemed it too expensive. Each year, the number of court-appointed trial consultants in criminal cases increases. In some jurisdictions, it is now practically commonplace for public funds to be used to enable death-penalty defendants to hire trial consultants.[33] Yet jury consulting remains a largely hidden industry, peddling its wares beyond public view. When a new trade roams the halls of our legal system, aspiring to change America's road to justice, we had all best pay attention.

This book will reveal the tricks of the trade and explore the many ways in which trial consultants have infiltrated the courtroom. It will present cases where consultants arguably have been responsible for huge jury awards and controversial criminal verdicts. However, it is not our purpose to launch an all-out attack on this growing industry. Instead, we aim to pull back the curtains, allowing a fair assessment of a new phenomenon in American justice. We hope to reveal the threat—and sometimes the promise—of trial consultants, so that you, the reader, can judge for yourself.

This book addresses four central issues: (1) To what extent do jurors and juries reach their verdicts objectively? (2) How do lawyers and their consultants attempt to predict juror proclivities and use this information to stack and sway juries? (3) To what extent do their efforts succeed? and (4) How should judges, lawmakers, and the public respond to these challenges to the jury system?

Chapter 2 spotlights two recent and highly publicized cases: the 1997 murder trial of British au pair Louise Woodward, and Steven Pagones's defamation lawsuit against Al Sharpton, C. Vernon Mason, and Alton Maddox, for remarks arising out of the Tawana Brawley incident. In the first case, the defense employed a top consulting firm; prosecutors may also have used an outside consultant, although they have not confirmed doing so. The second case involved no trial consultants. Chapter 2 considers the power of juries, as well as the ability of attorneys and trial consultants to harness that power. Drawing on interviews with prominent litigators, we present their perspectives on the growing phenomenon of trial consulting.

Chapter 3 paints a portrait of the trial consulting industry, recounting its past, present, and future—as perceived by key players.

Chapter 4 focuses on consultants' attempts to profile and—despite their protestations—stack the jury. Here, we review the news from the laboratory, discussing what social scientists have learned about the effectiveness of jury selection consultants and, more broadly, the extent to which the personal characteristics and backgrounds of jurors can influence verdicts.

Chapter 5 evaluates the efforts of trial consultants to sway a jury once it has been chosen. In pursuit of this objective, consultants may design research to test arguments, guide case strategy development, and assist in the preparation of witnesses. Trial consultants offer many services beyond jury selection. Although these enterprises are less known to the public, they probably have greater impact on cases and, consequently, promise to shape to a larger degree the future of the industry and the American justice system.

Many of the most controversial verdicts in recent years have led to allegations about racial differences in jury decisionmaking and attorneys playing the so-called race card. No discussion about trial consulting or juror bias can proceed very far without grappling with the implications of race relations for the jury system. Chapter 6 discusses several prominent trials—including the murder trials of O.J. Simpson and the police officers charged with shooting Amadou Diallo—while offering a broader perspective on juries and race; it traces the history of all-white juries and changes in jury law, and it reviews the findings of relevant scientific studies.

Chapter 7, the concluding chapter, addresses the policy issues raised by juror bias and the trial consulting industry. To what extent do current laws and practices increase or restrain biases in the justice system? What can be done to minimize the role of inappropriate juror prejudice and, more generally, to improve the quality of jury decisionmaking? Should the trial consulting industry be regulated and, if so, how?

As we embark on this exploration of juries and trial consulting, we should perhaps add one caution: The proud and faithful citizen might wish to avoid examining the jury system too closely. As one jury scholar reflects, "I'm reminded of the old aphorism admonishing us that people who love sausages (and the law) should never watch their being made. Contrary to the rampant curiosity of most social scientists, I wonder if those who love the institution of jury decision making should not also avoid watching it being done."[34]

This book is intended for those who reject that perspective, preferring instead to know precisely what goes into their sausages, lest they confuse mere indigestion for dysentery—or vice versa.

2

JURIES AT WORK

A HIDDEN INFLUENCE

JUDGE DAVID PEEPLES of the 224th District Court in Bexar County, Texas, tells of a case in which a consultant helped a prosecutor pick a jury. A prospective panel member admitted during voir dire that he knew the defense attorney and even regarded him as something of a friend. But the prosecutor's trial consultant noticed that whenever the defense lawyer posed a question to this juror, the juror would fold his arms tightly and display all the presumed portents of negativity. When the prosecutor asked a question, however, this fellow would relax his arms and display an array of sympathetic nonverbal signs. Although the prosecutor wanted to strike the incongruous man from the jury, he ultimately bowed to the advice of his expert, and the juror remained. To their dismay, the juror turned out to be the defendant's strongest advocate during deliberations. Judge Peeples concludes that this man had, in all likelihood, intentionally deceived the jury consultant. The judge further recounts that, to his knowledge, this was the only case in his court in which a jury selection consultant was used. Then he adds an important caveat: Consultants probably have been used in his courtroom more often, but their presence is rarely revealed.[1]

Consultants themselves can seldom say with confidence whether the other side is employing a jury expert. When asked, they may answer, "I assume they were used, because so much money was at stake," or "I thought I saw someone who might have been a consultant, sitting next to one of the attorneys." When consultants are well-known, of course, it is easier to spot them in the courtroom. But many trial consultants advise their clients without ever setting foot in the courthouse. Even after a case has concluded, attorneys and their consultants are often left wondering whether the other side used experts in jury selection and case strategy development. And the public generally learns of consultants only what the attorneys want them to know, perhaps to gain a real or perceived tactical edge.

When trial consultants work on a case, the key question is: Did they make a difference? When they are not used, the question becomes: Could they have mattered had they been hired? Most consultants are quick to point out that it is simplistic to equate successful consulting efforts with winning a case and unsuccessful ones with losing. The truth about consulting is—undeniably—more complex. But lawyers and the public are often left with little information about the effectiveness of trial consulting, beyond the self-interested, self-protective, and self-aggrandizing statements of the consultants themselves.

In this chapter, we introduce some questions frequently asked about juries, trial consultants, and justice. To what extent do jurors' decisions stem from their personal characteristics and traits rather than from the evidence developed at trial? Are ordinary citizens equipped to deliver just verdicts in complex cases? Can attorneys manipulate trial outcomes through selection (or deselection) of jurors? Finally, are consultants able to improve substantially the capacity of lawyers to pick sympathetic jurors and formulate effective trial strategy?

The two cases we discuss appeared prominently in the American mass media, and in each case the jury verdict surprised legal pundits. Many traced the verdicts to the particular composition of the deliberating panels, arguing that small changes in jury composition might well have led to dramatically different outcomes. Still, jurors in each case struck most observers as sincere in their commitment to fulfill their civic duty.

Concerns highlighted by these trials are not atypical; what they reflect, instead, are the ambiguities, afflictions, potentialities, and soft spots of the jury system itself. The first case is a criminal trial in which the defense team hired the National Jury Project, a well-established leader in the jury consulting industry. The prosecution neither admits nor denies having employed outside experts, but it does acknowledge having used some approaches generally associated with trial consultants. The second case is a civil suit in which neither the plaintiff's attorney nor the defense team used consultants.

A GAME OF CHANCE? THE
MATTHEW EAPPEN MURDER TRIAL

> I loved Mattie's weight in my arms, his head on my shoulder and his soft breath tickling my neck, and his gentle hand caressing my skin, and I loved to snuggle and get cozy with my two boys. . . . I get flashbacks of what I envision happened to my innocent, defenseless little Mattie. I am sickened to think he was crying for help and was instead beaten by hands that were supposed to be caring for him.[2]
>
> —Deborah Eappen, October 31, 1997

> I'd just like to maintain my innocence and say that I'd never have hurt Mattie and I never did hurt Mattie and I don't know what happened to him. I'm not responsible for his death. I didn't kill Matthew Eappen. That's all.[3]
>
> —Louise Woodward, October 31, 1997

Sunil and Deborah Eappen, both physicians, had hired Louise Woodward, an eighteen-year-old from Elton, England, to care for their two sons. On February 4, 1997, while in charge of the boys, Woodward notified police that Matthew, the younger child, was having difficulty breathing. Paramedics found him with a two-and-a-half inch skull fracture and bulging eyes, symptoms that sometimes signal a condition known as shaken baby syndrome. After several days on life support, the eight-month-old died. An autopsy revealed a month-old wrist fracture in addition to the fractured skull.

Woodward was charged with murder. According to prosecutors, Woodward had admitted that she shook the infant, dropped him on the floor, and tossed him on a bed. They maintained that the au pair had grown frustrated with the demands of her job and Matthew's uncontrollable crying. According to state medical examiners, the infant had hit the floor with a force equivalent to a fall from a second-story window. Injuries from the fall and the shaking, according to the prosecutors, had caused Matthew's death.

The defense presented a very different story, maintaining that Woodward had never confessed to abusing Matthew and, indeed, was not responsible for his death. They held that a prior undetected injury must have caused the baby's skull fracture. The defense also suggested that Matthew may have had a genetic defect or, alternatively, that his two-year-old brother Brendan—the only other person home at the time—might have caused the fatal injury. Prosecutors responded that no two-year-old could have struck Matthew with force adequate to cause such injury and that insufficient evidence existed to support the prior-injury theory.[4]

Jurors in the British nanny trial, as the case came to be called, had to decide several matters before they could arrive at a verdict. A great deal rested on their interpretation of expert medical testimony concerning the extent to which Matthew's injuries fit the pattern for shaken baby syndrome. To this end, they needed to pass judgment on testimony that the baby had suffered from a previous injury or illness from which he may have died. Additionally, jurors had to determine whether Louise Woodward acted with malice, that is, whether she acted intentionally and created "what a reasonably prudent person would have known was . . . a plain and strong likelihood that death would result."[5] To return a first-degree murder conviction, the jurors would also have to conclude that Woodward acted with either extreme cruelty or premeditation. To reach a verdict of second-degree murder, they would need to find that she had acted intentionally and with malice but without premeditation or extreme cruelty.[6]

Critically, Woodward (on advice of counsel) had opted to remove the possibility of a manslaughter verdict, thereby forcing the jurors to choose among acquittal, second-degree murder, or first-degree murder. At the outset of the trial, the prosecution had charged Woodward with murder only; midtrial the prosecution requested that the jury also be instructed on the lesser included charge of manslaughter. The defense vigorously objected (gambling that the jury would rather acquit than convict on murder), and the judge ruled against including the manslaughter charge in the jury instructions.

The stakes were indeed high: If the jury convicted Woodward of murder, she would be sentenced to life in prison, with the possibility of parole only if the conviction was on second-degree murder. In contrast, a manslaughter verdict carried with it a maximum of twenty years in prison, with a shot at probation.

The defense lawyers wanted to eliminate one worrisome possibility: The jury, if it thought the evidence was insufficient to convict Woodward of murder, might compromise and render a verdict of manslaughter rather than acquit.

Under the law, to convict Woodward of manslaughter the jury would have had to conclude only that she had acted recklessly and with disregard for human life—but as a result of the defense gamble to keep manslaughter off the table, that option was not available to them.[7]

On October 30, 1997, after deliberating for close to thirty hours over a three-day period, the jury returned a verdict of second-degree murder. Sentencing was set for October 31, and under the Massachusetts sentencing guidelines Woodward faced life in prison.

Several members of the jury spoke to the press after the case. Juror Stephen Caldwell's comments on ABC's *Good Morning America* provide perhaps the best insight into what happened behind closed doors. He explained, "Nobody wanted to find a 19-year-old woman from another country who has come to America under these circumstances guilty of murder and put her away for life." Yet they felt as if they were in a "no-win situation," and ultimately one consideration proved decisive. Caldwell, the father of three boys, explained that there was "no way we could face the Eappens or the citizens of the Commonwealth and say, 'We think she did it, but we're going to let her go.'" The jurors arrived at their conclusion, in large part, because they believed the prosecution's medical experts over those of the defense.[8] The remarks of another juror (who asked to remain anonymous) indicate that the jurors considered the judge's instructions with care. She commented, "I don't think any of us thought she tried to murder him but the basis was: 'Would a reasonable person have known that such actions would have caused harm to a baby?' And we felt a reasonable 18-year-old would know that hitting a baby's head against a wall would cause harm."[9] Another juror, Jodie Garber, confirmed that the verdict rested on interpretation of medical evidence that excluded, in the eyes of the panel, the possibility of an accident and pointed to Woodward. She added that "nobody liked the finding we felt compelled to reach. Nobody was happy having to do this. . . . She's a kid going to jail and the baby's dead, so what's going to come out of this that's good?"[10]

Garber told reporters that she and the other jurors would ". . . rather have had a chance to consider a manslaughter option."[11] Caldwell agreed, saying, "I think if other choices were available to us then potentially manslaughter may have been the verdict."[12] Still, ten of the twelve did not speak to this matter, and even Caldwell and Garber remained tentative. One anonymous juror took offense at some publicized speculation that one of Woodward's attorneys, Barry Scheck, was a motivating factor in the verdict, presumably because of his forceful style and/or his association with the O.J. Simpson defense. She said, "The craziest thing I heard someone say is that we came to our decision because of Barry Scheck. That we hated Barry Scheck and that's how we came up with the verdict. That is just crazy."[13]

The jury's verdict was wildly unpopular in some circles. A network of protests filled the World Wide Web, calls to Boston talk radio station WRKO ran 50-to-1 in favor of Woodward, and scientifically designed polls indicated widespread disagreement with the verdict.[14] Protesters outside the courthouse carried signs saying, among other things, "IQ Tests for Jurors."[15] A British human rights organization, Fair Trials Abroad, added to the clamor. Stephen Jakobi, its director, wrote:

> As far as I'm aware . . . America has the only system in the world that leaves the layman, unaided, to wrestle with complex cases. In Thailand, for example, the absence of a jury means that evidence is processed by highly educated Thai judges far more able to grasp the kind of convoluted medical evidence that this well-meaning but ill-schooled American jury was faced with. When we can say that Louise Woodward would have been better tried in Bangkok than in Boston, it's a major cause for concern.[16]

According to writer Maggie Scarf, sympathy with Woodward's plight

> . . . spread with the whoosh of a brush fire, not only in her native England, but also, to a lesser extent, on this side of the Atlantic. This surge of positive feeling was accompanied by mounting indignation at the baby's bereaved parents, especially Deborah [Eappen], who chose to work part-time rather than stay home with the baby herself. In the strangest of moral turnabouts, the Eappens somehow metamorphosed into the bad guys.[17]

In this highly charged atmosphere, a most unusual thing happened.

On the morning of November 10, 1997, as she had for a number of days, Louise Woodward opened her eyes in the bare cell of a maximum security prison. Convicted of murdering Matthew Eappen, she had been sentenced to life imprisonment, with the possibility of parole after fifteen years. But the next day, November 11, she awoke to the luxury of the Hyatt overlooking Boston Harbor, welcomed by a supply of Ferrero Rocher chocolates.[18] Invoking a rarely used power, Judge Hiller Zobel, who presided over her trial, had reduced the jury's verdict from second-degree murder to manslaughter and, shortly thereafter, sentenced Woodward to time served.[19] As the prosecution later lamented, the judge ". . . in effect . . . . treated the defendant as though she had been acquitted."[20] The jury's verdict would have sent Louise Woodward away for many years; the judge set her free.

In light of Judge Zobel's decision, one might reasonably ask in what ways the jurors had failed as they carried out their assigned responsibilities. Yet in his published decision, Zobel identified none. Indeed, he went out of his way to exonerate the jury, saying, "All of us—the prosecution, the defense, the Court, and the public—owe deep gratitude to the jury here, deliberating jurors and alternates alike, who gave of their time and effort and, in the aftermath, their privacy. Neither they nor anyone else should interpret today's decision as in any way a criticism of them."[21] Thus, we are left with the troubling dilemma of how a responsible jury can carry out its task admirably, commit no errors, and still arrive at a result so far removed from what a judge considers acceptable.

The judge's written opinion started by quoting John Adams's exhortation that the law remain "deaf as an adder to the clamours of the populace."

Earlier in his career, Zobel had edited a collection of writings by Adams; he apparently held the founding father in high regard. Zobel declared in the preamble to his reduction of the Woodward verdict that judges "must follow their oaths and do their duty, heedless of editorials, letters, telegrams, picketers, threats, petitions, panelists, and talk shows."[22]

Yet some observers at the time expressed concern that Zobel's principled declaration of judicial independence accompanied deeds that were highly consonant with the utterances of vox populi. Brandeis University professor Jeffrey Abramson quipped that ". . . the gentleman protests too much."[23] Similarly, Terry Moran concluded in *New Republic* that ". . . by the sound and fury of the media, Hiller Zobel was swept away."[24] Abramson's problem with the Zobel decision goes beyond the particulars of this case, saying that it "reinforces a growing perception in many corners that the jury was once upon a time, a long time ago, a good place to resolve disputes, but that it's simply not up to the task in a complicated world."[25]

Posttrial remarks from the members of the jury suggested a temperate, reasonable, and fair-minded atmosphere of deliberations. It must be noted, however, that juror comments after a unanimous verdict nearly always present a decision in a favorable light, and only under the rarest of circumstances do panel members ever confess to irrational or extralegal motivations. The interpretation of posttrial remarks raises several other problems. For example, unless everyone speaks to the media, a few jurors generally dominate, and it is their interpretations that prevail. Additionally, such interviews can expose the intellect and thought processes of jurors to public scrutiny. In this trial, juror comments did not reflect badly on their intelligence or sense of fairness. However, the suggestion that they may have preferred to convict on manslaughter proved damaging to the perceived integrity of the second-degree murder conviction.

The most frequent objection to the jury's verdict of murder did not highlight jury failure at all but rather a failure to present the jury with tenable options. After charging Woodward with murder, the prosecution switched midstream and asked the court to instruct on manslaughter in addition to murder. Then the defense objected in a deliberate gamble, and Zobel ruled in their favor. Thus, the jury's apparent dilemma derived most directly from defense strategy. Yet some also blamed Judge Zobel for permitting the maneuver, as well as the prosecutor for "overcharging" (had the prosecution not charged Woodward with murder in the first place, the defense could not have avoided the manslaughter charge). Still, as defense sympathizers pointed out, if the facts did not support murder, then the error—if one believes the murder conviction to be in error—still belonged largely to the jury.

Would another panel have processed the evidence differently and concluded that the British au pair was innocent? Perhaps even the alternate jurors who heard the case would have arrived at a different decision. This, in any event, was the theory offered by defense attorney Barry Scheck on Court TV's *Cochran and Company* several days after the verdict. He commented:

> I think that the worst thing that happened to us was one of these peculiarities of the jury system in Massachusetts, that we had picked 16 people for the jury and we were counting on having 4 people on that jury that were comfortable with technical evidence. We had a grad of Harvard Law School, an electrical engineer, an [actuary] who had a grad degree and a fellow involved in construction who deals with data all the time to make decisions. I'm not talking about an issue of intelligence, it's more that you wanted to get people on that jury that felt comfortable making a decision based on assessment based on scientific and technical evidence. By the luck of the draw we lost those individuals. . . . I think that the scientific evidence was not as important to [the seated panel] in their deliberations as it should have been. The evidence before the jury is very clear that this was an old injury.[26]

Consistent with this theory, one of the alternate jurors reported that he and the other alternates were "heartsick" at the finding of second-degree murder.[27]

Not surprisingly, Gerard Leone, the lead prosecutor in the Woodward trial, and Martha Coakley, a member of the prosecution team, do not agree with the defense team's assertion that inclusion of the alternates on the panel would have changed the outcome.[28] Leone and Coakley are correct that one cannot infer with confidence from posttrial remarks that the alternates would have voted to acquit had they actually deliberated. In the jury room, the juror stands on the frontline. Unlike the alternates, the seated jurors had to face squarely the moral and social consequences of setting Woodward free. Moreover, because the alternates did not deliberate, they did not hear the arguments raised by other members of the jury, some of whom may not have been so ill-equipped to assess the evidence as Scheck implied. And as Leone pointed out, alternates can, in some instances, "feel miffed at being left out" of a decision after investing so much time hearing a case; this can exert an unknown and unpredictable influence on their posttrial comments to reporters.

Coakley also noted that a couple of the alternates were more vocal than others, and one who said he had reasonable doubt about Woodward's guilt himself highlighted that he had not deliberated as the seated jurors had. Leone added that the defense, by asserting that the alternates would have made a difference, sent an "arrogant and absolutely incorrect" message impugning the seated jurors as ignorant or stupid. The prosecution contended that the deliberating jurors understood the evidence and properly applied the law to the facts. "The people on that jury were not ignorant. . . . [The defense claims that] the jury wasn't intelligent because it didn't agree with their position. . . . If the jury doesn't agree [with you], that doesn't mean you attack the jury."

Although Scheck's comments indicate that the defense would have preferred a more technologically or scientifically savvy jury, posttrial comments from another member of the defense team suggest that *less-educated* jurors of lower socioeconomic status might also have delivered a prodefense verdict. According to defense attorney Andrew Good, "We [originally] thought a smarter jury would be better for [the defense]. Research showed that they could follow scientific evidence better. In hindsight, this was a mistake. The people who came up to me all the time in the street [in support of Woodward]—a lot of them were working-class people."[29] The implication here is that the seated jurors judged Woodward harshly in part because they did not identify with her to the same extent as working-class jurors might have. Thus, the Woodward defense apparently believes that it could have fared better had the panel been lower in socioeconomic status, higher in analytic ability, or perhaps some combination of both.

We cannot be sure whether, or to what extent, the composition of this or any other jury determines a particular verdict. But we can speculate about the likely impact made by trial consultants in the Woodward case. We must, of course, temper our speculation with an awareness that attorneys and consultants in most prominent trials often recount events incompletely or in a way that enhances their own image. Professional tactics and various ethical guidelines further limit what lawyers and their hired experts will reveal, even after a case has concluded. Still, lawyers on both sides of this case, within understandable restraints, shared significant information about their trial tactics.

On behalf of the defense, the National Jury Project conducted trial simulations and aided in jury selection.[30] The National Jury Project has perhaps the longest pedigree in the business, dating back to the 1970s. According to attorney Andrew Good, National Jury Project's principal contribution to the case was to run trial simulations, in which jury-eligible people heard the basic facts and arguments relevant to the case. Although Good did not wish to disclose specifics concerning the conduct of these simulations, it is reasonable to assume that they were competently designed; the defense team's consultant, Elissa Krauss, is coauthor of *Jurywork*,[31] widely acknowledged as one of the premier how-tos of trial consulting.

Did the simulations help? Good does not jump to judgment on this matter, claiming that "it's hard to say," but finally decides—"in hindsight, no." The purpose of the simulations was to understand the issues that would be relevant to the jury. But Good explains that the simulations ultimately did not matter much, mostly because of what he refers to as ". . . the inherent vagaries of a trial." He notes that "there's a problem with the [trial simulation] technique. . . . How do you simulate Mom and Dad [the Eappens] grieving on the stand? . . . The problem is that simulations are always different from reality." Good does not blame National Jury Project. He explains: "I'm not saying and I don't want to be understood to be saying that the consultants did anything wrong. It's just that I'm not sure the entire enterprise isn't a lot of hocus pocus in the end. The truth is, it's all a crapshoot." He issues this verdict on trial simulations for the Woodward case and many others, but not for all cases. He has used trial consultants in other cases and thinks that "sometimes, in some cases, you have a damn good idea about everything and you really can lay it out in a fairly reliable way. Then, the information [gained] from simulations can be useful."

As to whether the simulations played a role in the defense team's decision to deprive the jury of the manslaughter option, Good says, "We knew [on the basis of research] that if we presented manslaughter to the jury, that was going to be the verdict." The defense attorneys were also convinced that a murder conviction was inconceivable, but Good would not provide details on whether pretrial studies addressed that question. Certainly, most proponents of trial simulations would see such an issue as eminently addressable through research. Good's ultimate judgment? "In my view, this jury went wildly off-track in a way no simulation could have predicted."

The defense team also enlisted the National Jury Project for assistance in selecting a jury. Good claims that the consultants were ". . . not a lot of help in selection," again not through any failure to do their jobs competently. He explains that court rules and practices in the jurisdiction limited the ability of the litigants to conduct a thorough voir dire. The consulting firm helped the defense prepare written questionnaires to screen prospective jurors. They also assisted the defense in obtaining "individual sequestered voir dire," rather than group questioning conducted in public. But the court did not permit many of the questions that the defense attorneys and their consultants wanted to ask. Using consultants for jury selection, according to the defense attorneys as well as the prosecutors, is extremely difficult in Massachusetts. As in some other jurisdictions, attorney-conducted voir dire is not permitted, so the judge asks the questions. The extent of voir dire, in many cases, is simply to ask prospective jurors, "Do you think you can be fair?" Still, although Good believes the jury went off-track, he does not attribute the verdict to a failure in the jury selection process. He recalls that the defense team, right up until the verdict, thought that the seated panel "was okay. Not nirvana, but some were pretty good." Had the four alternates served, he believes they would have carried the jury to an acquittal. Prior to the verdict, however, he still believed that even without the alternates his team would probably win.

The prosecution would neither confirm nor deny that it used outside trial consultants. According to Leone, the prosecution's pretrial preparation did include some methods for identifying issues and factors significant to the case, and these methods helped to guide jury selection and contributed to the setting of trial strategy. For example, Leone reports that the prosecution conducted informal focus groups around a conference table with members of the team as participants; but rather than take the roles of prospective jurors, they reflected on the issues as experienced attorneys.[32] In jury selection, the prosecution preferred "contemplative" jurors who would "weigh the evidence in a common-sense manner." Woodward seemed mainstream—young, white, of apparently middle-class background—and she was charged with a serious crime. "We didn't want jurors who would jump to conclusions or be judgmental," says Leone. Woodward was, he explains, "fairly vanilla in her social and personal characteristics," and he preferred jurors who would not make decisions based on their prior beliefs about what such a person was capable or incapable of doing to an infant.

Prosecutors also recognized from the outset that jurors would hear much medical evidence and scientific testimony from experts. "We looked at how people would assess the evidence," according to Leone. On this matter, the prosecution preferred jurors with sufficient intellectual self-confidence to question doctors' views, assess conflicting expert opinions without tossing their arms in the air in despair, and—finally—"... make a definitive judgment even though they were faced with experts who disagreed."

The prosecution also considered how jurors would assign responsibility for what happened. They were especially concerned that "... many people were judgmental toward [Matthew Eappen's parents]. They held them liable for placing [their children] in the care of a relatively inexperienced and young person." Likewise, the prosecution feared jurors who were very young. They believed that such jurors might be overly sympathetic to Woodward out of a sense of "there, but for the grace of God, go I."

According to Coakley, the prosecutors preferred people who had children of their own, because they would understand that ". . . children can be annoying and cry a lot but it is very difficult to seriously injure them by accident." She further recalls that they wanted women more than men, ". . . because men might be more likely to sympathize with a young woman away from home." Not surprisingly, the prosecution, according to Coakley, preferred women who worked outside the home, because they would be less likely to blame the Eappens.

Despite this fairly specific sense of whom they preferred, Martha Coakley observed, "we ended up in many cases looking for the same jurors as the defense. We could agree on a lot [of prospective jurors]. Many were equally acceptable to both sides." This was most apparent in the declared preference of both sides for educated jurors who, they reasonably believed, would have an easier time understanding the complex medical evidence.

Of course, most of the maneuvers carried out by the defense, the prosecution, and their advisers were designed to influence the jurors. But in this unusual case, the decision with the greatest consequence was made by Judge Hiller Zobel.

Judge Zobel provided a detailed explanation of his rationale in his written decision.[33] He did not, it should be noted, grant the defense everything it had sought, specifically rejecting a finding of not guilty. Without indicating how he would have processed the evidence, he explained that it was ". . . unquestionably within the jury's province" to disbelieve ". . . all the evidence contradicting the government's hypothesis." He further concluded that the jury's verdict was ". . . not against the weight of the evidence."

Nevertheless, Judge Zobel found a way to change the outcome of the Woodward trial. He interpreted Massachusetts law as permitting a reduction in the level of a conviction ". . . . *for any reason that justice may require.*" A judge in Massachusetts, he explained, ". . . must decide whether failing to reduce the verdict raises a *substantial risk* that justice has miscarried." Although the power he invoked was designed to be used sparingly, its scope can be interpreted broadly. In any event, Zobel explained that he believed

> that the circumstances in which [the] Defendant acted were characterized by confusion, inexperience, frustration, immaturity and some anger, but not malice (in the legal sense) supporting a conviction for second degree murder. Frustrated by her inability to quiet the crying child, she was "a little rough with him," under circumstances where another, perhaps wiser, person would have sought to restrain the physical impulse. The roughness was sufficient to start (or re-start) a bleeding that escalated fatally. . . . Had the manslaughter option been available to the jurors, they might well have selected it, not out of compromise, but because that particular verdict accorded with at least one rational view of the evidence, namely: (1) Matthew *did* indeed have a pre-existing, resolving (i.e. healing) blood clot; (2) Defendant *did* handle him "roughly"; (3) the handling (although perhaps not the roughness) was intentional; (4) the force was, under the circumstances, excessive, and therefore unjustified; (5) the handling *did* cause re-bleeding; and (6) the re-bleeding caused death.

Although he acknowledged that the defense had itself requested the exclusion of the manslaughter option and that he had granted that request, Judge Zobel declared that a court is not a casino, meaning that the interests of justice must ultimately override a litigant's gamble.

Thus, the judge presented his decision as, in some sense, a fulfillment of the jury's true desire. But taken in conjunction with the vastly reduced sentence—time served—the judge's rationale is not entirely convincing. Rightly or wrongly, some members of the jury supported the guilty verdict in part because they felt that they could not face the Eappens if they acquitted Woodward. Posttrial comments also suggest that the jurors did not believe the defense team's medical experts and therefore could not have accepted the judge's manslaughter scenario. After hearing of the reduced sentence, one juror exclaimed angrily: "I'm flabbergasted. I'm appalled. This is a complete injustice to that child's life, and this is not a reasonable sentence. . . . I cannot fathom the sympathy that has been given to Louise Woodward. . . . [She] served 200-some-odd days, and that baby will never be able to take 200-some-odd steps."[34] Other jurors did not comment on the reduced verdict, but assessments of its fairness are probably more connected to opinions about the sentence than whether the verdict should have been murder or manslaughter—something widely regarded outside the legal community as more or less a technical issue.

Critics of the jury system often claim that jurors bow to public sentiments. In this case, however, the jury made an unpopular decision while the judge's reduction of the verdict coincided with popular opinion. One poll found that 52 percent of those surveyed approved of the reduction to manslaughter while only 30 percent disapproved. Still, only 37 percent approved of Woodward's release, far less than the 52 percent who thought she should serve at least a bit more time behind bars.[35] In any case, a judge has access to information that the jury does not hear. The rationale for shielding a jury from outside information is that such information can unfairly prejudice jurors. One might ask whether it is reasonable to assume, in general and in this case, that a judge would be immune to the effects of such inadmissible information. One might answer, of course, that judges, by virtue of their training, intellect, and moral integrity, possess a superior ability to compartmentalize, discount, and appropriately process potentially biasing facts.

In this case, the jury's decision to believe the prosecution's medical evidence may well have rested on solid ground. Although defense attorney Barry Scheck spoke disparagingly of the panel's ability to understand the scientific facts, the jury's position received impressive support after the trial. For example, a letter signed by forty-nine medical experts in child abuse asserted, "The prosecution put forward well-established medical evidence that overwhelmingly supported a violent shaking/impact episode on the day in question."[36]

Of course, only experts can resolve such matters, and when they disagree laypeople may be forgiven for disagreeing as well. But why should we suppose that the judge was better able than the jury to resolve this matter or seclude his intellectual judgment from emotional influence? Perhaps in a case like this—where many emotional triggers are coupled with difficult scientific evidence—one's ultimate opinion is largely a consequence of social, psychological, and attitudinal characteristics. Perhaps it depends less on the evidence and more on the individuals with whom one identifies most readily—the Eappens or Louise Woodward. The judge called his sentence a way of bringing "the judicial part of this extraordinary matter to a compassionate conclusion."[37]

Judge Zobel is a respected jurist. Although appalled by the sentence, prosecutor Martha Coakley believes that he "did what he felt in his conscience was the right result." Zobel's decision might be justified on the old edict that the tie goes to the runner (i.e., a close criminal case should go to the defense), for jurisprudence in America is based on a preference for setting the guilty free over imprisoning the innocent. But the decision can be called "compassionate" only if one accepts Louise Woodward's version of the facts, a version at odds with that embraced by the jury. The judge never explicitly adopts or defends such a position, and to do so would be to reject the conclusions of numerous physicians with expertise in the subject.

Coakley objected that Judge Zobel ". . . stepped in . . . and created in his decision a whole scenario that was never argued by anybody, was certainly never presented and which even today the defense says, 'We don't agree with that.' So to the extent that he's followed his own conscience, that may be, but it's a decision that it seems to me is outside what the jury rejected." She further objected that determining Louise Woodward's state of mind was ". . . the quintessential jury decision."[38] She continues:

> If they didn't find that state of mind, they should have acquitted her. They were told that by the judge, they followed his instructions. . . . To the extent that you say, was it murder or manslaughter and how much time should she do, to some extent those are always judicial decisions. But to say, well, we're going to disregard the jury verdict even though there was enough evidence for them to find, and indeed Judge Zobel said, I find the weight of

the evidence is with the jury's verdict, it was really an end run around [the jury] to say, well, I'm going to do what I want, to some respect, I'm going to reduce it and I'm going to give her time served.[39]

Coakley added, on the day of the sentencing, "I think we felt even as he said this afternoon, 'I will sentence her as if this jury returned a verdict of manslaughter,' that the sentence that followed wasn't expected, it didn't really make sense in light of everything he said. It doesn't sit right in the sense of the jury verdict, and what they said, and his also saying [that] Louise Woodward is responsible for this child's death."[40] Prosecutor Leone concurred. He contended that Judge Zobel "was not at all right in his description of what the jurors might have been thinking. If that is what they were thinking, they would have been duty-bound to acquit [rather than return a murder conviction]. What the judge did was to take the middle-ground position. . . . My impression is that the jurors felt let down by the court and the system. Their very contemplative process was given short shrift."

Bruce Fein, a former United States deputy attorney general, also criticized Judge Zobel's actions, writing that "Jury verdicts command the confidence of the community that justice has been done. That is because jurors represent a cross section of the people. They collectively possess an understanding of the many facets of human nature and of circumstances that may have led to the crime. No single judge holds such moral breadth. Indeed, judges typically experience the world through the political upper crust."[41]

Fein's argument is the classic one in favor of juries drawn from the populace. But whether justice has been done is called into question when a defendant goes to jail on the basis of a conviction by a panel of twelve, while the alternates who sat beside them throughout the trial announce publicly that they would not have arrived at a similar conclusion of guilt. Whether the alternate jurors might indeed have decided differently had they been seated around the deliberation table may not matter, for their declaration alone reinforces public perceptions that jury decisions can be a game of chance.

CONSCIENCE OF THE COMMUNITY:
THE PAGONES DEFAMATION SUIT

Slander: defaming a reputation. No one dies at the hands of another. No one is assaulted or maimed. Houses do not smolder in ash. Indeed, children still chant that "sticks and stones may break my bones—names will never hurt me." But William Shakespeare, in the tragedy *Othello*, offers a more apt portrayal of the injury suffered as a consequence of defamation, through the words of the villainous Iago:

> Good name in man and woman, dear my lord,
> Is the immediate jewel of their souls:
> Who steals my purse steals trash; 'tis something, nothing;
> 'Twas mine, 'tis his, and has been slave to thousands;
> But he that filches from me my good name
> Robs me of that which not enriches him,
> And makes me poor indeed.[42]

Slander suits carry us directly to the heart of the jury's role in determining and, in some sense, defining truth. After concluding that a plaintiff has been defamed, the jury must evaluate damages, determining in dollars and cents how much harm a person's good name has endured. Additionally, the jury can levy a sum designed to punish the defendant and deter similar behavior by the same defendant or others in the future.

In this particular defamation trial, the six-member jury exerted an influence that went far beyond the specific questions of the case, possibly bearing on a New York City mayoral candidate's political future and, more significantly, on the rules under which our society conducts political and social debate.

By November 1997, when the actual courtroom trial began, most New Yorkers old enough to remember the Tawana Brawley incident had filed it away under old news. The angry rallies had not been forgotten, but many wished they could be. Exactly ten years earlier, in November 1987, the New York metropolitan area and much of the country learned of a fifteen-year-old black girl from Wappinger Falls, New York, who had been discovered in a garbage bag, partially unclothed and smeared with feces. Racial slurs had been scrawled on her skin. She claimed that a gang of white men in Dutchess County, New York—including a man with a badge—had abducted and raped her repeatedly over a four-day period. At first, most people believed Tawana Brawley, or at least were willing to give her the benefit of the doubt. After all, who would concoct such a story? But in the weeks and months that ensued, various loose ends and inconsistencies led many reasonable people—white as well as black—to doubt elements of her story.

Getting to the truth was no simple matter because three firebrand black leaders—attorneys Alton Maddox and C. Vernon Mason, with relative newcomer Reverend Al Sharpton—had come to Brawley's aid and turned the case into a cause célèbre in some parts of the black community. As one reporter put it, "The incendiary story preoccupied New York for much of 1988 and became a surrogate for discussions about race in society."[43] The three advisers held many demonstrations charging cover-ups and racism in the investigation of the Brawley case. Using inflammatory language, they accused then-Governor Mario Cuomo and New York Attorney General Robert Abrams of participating in the alleged cover-up. One of the advisers even suggested that Abrams used pictures of Brawley as a masturbation aid. But the regularly promised supporting evidence of a cover-up never materialized. At every step, Brawley and her three advisers failed to cooperate with police investigators and the grand jury.

Maddox, Mason, and Sharpton repeatedly accused Steven Pagones, at the time an assistant district attorney in Dutchess County, of participating in the alleged rapes—accusations that ultimately drove Pagones to file a lawsuit against them and Brawley for defamation. Their accusations did not stop with rape. Part-time police officer Harry Crist Jr. had died shortly after the alleged attack on Brawley, apparently as a result of a suicide now generally believed to be unrelated to the Brawley affair. But—at the time—Sharpton, Maddox, and Mason said they smelled a rat, claiming that Crist had also participated in the alleged rapes and that Pagones had murdered his friend to keep him from confessing to the crime.

About four months after the Brawley incident, Sharpton accused Pagones of rape on WWOR-TV, New York, and asked: "Now if he didn't do it, why isn't he suing us?"[44] In May 1988, Sharpton repeated himself on Geraldo Rivera's popular TV show: "We have challenged them [Pagones and a state trooper also accused] to sue us and we'd bring Tawana into court and prove they did it."[45] On ABC's *Nightline*, on June 16, he went a step farther: "We have the facts and the evidence that an assistant district attorney and a state trooper did this."[46] More than a year after the purported attack, C. Vernon Mason declared at Harvard Law School: "I want to repeat to everyone within the sound of my voice that Steven Pagones, Scott Patterson [the state trooper] and Harry Crist, amongst others, raped, kidnapped and sodomized Tawana Brawley."[47]

By that time, most reasonable people had stopped listening. The version of the Brawley incident that emerged from the 1988 grand jury report, issued after a seven-month investigation into the alleged incident, was fastidious and detailed—and unwavering in its conclusions that the reported incident had not occurred. The report stated that "we conclude that Tawana Brawley was not the victim of a forcible sexual assault by multiple assailants over a four-day period. There is no evidence that any sexual assault occurred." It continued that "there is nothing in regard to Tawana Brawley's appearance on November 28 [when she was discovered] that is inconsistent with this condition having been self-inflicted." The grand jury determined that there was "no evidence that a cover-up occurred or was attempted in this case."[48]

Regarding Pagones, the conclusions were crystal-clear:

There is no forensic or other evidence that in any way connects Mr. Pagones to any incident involving Tawana Brawley. The testimony of Mr. Pagones, his witnesses and documentary and photographic evidence were credible and persuasive and established Mr. Pagones's whereabouts for virtually every hour of the period between Tuesday evening, November 24, 1987 and Saturday afternoon, November 28, 1987. Steven Pagones had no connection with any incident involving Tawana Brawley during those four days.[49]

Brawley, according to some reports, made up the story to avoid punishment for her absence from home, although the grand jury report did not draw any conclusions on this matter.[50]

When a private citizen sues for defamation, he or she basically needs to show that a statement was untrue, that it has damaged his or her reputation, and that its publication was the result of some fault on the part of the defendant, if only negligence. But as a result of the U.S. Supreme Court's landmark ruling in *New York Times v. Sullivan*, when a public official sues for defamation, he or she must prove *actual malice*, that is, the defendant made the defaming statement with knowledge that it was false or with reckless disregard of whether it was true or false.[51] The logic behind this tougher standard is to encourage open and robust political debate without fear of legal reprisal.

By design, such cases are difficult to win. As one observer of the Pagones lawsuit commented, that meant that Pagones would have to ". . . furnish evidence that burrows into the defendants' states of mind—that catches them not in irresponsible hyperbole but in something akin to a deliberate lie."[52] Herschel Fink, an attorney who frequently defends news organizations against libel charges, explains, "The essence of the defense is not whether the statement is true but whether or not the defendant believed the statement was true." He continues, "It is sometimes said that an empty head but a clean heart is good enough to win a libel [or slander] case."[53] Pagones was designated a public figure by the court because he was a Dutchess County prosecutor when he was accused by Brawley and her advisers of assaulting her. Thus, he faced an uphill battle to win his defamation case against his accusers.

Thirty-six years old at the beginning of the slander trial, Pagones says he brought the suit to seek closure and restitution for the massive disruption in his life caused by the false allegations. Among other things, he claims that his health fell to pieces, he couldn't sleep, and he received death threats. His family suffered as well; as a result of the death threats, he and his wife were married in the presence of armed guards. "They've made allegations that will be with me for the rest of my life," he asserted. Someday, his children would want to know why he had been accused of rape. He hoped a judgment in his favor would help provide a satisfactory answer. "These men are dangerous," Pagones's lawyer said, referring to the defendants in his summation. "They are bad. They are evil. Don't let them get away with this." Pagones thought his suffering merited a hefty sum, and he sought $395 million—although, significantly, this amount was never revealed to the jury.

C. Vernon Mason and Alton Maddox, both well-known black activist lawyers at the time of the Brawley incident, had receded from public view by the time the defamation trial began in late 1997. Mason had been disbarred in 1995 for sixty-six instances of professional misconduct with twenty clients.[54] Maddox had been suspended from practicing law because of his refusal to cooperate with an ethics panel investigating his conduct in the Brawley affair. For her part, Brawley, who had moved from the area and kept a low profile in the years since she first appeared in the news, now emerged briefly into public view to declare that she had always told the truth. At a small rally in a Brooklyn church in early December 1997, just as jury selection was starting, Brawley (now known as Maryam Muhammad) said, "If I had read everything I heard said about me in the last 10 years, I would think it was a hoax, too. But it happened to me, and I'm not a liar. I'm not crazy." Twenty-five years old at the time of this rally, she attempted to explain her earlier silence: "Now it is my turn to fight. . . . I was afraid before . . . I was afraid because I was ignorant. . . . What happened to me happens to hundreds of thousands of women every day."[55] But still, Brawley provided no details to support her story and refused all opportunities to present her version under oath, maintaining her silence throughout the slander trial.[56] (She was a named defendant but failed to respond to the lawsuit; a default judgment was later entered against her.)[57]

Most attention in the defamation case centered on Sharpton, who had recently come close to forcing a runoff in the New York City Democratic primary race for mayor. Since the Brawley affair, Sharpton had abandoned some of his most extreme rhetoric and attempted to reposition himself somewhat closer to the mainstream of New York politics.[58] He had already declared his intention to run in the next mayoral race. In the summation at the slander trial, Sharpton's lawyer portrayed him as a noble civil rights leader, saying, "He came to the aid of a family in need—a young girl in particular—and made a call for justice."[59] His lawyer had earlier explained to the jury in his opening statement, "I am not here to prove to you what happened to Tawana Brawley. In fact, I am here to prove nothing at all. . . . This case is not about truth in the end. What this case is really about is whether a man—and in this case that man happens to be Reverend Sharpton—has a right to believe a 15-year-old girl."[60] Maddox and Mason continued to accuse Pagones of raping Brawley and murdering Crist. Inside the courtroom, Sharpton did not join them—although, outside, he continued his "verbal dances around the question."[61] Testifying in February 1998, Sharpton explained: "I'm of the opinion he was identified and should have been prosecuted."[62] Asked whether, at the time, he had discussed details of the story with Brawley, Sharpton said he had not. "I would not engage in sex talk with a 15-year-old girl."[63] Later that day, outside the courtroom, he recast the lawsuit as a status-enhancing event: "I've been indicted, I've been stabbed and now I've been sued. I have every base covered being a great civil rights leader."[64]

New York Times columnist Clyde Haberman suggested that "finding out whether there was any reality to her accusations never flashed on [Sharpton's] radar screen."[65] Many observers agreed. But responsibility fell to the jury to decide whether the advisers' failure to verify the accuracy of Brawley's accusations amounted to knowing falsehoods or reckless disregard for the truth.

From the very outset of the trial, lawyers representing Brawley's former advisers denounced the racial composition of the jury pool.[66] Outside the courtroom, Maddox, who represented himself during the trial, announced that the pool had been clearly stacked in favor of the plaintiff. "I suspect that what happened was that over some barbecue in the summer, all of Steven Pagones's friends were put in the jury pool," he charged.[67] But Michael Hardy, Sharpton's lawyer, rejected this inflammatory approach. Inside the courtroom, the defendants' attorneys presented two arguments. First, they claimed that a fair trial could not take place in Dutchess County because the Brawley case had brought protests and exhortations of racism there ten years earlier. This, they concluded, had hopelessly contaminated the community with negative predispositions toward Brawley's advisers. Second, they suggested that the jury pool lacked a sufficient number of blacks, as compared to the proportion of blacks in Dutchess County.

After some consideration, Justice S. Barrett Hickman, the presiding judge, rejected both contentions. Personal conflicts, associations with the Pagones family, and other reasons led to the elimination of scores of potential jurors from the original group. By the end of the second day of jury selection, seventy-eight people remained in the pool from which the jury would be selected. Of these, at least six individuals, or more than 7 percent of the pool, were black, about the same percentage as in the Dutchess County population as a whole. Justice Hickman denied the defendants' challenge to the racial composition of the pool, finding that the pool represented both the random selection process and the Dutchess County population. However, recognizing the sensitivity of the case, he granted the defendants seven peremptory strikes and the plaintiff five. (Typically, each side in this jurisdiction gets only three.) Both sides questioned jury prospects, more than a few of whom expressed concerns about their ability to serve impartially. Others were dismissed by the court or struck by one of the lawyers. For example, the judge dismissed one man because he had been a police officer in a nearby town.[68]

In the end, six jurors and five alternates were seated.[69] The seated jurors included three men and three women; four were white and two were black. They ranged in age from thirty-one to forty-seven. The men included a thirty-seven-year-old white toolmaker, a forty-five-year-old black IBM manufacturing engineer, and a thirty-two-year-old white pharmaceutical warehouse worker. The women included a forty-year-old black postal distribution clerk, a forty-seven-year-old white salesperson for advertising space in telephone directories, and a white woman who worked for a commercial bank.

Frank Bruni, who covered the case for the *New York Times*, commented, "What is most striking about [the jurors], as a group, is how many said they had never formed any strong, conclusive opinions about what happened to Ms. Brawley, even though her accusations, along with the findings of the grand jury, dominated headlines and TV newscasts for weeks."[70] He further noted that half of the jurors said they had extremely limited awareness of who the defendants were. The other three did not express any negative opinions about the defendants or their roles in the Brawley affair. Several said they valued the right to hold demonstrations and voice controversial opinions.

Two months into the trial, Justice Hickman excused one of the jurors, replacing her with an alternate. Earlier in the trial, the defendants' attorneys had alleged that the replaced juror, the advertising salesperson, had demonstrated partiality in favor of the plaintiff. Spectators had overheard her muttering "thank you" when Pagones's lawyer described a defense motion as "frivolous" and an "insult to this court."[71] A note from the jury complained that the woman's expressive reactions in the courtroom were inappropriate. At the time of those incidents, the judge allowed her to remain on the panel. But several days later, she asked to be excused on grounds of financial hardship. She was not drawing a salary from her job and could not get by on juror pay, about $30 per day. The replacement juror, first on the list of alternates, was a forty-five-year-old white male who worked with troubled children.[72] The jury composition was now three white men, one black man, one white woman, and one black woman.

The trial was long. Justice Hickman had originally estimated that it might conclude around Christmas 1997. In January, observers predicted it would last until March. It ended in late July. Along the way, jurors witnessed the sort of bombastic lawyering normally reserved for TV courtroom dramas—mostly, but not exclusively, from the defense. At every step, the defense team charged that they and their clients were being subjected to a racist and unfair system of justice.[73]

On July 13, 1998, the jury found all three of Tawana Brawley's former advisers liable for defamation—although not on all counts. Two weeks later, they awarded a total of $345,000 to Pagones—about one-tenth of 1 percent of the amount he originally had been seeking. The jury awarded just $15,000 in compensatory damages; the remainder represented punitive damages. The jury set Sharpton's share of the total damages at $65,000, Maddox's at $95,000, and Mason's at $185,000.

The jury's decisions cannot easily be labeled outrageous. All the litigants claimed victory, and all were somewhat disappointed.[74] After all, the jurors had endeavored to distinguish among remarks about Pagones that had been expressed as opinions and those set forth as facts, finding liability for the latter but not the former. They assessed greater punitive damages against Mason and Maddox because their defamatory comments occurred after the grand jury report appeared.[75] Posttrial statements by several jurors suggest that most, if not all, wanted to do the right thing. And some uttered hopes that the healing would begin and that all sides would move on.

From the jurors' posttrial comments, we can discern much—but not all—of the reasoning and interpersonal dynamics behind the verdict and the award. Only five of the six jurors signed the verdict sheet finding Brawley's former advisers liable for defamation. The woman who did not, Althea Williams, a postal clerk, was one of the two black jurors. At the conclusion of the second phase of the trial, after the damage awards were announced, the judge polled the jury. Williams said that she also did not support the damages decisions, although she had previously signed the damages verdict sheet. After the trial, Williams chose not to speak with reporters except to say, "I have a right to my opinion. But I'm not prejudiced against anybody. Everybody sat in that courtroom for eight and a half months."[76] According to another juror, Williams "always" said: "I grew up in New York City. I've seen other people who wanted for things and had no way to get them except through people like Al Sharpton."[77]

One of the white male jurors, Mark Urbin, the thirty-seven-year-old toolmaker, said that he believed the disagreeing juror had made up her mind months before the end of the trial when he (and another juror) noticed her playing an electronic game during questioning conducted by Pagones's lawyer. Also according to Urbin, during deliberations Williams relied on arguments that in Urbin's opinion were racist and unproductive, referring to the grand jury report as a "white man's bible" and speaking of how "her people" were oppressed for 200 years.[78] After the trial, Urbin said of Williams: "She believed in Tawana; all the rest of the jurors believed in the evidence."[79] One afternoon, a court officer brought deliberations to an early end when they grew heated and threatened to boil over. Urbin and Williams, according to other jurors, were yelling at each other when Williams became very agitated and jabbed a pen toward Urbin.[80] For his part, Urbin may have been the most aloof member of the jury and the least sympathetic to Brawley's advisers.[81] By trial's end, several jurors commented that they felt warmly toward Williams. This was especially true for Glen Heinsohn, a white juror who—like Williams—had grown up in New York City. He reported that he and Williams became friends during the long trial, sharing memories of the Bronx.[82]

Notwithstanding the conflict between Urbin and Williams, one cannot easily say that this jury was divided along racial lines. Of the two black jurors, only Williams failed to sign the verdict sheet. And in interviews after the trial, some of the jurors said that she had participated in deliberations and voted with the majority much of the time.[83] The other black juror, James Boone, signed the verdict sheet and apparently had no noteworthy conflicts with other panel members. Several jurors remarked that Boone, an IBM engineer, saw the essentials of the case as they did.[84] Just before making the liability decisions, a juror reported to the judge that the panel split 3-to-3 on some of the counts; these disagreements could not have been due to racial differences alone.[85]

All three of the white male jurors later spoke with the media and indicated that they held positive feelings for the defendants. Patrick Cody, the warehouseman, said, "They are strong men. I believe in what they do. I just think they should have went about it in a different way."[86] Glen Heinsohn commented, "I hope the healing begins and to Reverend Sharpton, you've always been a favorite of mine since the beginning and I thought that was going to get me thrown right out [during jury selection]. But to paraphrase [a character from] the *Grapes of Wrath*, 'Keep up the good fight,' you know, be there. There are people here that need you." He further remarked: "He's a likable guy . . . I've heard him on the Imus [radio] show."[87] Even Mark Urbin expressed some admiration for Sharpton, saying, "He does a good job at what he does."[88]

Prior to the jury's decision on damages, Sharpton told a radio audience that he would fight the real battle in the appellate courts because, all along, he believed that the Dutchess County jury was biased.[89] Around the same time, a reporter interviewed residents in the Brooklyn community of Bedford-Stuyvesant, a low-income black neighborhood and

Sharpton stronghold. He heard many opinions along the lines of, "They're just after him [Sharpton], as they are after all black men, any black men who speak up for themselves."[90] After the damages were announced, tempers cooled somewhat among the defendants and their supporters—although they still planned an appeal.[91]

The majority of the jurors wanted to deliver a message to Sharpton, Maddox, and Mason. Although they liked the defendants, they also liked Pagones and felt that he had been wronged. They did not arrive at any firm conclusions about what did or did not happen to Tawana Brawley, but—as one said—"Steve Pagones did not do it. That was the overriding fact here. Was Tawana abducted? We don't know."[92] They wanted to say to the defendants, "Do your homework before you shoot your mouth off."[93] But they did not want to destroy the defendants and they felt no animosity toward them.

They expected to please Pagones with the damage awards. One juror explained that Pagones had "said it himself: He didn't want to hurt these guys." They recalled testimony that Pagones was more interested in clearing his name and in accountability than in receiving a large sum of money. When told that Pagones had been seeking $150 million (Pagones had lowered his sights from $395 million after the jurors had determined that not all statements alleged in his original complaint were defamatory), the jurors said they were surprised. Neither side had told them the amount Pagones was seeking. Juror Glen Heinsohn explained that they thought that $345,000 was a tremendous amount of money compared to what they typically earned; he made $20,000 a year.

They had apparently never considered levying a sum anywhere close to what Pagones had been seeking. They set the actual damages suffered by Pagones at $15,000—just $5,000 per defendant; the rest of the award was designed to punish. Although Pagones said he could live with the jury's award, he had spent roughly the same amount in litigating the case. Plainly, it was a disappointment. To Sharpton, far from being an unambiguous rebuke, it was a victory. Sharpton claimed, "As I run for mayor in 2001, it's now going to be very difficult for anybody to raise the issue because of the size of the award."[94] He also remarked, with some justification, that ". . . this jury may disagree with some of what I did in the Brawley case but they clearly said they did not question my motives and they clearly said that I should continue in what civil rights work I'm doing."[95]

Many questions emerge about the connection between the composition of the jury, the verdict, and the award. Had there been even one more juror with views similar to those held by Althea Williams, we might well be telling a different story. Presumably, such thinking was at the root of the defendants' desire to change venue or increase the number of blacks in the jury pool. Conversely, the award could well have been larger had Williams not served. Although the other jurors rejected her perspective, they were, to varying degrees, influenced by her presence and the issues she raised. She altered the tenor of deliberations and affected the size of the award.

Posttrial interviews with some of the jurors revealed that the four white jurors sought significantly higher damages than Williams, who wanted to keep damages as low as possible—and Boone was undecided. Heinsohn had initially wanted to award $1.5 million but lowered his number because he hoped to achieve a consensus that included Williams.

Boone, also, was influenced by Williams. He describes himself as racially mixed and notes that he grew up among whites in Arizona. Discussing his decision, he commented, "Among those who perceive me as black, they would look at me and say, 'You have to do things based on your black culture.'" Although undecided at first about the damages and in agreement with the white jurors on many issues, he ultimately went along with Williams, seeking to keep damages low.[96]

The whites who served on the panel expressed a strong desire for healing, reconciliation, and racial cooperation.[97] The jurors had been selected in part because they appeared to lack knowledge and strong feelings regarding the plaintiff, the defendants, and the Brawley case. (Heinsohn, the juror who confessed that Sharpton was a "favorite" of his, did so after the trial and not during jury selection.)

After the jury found the defendants liable, Sharpton's lawyer argued that an award of millions of dollars would prove that "black people in America have no rights." He continued, "If that is the statement you want to make, make it. But the world would then know what a farce of justice this trial really is."[98] Describing his client as a brave civil rights leader, he urged the jurors not to give Sharpton the "financial electric chair." The defense also argued that Pagones's reputation had not really been damaged, because his friends did not believe the accusations against him. To jurors who respected all three defendants, it may have been painful to find the defendants liable in the first place, and the jurors may have seized on the opportunity, suggested by Maddox, to make "some adjustments" to the liability verdict by awarding only a nominal amount in damages.

The question arises whether jurors who came to this trial with extremely limited knowledge or opinions about the highly publicized Brawley case were in the best position to decide the issues. Stated more generally, one may ask whether jurors who are relatively uninformed and/or unconcerned about current events are well suited to render justice. Do such jurors represent the "conscience of the community"? Are they likely to be more subject to manipulation by the attorneys? Or are jurors with relatively little information about a case and relatively weak feelings about the litigants likely to be more objective? In this trial, many prospective jurors with strong feelings—feelings that were likely shared by many in the community, that were disproportionately antidefendant in this venue—were excused during jury selection. How might the verdict and award have changed had they been permitted to serve?

This lawsuit raises another question: What determines the size of a jury award? Pagones and his lawyer might have overplayed their hand, asserting again and again that this case was not about money. Seeking to please everyone, the jurors thought they had found a Solomonic solution. Had the $150 million figure been presented to the jurors, they would have been forced to see a far smaller award as a defeat for Pagones.

Interviewed several months after the jury verdict, both Pagones's attorney and Sharpton's stated that they had not employed trial consultants, whether for jury selection, case strategy development, witness preparation, or anything else. Michael Hardy remarked that his best "consultant" was his client—Sharpton—who had "good insights into these types of things."[99] Hardy also explained that as a rule he did not use trial consultants—mainly because of the expense. However, in his opinion, this did not pose much of a problem in the case, especially because Sharpton had a circle of personal advisers and friends with whom he consulted regularly regarding his testimony and other matters. Moreover, Hardy and his team pretested their arguments in the age-old, unscientific manner—trying them out on associates and staff.

During jury selection, Hardy aimed to seat predominantly middle-class, well-educated jurors and sought women over men. He believed that educated, middle-class jurors would be more likely to embrace his arguments concerning free speech and public debate and—perhaps—were less likely to hold racist views. Sharpton's codefendants didn't share Hardy's preferences; Mason's attorney and Maddox apparently sought out less-privileged, working-class jurors, probably because they believed them less likely to identify with Pagones, a prominent professional. As it turned out, Hardy did not get the panel of jurors he sought, and the final group more closely approximated the profile desired by Sharpton's codefendants.

Hardy would have preferred more black representation on the panel, but he agrees that the seated jurors turned out far better from his perspective than they might have, and they showed special sympathy for his client. He believes that the age of the jurors was one source of their apparent open-mindedness to Sharpton. Predominantly thirty-five to forty-five, most had come of age during the civil rights era of the 1960s and, in his opinion, were apt to be fairly comfortable with outspoken civil rights leaders and their causes. Although it was not part of his original jury selection strategy, Hardy acknowledges that the working-class status of some jurors ultimately helped the defense, as these jurors apparently believed that the damages they awarded to Pagones constituted a very large sum of money.

In the final analysis, however, Hardy does not see the composition of the jury as decisive. He believes that it was his closing argument that won over the panel for Sharpton. His summation emphasized Sharpton's lack of malice and his reliance on the story told by Brawley and her family. According to Hardy, this argument rang true with the jurors, persuading them that Sharpton believed what he was saying about Pagones at the time that he said it. Had Sharpton been tried apart from his codefendants, his attorney suspects that he may not have been found liable at all.

Hardy speculates that Pagones's counsel had employed a trial consultant, at least to prepare Pagones for taking the witness stand. But William Stanton, Pagones's attorney, is convincing in his denial. He states that he did not use a trial consultant in this case, and—in fact—has never used one in any trial.[100] Stanton elaborates, "I'm from the old school. I truly believe that if you are honest with the jurors, they will be honest and fair with you. I think you can do better relying on your common sense and everyday life experiences." He also believes that during voir dire a trial attorney, rather than searching for "perfect jurors," should strive to create a "good, honest rapport" with prospects, whomever they may be. He asserts that in this trial he wasn't looking for any particular "type" of juror: "In Dutchess County, we have basically middle-income, white and black jurors. I just wanted a cross-section of the community."

Stanton speaks in tones that are respectful of the sanctity of the jury system. And he claims that these particular jurors carried out their civic duty responsibly. "They served eight and a half months. They were there every day. They are exemplary of the type of jurors we have in Dutchess County." As to why the damages award was so low, Stanton suggests that most verdicts are a compromise and agrees that here, in particular, the jury was influenced by Pagones's own assertions at trial that he didn't care about the size of the award.

Stanton does not publicly acknowledge the low damages award as an implicit defeat for Pagones; neither does he state that any of the jurors were biased either toward the defendants or against the plaintiff. He notes, however, that during jury selection the judge "gave the defendants a lot of leeway in challenging for cause. This allowed them to store up a lot of peremptories. I wasn't able to save my peremptories." Perhaps this implies some dissatisfaction with the panel. But at least publicly, Stanton does not second-guess his performance during voir dire or criticize the results of the trial. When asked whether Pagones, given the chance to do it over again, would still say that the size of the award didn't matter to him, Stanton responds, "Yes, because that was the truth."

Stanton's relative inattention to the particular composition of the jury may resonate with some who possess a civic-minded sense of fair play, but one wonders whether a trial consultant might have improved his client's situation. As noted, this lawsuit highlights the potential vulnerability of some juries to slight changes in composition. It further seems that the well-intentioned, open-minded jurors in this case embraced the view that a just outcome exists at about the midpoint between two competing sides. But that is not always the case—and compromise does not always result in justice.

The outcome in this case—and the jurors' reflections on how they arrived at the damages figure—brings to mind the focus groups from the MCI antitrust lawsuit discussed in Chapter 1. In that case, pretesting MCI's trial strategy with focus groups revealed that MCI would be more likely to win a very large judgment if it did not specify the amount of damages it was seeking.[101] In the Pagones case, research might have pointed to the opposite tactic—or at least provided insights into jurors' likely preconceptions about different-size awards. Of course, in this trial, as in others, it is difficult to assess the quality of the jury outcome because of the lack of an objective standard for comparison. As a practical matter, it seems likely that a fairly large percentage of the Dutchess County population would have valued the actual damages suffered by Pagones far in excess of $15,000. One can almost hear them ask, "Who among us would choose to be subjected to years of threats and false accusations for that sum?" Alternatively, other prospective jurors—presumably harder to find in Dutchess County—might have stood their ground against *any* punishment of civil rights leaders who volunteered their services on behalf of a teenager in need. Still others might have argued that though Sharpton and his associates may have been careless or insincere in this instance, a large punitive damages award might stifle altruistic advocacy on behalf of people in need in the future.

Jury consultants looking back at this case might identify many areas where their services could have proven useful. Perhaps most significant, trial consultants might have assisted Stanton in identifying the predispositions, attitudes, and views of the prospective jurors. They might have attempted to steer him toward a panel of jurors who were: (1) more mainstream and, therefore, less likely to view Sharpton, Maddox, and Mason as important civil rights leaders; (2) more aware of the history of the Brawley affair; (3) more likely to view the injury to Pagones as serious and severe; and (4) more comfortable thinking in terms of large damage awards. By conducting mock trials and focus groups, trial consultants might have pretested many of Stanton's theories regarding the case—most important, perhaps, evaluating in advance the impact on jurors of Pagones's declaration that the case wasn't about money. They might also have assessed the extent to which the jurors accepted the image of Sharpton and the other activists as civil rights leaders, perhaps developing and pretesting methods for countering this image.

Given the constraints of the venue where the case was tried, trial consultants might not have expected to fare so well in producing a more sympathetic panel from the perspective of the defendants. However, they might have been instrumental in resolving the question of whether educated, upper-middle-class jurors were more or less desirable than less-privileged, working-class ones. Additionally, according to Hardy, the jurors believed that Sharpton acted without malice and, therefore, should not have judged him liable. He thinks the verdict against Sharpton may have resulted, at least in part, from an inability to divorce him psychologically from his codefendants. Thus, although Hardy recounts the case as a successful endeavor, he might still have benefited from focus groups exploring how best to drive home his case theories to the jury. (Sharpton's codefendants appeared to use the lawsuit as an occasion for propagating their personal agendas and politics and, consequently, would probably not have been receptive to strategic tips.)

Had they been asked, trial consultants would likely have been able to offer an array of services relevant to this case. In retrospect, it seems that the lack of trial consultants may have hurt Pagones more than it hurt Sharpton and his codefendants.

In any event, this case—despite its controversies—reveals a jury system that is far from a shambles. In a racially charged atmosphere created in part by the facts of the case and in part by the attorneys and litigants themselves, these jurors apparently worked hard to deliver decisions that they believed were fair, just, and racially unbiased. The result provoked relatively few passionate denunciations from either side. Indeed, these jurors succeeded in delivering a verdict that allowed both sides to claim victory.

WHEN HIRED GUNS HIRE GUNS

The Woodward and Pagones cases focus attention on the power of juries. What do attorneys involved in those cases conclude about the potential of trial consultants to harness and direct this power? Woodward defense attorney Andrew Good, who has used consultants on several occasions, wonders at cynical moments whether trial consulting amounts to anything more than hocus-pocus. He reasons that the effectiveness of trial simulations depends on the extent to which you can present your case reliably and realistically to the mock jurors. He concludes: "I know lawyers who swear by this. I don't."

Woodward prosecutor Gerard Leone believes that consultants probably can be helpful but cautions that no "experienced trial lawyer should rely more on a consultant than on [his or her] own gut feelings. . . . When you rely too much on research or listen to people outside the courtroom, it can lead to very wrong decisions." His associate, Martha Coakley, explains that in the district attorney's office usually "we don't have the budget for consultants. It's just not in the cards. [Besides,] most cases for the state are pretty straightforward. I'd say [trial consultants are] of limited usefulness. Of course, the more information one has, the better. . . . But [consultants] are not outcome-determinative."

Michael Hardy, Al Sharpton's attorney, claims little experience with trial consultants in his practice but appears receptive to the idea that they could prove useful in some "big-number cases." William Stanton, Pagones's attorney, has never used a trial consultant and believes ". . . you can do better relying on your common sense and everyday life experiences."

These assessments of trial consultants hardly amount to a resounding endorsement. Yet the industry has been growing steadily, and many of the nation's top lawyers would not think of trying an important, high-profile, or potentially costly case without using trial consultants whose fees run into the tens or hundreds of thousands of dollars. Why have so many of these prominent litigators, normally a self-confident group, grown dependent on jury consultants for their largest and most significant cases?

According to Bob Wallach, a San Francisco attorney who has been in practice for forty years and was among the first to use trial consultants, the answer can be summarized in one word: fear.[102] New York lawyer George Graff agrees: "You do it because you're afraid not to."[103] Although most civil jury trials result in verdicts for the defense, litigators— particularly those representing corporate defendants with deep pockets— live in mortal fear of juries. These attorneys and their clients cringe at any uncertainty and loss of control, and juries in recent years have returned some astronomical and well-publicized awards. On the plaintiff's side, fear centers on the antilawsuit, antilawyer juror who is fed up with huge judgments.

Everything depends on jurors and their thought processes, but the typical trial lawyer who handles large civil cases might personally spend only a few hours each year conducting voir dire questioning. Remarking on the growing consulting phenomenon, Wallach says, "It's only going to get bigger, because more and more lawyers will get to be sixty years old, having tried only five or ten cases. And the bigger it gets, the less expensive it's going to get."[104]

Moreover, attorneys seldom receive clear and interpretable feedback on how well they have performed their task, so it is very difficult for them to improve their skills or develop genuine confidence in their judgments. "We want to know what the jury's hot buttons are," says one plaintiffs' lawyer.[105] Attorneys traditionally have used their intuition to locate these hot buttons, but those who handle the largest cases are increasingly reluctant to do so. According to Wallach, "One of the problems with being an experienced trial lawyer is that you have a tendency to move away from the people who are your jurors. Being more affluent, your friends are professionals" and it is easy to lose touch with the likely reactions of those from other life circumstances. Thus, the attorney might gratefully put jury selection and analysis in someone else's hands.[106]

Geography and local court rules influence how frequently jury consultants are used and for which purposes. Jurisdictional variations in the permitted number of peremptory challenges are especially significant. In addition, some states permit attorneys to ask voir dire questions, allowing considerable leeway in the topics about which they may inquire. In other states, judges tightly control voir dire and, as a result, render jury selection consultants less consequential. Additionally, some states, including New York and California, draw their juries from highly diverse pools. In these unpredictable venues and in ones in which plaintiff-oriented juries commonly raise the stakes, lawyers might be more willing to invest in the services of a trial consultant.

Some attorneys will use full-blown trial consulting services only when the case is an "absolute company-breaker." Others purchase the full panoply for their largest cases and more limited assistance in smaller ones—where a client can more easily absorb any likely loss. Sometimes, it makes economic sense to delegate certain tasks to a trial consultant even when attorneys could do them just as well—because consultants' hourly fees are generally less than those of top attorneys.

In describing the heart of the consultant's task, Mike Cobo, a principal of DecisionQuest, explains that "we have to focus [attorneys] away from the legal issues and towards . . . the salient themes to jurors."[107] Judy Rothschild of the National Jury Project agrees, noting the predicament of an attorney preparing for a big case: "You may not remember what your first questions were. You've been working with the same witnesses on ten different occasions. It's easy to lose perspective. You really can't be sure how the testimony is going to come across."[108]

Miami consultant Amy Singer stokes lawyers' fears when she writes, "Attorneys often assume they are in touch with the key issues of the case, only to learn through jury simulations that what they considered important is not what is important to jurors." But she also offers a remedy, suggesting that approaches designed to identify juror bias during jury selection have ". . . proven reliable in thousands of civil cases" and that savvy lawyers can use a wide range of research services to reduce other uncertainties as well.[109] With so much at stake in a highly pressured situation and so little concrete information available, one can easily understand why so many attorneys have signed on with consultants who promise, with varying degrees of certitude, to deliver the critical goods.

Eric Oliver, another consultant, explains that trial lawyers "are often accurately accused of acting rather insecure about the opposition gaining any edge, and they will grab a jury consultant immediately, regardless of what they might think about the field, just because the other side has hired one. Much of this superstitious behavior . . . emerges from the fact that attorneys, like everyone else, have no real clue as to how people actually go about making judgments. In that environment, experts selling odds on potential bias start looking pretty good."[110]

There may be another, darker, reason to hire a trial consultant. In an unusually frank interview, consultant and jury researcher Gary Moran suggests that lawyers sometimes hire consultants for a variety of reasons unrelated to the services listed in their brochures.[111] "A key strategy," he explains, "that's used almost always in all criminal defense work is delay, delay, delay. Somebody may die. Somebody may be intimidated. Delay. So my purpose, ostensibly, [is to help obtain a] . . . change of venue but the facts of the matter are that I'm in there really to add one more stack of paper, one more diversionary tactic." He adds somewhat cynically, "So that's a professional service. Yes, of course it is because I'll do a survey. . . . [The change of venue] is not going to be granted anyway. The judge is going to sit there and sit there and after four hours, when you're thinking, 'Is he alive or is he dead?' he will finally utter the magic word—'Denied.' And then we all move along."

And, lastly, there is the matter of taking credit for a win, but sharing the loss. Moran recounts a first-degree murder case against a young man whose father had won the lottery shortly after his son's arrest. The son had beaten a woman to death, and it was fairly obvious that he was going to be found guilty. The prospect of finding a sympathetic jury was near nil. Moran recalls, "Why did they hire me? Well, I'll tell you. . . . One, the lawyer likes me and, I mean, I'm not going to hurt anybody. Two, he could blame me. [The lawyer] said, 'When the jury's picked, I'm going to blame you.' I said, 'Fine . . . blame me.'"

Moran obviously delights in revealing the underside of the business, although his cynicism appears bounded by a desire to provide as useful a service as possible. In Chapter 3, we hear more about the business of trial consulting—from consultants as well as their critics—and consider where the industry has been and where it is headed.

3

THE JURY PERSUADERS

BIRTH OF A PROFESSION

IN 1972, PHILIP BERRIGAN, THE RADICAL PRIEST, stood trial on conspiracy charges along with a handful of other protesters. According to the prosecution, these defendants—part of the Catholic Resistance to the Vietnam War—had conspired to raid draft boards, destroy conscription records, blow up underground electrical conduits in Washington, D.C., and kidnap Secretary of State Henry Kissinger. A group of social scientists headed by Jay Schulman, Richard Christie, and Philip Shaver signed on to the defense team—not to earn large consulting fees but as a contribution to what they perceived as a morally compelling cause. The involvement of Schulman and his associates in the trial is generally acknowledged as the first known instance of systematic, or scientific, jury selection.[1]

The social scientists never saw their task as stacking the jury. Indeed, they suspected that the government had attempted to do just that by trying the case in Harrisburg, Pennsylvania, which everyone presumed to be conservative territory. Pretrial polling revealed that eight out of ten registered voters in the area held views *unfavorable* to the defense. The consultants' task, as they saw it, was to help the defendants—the so-called Harrisburg Seven—get a *fair* jury, one that was not biased against them but also not biased in their favor.

Using methods of survey research that were standard at the time, Schulman's team sought to paint profiles of the most and least desirable jurors. They did this by probing respondents' attitudes about issues in the trial and obtaining various kinds of background information. The researchers attempted to gauge—among other things—trust in government, belief in the legitimacy of protest, and prior knowledge about the defendants.

To the surprise of defense counsel, the research team determined that college-educated jurors were apt to be *more* conservative and, therefore, worse jurors from the perspective of the defense. More intuitively, bad jurors for the Harrisburg Seven were also likely to be Episcopalian, Methodist, Presbyterian, or fundamentalist. Subscribers to *Reader's Digest*, members of local civic organizations, and Republican businessmen would also be more likely to convict the defendants. Those who were likely to favor acquittal included female Democrats with no religious preference who worked in white-collar jobs or skilled blue-collar jobs.

The consulting team rated the prospects in the Harrisburg jury pool for the extent to which they conformed to the profile of the prodefense juror derived from the survey findings. Although the prosecution eliminated several of the defense's top choices for the panel, the final twelve jurors seemed far better than those with whom the defense might have ended up. And as it turned out—fair or not—the twelve impaneled citizens hung on all the major conspiracy charges, a gratifying result for the defense. The jury delivered only one minor conviction, on a charge of smuggling letters out of prison.

As if that were not enough, a posttrial survey of some of the original interviewees revealed that a majority still leaned toward convicting the Berrigan group on at least one of the conspiracy charges. Thus, it seemed to some observers not only as if the jury selection advisers had made the crucial difference but also as if they had documented their impact through posttrial research. Who could deny the thrust of the jury's verdict? Trial consulting was off to an auspicious start.

Following the Harrisburg conspiracy cases, early jury consultants continued to build a reputation for effectiveness. One pillar of this image was the Joan Little case.[2] In August 1974, Clarence Alligood, a night jailer, had been found dead—apparently murdered with an ice pick—in a locked cell in the women's section of a jail in Beaufort County, North Carolina. Little, a black woman and the former occupant of that cell, had escaped, but she later turned herself in to the police in Raleigh. She contended that Alligood, who was white, had raped her and that she had, indeed, killed him—but in self-defense. Law enforcement personnel embraced an alternative theory: that she had lured him into her cell, perhaps with the promise of sexual favors, only to stab him at the first opportunity. Little's attorney did not want to leave this critical question in the hands of jurors from Beaufort County, many of whom he believed to be racist.

John McConahay, a Duke University psychology professor, led a team of social scientists who hoped to help Little in her defense. First, they polled a sample of the public and found, in line with their expectations, that two-thirds of the residents of Beaufort County believed that black women had lower morals than white women and that blacks were more violent than whites. The surveys additionally revealed that three-fourths of the residents of Beaufort County had heard of the jailhouse killing. In this regard, however, they did not differ substantially from other residents of the state. More important, the research suggested that residents of Beaufort County were twice as likely as residents of some other parts of the state to prejudge Little as guilty. Armed with these results, Little's lawyer succeeded in having the trial moved to Wake County, a locale deemed far more favorable to the defense. Polling evidence also helped eliminate from consideration several other venues apparently as biased as Beaufort County.

Next, McConahay's group built a mathematical model of the ideal defense juror for the Little case. They did this by studying how a large variety of background factors combined to influence a juror's predisposition toward the defendant. The researchers concluded that the most favorable jurors would be Democrats or Independents, younger than forty-five, residents of the city of Raleigh, with a college education. As in the Harrisburg Seven case, the defense then used this profile to help select jurors. The Little trial lasted five weeks, but the jury needed only a bit more than an hour to acquit Little of all charges. Her attorney then announced, with that peculiar machismo that often characterizes trial lawyers, that he had purchased the verdict with a large defense fund—used, among other things, to pay for substantial jury research.

During the early and mid-1970s, Schulman, McConahay, and a number of other academic social scientists offered jury selection services in several highly politicized and heavily covered criminal trials of the era. These included the Angela Davis trial, the trial of the Indian militants from Wounded Knee, the Attica prison rebellion trials, and the Vietnam Veterans Against the War trial, among others. Most of these cases involved left-wing activists, but jury selection experts also assisted in the defense of former Attorney General John Mitchell and Watergate defendant Maurice Stans.[3] Such cases typically ended with the consultants claiming victory and the attorneys with whom they worked backing up their claims.

An audit of trial consulting's first decade sometimes leaves the impression that the field sprung into existence like Athena, fully developed, armored, and rearing for battle. But the first consultants did not have to build their arsenal all the way up from the ground. Several trends propelled and sustained the development of the field.

News came from the business world and academia of a set of tools that might give the forward-looking and innovative attorney an edge over less progressive peers. Advances in academic jury science contributed to the development of the consulting industry. Academics saw a place where their theories could prove useful, while consultants hoped to derive added respectability from their associations with colleges and universities.

More directly, the market research and advertising industries had achieved well-documented success with focus groups, quantitative surveys, statistical analyses, consumer profiling, and a variety of other techniques. Trial consultants drew eagerly on such principles; perhaps this is why some practitioners refer to their methods as "basic" or "far from rocket science." Although lawyers did not always find the metaphor of "selling a product to the jury" an ego-enhancing one, many stood ready to profit from these methods if they proved germane to their work.

At the same time, immigration patterns and major changes in the law had brought to panels many people from backgrounds that did not approximate those of an earlier era. Blacks, Hispanics, Asians, and others left lawyers uncertain about whom to select during voir dire and how best to get their points across throughout the trial. Many lawyers sensed opportunity if only they could decode and harness the mind-sets of these new jurors.

The practice of law also changed in ways that benefited trial consultants. Most lawyers were spending less and less time in the courtroom. But within the profession, the need for an explicit focus on trial advocacy had been recognized. In the mid-1960s, Boalt Hall, the law school of the University of California–Berkeley, began teaching trial advocacy by videotaping students as they delivered opening statements, interrogated witnesses, and carried out other mainstays of the courtroom lawyer. The subsequent spread of trial advocacy training throughout U.S. law schools can be viewed as a precursor to the mock trials that consultants so often arrange.[4]

Perhaps attorneys had always thought of themselves as actors; now they started to think of themselves as communicators in a courtroom setting. In many ways, the tools in the trial consultant's arsenal enhanced the techniques that attorneys—or, at least, some attorneys—had been using for years. But lawyers had never followed the requirements of the scientific method to any meaningful degree. By the late 1980s, attorneys had become a fertile market for those who studied and sold scientifically gathered insights.

The industry was burgeoning.

PORTRAIT OF A CONSULTANT

Trial consulting has come a long way from its origins in political activism. During the 1980s, one firm, Trial Behavior Consulting, Inc. (TBCI), served as consultant for the defense in more than 150 asbestos-related trials. Across the country, thousands of plaintiffs were suing corporations for illnesses that purportedly arose out of their exposure to asbestos. In connection with this litigation, David Island, TBCI's founder, claims to have spearheaded the development of written juror questionnaires as a tool to select members of a jury (although this claim is difficult to verify). In 1986, he served as president of the recently formed American Society of Trial Consultants. He now estimates that, all in all, he has picked between 300 and 400 juries in many different parts of the country. In addition, he has prepared perhaps 1,000–1,500 witnesses.[5]

Recently, Island offered some frank reflections on the trial consulting business in an industry newsletter:

> There is no Bible, no manual, no ritualistically correct way of doing anything in our field. Other than engaging in some grossly negligent behavior, we are on our own. Consequently, an aura of personality-cult surrounds our profession. Clients stick to us because they like us, because of who we are as people, because of our experience, . . . because they get along with us and because we have done good work for them—all according to their standards. There may be good chemistry operating, but not necessarily good work being done, were the work to be judged by some objective standard or peer review.[6]

Island, like many consultants who have been around the business for more than a decade, thinks of himself as a pioneer. Also like many consultants—veteran and neophyte—he came to the field, more or less, by accident. After receiving a Ph.D. in educational psychology from the University of Minnesota in 1967, Island spent his early career in academia. In 1980, while on the faculty of California State University–Sacramento, he became involved in a research project assessing the impact of TV cameras in the courtroom. His research team concluded that in-court cameras were not harmful.

But far more significant for Island's future career, the study team noted considerable differences between effective and ineffective attorneys. The team was also able to predict trial outcomes based on its ratings of attorney competence. Building on this finding, Island developed training programs to teach attorneys how to improve their communication with juries.

One attorney he met in the midst of this endeavor inquired whether he had ever helped to pick a jury. He said he had not but agreed to try at no charge—on one condition. "If we win, you've got to be the president of my fan club for life." Island recalls, "We did. And he did. He is to this day one of my clients."

Although Island soon became aware that several other consultants had started doing similar jury work around the same time and that a few had started several years before, he had not heard of the jury consulting field

when he began. It was, he notes, "one of these . . . spontaneous generation things where independently, all over the country, the same thing was
happening."

Island headed TBCI from 1984 until 1990, when he sold his financial
interest to a holding company. For the next five years, he consulted to his
former company as an independent contractor from his home. Then, in
1995, he joined Forensic Technologies International (FTI), lured—he
says—by the money and because he found that he really did like going to
work each day. FTI today is one of the giants of litigation consulting, offering a full range of scientific, engineering, graphic design, and other expertise in addition to jury research. Over the years, it acquired several for-
merly independent stars of trial consulting, including Art Patterson,
Jo-Ellan Dimitrius, and Edward Bodaken. By many accounts, this strategy has turned FTI into one of the two top firms in trial consulting,
along with DecisionQuest.[7]

It can be a tough business. Island recalls the first time he lost big. He
was working with an attorney defending one of the largest banks in the
world. The bank had loaned upward of $10 million to a California straw-
berry farmer. The farmer couldn't make his payments, so the bank called
the loan. Subsequently, the farmer went bankrupt and sued the bank, alleging that the bank had engaged in improper lending practices. Island's
role in the lawsuit on behalf of the defendant included designing the jury
questionnaire and assisting in selection of the panel.

Still smarting from the memory, he describes the phone call from the
attorney telling him of the verdict against the bank: "$60 million." He
said, "You've got to be kidding." "I am not kidding," the lawyer replied
gravely. "Have you ever thought of going into another line of work?"
Island is willing to tell us this story today because, after a few years, the
client rehired him, and they presently have a good working relationship.
But the case drives home the intensity of the work. "Jury selection,"
Island explains, "is very difficult. It's very tense. A lot rides on it. And of
course if one of the most famous lawyers in San Francisco loses $60 mil-
lion dollars for one of the largest banks in the world, who's he going to
look at but his consultants? Right?" Then, he adds cheerfully, "In fact, it
was . . . the economics consultant. . . . who did make some mistakes."

Island explains that a good jury expert does not necessarily aim for a complete victory. "Sometimes the cases are really, really bad for your client." Then, the idea is damage control. Often, he asks his clients, "Do you want to win this case or do you want to work on how little you lose?" This distinction matters greatly because "the jurors who will [award large] damages look different from the jurors who will find liability." Sometimes the likely make-up of the jury pool makes a loss unavoidable. "We know," he explains, referring to his database, "that in certain venues, eighty percent of a certain ethnic group are going to go against a corporate defendant, just out of the box. We know that."

One particular sexual harassment case, he believes, illustrates why attorneys should listen to their consultants. A male deli manager working for a large supermarket chain supervised a number of female workers. He had allegedly coerced one of them into performing oral sex in exchange for better schedules and, possibly, a raise. The worker complied but, some time later, filed a lawsuit against the supermarket chain. The company's law firm retained Island.

He recalls, "There was hardly any contention about whether or not the act happened. There was some issue, you know, she wasn't bound and gagged. Why'd she do it? Why didn't she kick him in the groin and get on with it. And so there was some complicity on her part, perhaps. But still, a horrible case. A horrible case. . . . To take to trial? . . . You, the supermarket chain, you want the headlines about this stuff. . . . ?"

Island conducted focus groups and mock trials to determine the likely outcome of the case, including the probable damages that a jury would award. The case was to be tried in a politically liberal venue—one in which, presumably, prospective jurors would be predisposed to sympathize with an alleged victim of sexual harassment—and some of the mock jurors were saying $80 million. Others were saying the harassment hadn't happened.

After doing considerable research and analyzing the results carefully, Island was able to offer his client some guidance. "How much do you think this case is worth?" the lead attorney asked. Island predicted that the verdict in that particular venue would come in at $1–5 million. He recommended that the supermarket settle the case. "[But] they took it to trial. I helped pick the jury," he recalls. They wanted to win.

The trial lasted four weeks. "Horribly long, horribly awful," Island laments in retrospect. The jury awarded $300,000 in compensation for lost wages, along with *$3 million* in punitive damages. The punitive damages, according to Island, probably stemmed from the supermarket's failure to fire the deli manager. (In fact, the supermarket sent the deli manager for management training after receiving the complaint from the female employee.) But Island sees this as "a case that should never have gone to trial."[8]

Although jury consultants are often portrayed as amoral—hired guns—Island does not easily fit this image. He seems sincere about addressing moral and ethical dilemmas. "If you don't think through the ethical issues, I think you'd be a bad trial consultant," he declares. From time to time, he ruminates about the substance of cases. "I ask myself . . . Do I believe this case? When I know, for example, that these people polluted the environment and here I am working for them." But this is not where he sees the most difficult ethical dilemmas. After all, he explains, large corporations deserve their day in court.

Although he thinks Jo-Ellan Dimitrius did a "fabulous job" for O.J. Simpson, he firmly declares that he could never have worked on O.J. Simpson's criminal defense ". . . because he did it." Island claims special expertise on the matter because he has coauthored a book on domestic violence. His book—*Men Who Beat the Men Who Love Them*—deals with domestic violence in the gay community.[9] But many of the issues are similar, and like others, Island sees the Simpson case as a classic instance of domestic abuse turned extreme. He adds, "There are parts of me that I simply cannot put aside and work effectively." He avoids criminal cases because "I don't have the stomach for criminal stuff. I couldn't stand it." And he would be unwilling to assist in the defense of a company being sued for dismissing an employee with AIDS. Most ethics are personal, he concludes.

Island is also concerned about the ethics of witness preparation, which constitutes a large portion of his work. Breaking his usual rule about not participating in criminal cases, he played a small role in the William Kennedy Smith rape case. Island would not say much about this because he signed a nondisclosure form in connection with his services, in which he agreed, among other things, not to write a book about the case. He spent three days preparing witness Patrick Kennedy, son of U.S. Senator Ted Kennedy, for trial. Patrick was key to the case because he had been with Smith, the senator's nephew, for the entire evening except for the time of the alleged sexual act.

Island's main task was to help Patrick Kennedy appear as a neutral observer, rather than as an advocate of the Kennedy family. The goal was to get Patrick to tell—very simply—what he knew. Island explains the ethical way to prepare a witness: "My role is never to script someone, you know, say 'This is what you need to say.' Never. Ever. That would be unethical." Instead, he might ask a witness to "try it again" in order to more clearly convey what he or she really means. He spends days and days doing this. Island apparently believes he is able to keep from crossing the line from witness preparation to scripting.

He raised several other ethical dilemmas during our interview. Still, he never questions the ultimate morality of engaging in the business of jury consulting—assisting in jury selection or conducting focus groups, mock trials, witness preparation, and so forth. Like all consultants, he argues that these techniques—the staples of the jury consulting industry—constitute a legitimate part of an attorney's arsenal in an adversarial system. In his view, they might be used ethically or unethically, but—in themselves—they are acceptable.

POWERFUL MANIPULATORS: FACT OR FICTION?

John Grisham, in his best-selling courtroom thriller *The Runaway Jury*, fuels perceptions that jury consultants are up to no good. His fictional consultant, Carl Nussbaum, gets $1.2 million to pick the perfect jury.[10] The fee hardly matters to Nussbaum's client, Big Tobacco. After all, the industry fears a precedent-setting monster of a verdict, one that would threaten its very lifeblood. The only question is whether Nussbaum's tricks are equal to the task. His team of psychiatrists, sociologists, handwriting experts, law professors, and others employs the latest in social science, conducting a flurry of community surveys, simulations, and focus groups.

The fictional plaintiffs counter with their own jury experts, no less imposing. Both sides go beyond traditional methods of scientific research, flirting—Grisham writes—"around the edges of laws and ethics."[11] Nussbaum's team launches extensive investigations of 196 members of the jury pool, tracking them through their daily routines, snapping photographs, and recording their conversations at every opportunity. His goal is to unearth that one telling detail that tips a juror's hand and reveals his or her likely vote. Although Nussbaum seems to stop at nothing, many of his methods would probably be legal in most jurisdictions.

Grisham's fictional consulting team judges a doctor's wife particularly promising for the defense—except for one thing. She belongs to two health clubs and has "the precise appearance of one who aspired to look forever athletic."[12] The consultants wonder whether the prodefense proclivities they infer from this woman's position in life would be outweighed by a preoccupation with health matters. The question soon resolves itself when a photographer, at 100 yards, catches her sneaking a cigarette in the park. Knowing this, the tobacco attorneys will do all they can to include her among the final twelve.

The bevy of trial consultants conjured up by Grisham scrutinizes every scratch, squirm, and wiggle offered up by the unsuspecting but dutiful citizens in the pool of jury prospects. Needless to say, Grisham's jury specialists glean far more from jurors' questionnaires than face-value responses; handwriting experts follow each loop and cross in penmanship, trying to discern moods, traits, and attitudes. When the lawyers finally exercise their right to strike jurors from the pool—ten strikes each in this case—they are able to draw on far more than gross stereotypes and lawyerly intuition.

Grisham rouses his readers, in part, by playing on fears that the American justice system has been hijacked by crafty attorneys and immensely effective hired-gun social scientists. But, in later chapters of his book, tobacco industry higher-ups grow nervous that their experts have let them down, and so they order jury tampering of an obviously criminal variety. It soon becomes clear that the consultants, despite their touted excellence, have failed to discover several critical attributes of the jurors. Ultimately, the plot revolves around what jury consultants call a "stealth juror"—one who conceals a strong personal agenda in order to get seated on a panel.

Referring to Grisham's stealth juror, two prominent trial consultants maintain that "In reality . . . . jurors who distort the truth to avoid being excused during voir dire are not uncommon. From the Dalkon Shield cases in the early 1980's to the Agent Orange cases, a number of prospective jurors have attempted to conceal extremely strong biases. Because their prejudices are not overt, these jurors generally cannot be excused for cause, and thus become the highest priority for peremptory strikes."[13] They explain that the most significant and obvious reason that a biased juror might want to appear neutral is "a covert desire to punish one of the parties to a lawsuit."[14] Thus, in their view, trial consultants can make an important contribution to justice by effectively identifying and derailing stealth jurors, ones similar to—although perhaps not as clever as—the amazing juror who delivered $400 million in punitive damages in *The Runaway Jury*.

Outside the industry, however, few have cast trial consultants in so noble a role. Since the birth of this field in the early 1970s, many critics have assailed the ethics of scientific jury selection and related consulting services. As early as 1974, sociologist Amitai Etzioni referred in the *Washington Post* to the field as "social science jury-stacking," concluding that "man has taken a new bite from the apple of knowledge, and it is doubtful whether we will all be better for it."[15] Several years later, he commented, "The affluent people and the corporations can buy it, the poor radicals get it free, and everybody in between is at a disadvantage."[16] In 1992, *Business Week* ran an article entitled "The Best Jurors Money Can Pick."[17]

Two of the most articulate recent writers on the jury system, Jeffrey Abramson and Stephen Adler, have both spoken unfavorably about consultants. Discussing consultant-stacked juries, Adler writes, "Why should we defer to the decision of a group of individuals who have been selected for their likely partisanship and then persuaded by many of the same techniques that sell soap and breakfast cereal? When verdicts come to seem more manipulated than majestic, one thinks of *Brave New World* more readily than *12 Angry Men*."[18] Elsewhere, he adds, "Jury consultants have evaded restrictions so far, but nothing in the Constitution safeguards them. We can and should ban their use."[19] Abramson says, "The spectacle of inquiring into a person's religion or national origin, only to strike the person if the answer is one way rather than another, should be enough to indicate the underlying tension between traditional norms of blind jury selection and the new science."[20]

Following the O.J. Simpson trials, critics of jury consulting grew more vocal. One critic complained, not atypically, that "the jury system is distorted by demographics. It is compromised by consultants. It topples headlong into the racial chasm that divides city from suburb. There doesn't even seem to be a consensus anymore about what a 'jury of one's peers' means. In fact, that's the last thing many attorneys want and they'll pay a lot of money to make sure they don't get it."[21] Judge Harold Rothwax, a tough-minded but generally thoughtful jurist, once suggested that one lesson of the Simpson criminal trial was that ". . . jury selection is hostage to peremptory challenges that, with the help of scientific jury experts, can mold a jury in the hope that it will be swayed by emotion and innuendo, not fact."[22] A well-known former judge, Burton Katz, objects: "Lawyers misuse . . . [consultants] to skew jury selection to their side. If nothing else, this creates bad impressions of our system."[23]

Even the *Harvard Law Review* joined the condemnation of jury consultants in the aftermath of the Simpson trials: "Although there may be nothing inherently illegal or insidious about the consulting industry, its absolute freedom from legal or ethical regulation by the court system is troubling."[24] It is fair to say that jury consultants, in the eyes of many, have emerged as the nemeses of modern American justice.

One might ask why trial consultants have generated so much controversy. After all, most cases never get to a jury, and only a small percentage of these involve consultants. Only 2–3 percent of tort filings make their way to a panel of peers. Far more often, plaintiffs abandon their claims, judges resolve them prior to trial, or—more commonly—the parties agree on a settlement.[25] Juries also decide relatively few criminal cases. More than 90 percent of criminal convictions come from negotiated pleas of guilty.[26] One study showed that, in many jurisdictions, only about three or four out of every 100 arrests proceed to a trial by jury.[27]

And of the 150,000–300,000 cases decided by juries each year, perhaps fewer than 10,000 involve consultants.[28]

We cannot, however, underestimate the significance of juries. Nearly everything that happens in the American justice system depends—directly or indirectly—on juries and their presumed patterns of decision-making. Political scientist and attorney Jeffrey Abramson explains: ". . . It is the background existence of the right to a jury trial, and predictions about how juries would decide cases were they to get them, that drives parties to settle or plea bargain in the first place. Those who argue that the jury is unimportant because jury trials are infrequent thus mistake the tip of the iceberg for the whole."[29]

Similarly, trial consultants make an impact on the justice system far out of proportion to the number of cases in which they participate.[30] The very largest civil suits nearly *always* involve consultants, usually on both sides. Many attorneys report that when the stakes are high enough, using outside jury experts is standard procedure. Trial consultants often help one or both sides in important criminal cases, too, especially those that generate a lot of media attention.

One jury consultant after another declares that business is good and, barring changes in the political or legal environment, likely to get much better. Ann Harriet Cole, a Manhattan-based consultant and president of the American Society of Trial Consultants, said to a gathering of new consultants: "Business is burgeoning. Most people are turning away work, referring it to colleagues. We're not seen [by attorneys] as some weird thing, but as something they need to do or they may not be doing all they can for their clients. It is a growing field, not a profession with finite opportunities. The more people, the more opportunity."[31] Elsewhere, Cole writes that

our profession has finally arrived. I know this is true because when I tell folks that I meet socially, not just high stakes civil and criminal attorneys, that I'm one of those people who work with lawyers to define trial strategy, find the 'story' in every case, prepare witnesses to testify and . . . help select juries—that in short, I'm a litigation consultant, a trial consultant or a jury consultant (which one falls out of my mouth depends on whim and mood of the moment), most of them have a sense of what I mean and also know that I'm *not* some shady kind of private investigator who attempts to tamper with an actual jury. Ten years ago . . . that mostly wasn't the case. Sixteen years ago when I first paid my dues and showed up at the 1983 ASTC Conference in Chicago that surely wasn't the case.[32]

Trial consultants are no longer the rare birds they were in the 1970s. They are understandably eager to quote a New York lawyer who told a journalist in 1989, "It's gotten to the point where if the case is large enough, it's almost malpractice not to use them."[33] Although this assessment certainly constituted an overstatement when it was made and probably still does today, many of the nation's top attorneys share the belief that trial consultants can be decisive in civil and criminal cases.

Yet few attorneys, let alone the public, know much about who these behind-the-scenes players are or what they do. As Solomon Fulero, an academic jury researcher and occasional consultant, notes: "There's much more of this going on than people know. But it's not generally made known publicly."[34] Indeed, lawyers typically *want* their consultants to stay behind the scenes. Consultants themselves often show little awareness of what goes on in the industry beyond the confines of their own firm.

In the next section, we examine more closely the people who make up the trial consulting industry, seeking to understand their backgrounds, motivation, and outlook.

TRADING SECRETS

With the temperature topping 100 degrees, San Antonio, Texas, seemed an appropriate venue for the annual gathering of those so often characterized as the devil's handmaidens. But even in sweltering heat and beneath a dark blanket of smog that had blown over from a Mexican forest fire, the city offered a pleasant setting for the annual meeting of the American Society of Trial Consultants. La Mansion del Rio, the hotel that hosted the event, might be described as charming but not prohibitively expensive, hardly a monument to avarice or conspicuous consumption. Built in 1852 as a school for boys, the edifice reflects the city's

Spanish heritage. It is located on the banks of the cascading San Antonio River along the famous Riverwalk and stands under towering cypresses, only a few blocks from the Alamo fortress. Despite the ostensible conference objective of exchanging ideas and information, there may well have been a greater truth in the hotel's motto: "La Mansion del Rio . . . . what you come to San Antonio for."

After all, explained David Island (who did not attend the conference), "trial consultants, by and large, are loathe to share with each other anything substantive about what they know."[35] Howard Varinsky, another prominent consultant who did not attend, agrees: "We don't really share knowledge the way other professions share knowledge. We try to protect our little insights and methodologies, more often than not. . . . What you find at conferences is geared toward the beginner . . . basic . . . platitudinal. . . . Knowledge is protected by each firm."[36] Most consultants are very tight-lipped about what they do on the job, in part to protect client interests and confidentiality, but also because, as several concede privately, this is a somewhat paranoid field. In this business, many of the firms refer to much of what they do as "trade secrets."

Island reflects, "Our work is very solitary and almost frighteningly lonely."[37] Many trial consultants admit to a need for professional support and community. Some did expect to find this in San Antonio. Others came to the conference not so much to learn as to strengthen their career identity, to add to their self-image as members of a legitimate, scientifically based, ethical profession. In any event, the conference provided a rare opportunity to observe trial consultants during their moment of reflection, sociability, and even—on occasion—openness. These observations can help us to discern what motivates them, as well as how they perceive the politics, ethics, science, and business of their profession.[38]

With pay reportedly so high, outsiders might see motivation as obvious. But things are not so simple. Many trial consultants started out in academia and most left (or never entered) the profession for which they originally had trained. At one meeting in San Antonio, people around the room spoke of their academic backgrounds. They had Ph.D.s in communication research, clinical psychology, social psychology, organizational behavior, political science, sociology, counseling, and mass communication. Several were attorneys who had tired of legal practice. One held an M.B.A. Quite a few had multiple graduate degrees. Numerous consultants readily acknowledge that they originally entered the field largely because prospects for academic employment were poor when they completed their graduate degrees. But none mention any regrets.[39]

Robert Hirschhorn, who worked for the government on the Whitewater matter, for Terry Nichols in the Oklahoma City bombing case, and for William Kennedy Smith in his rape trial, followed perhaps the most unusual path into the consulting business. In the mid-1980s, he had been a young Texas lawyer handling what he considered to be an "impossible" case when a colleague suggested that he hire Cathy Bennett, a rising star in jury consulting. Hirschhorn recalls that he ". . . hired her so that when we lost I could blame it on her," but he never got the chance.[40] "In the few days we worked together, she changed my perception of law practice and jury selection."[41] Hirschhorn won the case, married Bennett, and joined her firm as a full-time consultant. He told her, "I want to stop practicing law and I want to learn to do what you do."[42] When, several years later, Bennett died of breast cancer at age forty-one, Hirschhorn assumed the presidency of the firm, which retains the name of his late wife.

Nearly all trial consultants describe the field as a good place for intellectually creative work. For example, Cynthia Cohen, a solo practitioner in Manhattan Beach, California, wrote a doctoral dissertation for the Annenberg School of Communication at the University of Southern California entitled "Communication Skills and Cognitive Processes in Productively Reducing Uncertainty in Ambiguous Instructional Messages." Although it took a bit of translation, in substance her dissertation was a stepping-stone to her first job developing witness communication training for the then-prominent firm Litigation Sciences.[43] Some consultants, particularly in the early days, started doing jury work as a way of contributing to some favored social cause, for example, defending antiwar activists, although—in order to make ends meet—nearly all took on commercial work as well. To this day, the politics of trial consultants (who express any views at all) tends toward the left.

For more than a few consultants, the legal work environment holds significant appeal. Many share Howard Varinsky's satisfaction with "very stimulating" work and ". . . lots of interaction with bright people."[44] As consultant Florence Keller puts it: "Two of the most fascinating issues in the world are how people think and the laws that govern people. What could be more interesting?"[45]

FACING THE CRITICS

Despite these day-to-day rewards, the vast majority of consultants express deep concern that they are members of a profession under assault. Never have they sensed this more than now. Like others, Theresa Zagnoli, of the mid-sized Chicago firm Zagnoli McEvoy Foley, Ltd., sees a multipronged attack. She writes:

> Not since the conception of our profession have we faced such skepticism from within the legal field, attacks in the media and criticism from the general public. As we become more visible, we become more vulnerable. It may be constitutionally difficult to place statutory restraints on our profession . . . but as we communication experts know, the thrust of public opinion is often greater than the power of law.[46]

As a result of the public assault, trial consultants frequently view reporters with trepidation. Although they might like to avoid the media completely, they are drawn by a desire to promote and publicize their services. Ohio consultant and professor Moe Rouse reflects on the dilemma and warns, "Very seldom will you know how the reporter feels about what you do. Be careful of the reporter who appears to like you. Likely he or she thinks you are fooling around with justice!"[47]

Consultants find themselves in a double-bind. They need to be perceived as effective, even decisive, in order to get and keep business. Yet they cannot be viewed as too effective or too central to the jury system if they are to refute critics and ward off political, legislative, and judicial attacks. They must forever struggle to maintain a balanced and delicately nuanced image in the public eye.

The problem appears to go beyond their management of external impressions. Many, especially those who come from liberal or idealistic academic backgrounds, genuinely want to feel that they are efficacious in their efforts and socially constructive in their impact. At the very least, most seem to have a need to believe that they are not harming the American justice system.

To this end, trial consultants invoke many defenses of the industry. Most start by denying emphatically—sometimes angrily—that they stack juries. Ronald Beaton, an FTI affiliate, objects that "people who accuse us of stacking the deck give us too much credit. You can't stack a jury. You can only unstack one."[48] One consultant after another points out that they do not select jurors but only "deselect" them.

Moreover, consultants claim that they are simply doing what lawyers have always done during jury selection. The only difference, they say, is that whereas attorneys traditionally have drawn on ethnic, occupational, and other stereotypes, trial consultants approach the task more fairly and scientifically. Many take solace in the notion that they are delivering American justice into the hands of moderates and those most likely to decide cases on their merits. As Solomon Fulero explains, "The theory is you're going to get off the three that are most against your side and so is the other side and the middle is going to be left."[49]

If critics suggest that bigots and extremists would be eliminated anyway through the use of the challenge for cause, consultants respond with a plethora of stories about judges who fail to remove obviously biased jurors. Judy Rothschild of the National Jury Project, one of the pioneer firms, refers to an abundance of social science research that shows that people are reluctant to speak in public about their biases and, indeed, are often unaware of them.[50] According to Rothschild, people also cannot tell how their preconceptions will affect them in a particular case because they do not yet know the specific facts of that case. And even when jurors admit some bias, judges may remain reluctant to remove them.

Rothschild tells of a personal injury case in which a prospective juror, a doctor, asked during voir dire to speak privately with the judge. The physician explained that he had been the defendant in a medical malpractice case and, as a result of that case, had been divorced and forced to relocate his office. He didn't think he could be a very good juror. The judge responded, "Well, you don't know anything about this particular case. Could you be fair and just and judge *this* case on the evidence?" The physician answered, "I could try. I have some very strong views about personal injury litigation but I know it's my duty to set these views aside. I could try. I can't guarantee you I could do it but I could try." The judge said, "You've passed for cause," meaning he could stay on the case and that if the plaintiff wanted to remove him, it would have to exercise a peremptory challenge. In Rothschild's view, this juror was plainly biased and had tried to do the right thing. The judge missed the point, as might many others because, Rothschild argues, most judges are typically loathe to remove a juror unless the juror explicitly states that he or she cannot be fair.

Howard Varinsky makes a related point with the notorious case of John Walker, who was charged with, and later pled guilty to, spying against the United States. One prospective juror had been given a questionnaire asking, "What do you think should be done with people accused of espionage?" In writing, he answered, rather frankly, "Hang him by the balls." Later, in open court, the judge asked him a similar question, to which he more nobly replied that he would ". . . have to see the evidence."[51]

A frequent argument against trial consultants is that they tilt the scales of justice in the direction of the wealthy since only the rich can afford their exorbitant fees. Consultant Lucy Keele and most other consultants agree yet see this as an inescapable aspect of the American justice system. She explains: "Money affects everything in society. It affects the kind of school you go to, the type of job you get because you can buy nicer clothes. It affects justice in terms of the kind of lawyer you can get. We are an extension, obviously, if you have money and can afford these services, it will go better for you."[52]

But Solomon Fulero has a solution. Referring to the U.S. Supreme Court decision in *Gideon v. Wainwright*, which secured the right of counsel for indigent defendants in state criminal trials, he says:

> You could have argued, I suppose, "I've got the solution. Since only the rich have lawyers, we'll ban lawyers. Right?" And, of course, that's not what the Supreme Court did. They leveled the playing field by providing lawyers at public cost to criminal defendants who can't afford them. If

. . . [trial consultants] are really effective, what you do is level the playing field. Provide them at no cost, at least in cases where it's an issue.[53]

Another oft-heard criticism of jury consultants is that "clever consultants can use the peremptory challenge to stack juries or 'dumb them down,' arriving at the least sophisticated or educated group" of jurors.[54] Indeed, recent cases in the public eye have left few members of the general public believing that the role of the consultant is to *increase* the intelligence level of juries. Yet many jury selection experts claim that their goal is, in fact, to identify and seat intelligent jurors. Says Florence Keller, who typically consults in civil cases involving large corporate clients, "There is a feeling that we are the scum of the earth. Here's how I answer that. . . . I always end up with a smart jury. That's really what I want. Maybe because [I work mainly with] . . . intellectual property cases." She continues: "We do our work. The lawyers do very well in preparing. If I can get a smart jury that isn't very, very biased against us, we're going to win."[55]

And criminal defense attorneys and their trial consultants frequently note that many jurors start out with a strong proprosecution bias; large numbers improperly presume guilt rather than innocence at the outset of the trial. Consultant Gary Moran, an academic, works chiefly for criminal defendants. He asserts that the defense wants people intelligent enough to consider the possibility that something is imperfect or improper in the government's case, even though the defendant is not necessarily squeaky clean. Moran believes that prosecutors "are looking for dumb people, racist people, people who are hostile. That's what the government's looking for. The people the government tries to kick off juries are the most able people." He adds, "The defense is not looking for stupid people. . . . You are not going to be able to get twelve people so stupid that you can hoodwink them. But the government can certainly eliminate the few intelligent people because there are not many of them." Moran pinches his nostrils and comments, "This is the way jurors acquit people—by holding their noses."[56] The implication is that many defendants are rather unsavory characters who have probably committed some misdeeds. In this context, jury consultants for the defense might seek educated, broad-minded jurors who are thought to be more willing to embrace the legally ordained presumption of innocence. Of course, one can easily imagine that the consultants who work with prosecutors would argue that they, too, are in search of the more intelligent jurors. And, notwithstanding a famous debate between defense lawyers F. Lee Bailey and Percy Foreman concerning which one—in an illustrious career—had picked the stupidest jury, few attorneys or consultants will acknowledge that they are seeking intellectually deficient jurors.[57]

Trial consultants often portray themselves as enablers rather than disablers of the jury system. Indeed, the overwhelming majority of consultants describe themselves as fervent defenders of the jury system and, in many cases, as the grease that smoothes its sometimes creaky operation. David Island says, "If there's anything [trial consultants] probably all agree with, it's that the jury system is good. And it isn't just that we make our living in relation to it. But it's a philosophical, political posture we've taken as a group."[58]

Thus, in their view, when trial consultants help prepare witnesses to testify, they are not putting words in people's mouths (and certainly not suborning perjury). Rather, they are helping witnesses communicate their stories effectively. By removing personal affectations, stylistic idiosyncrasies, linguistic imprecision, and cognitive fuzziness, they are—in effect—helping the truth to work its way out. When they eliminate prospects from the jury panel, they are removing prejudice and helping to restore the system to its originally intended function. Similarly, when they pretest legal arguments before focus groups and mock juries, they are helping to ensure that the jury will hear the very best arguments that each side can offer.

A LOOK BACK, A LOOK FORWARD

Numerous scholars have revisited the early examples of systematic jury selection techniques and concluded that their impact was perhaps less impressive than was widely believed at the time. Concerning the Joan Little trial, for example, the presiding judge said that the case against her was one of the weakest he had seen in his twenty years on the bench. Thus, under the circumstances, even jurors who bought into negative stereotypes about black women might have had difficulty finding Little guilty beyond a reasonable doubt. The evidence may have determined the verdict. Who ended up on the jury—after all that research—may well have been irrelevant.

Similarly, the Berrigan verdict may have rested on a fairly apparent lack of sufficient evidence to convict. Those prospective jurors who said, after the trial, that they would have convicted on a conspiracy charge said so without hearing the courtroom proceedings. As Jeffrey Abramson has written, "Jury consultants are far too quick to assume that persons willing to presume a defendant's guilt in response to a poll question would also presume guilt if seated on a jury."[59] He further notes that the two jurors who held out for conviction in the Berrigan case had been judged favorably by the consultants. One was a woman, a member of a "desirable" religion (the pacifist Brethren Church), and the mother of four conscientious objectors. The other did not fit the desirable religious or occupational profiles, but the consultants believed he had the right attitudes toward social protest and the counterculture. This juror turned out to be a religious zealot who spoke of doing "God's work" on the jury and refused to listen to rational argument. In contrast to the consultants' expectations, the two proconviction jurors had formed a religious bond that worked against the interests of the Catholic radicals. One cannot even say with confidence that jury selection worked with regard to the other ten jurors who voted for acquittal, for this trial, like several other early trials involving jury consultants, was a conspiracy case, and conspiracy convictions are notoriously difficult to obtain. Any randomly chosen group of twelve jurors may well have produced the same result.

Plainly, a fair assessment of the role of the new jury selection techniques should start with the simple recognition that victory in a court case—as well as defeat—may arise from many sources. In subsequent chapters, we will take up the matter of what works and what does not more systematically. For now, however, it is worth noting that those attorneys who have the resources to hire consultants may also be those who are in the best position to prepare other aspects of their case carefully. They may be able to afford the best expert witnesses and to conduct the most comprehensive legal research. As a result, the observation that an attorney hired a consultant and then won the case really tells us very little.

By the year 2000, trial consulting had become an increasingly healthy, mature, and profitable industry—not big business but hardly small change. Its most renowned practitioners were no longer leftist university professors who donned neglected neckties to assist in courtroom battles during summer breaks. Tasteful suits and polished shoes became the norm as annual revenues for the industry reached $400 million.[60] The American Society of Trial Consultants, founded in 1982 with fewer than two dozen members, grew to a total membership of close to 400 by the summer of 1998.[61] Depending on whom one included under the heading Trial Consultant, some recent estimates placed the number of firms at more than 400 and the number of professionals in excess of 700.[62] Many trial consultants are solo practitioners, and quite a few offer services on a part-time basis, often while maintaining professorial positions in the social sciences, business, and law. But the trend, very clearly, has been toward larger firms.

During the 1980s, one company emerged, far and away, as the industry leader. Founded by Don Vinson, a former professor of marketing at the University of Southern California, Litigation Sciences worked on thousands of cases and spawned a whole industry of competitors. Phil Anthony, one of the principals of the firm, recalls that when they first incorporated in 1979 they successfully sold their services to only a handful of innovative trial lawyers.[63] "The vast majority would say, 'Absolutely not. I'm not going to do that.' . . . So the whole world has changed. . . . . Today, trial consulting is almost a standard part of trial preparation in any case of any substance." When he speaks of substance, of course, he means cases where a very large amount of money is at stake. "It's applied in cases where exposure is as low as anywhere from a million to a half-million dollars. Below that, it doesn't make too much sense." Litigation Sciences made its reputation ". . . on the basis of being the firm which works on behalf of corporate defendants . . . the majority of the time." He adds, "We specifically sought out corporate defendants as clients. We did not seek out criminal cases or cases on behalf of plaintiffs." The strategy paid off. In the early years, Litigation Sciences grew rapidly, according to Anthony, at the rate of 54 percent a year for more than a decade. The firm had more than 300 employees and consulted in all fifty states,

Guam, Puerto Rico, and other countries. Many of their biggest cases in the early years dealt with antitrust litigation. Product liability cases predominated for a time in the 1980s. By the end of that decade, annual revenues reached $30 million.

The firm did so well that it attracted the attention of Saatchi and Saatchi, the advertising giant, which was in the midst of its move into the consulting arena. Vinson and the other principals decided to sell Litigation Sciences, believing that the affiliation with Saatchi and Saatchi would enable the jury consulting firm to grow even bigger. According to Anthony, when Saatchi and Saatchi chose shortly afterward to exit the consulting world, he, Vinson, and the other principals from the original firm tried to buy it back. The offer was rejected. "So we quit. We had a noncompete agreement so we actually waited for what amounted to a couple of years and then we started DecisionQuest." The new firm was launched in 1992 by senior personnel of Litigation Sciences: David Davis, Ross Laguzza, Reiko Hasuike, Mike Cobo, Layne Hastings, Allan Colman, and Phil Anthony. Don Vinson joined the firm a year later. Not surprisingly, the Litigation Sciences division of Saatchi and Saatchi soon petered out.

DecisionQuest has succeeded in recapturing its predecessor's position as the industry leader—although FTI, National Jury Project, and a few other firms are formidable competitors. The firm, now a division of the consulting corporation Dames and Moore, has annual revenues of $40 million and employs about 200 people in thirteen offices. It offers a very wide array of trial support services. "What we do," explains Anthony, "will cost anywhere from a low of ten thousand dollars to upwards of a couple of million dollars. . . . The average to do something meaningful is probably a hundred to two hundred thousand dollars."

But size does not necessarily equal quality, and attorneys frequently have no way of judging whether the services they receive from Decision-Quest and other large firms are really better than, or even as good as, the advice they would get from, say, a professor who consults part-time. In the absence of reliable information, many feel safer with the industry leaders. But others suggest that prospective clients should select their advisers based on the quality of their scientific training. Jury researcher

Michael Saks says: "I would trust somebody who . . . [came from] any kind of graduate program that was very serious about its research methodology. I don't care if they're psychologists or communications or educational researchers if they really understand that they need to have an empirical basis for what they're doing." Such services need not be high-priced. He continues, "Some of the best services that . . . [consultants] can provide don't cost so much, namely, running some videotapes of what your basic case consists of past a sample of people who are drawn from the jury-eligible population. . . . Given a couple of weeks and not too many thousands of dollars, you actually could get a read from these people on how your case is coming across . . . and probably make some useful adjustments at trial."[64] Professor Solomon Fulero agrees: "Jury selection firms make a big deal out of it—whip it up into something that will cost you a hundred to two hundred thousand dollars. I think this can be effectively done for as little as five to fifteen thousand dollars. I think that most attorneys are not aware of that." He adds, "For a little investment, they can get fairly effective [information]—if you leave off the frills and bells and whistles and things that I think aren't very effective."[65]

Consultant Howard Varinsky, coming from a background in social work, thinks the best consultants have superior insight. He explains, "I judge competence not by degree and not by knowledge of methodology, not by knowledge of quantitative analysis. I judge competence by sharpness and intuition—by how people in the field think about information and juror processing, not necessarily how they derive their information. . . . I want to see wisdom there."[66] Of course, the split between the scientific approach and the intuitive one redounds throughout psychology and the social sciences. And debates over the relative advantages of big and small firms similarly reverberate throughout the business world.

As trial consulting finishes its first quarter-century, one might pause to assess some ways in which the industry today differs from its early years. Most notably, trial consultants place far less emphasis on jury selection than they did in the past. One after another comments on this shift. Howard Varinsky remarks, "We all started off as jury selection consultants but realized that there's much more to it."[67] Phil Anthony agrees, calling jury selection "a very minor part of what we do . . . . [which] has minor importance relative to the presentation of the case." He explains,

> We try to determine what's the best case . . . [an attorney] can put on rec-
> ognizing that . . . . [he or she is] going to get a cross-section of all kinds of
> people serving on that jury. I'm not going to be able to predict what that
> jury looks like. I'm not going to be able ever to really know what any one
> of those people is thinking or where they come from but rather [I should
> strive] to put on the best case I can put on, maximizing the positive aspects
> of my case and minimizing the negative aspects. And that's where we spend
> ninety percent of our creative energy.[68]

Florence Keller, from a smaller firm, echoes the new consensus: "Select-ing a jury or deselecting a jury is in many ways the least important thing we do."[69] Professor Michael Saks concludes: "I think the firms have shifted. If you look at what they were doing twenty years ago, selecting a jury was what it was all about. Now, the focus is much more on shaping the evidence . . . . [and] preparing the witnesses."[70]

Many attorneys first come to trial consultants for assistance with choosing jurors. Nearly all the firms will provide this service, but they will also attempt to sell the attorney a range of services deemed more effective. As a result, many consulting firms now promote themselves as full-service operations and emphasize case strategy. Promotional brochures typically offer case analysis, trial simulations, evaluation of opening statements and closing arguments, witness evaluation and preparation, preparation of voir dire questions, jury selection assistance, settlement evaluation, post-trial interviews, change of venue evaluation, jury composition challenges, community attitude surveys, courtroom graphics, continuing legal edu-cation, and other services.

Despite the deemphasis of jury selection services, trial consultants still assist in choosing thousands of juries each year. In contrast to earlier years, however, they are paying less attention to demographic predictors like race, ethnicity, age, sex, religion, economic status, and occupation. Today, they typically look much more carefully at a prospective juror's attitudes and values. DecisionQuest's Mike Cobo explains: "Our research has found that there is nothing that's demographically matched to who is a plaintiff-oriented juror and who's a defense-oriented juror and that's years and years and years of cases and tens of hundreds of thousands of jurors that we've interviewed. What we do know is that there are attitudes, values and beliefs that drive people to make certain decisions."[71] But to learn which attitudes and values will affect judgment in a particular case, trial consultants cannot draw on previously gathered data. Each trial requires new research.

During the past fifteen years, jury consulting has become increasingly corporate and bureaucratic. Some, like professor Fulero, lament this change:

> This whole thing started as an academic enterprise. It was a set of social scientists who were being presented with an applied legal problem. . . . Very quickly, after the political trials, it became a general academic problem. How good are lawyers at this and what can we do? . . . A lot of people—a lot of the psychology people—who got into this in the seventies were intrigued by that. They viewed the jury as a laboratory, as applied social psychology. . . . And if you could make a little money on the side along the way—that was fine. . . . But it very quickly turned into big business. I think when that happened, I think something was lost. That is what concerns me . . . I guess I'm worried [that what is being sacrificed is] . . . academic integrity.[72]

The concern that Fulero voices is that large firms may be less willing to follow through on the implications of scientific research if their business interests would take them in a different direction. Put another way, how might established firms respond to evidence that one of their most profitable techniques had little scientific validity?

Nevertheless, professionalization and greater pressure to engage in pro bono activities have accompanied the increasing bureaucracy of the industry.[73] Thus, many consultants have called for an enhanced code of ethics, perhaps in part because they believe such a code will help establish the profession and protect it from political and judicial onslaught. In a recent survey of members of the American Society of Trial Consultants, 96 percent of those who were aware of the society's Code of Professional Standards rated it "very" or "somewhat" important.[74] Perhaps more telling, however, a substantial percentage of the membership remained unaware of the code's existence despite the fact that subscription to its minimal standards was a mandatory condition of membership.

The questions considered in the society's code are not the big ones. Instead, like most codes of professional ethics, the industry's current code deals more with the need of practitioners and attorneys for rules of engagement in business activities. For example, is it ethical for a consultant to work for one corporation when he or she has previously worked for an opposing party? To what extent may insights from prior work be brought to bear on a new project? If one works typically for plaintiffs in a certain type of litigation, is it reasonable to occasionally work for defendants, and vice versa?[75] Is it acceptable to publish win/loss rates even though such figures are perhaps devoid of meaning and likely to mislead potential clients?

Another troubling dilemma for practitioners concerns what to do when a client requests services that either will not help or cannot be provided within the available budget. Gary Moran describes the problem: "Just because there is a lot of money at stake is no reason to use a service if you have no reason to believe it will work. . . . [A doctor may say,] 'You have a metastasized malignancy, there is nothing I can do for you and there is nothing medicine can do for you; we're going to try to keep you comfortable; get your affairs in order, you'll be dead in six months.'" He continues: "Now you are clearly in a bad situation but this is not a reason to go have a coffee enema in Tijuana. . . . The fact that your life is at stake doesn't change the reality that coffee enemas are useless."[76] Well-known jury researcher Michael Saks, who generally views jury consulting with the detachment of an academic observer, also addresses the issue, pointing out that perhaps the consultant should simply say, "No, I'm sorry. We can't help you." He, too, invokes a medical metaphor:

It's like a patient coming to a doctor and saying, "I know I should have come to you earlier when I felt the lump and I'm here kind of late in the game. And I don't have insurance. I can only pay you — here's my passbook savings account. There's five hundred dollars in there. Do for me what you can." Should the doctor say, "Get lost. We can't do a good job for you"? Or should the doctor say, "I'm only going to be able to do something very limited but that's what you want"? They could say, "Here's what works. But here's what I can give you—given the time and the money. If you want to purchase that, I'll give it to you—with the understanding that. . . ."[77]

Saks's position seems reasonable enough, but one wonders how many consultants running a business with an eye on the bottom line will capture its subtlety.

The drive toward professionalization has raised questions concerning the appropriate training of consultants. Professions, after all, are supposed to possess some shared core of knowledge. Yet so many diverse academic backgrounds are represented among current practitioners, and so little in methodology is willingly shared among consultants, that efforts to standardize training have thus far failed to congeal. Nonetheless, a few graduate programs offer training useful in the preparation of professional trial consultants. The University of Kansas offers a legal communication emphasis in its communication studies doctoral program. Students can take courses like "Persuasion Theory and Practice," "Argumentation," "Nonverbal Communication," "Legal Communication," "Small Group Communication," "Psychology and the Law," and "Forensic Psychology." The University of Nebraska offers a variety of joint degree programs that focus on jury behavior and are suitable for those who wish to become trial consultants. More recently, Towson University in Maryland has launched an interdisciplinary program—to obtain a "University Certificate in Litigation Consulting"—for students with graduate degrees who wish to build on their prior training to become jury consultants.

It remains to be seen how far the movement toward professionalization will go, as well as what protections it will provide. Perhaps it will merely serve to limit the number of competitors on the market. Even with a minimally restrictive code of ethics, calls for formalized grievance procedures and enforcement provisions have already encountered substantial resistance within the profession and are likely to encounter much more.[78]

There appears to be little hope for a powerful, industry-generated ethical code with teeth.

One final development in the trial consulting industry may prove very consequential for the future. In recent years, several solo practitioners and smaller firms have started to offer low-cost consulting services. For example, in the late 1990s, The Litigation Edge—a Denver-based consulting group—introduced a service called "The 999 Focus Group," where research would be conducted for $999. The firm's website offered the following description:

> You fill out our questionnaire and we present your case to a panel of jurors for immediate jury feedback. This service enables you to get a juror reading on your case, find out where the problems lie and assess what your case is worth (if the jurors find liability). Our report will consist of the jurors' comments regarding the various aspects of your case, recommended *voir dire* questions and our general psychological recommendations based on the jury's response to the key issues and our assessment of the problems revealed by the research.[79]

Marjorie J. Sommer, a principal of The Litigation Edge, reports that the price for the low-cost research has increased to $2,000 (in 2001) and is now called the "Mini-Max Focus Group"—for *mini*mum price and *max*imum information. She notes that The Litigation Edge offers a full array of trial consulting services, none priced above $20,000. "And you wouldn't believe how much our clients get for those $20,000," she boasts.[80]

With prices such as these, the stakes in a trial need not run into the millions in order for lawyers to give jury experts a crack at a case. The Wilmington Institute Network offers a service called the "Virtual Jury." As they explain it:

> The Online Focus Group is here! It is excellent for measuring attitudes towards your important case. It helps you decide whether to try or settle your case. Test your case themes and design your visual evidence. Empirical

group research is now affordable for every case. . . . It is cost-effective and time-efficient. Any venue may be accessed at a fraction of the cost of traditional in-person focus groups and mock trials.[81]

The low-price end of the consulting market remains the great untapped and untested business source for consulting firms. If professors Saks and Fulero are correct in their assessment that useful services need not cost in the tens or hundreds of thousands of dollars, then trial consultants—for better or worse—may be able to assist in far smaller cases than they generally have in the past. If, in contrast, consultants who cut corners are losing the wheat along with the chaff, then the industry may remain cost-effective only for the largest cases. Another possibility is that firms like The Litigation Edge may not be able to endure very long providing even the most basic services at the prices advertised. In any event, prices have been going up at some top firms, whereas others have opted for keeping prices low and increasing the size of their market. Should these latter firms succeed, jury experts may very well transform the way much litigation is carried out in the United States.

In the long run, however, the trial consulting industry cannot thrive unless the services it provides are effective. And it is to this matter that we now turn.

4

NEWS FROM THE LABORATORY

SO MANY CLUES, SO LITTLE TIME

DR. JO-ELLAN DIMITRIUS tells of the daunting, high-pressure task she faces each time she tries to select jurors sympathetic to her clients. A prospect might, for example, be short, dark-haired, well-dressed, college-educated, and married with two young children. He might teach high school history, love gardening, enjoy old movies, and belong to the rotary club. He might also speak with a slight Southern accent and come from a large, close family. That man has a thousand other characteristics as well but she, the jury consultant, has only five minutes to determine whether he would give her client a fair hearing. "So many clues, so little time!" she laments; "a wrong decision could literally be fatal to my client."[1]

Many of America's most prominent attorneys apparently believe that Dimitrius can pierce, dissect, and interpret such complexities with great skill. Although her celebrity status stems mainly from her work for the de-fense in the O.J. Simpson criminal trial, she has also attracted public at-tention as a trial consultant in the Reginald Denny, John du Pont, and McMartin preschool cases. Some people even blamed her, in part, for the 1992 Los Angeles riots because she had helped choose the panel that let off the officers charged with brutalizing Rodney King. After the Simpson verdict, people yelled at her in the streets, accused her of fomenting a race war, and even threatened her life.[2] All in all, Dimitrius has been retained in more than 600 jury trials. An attractive woman in her early forties, she stands by most accounts near the pinnacle of her profession. Several years ago, *American Lawyer* magazine went so far as to dub her the "Seer," presumably because of her ability to penetrate the mysteries of panel selection and to forecast juror proclivities. Dimitrius drew one of the top hourly rates at FTI/Consulting, a leading trial consulting firm, and remains as sought after as any trial consultant in the country.[3]

Although the market appears to have spoken, one might reasonably inquire whether the services she and other consultants provide truly merit such confidence and, if so, what combination of talent, training, and methodology has made her so effective. During the Simpson trial, she used many focus groups, an eighty-five-page juror questionnaire, an eight-question predictive model, and other tricks of the trade.[4] But Dimitrius does not see her profession as one that is, at its core, scientific.

In her 1998 book, *Reading People*, she explains:

> Some of those who read people for a living, as I do, rely almost exclusively on scientific research, surveys, studies, polls, and statistical analysis. Others claim to have a God-given talent. My own experience has taught me that reading people is neither a science nor an innate gift. It is a matter of knowing what to look and listen for, having the curiosity and patience to gather the necessary information, and understanding how to recognize the patterns in a person's appearance, body language, voice, and conduct.[5]

She asserts,

> *I never guess* about who should sit on a jury. But intuition is not guesswork, and it has always played a major part in my work. Over the years, I have learned to pay close attention to my deeper feelings about people and situations. Often, sudden flashes of intuition have led me to conclusions about people that appeared, at first, to be totally at odds with the rational workings of my mind. And on most occasions, these intuitive conclusions have turned out to be right.[6]

Although she holds a doctorate in criminal justice and has studied psychology, sociology, and statistics, Dimitrius believes that her strength is a capacity to "see the pattern of someone's personality and beliefs emerge from among often conflicting traits and characteristics."[7] As a consequence of "reading" tens of thousands of people in and out of the courtroom, Dimitrius claims that she has "amassed a very large subconscious database of various human characteristics and what they are likely to mean in various people under different circumstances."[8] This database forms the foundation for her "intuitive responses to people and situations."[9]

She describes her routine when in the courtroom:

> I constantly watch jurors, witnesses, lawyers, spectators, and even the judge, looking for any clues about how they're responding to the case and the people presenting it. I listen carefully to the words that are spoken, and to how they are spoken. I pay attention to the way people breathe, sigh, tap their feet or fingers, or even shift their weight in a chair. As the jurors walk by I notice any unusual smells—heavily applied perfume, body odor, the scent of medication. When I shake someone's hand I take note of the feel of his handshake. I use *all* of my senses, *all* of the time.[10]

Discussing a juror's intonation, she remarks: "It's easy to notice the message someone sends with a pouty, sad, or frustrated tone of voice, but a fleeting note of anxiety, fear, or embarrassment may slip right past you if you don't pay close attention. I've trained myself to listen for these vocal clues and recognize their nuances, since such a momentary glimmer may be the only tip I get about a prospective juror's doubts or true feelings toward a client." If indeed Dimitrius possesses such talent, one can understand why lawyers would pay handsomely to draw on it.[11]

Recounting how she convinced a reluctant defense team to retain one man on a jury, she notes with satisfaction that "the man became an active participant in the jury deliberations that resulted in our client's acquittal."[12] Elsewhere, she notes that her gut feeling told her to retain a juror about whom there had been some concern and that "we left her on the jury, which found my client not guilty."[13] A skeptical reader might be left wondering whether these tales and others in her book reflect the consistent efficacy of the consultant's methods or, perhaps, some biases in the memory, evaluation, and presentation of evidence. One might, after all, be inclined to remember successes more than failures, despite the best of intentions. And in trials where an entire jury votes to convict or acquit, one could infer that the facts of the case were sufficiently powerful to override any preexisting tendencies.

During the past few decades, numerous researchers—mainly social psychologists—have attempted to probe the mysteries of person perception, using carefully crafted scientific methods. Hundreds—perhaps thousands—of studies have looked at the ways people try to discern the personalities and motives of others. They have also gauged the accuracy with which people draw such inferences.[14] One might not expect Dimitrius to cite, review, or even summarize this work in her book (intended primarily as a self-help manual) and, indeed, she rarely refers to this huge body of social science—much of which bears directly on her theories and methods. Sometimes, studies confirm her approach, sometimes they call it into question. But Dimitrius's pool of insight apparently flows from a different stream—her own.

A central conclusion that emerges from the social psychology of person perception is something with which Dimitrius would most likely agree: When a person is attempting to deceive another, he or she is most able to control information conveyed verbally and far less able to prevent lies from seeping through nonverbal channels, including tone and voice quality. Nonetheless, studies also show, consistently, that people generally cannot detect and interpret reliably the nonverbal signs of deception. The typical person does better at this task than one would expect from chance alone—but not much better.[15]

After reviewing more than thirty studies, one psychologist explains this phenomenon by alluding to a bad match between behaviors that *really* tip off deception and those that people use to detect lies.[16] In other words, we have all sorts of theories about how to tell when someone is lying, and our theories, more often than not, are dead wrong. Moreover, we don't have much sense of how well we are doing at detecting deception. Thus, whether correct or incorrect, we typically express considerable confidence in our judgments.[17]

One 1991 study focused on professionals who, in their line of work, frequently had to sniff out lies. The sample included (among others) police detectives, trial judges, psychiatrists, and those who administer lie-detector tests for the government. These experts viewed brief videotapes of women who were, by arrangement with the experimenter, either lying or telling the truth about their feelings. Contrary to what we might expect, none of the experts did significantly better than chance at identifying the liars, and none did better than a sample of college students who were assigned the same task.[18]

Another study looked specifically at jury selection strategies, comparing experienced trial attorneys to a sample of undergraduate students. Again, the experts failed to demonstrate expertise. Given an abundance of potentially relevant facts about the jurors, both groups used the same information and employed strategies that were essentially indistinguishable.[19] The researchers quipped, ". . . Not only is jury selection by attorneys an art, but it is a lay art. Attorneys used the same stereotypes that civilians used, and in as cognitively simple a manner."[20]

Such research disputes the claims of practitioners like Robert G. Begam, former president of the Association of Trial Lawyers of America, who asserted that litigators ". . . are acutely attuned to the nuances of human behavior" and, therefore, able ". . . to detect the minutest traces of [juror] bias or inability to reach an appropriate decision."[21] Nobody can rule out the possibility that particular lawyers have extraordinary intuition or perceptiveness when it comes to reading people. But, generally speaking, there is reason for skepticism—especially when one considers similar research on the expert judgments made by clinical psychologists. Here, too, evidence suggests that professionals—when presented with scenarios based on limited information—reason fallaciously and similarly to novices.[22]

Still, Jo-Ellan Dimitrius might well respond that none of these findings are especially surprising and that none bear on her accuracy in decoding nonverbal messages. Moreover, none of the people studied by the academic researchers had been trained in her approach. She might also point out that the inability of attorneys to move beyond stereotypical approaches to jury selection hardly calls her own skills into question; indeed, it highlights the importance of the service she provides. She might even note that the latest research on lie detection endorses an approach rather consistent with her own. According to Paul Ekman, a leading researcher who has studied exceptional detectors of deception, no behavior or signal in itself provides a sure-fire sign of deceit and, consequently, the lie catcher must figure out the meaning of particular signals in each individual case.[23]

Other jury selection consultants might remark that their methods draw far less on intuition and subjective people-reading skills than Dimitrius suggests, far more on established scientific methods. Some might argue that their value to an attorney stems not from any superior insight or intuition they possess but rather from their ability to focus on jury selection while the lawyer is preoccupied with other matters. Still others would concede that consultants are not very effective in selecting sympathetic jurors and that their primary usefulness comes from running mock trials and focus groups used to craft juror persuasion strategies.

What might *Consumer Reports* magazine say about jury selection consulting? Are attorneys getting good value on their dollar? In our search for an answer, consultants' tales—tall and otherwise—can only get us so far. Professors Lawrence Wrightsman and Saul Kassin are surely correct when they argue that ". . . juries cannot be evaluated by case studies, autobiographical accounts, and news stories, no matter how vivid and compelling they may seem"[24] and that "just as anecdotes cannot affirm the effectiveness of scientific selection methods, neither can they affirm their ineffectiveness."[25] To address these concerns, we must delve deeper into the psychology of juries that has developed over the past half-century.

PEERING INTO THE MYSTERIOUS BOX

The jury is a "black box": We know what happens before it gets a case and we know what decision it renders, but nearly always we can only speculate about what happens in between.

No one has ever probed a jury's deliberations more carefully than Victor Villaseñor, the highly regarded novelist of the Mexican American experience and author of many critically acclaimed books. Upon hearing in May 1971 that Juan Corona, a fellow Chicano, had been charged with more than two dozen brutal murders near Yuba City, California,

Villaseñor—then a fledgling reporter—recalls thinking that no one man could possibly have committed so many atrocities. His earliest research into the case seemed to reinforce his suspicion that Corona might, in fact, be innocent and the victim of ethnic bigotry. However, by the time the case went to the jury in January 1973, Villaseñor no longer remained convinced of Corona's innocence.

Neither the defense nor the prosecution crafted an iron-clad case. Struck by the complexity of the task confronting the jurors and, later, by how well they had carried out their civic responsibilities during eight long days of sequestration, Villaseñor decided to write a book on the case from the perspective of the panel members.[26]

The jury convicted Corona. Villaseñor then, spent many months interviewing the twelve jurors, along the way amassing 2,000 pages of notes and hours of taped conversations. Whenever possible, the careful reporter checked jurors' recollections against each other, noting that ". . . four people could each recall a specific incident on a specific day as having happened quite differently."[27] Often, however, conflicting memories later reconciled into a consensus after discussions, questions, and—occasionally—reenactments. The reader of Villaseñor's book is left agreeing that the author's report of what transpired in the jury room ". . . was as close to the truth as is humanly possible."[28]

The Corona jury, like many juries, included a wide range of personalities—strong, weak, colorful, bland, loud-mouthed, soft-spoken, abrasive, and agreeable. Although all heard the same evidence, each initially processed it in his or her own way—sometimes reflecting biases and predispositions brought with them into the courtroom. In the end, one anchor alone seemed to keep deliberations on target despite personal conflicts and situational pressures—a shared perception of the weightiness of the task they faced as a group. The fairness and skill with which these untrained neophytes apparently sorted, evaluated, weighed, considered, and reconsidered the evidence is impressive. The reader sets down the volume with the belief that he or she has eyed the unseeable, feeling not unlike the proverbial fly on the jury room wall.

Yet upon reflection, even Villaseñor's wonderfully textured, balanced account leaves some doubt whether we really have the whole truth and nothing but the truth about what went on during deliberations. One juror—the last to hold out against conviction—informed reporters that she had been pressured to change her vote. The headlines, following a news conference with the defense attorney, charged jury tampering. To this day, Juan Corona proclaims his innocence, objecting that the jury so honored by Villaseñor had not overcome its limitations but succumbed to them. His self-serving protests may be easy to dismiss. But suspicion of jury misconduct figured prominently in several appeals and an order for a new trial (in which Corona was again convicted).

Even when a talented and fair-minded reporter is willing to devote years to understanding and deciphering jury deliberations, we remain uncertain about what happened behind closed doors. Whenever a case captures the public eye, Court TV and the other mass media trot out jury experts who feed what is generally a short-lived but intense hunger for insight into, first, what a particular jury is likely to do and, later on, why it did what it did. Some of these experts are experienced litigators, constitutional scholars, social scientists, and professional jury consultants. But regardless of background, few have ever witnessed a real jury in deliberation.[29]

Their conclusions may be wise or misguided, upbeat or pessimistic, civic-minded or self-serving. But they are always speculative.

One might wonder how studies of a black box, then, can ever move beyond speculation into the scientific realm. After all, how can scientists tackle a phenomenon that they cannot observe? At least as far back as the days of British philosopher John Locke, scientists have identified observation as the launching pad for knowledge, and jury deliberations take place beyond the reach of observation. But this problem is not insurmountable. Much of modern science deals with phenomena that cannot be observed directly. Consider, for example, the physics of the electron or theories about events in the distant past, like the creation of the solar system. Indeed, the entire field of cognitive psychology rests on inferences about what occurs in another black box—the human mind. In all these areas, scientists gather evidence indirectly, by simulating unobservable events and scrutinizing observable consequences of things that are, in themselves, unobservable. Nonetheless, the ability to see something directly is nearly always a desirable first step in social-psychological exploration, and the inability to watch actual juries deliberate has always stood as a major impediment to progress in this area.

Thus, when professors Harry Kalven and Hans Zeisel launched the historic Chicago Jury Project, their first thought was to try to obtain an exception to the rule so they could record actual jury deliberations. After some preliminary efforts (in which jurors were unaware they were being recorded), the researchers reluctantly abandoned this approach because of the public and political outrage it triggered.[30] The episode put an end to social-scientific recording of actual jury deliberations and effectively locked the jury door for three decades. By the mid-1990s, memories had faded sufficiently for the Arizona Supreme Court to authorize the placement of video cameras into several jury rooms during deliberations. This time, the jurors were told in advance and cameras were unobtrusively located. The result was a fascinating TV broadcast that publicized many concerns about the jury system.[31] But, to date, no serious scientific analyses of these or any other actual jury deliberations have been published.

Unable to proceed with their plan for recording deliberations, Kalven, Zeisel, and their colleagues went on to develop other methods for studying the jury, culminating in the 1966 publication of *The American Jury*, widely regarded as the most influential book ever written on the topic.[32] One key part of the project examined 3,576 criminal jury trials by mailing questionnaires to trial judges and asking them to report, for cases tried before them, "how the jury decided the case, and how they [the judges] would have decided it, had it been tried before them without a jury." Judges were also asked to provide additional descriptive and evaluative comments about the case, the parties, and counsel.[33] Although this approach has obvious imperfections—most notably its heavy reliance on the recollections and opinions of ego-involved judges and its inclusion of a very biased sampling of cases—the study provided the first significant empirical insights into jury behavior.

Kalven and Zeisel reported that judges and juries agreed on 78 percent of criminal verdicts—64 percent of the time agreeing to convict, and 14 percent of the time agreeing to acquit.[34] Ever since, scholars have pondered the meaning of the 22 percent disagreement between judge and

102 News from the Laboratory

jury. Is it cause for celebration, despair, or something in between? The researchers examined the disagreements and found that 19 percent of cases involved a jury voting to acquit while the judge would have convicted. The remaining 3 percent of cases had juries convicting where the judge would have acquitted. Thus, most of the time when the jury disagreed with the judge, the jury was more lenient—but it is hard to conclude that these discrepancies can be explained by jury error or incompetence. Many times, the disagreements were on cases that the judges considered very close calls; the judges themselves seldom felt that jurors had not understood the relevant issues.

Sometimes, jurors were more likely than judges to give first-time offenders the benefit of the doubt; sometimes, they apparently disagreed with the law and acted in accordance with their own views. Juries also were more likely to interpret the standard for conviction (guilty "beyond a reasonable doubt") in the defendant's favor. Sometimes jurors would make a judgment that the defendant already had been punished enough by the aftermath of a crime. Another reason for jurors' apparent leniency had to do with the way cases were selected for jury trial. If a defendant feels that he or she will get more sympathy from a judge, that defendant will not opt for a jury trial. Thus, part of the "leniency effect" may have to do with the particular mix of cases that end up before juries, not some overall tendency of jurors to acquit.[35]

Kalven and Zeisel also examined 4,000 civil cases and found, coincidentally, the same percentage of cases (78 percent) on which the judge and jury agreed. This total agreement included 47 percent of cases where judge and jury agreed in favor of the plaintiff and 31 percent where they agreed in favor of the defendant. About half of the disagreements (10 percent of the cases) involved a judge favoring the plaintiff while the jury favored the defendant; the remainder (12 percent) were the other way around.[36] As with the criminal cases, the issue emerges of just how much agreement there *ought* to be between judges and juries. If, after all, we knew judges were always right, we might have trouble defending a jury system in the first place.

The American Jury is a monumental work of social science, and it would take us far afield to review the many issues it probes so carefully.

This book rests on indirect and sometimes methodologically flawed studies of juries that deliberated more than four decades ago, but when it was published it established for many scholars and researchers an optimistic outlook on juries that still prevails. This image of the jury system also draws on the results of much more recent research inspired by the Chicago Jury Project.

Kalven and Zeisel wondered why the jury was not "more of a wildcat operation" and thought their single most significant finding was that the jury "despite its autonomy, spins . . . close to the legal baseline."[37] They attributed the success of the jury system in part to the "group nature of the jury decision" with its potential to "moderate and brake eccentric views."[38] Additionally, Kalven and Zeisel concluded that "the official law has done pretty well in adjusting to the equities, and there is therefore no great gap between the official values and the popular."[39]

Since the Chicago Jury Project, those who have sought to peer into the mind of the juror have relied most heavily on simulations, where the goal is to re-create as closely as possible the conditions of an actual courtroom. *If* this can be accomplished successfully, researchers can explore scientifically a tremendous array of important questions relating to the American trial system. The problem is that even though it is not difficult to set up some approximation of a courtroom, it is extremely tricky—and sometimes impossible—to create a *good* approximation, one in which the experience of research participants approaches that of real-world jurors.[40]

We never know the extent to which research subjects in simulated trials deviate from actual jurors in real trials. And more often than not, the summary trial in which the mock jurors have participated is quite different in pace, intensity, and clarity from the actual trial experience. Nearly always, experimental research considers only a small number of fact patterns, so we are left wondering how well the results will generalize to other circumstances—and, of course, every courtroom trial is, to some extent, sui generis.[41] When many studies have been conducted on a single topic, they can—through a statistical procedure known as meta-analysis—be combined to produce a whole that is greater than the sum of its parts and more likely to be generalizable than individual studies. But experimental research has been especially weak in addressing what researchers call "interaction effects"—for example, whether a member of a particular occupational group would be apt to convict a defendant of a particular ethnicity for a particular crime, or whether a juror's race plays a role in determining the size of a jury award for a particular type of tort.[42]

Thus, we must use caution not only in interpreting the claims of trial consultants but also in deciphering the findings of social scientists who have sought to evaluate them. Several decades of research have certainly started to fill in the once-empty canvas of understanding, but whereas some areas reveal sharp images, others seem more akin to a Rorschach inkblot onto which one can project only impressions, expectations, and desires.

To understand this immense body of research evidence, and how it bears on the jury selection consulting industry, we must address several questions. First, to what extent do jurors succumb to personal biases, dispositions, and inappropriate influences rather than rendering decisions based solely on the evidence? Second, which jurors tend to acquit and which to convict? Third, which jurors tend to award large damages in civil cases? Fourth, how well do lawyers pick jurors without the assistance of consultants? Fifth, can jury consultants make a difference and, if so, how much of a difference and under which circumstances?

THE JURY VERSUS THE EVIDENCE

All jury selection consulting rests on one assumption: The traits, attitudes, and background of a juror will bear significantly on how he or she decides a case. Thus, jury consulting pioneer Jay Schulman and his colleagues spoke, rightly or wrongly, of "a very obvious fact: the people who constitute the jury can have as much or more to do with the outcome of a trial as the evidence and arguments."[43] But what struck these early practitioners and countless legal pundits since as self-evident has seemed less apparent to many social scientists.

Two students of the jury system, Michael Saks and Reid Hastie, noted in the late 1970s that people might act with unusual fairness and objectivity when called on to perform their civic duty as jurors. They suggested that "common-sense assumptions that the personal politics and prejudice which characterize much of human life invade the jury box ignore the special situational characteristics of the court and the human relationships constructed there."[44] During the past two decades, quite a few social scientific investigations have lent support to Saks's and Hastie's position.[45] Although this line of research has not settled the matter once and for all, it appears that evidence determines verdicts far more often than jurors' backgrounds, personalities, attitudes, predispositions, beliefs, or other biases. Only rarely does an irresponsible jury bring in one verdict while the evidence points decidedly in another direction. In other words, when the evidence is strong, nothing else matters much, not the traits of jurors, the craftiness of lawyers, the skill of judges, or anything else. Even when evidence is more ambiguous, personal characteristics of jurors generally exert a relatively minor influence on verdict preferences.[46]

Indeed, social psychologists would not expect to find a stronger relationship between what a juror brings into the courtroom and how he or she decides a case. Several decades of exploration in many different domains of human behavior have led them to anticipate inconsistency among peoples' traits, thoughts, attitudes, and actions. As psychologist Martin Kaplan explains:

> The reasons for . . . [the] poor relationship between personal characteristics and juror behavior are clear. First, personality does not exert a consistent effect on behavior; its effect depends on the specific situation. . . . Second, personality is imperfectly related to attitudes, and it is the attitudes of jurors that we are trying to predict from these personal factors. Third, attitudes are imperfect predictors of behavior. To be more explicit, personality and demographic factors are general, and do not always show their effects in specific situations. . . . It is little wonder that general characteristics in jurors do not translate to their specific behaviors in a particular trial.[47]

Or as Michael Saks and Reid Hastie put it, "The jury, like most other human groups, functions according to its composition, its structure, the nature of the group process, and the task confronting the group. . . .

Research findings suggest that jury composition has little influence on the outcome of a trial relative to other variables under the lawyer's control."[48]

Those who believe in the jury system should take some solace in the relative potency of evidence in determining juror preferences. But they should not feel entirely comforted. After all, had juror personalities, attitudes, feelings, dispositions, and backgrounds proved decisive in typical cases, there would be little left to do save scrapping the system. And although research suggests relatively few cases turn on juror biases, a few incorrect verdicts may be more than we desire and more than we need to tolerate.

All it takes is one strong-willed person to hang a jury in a criminal case, one person bent on disobeying the judge's instructions, one person whose prejudice prevents him or her from hearing a witness, one person whose experiences have inclined against a decision based on the evidence. Even though most cases do not evoke strong personal biases in most jurors, some cases do. And when these cases are highly publicized, the consequences can be far-reaching, as they undermine confidence in the jury system as a whole—three decades of scientific evidence notwithstanding. In short, a little bias can sometimes go a long way.[49]

WHO CONVICTS, WHO ACQUITS?

If the verdict would turn on the evidence, it was going to be a bad day for Modesta Solano, a twenty-six-year-old mother of two charged with possession and transportation of drugs for sale.[50] Somewhat attractive with dark black hair and big eyes, Solano solemnly sat throughout her Arizona trial, her face betraying the seriousness of her predicament. Some time earlier, en route to Newark, New Jersey, she and Urbano Hernandez had been stopped in the Phoenix airport and caught red-handed with four suitcases of marijuana and cocaine. Both had been traveling under assumed names. Solano acknowledged that she agreed to accompany Hernandez on the trip but maintained that she had absolutely no idea what was in the luggage. Offered a deal by the prosecutor, Hernandez accepted and testified convincingly against his purported accomplice.

Needless to say, Solano's defense attorney assailed his credibility by calling attention to his powerful incentive to fabricate a story. After all, she noted, he had to do something to avoid a long prison sentence.

The most damning evidence in the case came not from Urbano but from Solano herself. Acting out of anger and frustration, she unthinkingly had shared some rather frank reflections during a telephone call from jail before her release on bail; this she did even though she had been informed that the conversation would be taped. In court, jurors heard a replay of Solano's remarks. She was heard to complain that "He [Urbano] f*****g told them that everything was mine. That he didn't have no bags with him. Nothing. Believe that shit." The person on the other end of the line asked, "That's what he said?" She answered, "Yep. That's exactly what he said. I told 'em, you're full of shit, two were mine and two were his. I'll take the blame for my shit, but I ain't taking the blame for his." More damning still, she mentioned the exact weight of the drugs in the luggage, something she could not have known unless she had been involved in the trafficking. Her lawyer explained the tapes feebly, suggesting that it is "survival of the fittest" in jail and that Modesta Solano had to assume a tough demeanor if she hoped to survive.

However, the defense attorney's real strategy was more sophisticated. She discussed possible sentences facing Urbano Hernandez, ostensibly to inform jurors about his incentive to lie but, in reality, to tip them off about the implications of a guilty verdict for Solano. Although the judge informed the panel that they could not discuss penalties, Solano's defense attorney hoped jurors would ignore this instruction and consider— openly or covertly, consciously or unconsciously—the fairness of imposing a substantial prison term on Solano when Hernandez probably was going to get a light one or even probation.

Almost always, we are left with little more than speculation about how jurors respond to lawyers' strategies and the evidence. But this case was different. It was one of several trials where the Arizona Supreme Court had authorized videotaping of jury deliberations, and CBS obtained permission to subsequently broadcast events in that jury room on national television. Of the eight jurors who debated the case, six quickly determined that the evidence was straightforward and damning: Modesta Solano knew what was in the suitcases, she had helped plan the crime, and she was, therefore, guilty as charged.

But two jurors disagreed. One was Alvo, a young, long-haired, and affable man who never clearly articulated why he wanted to acquit. At times, he appeared ready to go along with the consensus—especially if his became the sole deviating vote.

By far the more passionate opponent of conviction was Joe, a bright, intense, obviously sincere man. Partly bald, starting to gray, and in his midsixties, he had attended law school forty years earlier but never completed the program. Joe explained that Modesta Solano, in his mind, was "at best an accomplice"; were the jurors to convict, she would receive "a mandatory, more severe punishment" than Hernandez. Several others on the panel immediately objected that the judge had instructed them not to discuss sentencing. But Joe would not budge, claiming that it was immoral—regardless of what the judge said—*not* to consider the implications of their verdict.

According to Joe, the jurors faced two clear options: "She's either guilty with mandatory sentencing or she's not guilty." During the hours of deliberation that followed, Joe suggested other explanations for his reluctance to convict. He averred, "Younger people that drift, that are brought up with a whole different sense of morality, my grandchildren, they don't see things the way I do. I'll tell you that. And it's not a question of right and wrong. They just don't see things the way I do." Later, Joe added, "What bothers me most about this case is that the strongest evidence against her is her own words," objecting—incorrectly—that "basic to our law is the right not to incriminate ourselves."

Although Joe apparently did not believe that Modesta was, as she claimed, a bystander who did not know what was in the suitcases, he objected that the state's case was "very weak, not the strongest in the world." Yet his opposition to conviction seemed to have deeper roots—philosophical, psychological, or both. He argued that jurors must perform two tasks: first, determine guilt or innocence, and second, do justice. Most of the other jurors objected to this conceptualization of their role, accepting a more restricted, traditional, and legalistic definition.

After the jurors reported their deadlock to the judge, he sent them back to the jury room for one more try. But neither Joe nor Alvo budged. Joe later explained: "I was not going to do something that was against my beliefs and conscience and logic that would make me regret what I had done." The jury hung and the judge declared a mistrial.

Just where did Joe and Alvo's votes originate? In Alvo's case, there's not much one can say beyond sheer guesswork. Perhaps he didn't want to send a young mother to prison. Possibly, he did not agree with current drug laws. But Joe's extensive comments suggest several better-informed hypotheses—some stemming directly from his own arguments, others requiring a foray into psychology. He may indeed have refused to convict because of sentencing inequities concerning Hernandez and Solano or because of his mistaken understanding of the scope of the constitutional mandate against self-incrimination. His mention of his grandchildren as "younger people that drift" hints at some unmentioned personal issues that may have been decisive, perhaps experiences with relatives who had used drugs or had scrapes with the law. His early experience in law school may have given him the confidence to stand up against a "lay" group who saw the case differently. Alternatively, his abandonment of legal studies may have stemmed from dissatisfaction with the operation of the legal system or, even, have *created* such dissatisfaction. Perhaps Joe wanted to "outsmart" the prosecutor, proving that he was in fact as "good" as any lawyer who had completed legal training. In any event, his willingness to buck the judge's instructions may have had some connection to his abortive educational experience. All of these explanations are speculative, but the Solano case certainly highlights the potential impact of a strong-willed personality—or two. Several months later, the same case was retried with a very different outcome. After forty-five minutes, the new jury returned a guilty verdict, and Modesta Solano received a five-year sentence. Her lawyers said they had not been surprised, for they had expected a guilty verdict the first time.[51]

For three decades, social psychologists have sought formulas to identify jurors likely to acquit or convict. These researchers have been driven by a hope that one could predict how a juror would process, evaluate, and weigh evidence if one knew something about his or her demographics, personality traits, and/or attitudes. For example, older people might be more likely to vote guilty than younger ones. Shy people might be less likely than assertive ones to acquit. Gender, race, ethnicity, religion, income, education, and occupation might consistently incline a juror in one direction or another.

How do the many personality characteristics and traits measured by psychologists bear on a juror's voting behavior in criminal cases? What about the political opinions and beliefs people hold, for example, their degree of political liberalism, their views on abortion, their stance on capital punishment, their attitudes toward the justice system?

Dozens of studies have examined these questions from many different angles, using methods of varying scientific credibility. Some have asked mock jurors to evaluate evidence in simulated trials, focusing on their initial reactions to the case or allowing them to deliberate with other jurors. Other studies have questioned real jurors following actual trials to determine whether their perspectives were associated with differences in their personalities, views, or backgrounds.

When we step back and analyze this large and complex body of social science, a very clear problem emerges: Background, attitudes, and traits often make some difference in particular trials, but when we seek to identify a personality type that can predict voting predispositions across many criminal cases, we find that none exists. Thus, Shari Seidman Diamond, an eminent student of the jury system, concludes that ". . . there is no profile of the good defense (or prosecution or plaintiff) juror that can be used across cases. Characteristics that emerge as predictors on one case do not show the same pattern on another case." She further advises that: "The jury consultant who provides a profile of the good defense juror suitable for all cases and applicable to all communities is offering the most blatant voodoo voir dire advice."[52]

Still, social scientists have developed several measures that are *weakly* associated with a tendency to convict across cases. One of these instruments, the Juror Bias Scale (JBS) developed by psychologists Saul Kassin and Lawrence Wrightsman, consists of seventeen items.[53] For example, respondents indicate whether they agree or disagree that "for serious crimes like murder, a defendant should be found guilty so long as there is a 90 percent chance that he committed the crime." Or "in most cases where the accused presents a strong defense, it is only because of a good lawyer." Or "too many innocent people are wrongfully imprisoned." Given the ostensible relevance of these items to how a juror might weigh evidence, what is most surprising is that the scale predicts juror proclivities so poorly, even when the evidence does not point strongly in either direction. The Legal Attitudes Questionnaire, developed by psychologist Virginia Boehm, has also been of limited value in predicting how jurors will vote in a wide variety of cases.[54] Simply knowing a person's views on the death penalty will enable one to do a bit better than chance in estimating his or her likely vote in many criminal cases where the evidence does not strongly favor one side or the other. This is because jurors who oppose the death penalty are somewhat more likely to acquit.[55]

Still, nearly all jury researchers agree that the attempt to identify global "hard-liners" and "bleeding hearts" that convict or acquit in all, or nearly all, cases has been a failure.[56] What this means is that those interested in understanding and predicting how jurors will vote will find their best hope in *specific* characteristics for each case. In other words, aspects of a juror's background, personality, and beliefs that prove critical in one case—perhaps propelling someone powerfully toward advocacy of acquittal—might prove useless in the next trial, or even might push someone in the opposite direction.[57]

The need for a case-specific approach does not come as a disappointment to the trial consulting industry. If one set of characteristics were known to predict juror behavior across the board, lawyers would quickly master the type and devise ways of identifying sympathetic jurors on their own. If no general conviction-prone syndrome exists, however, consultants must conduct separate research for each particular trial where attorneys seek guidance. FTI's Arthur Patterson, one of the nation's leading consultants, explains:

> Given a particular case, with its setting, defendant(s), potential jurors, jurisdictional rules, evidence patterns, and other idiosyncratic features, there may well be individual factors that will have significant implications for

juror selection. The role of the scientific jury selector then, may be one of identifying both the salient characteristics of the case and the juror factors that may interact with these case characteristics, in influencing the verdict. . . . The case specific method is, in fact, the method used by experienced scientific jury selectors when given the time and resources to conduct the proper empirical research for the case.[58]

In theory, there may be a middle road between the failed search for a general tendency to convict (or acquit) and the expensive identification of profiles for specific cases. Patterson argues, "When time and/or resources prevent research on a specific case, the jury selector should apply only the previous research that has been shown to be generalizable to the specific case at hand."[59] This approach seems logical enough. If the same jurors tend to convict in the same sorts of criminal trials—defined perhaps by crime type, defendant characteristics, type of evidence, and other dimensions—then one should be able to use that information without going through the trouble and expense of new research. On this basis, the construction of a scientifically based manual for jury selection would seem possible.

However, at least two obstacles have stood in the way of this endeavor. First, no simple classification of cases is feasible; there are too many dimensions along which trials differ. The second problem concerns the availability of sufficient numbers of high-quality studies. Most of the research that has been conducted on jury selection has been proprietary, and consulting firms guard such findings carefully. Trial consultants frequently state that "our huge body of research tells us this" or "our file of studies on this sort of case tells us that" but, without open peer review by other scientists, observers should remain skeptical.

Published scientific studies are beginning to accumulate, but at this point our knowledge of which jurors tend to convict in various types of trials is sketchy. Researchers have examined criminal trials involving murder, rape, controlled substances, and other matters.[60] Usually, the best indicators of verdict preference turn out to be attitudes toward the case—often intuitively relevant ones—rather than juror demographics. For example, a series of studies found that disenchantment with psychiatrists and a distrust of the insanity defense inclined a juror to convict when an attorney mounted a defense of not guilty by reason of insanity.[61] Another study found that knowing a juror's feelings about lawyers and narcotics would be useful in predicting his or her verdict in a case involving an attorney charged with drug crimes.[62]

Even in rape cases, where women do convict somewhat more frequently than men, one can make a better prediction by knowing a juror's thoughts about rape than by relying on knowledge of gender.[63] Apparently, a woman's greater likelihood to convict derives not from something mystical about her gender, not even from greater punitiveness toward rapists, but rather from a gender-related tendency to believe the evidence in rape cases. When men share in that tendency, they too convict disproportionately.

At present, the attempt to devise profiles of conviction-prone jurors for categories of criminal cases has advanced no farther than the effort to discover global tendencies. Not much is likely to change even if scholars step up the pace of their work in this area. Research on juror behavior ages badly, becoming outmoded as the surrounding culture changes. And too many dimensions of a case have to be taken into account. For example, a defendant may be a white, wealthy, elderly female accused of shooting her husband because he was having an affair with a younger woman. There may be testimony from an eyewitness who can't speak English very well and the case may turn on some critical DNA evidence. Even if many studies had been conducted on the tendency to convict in murder cases, we would have reason to doubt their relevance in this specific complex instance.

Much also depends on the particularities of the parties involved in a trial. In criminal cases, those who wish to predict juror behavior must consider the impact of the *defendant's* race, ethnicity, age, wealth, education, appearance, attitudes, demeanor, and personality. Some defendants fare well or fare poorly across the board, regardless of who sits in the jury box. But many times, the characteristics that a defendant brings to the courtroom can be assets with some jurors and liabilities with others.

Perhaps the single most significant advantage a defendant can bring to trial is physical attractiveness. Mock trials and others studies have documented that for nearly all crimes beauty confers an edge, whereas ugliness evokes a tendency to convict. Although elements of beauty do reside in the eyes of the beholder, a cultural consensus has emerged around certain aspects of attractiveness; those who fit the desired mold fare better in many aspects of life than those who do not. In the legal system, they are less likely to get caught at illegal activities; if caught, they are less likely to be reported. And if a trial ensues, they receive more lenient treatment. In criminal cases, the attractiveness bias manifests most powerfully in studies of sentencing where unattractive defendants typically draw substantially longer sentences than attractive ones. The attractiveness bias extends to charges of rape, shoplifting, robbery, murder, and other crimes. A noteworthy exception concerns swindling, where an attractive defendant is thought to have used his or her appearance to help perpetrate the crime. Here, for once, the unattractive get the edge.[64]

In addition, jurors in simulated trials might start out somewhat inclined to convict the poor, the uneducated, those low in social status, and those with a criminal record.[65] However, few defendants in actual trials start out with all of the jury strongly biased for them or against them because of their background. More often, the characteristics of a defendant confer advantage or disadvantage only when considered in conjunction with the attributes of a juror. Thus, it is difficult to identify any consistent patterns based on defendant demographics such as race, ethnicity, gender, age, income, or education. For example, wealthy defendants might fare worse with some jurors and better with others. And it is not simply a matter of the wealthy favoring their own. What's more, wealth might be a blessing for defendants charged with some crimes and a curse for those charged with other crimes. The relationship between the race of a defendant and that of a juror is an especially complex matter.

The simplest rule regarding the relationship between the juror and the defendant is what social psychologists call the *similarity principle*.[66] It is also the principle most often used by attorneys to govern their own voir dire when no consultant has been retained. In most aspects of life, people prefer others who are similar to themselves. This principle governs how we choose our friends and mates; to some extent, it governs our initial inclinations to acquit or convict. We typically like people who resemble ourselves in background, ethnicity, and beliefs. But much of the time, people resemble us on a few dimensions and are different on others. There is no reliable way to predict when a psychological bond or identification will form.

Texas attorney Mike McCurley points to a child custody case to illustrate this point.

> An attorney representing the father may think that the best juror for his client would be a man. This would be based on the stereotype that all men would sympathize with a father seeking custody. This stereotype could prove to be incredibly false. Many men may feel that it is not the father's role to take care of young children. This bias may arise from a number of factors, but it is one that needs to be considered in evaluating the potential jurors. . . . The problem can also cut the other way in this example. The mother's attorney in this case might think that the best option for her client would be to put young mothers on the jury. This feeling would be based on the belief that most women would not want their children to be raised by anyone other than themselves. This presumption could also prove to be wrong because many mothers may not identify with this and may have wished that the father of their children had taken a more active role in raising their children. This may make them more sympathetic to the father who is fighting for the custody of his children in court.[67]

The odds, after all, of finding someone with characteristics and experiences closely matching those of a defendant or civil litigant are slim, and there is virtually no chance of finding twelve such people to sit on a jury.

Moreover, people can react negatively to the discovery that others like themselves have committed a crime or acted dishonorably. A rebound effect might lead them to judge "their own" with greater harshness than they would otherwise bring to bear. Jews might end up tougher on Jews, teachers on teachers, elderly people on other elderly people.

Thus, at least for the foreseeable future, the prediction of juror proclivities must occur on a case-by-case basis. And those who study individual cases will have to consider not only the specifics of the crime and the evidence but also the idiosyncrasies of the defendant.

WHO AWARDS THE BIG MONEY?

During the past decade, individual smokers, former smokers, and their families filed hundreds of suits against tobacco corporations, and until recently, nearly all of these had been resolved in favor of the companies.[68] But things began to change in the mid-1990s. A Jacksonville, Florida, jury awarded $750,000 to former smoker Grady Carter and his wife. Then another jury in the same state awarded $1 million to the family of Roland Maddox, who had died of lung cancer after smoking for fifty years.

A new record for this type of lawsuit was set in February 1999 when a San Francisco jury ordered Philip Morris to pay $51.5 million to a woman with inoperable lung cancer. Patricia Henley, the fifty-three-year-old plaintiff, had puffed away for more than thirty-five years, mainly on Philip Morris's Marlboros. She received $1.5 million as compensation plus an astronomical $50 million in punitive damages, more than three times the punitive figure sought by her attorney.

One juror explained the verdict, in part, as a consequence of disgust with efforts of cigarette manufacturers to cast doubt on the government's scientific reports that smoking was addictive and a cause of cancer. She explained: "With publicity and advertising, [the tobacco company] . . . . really tried to downplay it as a controversy between the Surgeon General and responsible medical people. It all seemed kind of deceiving, and they were kind of saying, like, 'Oh, this is just business.'"[69] The San Francisco jury's record did not stand for long. The next month, a panel in Portland, Oregon, hit the same corporation with an $81 million judgment, including $79.5 million in punitive damages.

Then, in July 2000, jury awards against the tobacco industry jumped into hyperspace when a Florida jury in a class-action lawsuit ordered a group of defendants to pay $144.8 *billion* in punitive damages.[70] The six-member panel included an assistant elementary school principal, another school employee, a welder, a telephone technician, a postal worker, and a bank teller. The jurors heard the case for two years but deliberated for a mere five hours before deciding on an amount. The six each named a figure ranging from $100 billion to $200 billion. Then, they averaged the numbers, arriving at their tidy sum.

It was the first time a class-action suit against Big Tobacco had gone to a jury, and panel members were, no doubt, influenced by the size of the class, an estimated 500,000 Florida smokers. As in previous cases against the industry, anger appears to have driven the verdict. "It was insulting," jury foreman Leighton Finegan said after the trial. "It's just the tobacco industry's mentality, that they are beyond challenge."[71] When attorneys for the cigarette makers suggested that their clients could afford to pay $150 million–$375 million, but no more, the wrath of the jurors increased. As juror Gary Chwast, a thirty-year-old postal worker, later told reporters, "I'm not an idiot. The C.E.O.s of the tobacco companies are making millions. Why are they making so much if the companies don't have the money? What are you not telling me? It offends me."[72]

Big dollar awards to individuals are mind-boggling at first, but this does not prove that they are unjust or irrational. Supporters of a tort system that vests great power in juror discretion note that punitive damages are intended to express the moral outrage of the community and to deter future wrongdoing. This, they maintain, can be accomplished only if awards are large enough to cause corporate giants to take note. They also must hurt sufficiently to outweigh the economic benefits derived from those who have been hurt by corporate policies yet deterred from bringing suit for one reason or another. Supporters also maintain that several posttrial mechanisms exist for reigning in jury excesses, and to date, cigarette manufacturers have proved particularly adept at utilizing them.[73]

Whatever the merits of huge awards against tobacco companies, what concerns us here is their variability. The cases discussed above and the hundreds of others still pending against the cigarette giants certainly involve different claims, facts, laws, attorneys, plaintiffs, defendants, and arguments, yet clearly they share a great many commonalities as well. We can therefore ask, What leads one jury to find liability while another does not?

Shortly after the Jacksonville jury hit Brown and Williamson Tobacco Corp. with a $750,000 judgment, another jury in Duval County, Florida, let R.J. Reynolds off the hook. They certainly had little sympathy for the defendant. A juror explained: "We had a hard moral dilemma on our hands in that we thought R.J. Reynolds knew more than they were telling

and should have told. . . . Had they asked different questions [on the verdict form], possibly, there would have been a different outcome."[74] Similarly, in July 1999, a Louisiana jury—by a vote of 11-1—cleared R.J.
Reynolds and the former American Tobacco Company in a suit brought
by the wife and children of a smoker who had died of lung cancer several
years earlier. The jury foreman reported that the "evidence was too
cloudy" to say that cigarettes were the sole cause of the man's death.[75]
This objection might plausibly be applied to most, if not all, tobacco
death cases.

Other types of civil litigation have generated similar concerns about
the variability of jury verdicts. For example, a Connecticut jury of four
men and two women told Trinity College to pay $12.7 million to a
woman chemist, Leslie Craine, who, having been denied tenure, sued the
school on the grounds of sexual discrimination.[76] The award included $6
million in punitive damages and $4 million for emotional distress, even
though many academicians, including an official of the American Association of University Professors, view Trinity's tenure system as being
among the fairest in the country.[77] The college tenure committee had rejected her on the grounds that, despite being a fine teacher, she had not
published adequate scientific research. Even professor Craine reports being ". . . kind of astounded at the award figure."

A federal jury in Manhattan surprised many observers when it determined that the National Basketball Association (NBA) should pay Sandra
Ortiz–Del Valle $7.85 million, also because of sexual discrimination.[78]
Ortiz–Del Valle had been denied a job as a referee; according to her
lawyers, the league offered varying reasons for not hiring her, reasons that
amounted to little more than a pretext for discrimination. The NBA's
lawyers objected to the award, which included $7 million in punitive
damages, noting that it was the only league that had female officials in
the first place.

Janet Peckinpaugh, a Hartford anchorwoman, charged that the managers at her local CBS TV station discriminated against her on the basis
of sex and age, breaching her contract, making false assurances about
long-term employment, and retaliating against her for complaining that
she had been sexually harassed by her male coanchor.[79] A federal jury of

five men and three women agreed with her on most of the allegations except for age discrimination. They awarded her $4.3 million in compensatory damages and $4 million in punitive damages ($1 million for sex discrimination, $3 million for retaliation).

Sensing the spirit of the times and fearing an adverse verdict, Miller Brewing Company decided to take preemptive action.[80] A manager, Jerold Mackenzie, had repeated a story line he had seen on the *Seinfeld* TV program to a female coworker and showed her a page from the dictionary with the word "clitoris" on it. (Throughout the television episode, Jerry Seinfeld cannot remember his girlfriend's name, only recalling that it rhymes with a part of the female anatomy. As the show concludes, her name [Dolores] finally comes back to him.) The coworker viewed the incident as sexual harassment. When she made an accusation, the company investigated, decided that the remarks constituted the last in a series of bad management decisions, and subsequently fired Mackenzie from his $95,000-per-year job. Unfortunately for the company, Mackenzie then sued for wrongful termination, and a ten-woman, two-man jury awarded him $26.6 million. Jurors later reported that ". . . just talk with no touching didn't strike [them] as that offensive."[81]

Sexual discrimination, sexual harassment, and tobacco cases all attract publicity and are to some extent politicized. But it is not just these sorts of cases that raise questions about jury consistency in the civil justice system. Consider a case where a store security guard handcuffed and threw to the ground a woman who he believed had shoplifted a soda. After a two-week trial where physicians and psychiatrists testified about the woman's physical and emotional suffering, a Baltimore jury deliberated for one and a half hours before deciding on liability and compensatory damages. Following a second trial for punitive damages, the jury deliberated a mere eight and a half minutes before determining that the guard had to pay the plaintiff $1,000 and that his employer, a security company, owed an additional $1.5 million. In Colorado Springs, security guards at a K-Mart committed somewhat comparable acts against two teenage girls whom they believed had shoplifted. The guards twisted the girls' arms behind their backs, pushed them against a wall, and strip-searched them. In this instance, the plaintiffs could not afford expert testimony, and a six-person jury awarded just $502 in compensation to each of the teenagers, along with $2 more to their mother. No punitive damages were awarded.[82]

The point here is not that all, most, or even many juries are making outrageous awards but rather that some do and some do not. Publicity frequently surrounds verdicts that are atypical, pathbreaking, or seemingly outlandish, especially preferring those instances where an unfortunate soul seems suddenly transformed into a lottery winner. We are much less likely to hear about verdicts that appear in line with expectations.[83] Still, huge awards, even when they are infrequent, exercise a powerful effect on the civil justice system. Their possibility elicits salivation from plaintiffs' lawyers and justifiable trembling in defense attorneys, particularly those who handle product liability, antitrust, medical malpractice, and discrimination cases.

For lawyers who handle civil litigation, the broad policy debates recede in importance, and the key question becomes, How can I identify jurors who will be sympathetic (or unsympathetic) to me, my client, my argument, and my witnesses? A 1998 Juror Outlook Survey conducted by *National Law Journal* and DecisionQuest revealed that potential jurors across the country are sharply divided on matters that may well influence their verdicts in lawsuits.[84] More than three-quarters of the respondents said that "whatever a judge said the law is, jurors should do what they believe is the right thing." Seventy-eight percent agree that "executives of big companies often try to cover up the harm they do"; one person in four agrees strongly. Two-thirds believe that lawsuits against product manufacturers have made products safer. More than one juror in five admits that they could not be "fair and impartial" if a case involved a tobacco company. Many acknowledged a similar inability to retain objectivity regarding asbestos and breast-implant manufacturers.

The survey also contained bad news for those who initiated lawsuits. Eighty-four percent of respondents agreed that "when people are injured, they often try to blame others for their carelessness." More than three in five supported limits on punitive damages levied against corporate defendants, and very large majorities thought that lawsuits had increased the cost of products (73 percent), medical care (89 percent), and insurance

(91 percent). The Juror Outlook Survey permits us to conclude that some prospective jurors possess especially negative attitudes toward corporate defendants, some toward injured plaintiffs, and some toward both. The survey further suggests that members of the public differ sharply on dimensions that seem relevant to their propensity to find for the plaintiff or defendant and, once they produce such a finding, to make large or small dollar awards.

Although we cannot be sure about the extent to which general pretrial attitudes will bear on verdicts in a courtroom, the survey findings raise some questions for litigators. For example, will potential jurors confess their inability to be "fair and impartial" during voir dire? And if not, how might an attorney identify unsympathetic jurors on the basis of their less-than-frank responses? When the jury pool seems stacked against an attorney's case, how might he or she prove this point in order to obtain a change of venue?

Attorneys on both sides want to identify jurors inclined to make large awards, especially those who might compensate plaintiffs handsomely for pain, suffering, and emotional distress. They also desire insight into a juror's openness to punitive damages.

Consultants think they can provide an answer. Ellen Leggett claims that her company's ". . . research has discerned a distinct 'punitive juror' profile that applies in many product liability cases."[85] According to Leggett, ". . . punitive jurors may be those individuals who are already feeling victimized in some way in their own life," and she notes that "a product liability lawsuit becomes an area for them to fight their victimizer in the form of a corporate defendant."[86] Punitive jurors may display generalized hostility, perhaps feeling that they have "played by the rules" but it has not paid off. Alternatively, their anger may stem from a recent life trauma or underemployment, given their level of education. She sees another warning sign in an unstable occupational history, particularly one including firings, layoffs, or forced transfers. White-collar workers facing unemployment can be dangerous for product liability defendants, for they are "articulate, educated and credible" and can be "a formidable punitive voice in the jury room," one that is "willing to take 'Corporate America' to task when given the opportunity."

Leggett also calls attention to prospective jurors who are "prone to identifying with a perceived victim, such as individuals employed in the social service field or nonprofit organizations. Their mission is to 'right wrongs' and jury service becomes an opportunity to save others from the dangers of what they perceive as an unsafe product." Finally, Leggett looks out for those who ". . . have little belief in their ability to control events in their own lives." Such individuals hope that someone will protect them because they do not believe they can do it themselves. Consequently, they hold corporate defendants to "very high, rigid and unrealistic standards."

Although Leggett's profile has some intuitive plausibility and purportedly rests on "years of research," no peer-reviewed studies or published evidence support it. More important, she herself concedes that ". . . determining whether this punitive profile applies in your action and whether particular jurors will be disposed for or against you will depend on the jurors' attitudes and experiences in areas relevant to your case. Determining which attitudes and experiences really matter, however, can be accomplished only through research conducted before trial with individuals living in your trial venue and eligible for jury duty."

Gold-standard research may not be cost-effective for many cases. Discussing sexual harassment and wrongful termination cases, attorney Craig White declares, "Honestly, most employment cases don't justify spending $10,000 to hire a jury consultant to perform a mock trial and/or help you pick your jury."[87] He suggests drawing on experience, prior research, and other sources to develop a low-cost profile of high-risk jurors for such cases. Thus, he suggests that a female plaintiff, bringing a wrongful termination and harassment suit, should avoid men, small-business owners, and older jurors. Not surprisingly, the plaintiff would also want to avoid those who believe: (1) most reports of sexual harassment are exaggerated, (2) efforts to hire and promote women have gone too far, (3) punitive damages are a poor way to punish corporations, and/or (4) laws and regulations have made it too difficult to terminate bad employees. Jurors would also be high risk if they (1) socialize in discriminatory organizations, (2) have themselves been terminated at their place of employment, (3) have been a defendant in a lawsuit, and/or (4) are employed in a male-dominated industry. Voir dire questions can sometimes assess the extent to which jurors fit this profile. As with Leggett's punitive juror profile, we might suspect that one who uses the wrongful termination/sexual harassment profile would do better than chance most of the time. How much better we cannot know, and without case-specific research, we might not be able to detect exceptions to the rule.

Back in 1989, jury researcher Edith Greene asked what we know for certain about how juries make damage awards and concluded, "What is perhaps most clear . . . . is that our understanding of these issues is in an extremely rudimentary stage."[88] More recently, some social scientists have suggested that juror decisions about damages might be more predictable than their judgments concerning civil liability and criminal guilt.[89] Although consultants and scholars alike warn against reliance on demographic stereotypes and the failure to consider specific aspects of a case, some have noted that, once liability has been established, there can be substantial commonalities in the damage-related issues confronting jurors across a variety of cases. Moreover, the award of damages might prove more subject to the influence of subtle preexisting biases. One would, after all, need to be very committed to one's biases in order to convict an innocent man or acquit a guilty one. But once the question becomes how much a corporation should pay, prior inclinations might indeed dictate the addition of a zero or two to the final sum. The trial consulting industry deals with this issue more than any other, with big-money civil cases providing most firms' bread and butter.

As a result of studies conducted during the past decade, a few things are becoming clear about the way jurors think and act concerning liability and damages. First, and perhaps self-evidently, jurors rarely make very large awards, and relatively few plaintiffs end up winning any punitive damages or compensation for pain and suffering. Second, jurors consider the severity of an injury not only in making decisions about damages but also—and inappropriately—in determining whether a defendant is liable in the first place. The worse the injury, the more likely a jury will find someone liable. Third, jurors can anchor their thinking on damages to figures that have been provided by an attorney, even when that number is not backed up by expert economic testimony.[90] Fourth, wealthy ("deep-pocket") *individual* defendants may or may not receive harsher treatment at the hands of juries, but corporate defendants probably do; they are more apt to be found liable and hit with higher damages.[91] None of these rules is hard and fast; each rests on multiple—but imperfect—studies. Exceptions abound.

A few recent studies suggest that consultants should pay great attention to the ways prospective jurors think about money.[92] According to this research, the average juror makes larger awards than the typical judge or lawyer would. And despite basic agreement on what makes an injury worthy of compensation, mock jurors tend to rate various injuries as substantially more severe than do lawyers or judges. The greatest disagreement occurs when people must translate perceptions of severity into dollar awards.

The same sorts of cases arouse jurors' outrage and desire to punish without regard to their gender, race, age, education, or income. However, even when they agree that they wish to punish a defendant, jurors from different backgrounds may well arrive at vastly different damage awards. People from similar backgrounds, also, may possess widely divergent perspectives on how much is a lot and how much is enough. In short, many people—perhaps most people—are essentially clueless when asked to express their punitive intent in dollars, the mode required by the legal system. Based on several studies, we are learning that to understand damage awards, especially punitive ones, we might need to focus on how jurors think about money at least as much as we concentrate on how they think about the issues involved in a case. Despite useful research on matters such as these, however, most insights into how juries decide about damages and which jurors are most willing to award the big money remain the untested opinions of practitioners.

Ronald Matlon, a litigation consultant and founder of the American Society of Trial Consultants, has offered a few generalizations about civil jurors that he deems "relatively safe to make."[93] Matlon maintains that women will award lower damages than men, except when the plaintiff is a woman. He further states, "Women favor young, handsome male lawyers and parties in litigation."[94] Younger jurors prove more lenient in assigning liability in civil cases. But older jurors will award lower damages. Black jurors, according to Matlon, favor perceived underdogs—white and black—and will award them large damages.

But Matlon sees social and occupational status as more reliable predictors of how jurors will decide civil cases. Low-income people favor plaintiffs, especially when they are also low-income. According to Matlon, plaintiffs' jurors also include butchers, printers, tool-and-die makers, accounting clerks, painters, bookkeepers, entertainers, artists, musicians, auditors, office machine operators, sales clerks, general clerks, realtors, brokers, and secretaries. Prodefense jurors include retired military personnel, insurance company employees, farmers, executives, professionals, retired executives, salespersons, electricians, draftsmen, and homemakers. However, teachers and homemakers are especially supportive of plaintiffs in negligence cases involving injuries to children. The spouses of blue-collar workers typically argue for the lowest damages, perhaps, according to Matlon, because "these people generally earn very small amounts of money and are not equipped psychologically to deal in large amounts of cash."[95] More generally, he concludes that jurors identify with parties in litigation who are similar to themselves; thus, "the greater the disparity in social status between a juror and a party in litigation, the more difficult it is for identification and empathy to occur between the two."[96]

Matlon's "relatively safe" rules have some foundation in published research, but as he acknowledges, they must all be qualified with a "sometimes." To the extent that research supports these assertions, it does so indirect and inconsistently.[97] The guidelines also can be self-contradictory. We do not know whether a lawyer who relied on such generalizations would do better than one who relied on chance alone, although it seems likely that there would be at least some marginal improvement. The biggest problems would occur when the particulars of a case call the rules into question or when, regarding a specific juror, the various rules point in different directions.

The way jurors perceive, feel, and think about the world and, more specifically, about our litigious society may tell us something about their tendency to award big damages. Elissa Krauss and Beth Bonorain, in their comprehensive guide to jury consulting—loosely based on published and unpublished research—believe that one key to a juror's willingness to spend a defendant's money lies in his or her attitude toward personal responsibility. They explain:

> At one extreme are people who attribute nearly total responsibility to the individual for shaping his lot in life. At the other extreme are those who attribute nearly total responsibility for success and failure to situational factors and emphasize societal conditions. Most people's views fall somewhere between these extremes. Depending on the facts and circumstances in a case, prospective jurors who are more inclined toward one end of the continuum may be more open to the plaintiff's presentation, or the defendant's. . . . Often practitioners assume that a juror's experience of personal hardship will be an asset for the plaintiff. However, experience alone does not determine a juror's attitudes; more important is the way in which the juror has interpreted and understood the experience.[98]

Bonora and Krauss also call attention to a juror's ability to tolerate ambiguity: "Jurors who seek simple answers to complex problems or who rush to closure find it difficult to hold named defendants liable when there is involvement by other unnamed defendants or even a tenuous basis to conclude that there was comparative negligence."[99] Going farther out on a limb, the authors note that "intolerance for ambiguity is frequently observed among jurors who abide by rigid, highly organized and deferential behavior patterns and activities. Such people may be found among those who are fervent members of certain religious groups or other organizations which reflect rigid worldviews and extremely hierarchical organizational structures."[100]

A juror's views on personal responsibility and his or her capacity to handle ambiguities can bear on the size of damage awards, but according to Krauss and Bonora, these traits relate more directly to the issue of liability. They, and many others, see the tendency to award or not award big damages as tied more closely to one's attitudes toward what some have called the "tort crisis." During the 1990s, legislatures transformed the landscape of civil litigation in many parts of the country, unleashing sweeping changes under the banner of lawsuit reform.[101] Various limits on punitive damages and other barriers have made it harder for plaintiffs to prevail. These alterations in the civil justice system have been both cause and consequence of parallel changes in public attitudes. More recently, top courts in several states have begun to overturn some of the recently imposed limits on civil suits; this too has kept the issue of tort reform high in the public consciousness.[102]

Bonora and Krauss, who work often for plaintiffs in civil cases, write that

> media and political campaigns concerning the clogging of the court system with record numbers of allegedly frivolous law suits—sometimes called the 'litigation crisis'—have increasingly caused jurors to become concerned with matters previously thought to be extraneous to personal injury litigation. Jurors often consider, for example, whether a large award will bankrupt a company, hurt an industry, set a 'precedent,' or encourage others to bring similar lawsuits. They consider the impact the award may have on the public. They may think of higher prices and increased insurance premiums or they may fear the effects a company's bankruptcy might have on a community. . . . Some jurors' fears about higher prices will prevent them from even considering substantial damage awards.[103]

Consultant Amy Singer comments similarly: "Interview voir dire panelists anywhere—small towns, medium-size cities, giant metropolises—and you'll find that a large number think . . . that jury awards are climbing out of sight and that this is a principal reason why manufacturing, insurance, and medical costs are also rising."[104] Those consultants who work primarily with corporate defendants generally downplay the prevalence of such attitudes and, in any event, view them as a necessary corrective for anticorporate attitudes.

How a person feels about torts and lawsuits, not surprisingly, turns out to be one of the most important personal characteristics bearing on the tendency to make large damage awards. For example, in one recent study of product liability cases, jurors who favored tort reform, believed awards too high, and thought many lawsuits frivolous were apt to vote against monetary damages or for smaller damages than other jurors.[105] According to other studies, these tort reformers are older, more conventional,

". . . anti-civil libertarians who feel somewhat powerless and alienated. They do not believe in imminent justice and they do believe in taking legal action in their own self-interest."[106] Interestingly, one study showed that attitudes toward tort reform not only predicted verdicts and award sizes in civil suits but also the tendency to convict in criminal cases.[107] Attitudes toward the tort debates can reflect some fundamental component of a person's worldview and, therefore, have implications even for matters where they would not, at first, seem relevant.

Many practitioners adopt the seemingly commonsense view that ". . . jurors do what everyone else does—they proceed in ways consistent with their biases."[108] But the truth is more complex. No very precise answer emerges if we ask "Who awards the big bucks?" The tendency to favor plaintiffs and award large damages, like the propensity to convict in criminal cases, is situation-specific. It depends on the particulars of the lawsuit, and without knowing these particulars, nothing can be said with great confidence. Certain rules can apply much of the time or for most cases. A young, low-income musician who tends to attribute success or failure to situations rather than individuals and opposes tort reform would certainly be a better bet for a similar plaintiff suing a large corporation in a product liability case. An older, high-income banker who thinks in terms of personal responsibility and favors tort reform would, no doubt, be a poorer bet. But lawyers do not often face such clear choices, and even when they do, the best bet can be a loser.

CAN ATTORNEYS PICK SYMPATHETIC JURORS?

Attorneys sometimes congratulate themselves on their ability to pick "winning" jurors, alluding to powers of perception that have been sharply honed over the years. Although difficult to rule out the possibility that an occasional attorney possesses such extraordinary skill, it seems far more likely that most trial attorneys employ selection strategies that do not differ markedly from those that would be used by nonattorneys. Probably, their choices are little better than hunches.[109] Some attorneys readily admit to this. As one unusually forthright primer to jury selection conceded: "It is, in the end, a guessing game."[110]

Manuals to lawyering have offered—and continue to offer—abundant advice on how to select a jury. Much of this advice is of obviously questionable value. Stereotypes used by attorneys over the years have been simplistic, self-contradictory, often bigoted, and devoid of foundation beyond the vagaries of experience. Thus, one reads that (from the defendant's point of view): "Generally speaking, the heavy, roundfaced, jovial-looking juror is most desirable. The undesirable juror is quite often the slight, underweight and delicate type. His features are sharp and fragile, with the lean 'Cassius' look. The athletic-looking juror is hard to categorize. Usually he is hard to convince; but once convinced he will usually go all the way for you."[111] Another antiquated authority urges plaintiffs to choose members of minority groups but notes a vital exception: "Plaintiffs should be very careful about taking a Jewish juror in a malpractice case against a doctor. . . . Most Jews want their sons to become doctors, 'my son, the doctor,' and they want their daughters to marry doctors. I have never figured out why, but they do."[112] Advice such as this appears less often than it once did, but similar, unfounded know-how can still be found in manuals for trial attorneys. On a positive note, inasmuch as the advice is so often conflicting, counsel will find it difficult to follow.[113]

Psychologist Reid Hastie has reviewed carefully the evidence on attorney effectiveness in picking juries and reasonably concludes that ". . . all evidence demonstrates a consistent lack of impressive attorney performance in this regard." According to Hastie,

> Attorneys disagree substantially about what information to rely on and which jurors to select, and consistently produce low levels of accuracy in judging juror verdict preference prejudices. Perhaps more importantly, even the heightened power of prediction of statistical models also demonstrates comparatively low levels of success in forecasting juror verdict preferences. Finally, considerable research on other similar 'clinical judgments' of peoples' future behavior also concludes that these judgments are sharply limited by a low ceiling on achievable accuracy, and jury selection conditions

are virtually a prototype of situations in which 'learning to judge' will be difficult or impossible.[114]

It's not that attorneys are especially poor judges of human behavior, it's just that they are facing an extremely difficult task. Indeed, Hastie notes one exception where juror backgrounds are sometimes predictive of their judgments, and in this instance, attorneys do rather well: the prediction of award sizes in personal injury cases. Here, juror income and occupation are easy to determine and can be tied to the magnitude of awards. Both plaintiff and defense lawyers can estimate with some accuracy how much prospective jurors are going to award. Still, this is an exception. Most of the time, attorneys have little idea how specific jurors are apt to respond to the arguments and evidence they offer at trial.

DO CONSULTANTS MAKE A DIFFERENCE?

Dramatic early successes surrounded jury consulting work for the defense in several highly politicized trials of the seventies. Yet the so-called success rates of consultants, even when they can be believed, tell us little about their efficacy.[115] As noted, clients who can afford jury consultants can also hire the best attorneys. And lawyers who bother to hire consultants are apt to prepare other aspects of their cases with equal care. Consultants themselves—especially when they speak off the record—betray concern about the tenuous foundation of scientific jury selection.

Although attorneys hardly agree among themselves on the usefulness of hired jury-pickers, enough apparently believe in their effectiveness to sustain a lucrative and growing industry. Some have suggested that we use the market as a barometer of consultant efficacy.[116] The trouble here is that a serious problem and a lack of good alternatives can create a market for ill-founded solutions, even quackery.

In a recent article on an unrelated matter—the effectiveness of alternative medicine—author Samuel McCracken notes,

Life, after all, is an unremitting sequence of anecdotal evidence. As individuals, that is all we have. If we are to make something of it, we must assemble, usually with the help of others, a vast array of anecdotes that can then be tested against one another and ordered according to some rational, even skeptical scheme, which probably will include statistical analysis. . . . The anecdotes presented by most advocates . . . concern instances in which a particular nostrum seems to have been effective. One does not often hear from supporters of *x* a striking account of how *x* failed, or produced unacceptable side effects. Yet nothing is likelier than that such tales exist.[117]

We should keep this in mind when we evaluate jury consultants just as surely as when we assess practitioners of alternative medicine.

Over time, we might expect the free market to weed out ineffective consultants, but the time-lag can be very long—especially because ineffectiveness, like effectiveness, is difficult to prove. Nothing occurs during or after a trial that can ever establish conclusively for an attorney that he or she has made a correct or incorrect decision by retaining a consultant. Yet by affirming belief in the usefulness of the consultants they have already hired, attorneys can avoid the unpleasantness of acknowledging that they bought a bill of goods.

The social science that bears on the question of consultant efficacy is unpalatably complex, and even the best of it by no means instills complete confidence. No study, let alone a body of research, has directly assessed the utility of jury selection consultants. More than twenty years ago, Michael Saks and Reid Hastie objected sensibly to those who were touting the benefits of the then-novel panel selection technology. They wrote,

> The evidence . . . that has most excited or frightened people about scientific jury selection is the fact that no one who has used . . . [it] has lost a case. This seemingly impressive evidence is really no evidence at all. One cannot know the meaning of such an outcome without comparing it to a control group. For example, suppose each time juries selected scientifically heard a trial, a second jury selected the traditional way also heard the case. We could then compare the verdicts rendered by the scientifically selected juries with those rendered by the traditional juries. . . . If the scientifically selected juries convicted at the same rate as the conventional juries, we could infer

that the selection had no impact on the jury's decision making. Only if the juries selected scientifically by the defense convicted less than their yoked counterparts, would we be able to be sure the technique was more effective than what lawyers did anyway. Such studies have not been made, so our knowledge on this question is less than certain.[118]

In 1990, Shari Seidman Diamond, who has conducted respected research in this area, reiterated Saks's and Hastie's concern, noting, "The demands of the courtroom preclude a full controlled test of the technique [of scientific jury selection] in the courtroom setting. In the ideal test . . . , a series of cases would be tried before multiple juries, some 'scientifically' selected and others traditionally chosen. A comparison of the verdicts rendered by the two types of juries would test the value of the method. . . . This direct test of . . . . [scientific jury selection] has not yet been done."[119]

Yet there is much indirect evidence suggesting rather strict limits on its potential effectiveness. For example, we know from a great deal of mock trial research that the strength of the evidence and other aspects of a case, most of the time, matter far more than who sits on the jury. A variety of juries hearing the same case will usually produce the same verdict. Thus, only when the evidence is balanced does the possibility generally emerge for scientific jury selection to clinch a verdict. Jury science rests on several testable assumptions, including: (1) that preexisting juror characteristics will predict tendencies to favor one side or the other; (2) that jurors will reveal to consultants sufficient information to uncover these characteristics; (3) that jurors' pretrial verdict preferences will determine their final votes, surviving whatever else goes on during the trial and in the jury room; (4) that court rules permit sufficient peremptory strikes to eliminate enough jurors to change the final verdict; (5) that preferable replacement jurors are available; and (6) that consultants are providing lawyers with jury selection insights that they do not already possess.

Court rules vary from one jurisdiction to another and one case to another, as does the availability of jurors who will be more sympathetic to one's side. But the relationship between juror characteristics and pretrial opinions about a case has usually been weak. In most cases, so has the connection between the pretrial opinions of a juror who disagrees with the majority and his or her final vote. Group deliberations nearly always reduce the impact of individual biases, mainly because it is extremely difficult to conceal such biases in the intense atmosphere of the jury room, and it is even harder to justify them.[120] Generally speaking, people's actions in court stem more from the facts of the case, circumstances, and situational pressures than from their backgrounds or consistently manifested traits of personality.

Skillful attorneys and their consultants may be able to probe prospective jurors and mine a few of their secrets, but there is also much that people successfully conceal, especially when it might reflect negatively on them. There is no evidence that either consultants or attorneys are especially good at detecting deceptive prospects. Neither is there data backing up the claim that attorneys will learn more about jurors during voir dire when they have been coached by psychologically trained consultants.

In particular cases, the profiles of desirable jurors may be fairly apparent, and lawyers' guesses may be as good as or better than scientific selection methods. More likely, both groups—lawyers and consultants—can pick sympathetic jurors in easy cases, and neither can pick them in tough cases. One example might concern murder cases, where nearly everyone—attorneys and consultants—agrees that attitudes toward capital punishment can be used to predict a juror's likelihood of convicting a defendant in the first place. Unfortunately, the few scientific studies that have attempted to address the question of the relative effectiveness of traditional and scientific selection methods have faced high methodological hurdles that they have not completely cleared.[121]

One student of the trial consulting industry concludes that social-scientific researchers are sharply split on the effectiveness of scientific jury selection and that empirical studies "have produced inconclusive findings."[122] We believe that while the experts may at first seem divided, they turn out—after a little probing—to agree on the facts and are only quibbling about whether these facts add up to a glass that is one-tenth full or nine-tenths empty. One social scientist calls for attorneys to be ". . . vigilant and critical consumer[s] of the services that are offered."[123] Another warns of throwing out the "baby with the bathwater."[124] Still another claims that a consultant's methods "occasionally identify a subtle, case-specific predictor of verdicts," although he concedes that "it is difficult, however, to cite even one convincingly demonstrated success of this type."[125] Finally, one writes, "Scientific jury selection helps one make educated bets. It is not magic. In fact, it appears to be a relatively weak device."[126] Despite differences in tone, none of these social scientists claims that scientific jury selection *frequently* proves decisive, and none suggests that it *never* works.

The best conclusion is that there are cases where jury selection consultants can make a critical difference but that such cases are few and far between. Scientific jury selection will be most likely to matter when: (1) cases are publicized, politicized, or unusual; (2) the facts of the case are likely to activate, inflame, or polarize jurors' attitudes; (3) the evidence does not strongly favor one party; (4) juror leanings are strongly related to observable demographics or otherwise discernible characteristics; (5) the attorney's case strategy depends heavily on certain assumptions made about the jurors; (6) the predictors of juror leanings are not obvious, or better still, they are counterintuitive; (7) attorneys are permitted to conduct voir dire, ask many questions, and distribute comprehensive juror questionnaires; (8) the jury pool is diverse; (9) the court permits many peremptory challenges; (10) the other side is not using scientific jury selection; (11) the attorney lacks familiarity with the jurisdiction; and (12) the budget permits well-designed pretrial research.

Sometimes, when big money (or one's life) is on the line, even a highly improbable glimmer of hope of a decisive edge will be worth a tremendous fee. Thus, huge corporations are willing to part with hundreds of thousands of dollars quite rationally when they face the prospect of payoffs in the tens or hundreds of millions. At the other end of the cost spectrum, general profiles of the conviction-prone juror—touted as applicable across the board—are not likely to be of much use. In civil cases, sweeping profiles can be slightly more effective in identifying those who are apt to award high or low damages.

Like the fanciful stereotypes about jurors that lawyers trusted in the past, scientific jury selection can help attorneys manage their stress far more often than it helps them capture a verdict. In many instances, it is merely a "placebo to build litigant and attorney confidence."[127]

By nearly all accounts, it is when trial consultants move beyond jury selection and into other realms that they have their greatest impact.

5

BEYOND JURY SELECTION

IF YOU CAN'T BE WITH THE JURY YOU LOVE . . .
LOVE THE ONE YOU'RE WITH

TAMPA TRIAL CONSULTANT HARVEY MOORE draws several images of his craft. A professor of sociology who once conducted studies of military deserters in Vietnam and motorcycle gangs, he suggests that "we're like stage managers. The judges control the courtroom. The attorneys try to put their best foot forward. . . . But the question is, what's your best foot?"[1] Moore objects when attorneys say that it is the facts that count in a courtroom and seems to portray himself as an expert guide to understanding and structuring the elements of a case: "There are no facts that count. . . . It's like when I was in astronomy class and they said, 'Pick out Pegasus.' Well, you can't see Pegasus in a bunch of little stars. The only people who are going to see Pegasus are those who've grown up in an ancient Greek culture. You have to make people see it."

Moore also likens himself to a marketing consultant: "Nobody would approach the sale of a new car or the selling of . . . [a] home without some attention to who the potential buyers are," he explains. "That's what we do, figure out what the potential buyers want." "Part scientist, perhaps part benign Rasputin" is how one reporter has described Moore.[2]

Trial consultants in their various roles might also summon forth images of the movie director, the ad man, the political speechwriter, the statistician, the acting coach, the storyteller, and even the astrologer. Once the jury has been selected, the task in many of these capacities is to sway the jury toward their client's side. And during the past decade, a consensus has grown among academics, practitioners, and trial attorneys that it is here rather than in jury selection that trial consultants can matter most.

It is easy to see why this may be so. Lawyers often attempt to gauge juror perceptions and reactions on the basis of their own, and when they do, they are frequently led astray. The problem is that many jurors and attorneys reside in different worlds. Social psychologists have noted that people, in general, tend to overestimate the extent to which other people share their opinions, attributes, and perspectives. They dub this tendency the "false-consensus effect," noting that it frequently leads to erroneous judgments.[3]

Two jury consultants have addressed the matter in an article titled "Attorneys and Jurors: Do They Have *Anything* in Common?" They claim that ". . . the attitudes, values, and beliefs of attorneys are derived from life experiences which are, by societal definition, not typical or 'normal.' Anthropologists might go as far as to say attorneys exist in a subculture of their own."[4]

Along similar lines, Tennessee lawyer Kathryn E. Barnett has written that "formal legal training may pose one of the largest obstacles to success for attorneys who evaluate and try cases."[5] The well-known litigator Michael Tigar supports this view. In a trial attorneys' guide to examining witnesses, he advises,

> Your task is to step outside of your education and upbringing and try to see the world from all the different perspectives that jurors will bring to bear. In argument, all trial lawyers use analogies from everyday life. Your analogies are worth nothing if they describe an everyday life that might be yours but is foreign to the jurors. You live in a law firm. You might hang out with people who make, or think they make, broad-gauge economic and social decisions, weighing and sifting and deciding at a distance. Most jurors deal with the consequences of those decisions—they buy the products, breathe the air, pay the prices, try to get along. . . . In twenty-five years of lawyering, I have found nothing so striking about my profession as its members'

cultivated ignorance of what people think of them and their clients. That sort of arrogance is costly.[6]

Tigar believes good trial consultants can help lawyers to bridge the gap between themselves and those on whom their success depends—the jurors. He contends that "in fairly large cases, a couple of good jury studies will be helpful—I am not talking about full-blown dress-rehearsals, but more modest efforts designed to make sure you are on the right track. Of course, in the 'big' case, the client may be able to pay for the full treatment."[7]

Jury scholar Shari Seidman Diamond also believes that consultants can help lawyers perceive more clearly the way a case will play, or is playing, before a jury. She explains: "Experienced trial attorneys are skilled communicators but they cannot see the themes of the dispute through the eyes of a juror. A pretrial test of juror reactions to the facts of the case and arguments that both sides are expected to make can provide a crucial warning that the message is unclear, that the theme initially selected is not plausible, that jurors will be bothered or unconvinced by parts of the message or that jurors are troubled by missing information that could be supplied."[8]

Even if the thoughts, emotions, and reactions of an attorney closely paralleled those of the typical juror, it might be foolish to substitute one's own impressions for systematic research. If attorneys possessed some special power to read juries and decipher their decisionmaking processes, they could, perhaps, do without the studies. Many experienced litigators indeed claim to possess such skills—and perhaps some do—but, for the rest, it is easy to see how focus groups, trial simulations, and related techniques might substantially improve the quality of judgments that must be made throughout a case.

Consultant Harvey Moore suggests that the needed technology ". . . is nothing more than journeyman social science research."[9] There have been no groundbreaking methodological innovations in the field. Competent consultants emphasize the proper application of basic social scientific methods to the specific goals and requirements of the trial team.[10] This task requires scientific training, creativity, homework, and—above all—familiarity with the context of the litigation.

Robert Minick, a DecisionQuest consultant, notes potential pitfalls encountered by the careless consultant: "If the case issues are presented to the wrong audience, an invalid result will occur. If a representative test audience is presented with a misleading summary of the issues on both sides of the case, an invalid result will occur. The importance of these two elements is easy to grasp. Satisfying the requirements for valid venue and case issue representation is not so easy."[11] Commonly used methods such as telephone surveys, focus groups, and mock trials have strengths and weaknesses that must be considered. Once a technique has been selected, countless small but consequential decisions follow—for example, how many focus groups to conduct or how closely mock jurors must match the actual ones. Careless handling of any of these choices may render the results of the research useless. Yet consultants who always promote the more expensive, blue-chip alternatives may engage in needless overkill and price themselves beyond the budgetary capacity of potential clients. An attorney must determine when a frugal, bare-bones study has departed so radically from the dictates of quality research as to become wasted effort. On this matter, consultants disagree—and often in ways that parallel their economic self-interest.

There is no universally accepted vernacular among trial consultants, so firms can appear to do different things but actually provide similar services. Aside from jury selection work, the efforts of trial consultants can be divided into five main categories: (1) predicting how jurors will decide; (2) developing strategies, themes, theories, and stories for arguing a case; (3) preparing witnesses; (4) training attorneys; and (5) conducting posttrial juror interviews.[12]

FORECASTING TRIAL OUTCOMES: TO SETTLE OR NOT TO SETTLE

A trial usually occurs because one or both sides remains uncertain about how the jury will decide the case. In a civil suit, the plaintiff and defendant often go to court because they arrive at different answers to the same question: "How much is this case worth?" In a criminal case, shared expectations of a conviction will often yield a plea bargain. Trial consultants assert that their services, by reducing uncertainty concerning the outcome of a jury trial, provide a catalyst to settlement and thereby benefit an overburdened justice system.

For example, consultant Amy Singer argues that ". . . a careful intelligence survey enables an attorney to . . . present reliable data projecting that a jury will support a plaintiff's position, and . . . . present a settlement demand that is less onerous to a defendant than a projected jury verdict."[13] Under such circumstances, the defendant will probably settle. She shares an example, omitting several identifying features to protect the confidentiality of her client, the plaintiff.

A mother purchased a product that met all industry standards and worked entirely as intended. She tried to keep it away from her small son, but he soon discovered and handled it. The boy was severely injured, and his mother sued the manufacturer. Several years earlier the company apparently had obtained a patent to make a childproof version of the product, but it had not followed through to incorporate the safety feature. Still, Singer reports, "it seemed unlikely that jurors would find the product unreasonably dangerous or defective or the manufacturer negligent for not warning users of possible danger."[14]

A survey of potential jurors yielded surprising results. According to the research, the best strategy for the plaintiff would be to emphasize that the mother had made an effort to prevent an accident by keeping the product hidden but that the manufacturer made no similar effort to produce a safer product even though it could have done so. Survey respondents proved overwhelmingly responsive to this approach. According to Singer, "It could be projected that over 92 percent of people living in the jurisdiction would agree that the manufacturer should be held liable for damages and that an award of $2 million was fair."[15] The plaintiff's attorney shared these results with the opposition, and the parties quickly agreed on a settlement.

Consider another case, this time where the defense retained a jury consultant.[16] A university teaching hospital permitted a relatively inexperienced intern to attempt to deliver a baby—unassisted. During the delivery, complications developed, and, according to the plaintiff, the hospital staff failed to take appropriate measures. The intern appeared to confirm this view partly by admitting that there were certain things he could have done—things he "didn't think of"—that might have made a difference. Although the defense attributed the baby's problems to an infectious disease and claimed that the infant was saved only though the hospital staff's superb medical intervention, there was a strong temptation for the hospital to settle for a "few" million dollars. The urge arose from the possibility of a jury verdict of, perhaps, $20 million, including $15 million to cover the child's future needs.

But jury research convinced the defendants that they were not likely to be hit with such a monster judgment. Several simulated panels returned verdicts for the defense and gave them confidence to adopt a tough negotiating stance. Ultimately, the case went to trial, and the jury did not buy the plaintiff's argument. Without the knowledge gleaned from the pretrial research, the defense might have opted to settle rather than proceed to trial. As the authors of a guide to jury research for insurance claims managers point out, "It is not uncommon in cases with catastrophic injuries to place some amount on the settlement table. While it seems logical to pay $500,000 to settle a case that has a potential $5 million exposure, the logic quickly fades if the true value of the case is $0."[17]

Defense attorneys and their clients often use surveys and other pretrial studies to red-flag dangerous cases. Consider two similar cases where the same state was sued for negligence. In the first case, no trial consultant was retained. Here, a convicted thief and burglar was released on parole and, shortly afterward, murdered an elderly couple. The parolee, it turns out, missed a few scheduled appointments, and the parole officer failed to make a required home visit. An adult daughter of the couple sued, asserting that parole should have been revoked. The defense team reviewed verdicts from similar cases and concluded that the jury would grasp the predicament of the state, comprehending the difficulties inherent in predicting and preventing the violent act. Thus, the defense anticipated that the panel would attribute most or all of the fault to the murderer himself, placing none or perhaps a very small percentage of the blame on the state. But to the surprise and dismay of the defense, the jurors returned a verdict of $3 million and found that most of the fault rested with the state—not the perpetrator.

The authors who report this case—two insurance claims adjusters and a jury consultant—believe that the verdict did not come from a rogue jury and that the outcome was indeed predictable. They cite a somewhat similar case in which a previously nonviolent probationer embarked on a spree of rape and murder after his release. The defense hired a trial consultant to study how panels of jurors from the same venue would react to the case. The research revealed several beliefs that might apply to jurors in the first case as well. Most participants in the research panels apparently believed that parolees and probationers resemble "wards of the court," meaning that a governmental agency assumes full responsibility for knowing where they are at all times. Moreover, the average juror wants to believe that violent tragedies are preventable and that they do not occur at random—only when somebody screws up. Similarly, they reject the notion that such crimes are part of the harsh realities of life, and they lack sympathy for an overburdened and understaffed bureaucracy. They expect agents of the government to follow every aspect of established procedure, and when they do not, then jurors see a breach of policy that is tantamount to negligence. Finally, some jurors in the study seemed apt to attribute most of the fault to the government because they realized that the imprisoned murderer would be unable or unlikely to compensate the victim. Thus, the pretrial jury research suggested that the defense would not prevail and that a large settlement might still be less expensive than a jury verdict. Accordingly, the parties settled.[18]

Either side can use focus groups and surveys early on to determine whether it makes sense to pursue a settlement or to adopt an aggressive stance, proceeding to trial if necessary. Sometimes, pretrial research can help to resolve disagreement on these matters within the team of the plaintiff or the defense. Several prominent attorneys admit using mock juries to help convince their clients "what they're up against," thereby encouraging them to settle when they might otherwise be recalcitrant.

But perhaps the most promising use of such studies, from a policy standpoint, is when they are shared with the opposition. By narrowing the gaps in perception between the parties, pretrial research can become a useful aid to settlement in the civil justice system. By enabling lawyers to peer into the future, jury studies can encourage nontrial solutions to criminal matters as well. When defendants realize that they are likely to be convicted, they become more receptive to plea bargains. Likewise, when prosecutors learn that acquittal is likely, they might be more inclined to drop charges or consider a plea to a lesser offense.

TRY, TRY AGAIN: THE QUEST FOR A WINNING STRATEGY

Several years ago, Claude "Mountain Man" Dallas, a former trapper, escaped from an Idaho prison where he had been serving a thirty-year term.[19] After Dallas spent eleven months as a fugitive, authorities finally captured him in California. He looked like a different man, having undergone facial plastic surgery during his months on the lam. Under the law, a person could justify escape only on grounds that while in prison he was in imminent danger and—equally important—that he planned to turn himself in immediately upon reaching a safe haven. To make this case would be no mean feat for an eleven-month fugitive who had voluntarily altered his facial features.

But Dallas had an explanation. He had been serving time for voluntary manslaughter of two game wardens, and as he told it, the prison guards considered him a cop-killer. He feared for his life. According to Dallas, the only reason he had not turned himself in immediately was because he had been waiting for the population of prison guards to turn over. It would not be safe for him to return to the same guards who had threatened him.

It was quite a story. But would the jury believe it? To find out, his attorneys hired California consultant Howard Varinsky to run a study. Varinsky's team presented an abbreviated version of Dallas's story to mock jurors. They didn't find it credible and, subsequently, voted to convict. But then the defense team floated another strategy, one they had initially judged to be weaker. Dallas, they argued, had been the target of harassment in prison. Abandoning the turnover-of-the-guards theory, they now maintained that the scared fugitive had not turned himself in immediately because he had been trying to earn enough money to support a lawsuit he wished to file. His goal was to sue the prison officials to force them to guarantee his safety while incarcerated. The mock jurors found this story much more compelling and voted to acquit. In the actual trial, Dallas's lawyers used the earning-legal-fees theory and obtained what has to be viewed as an unlikely acquittal. In this case, the lawyers had two theories, neither of which seemed a likely winner. The jury research identified which of the two had a better shot. The lawyers followed the advice—and were glad they did.

Many lawyers claim that trial consultants are most valuable when they conduct focus groups and trial simulations to help formulate and evaluate case strategies, themes, and approaches. Why risk making an argument before the real jury when you can try it out with surrogate panels? Attorney Peter Gelblum, whose firm successfully represented the Goldman family in the O.J. Simpson civil suit, explains: "One thing a lot of lawyers tend to do is to put too much emphasis on legal arguments and on logic and rationality when that is not necessarily what sways a jury."[20] He judges trial consultants to be most valuable when they enable attorneys to learn, in advance, how well their arguments are likely to be received. Sometimes, Gelblum notes, trial consultants afford an opportunity to try out arguments "that you never even plan to make," just to be sure that one is not overlooking a perspective or detail that might prove significant to a jury. In his work on the O.J. Simpson case, however, Gelblum reports that jury research did not reveal any hidden strategies.

One very clear and important finding from the mock trials of the O.J. Simpson civil case was not much of a surprise to Gelblum. He recalls: "By far the most important thing we learned . . . was that, among Simpson supporters, the depth and strength of support for him overcame all rationality; it was mind-boggling." He says that at one point after presentations had been made to the mock jurors and they had finished deliberating, one group was asked: "What would you say if we had presented the following evidence to you. The murderer wore size-12 Bruno Magli shoes and this was established beyond dispute. Simpson denied ever wearing size-12 Bruno Magli shoes. A photo which you can assume is accurate shows him wearing size-12 Bruno Magli shoes within months of the murder. Do you think that's pretty decent evidence?" "With barely a beat," Gelblum recalls, "one black woman supporter said, 'No. Somebody could have stolen them from him.'" He claims that many of Simpson's supporters possessed this type of rigid loyalty by the time of the civil trial. The response was so irrational that the research taught him "that it was not possible to change their minds." In this sense, the mock trials did not suggest a means of altering the perspectives of jurors unsympathetic to the plaintiffs but rather the importance of keeping them off the jury in the first place.[21]

However, the research did reveal that among some people who were Simpson supporters there was one way to make a dent in their loyalty. In the mock trials, Gelblum explains, "the only thing that moved them toward our side was Simpson implicating himself. Hearing him say something that appears to be a lie." Along these lines, getting Simpson's own friends to contradict him was apt to be reasonably effective. Gelblum recalls, "One of our favorite charts that DecisionQuest prepared for us was what we called the liar's board. . . . It said 'Either Simpson's lying or the following are lying.' It was four feet by six feet, filled with names and phone records—all of them contradicted something he said."

Gelblum and his associates judged the jury research results useful and interesting rather than essential, largely because the findings did not contradict any beliefs they possessed prior to conducting the research. But the tips that lawyers glean from focus groups and mock trials often play a far more central role in guiding the conduct of a case than they did in the O.J. Simpson civil trial. According to one consulting group's promotional literature, focus groups are "less elegant . . . and expensive and time consuming" than trial simulations, but they can "locate the 'natural' ways in which jurors might understand and structure a case. . . . A really good focus group will tell you how to get from a set of facts to an end result, and will simultaneously lay bare the hazards along the road."[22] Usually consultants conduct a series of groups, even when resources are constrained, as it seldom makes sense to rely on only one or two focus groups.

Several different procedures are used, but most consultants begin by recruiting small groups of six to twelve paid participants who reflect the community or the anticipated make-up of the jury. A neutral moderator or the attorneys then present a summary of both sides of the case, usually in a storylike, opening-statement style. The focus group participants discuss the issues of the case among themselves, occasionally asking the moderator or attorneys to provide additional information. Sometimes participants hear a judge's instructions and proceed to formally deliberate and arrive at a verdict. The final stage of the focus group usually includes postdeliberation discussions and question-and-answer sessions in which the sponsoring attorneys usually take part.

Everything is videotaped. Participants may also complete a written questionnaire designed to further convey their reactions to the case. The goal throughout the sessions is to gain insight into the thought processes of participants and to assess the persuasiveness of arguments, documents, and evidence. By clarifying the issues in the case, the attorney may, with the consultant's assistance, develop a more effective theme, reworking the opening statements, closing arguments, and everything in between.

For big cases, focus groups may be the first step toward a more comprehensive research program that includes full-blown mock trials. In a well-designed study, attorneys (sometimes in videotaped presentations) present both sides of a case to mock jurors in a real or carefully simulated courtroom setting. The presentation is designed to capture as much of the reality of the trial as possible, including voir dire, preliminary instructions to the jury, opening statements, direct and cross examination of witnesses, presentation of evidence, and closing arguments. Mock jurors typically hear extensive instructions from a mock judge and then deliberate to a verdict. As in the focus groups, extensive interviews follow in order to reveal more about the thinking of individual jurors as well as the group as a whole.

The Stanford-based Trial Analysis Group, a high-powered team of consultants, offers two pieces of advice on how to conduct mock trials correctly. First, they claim:

> Jury simulations are useful in direct proportion to the degree to which they are veridical. Composing a mock jury from the staff of your law office, from your family or with a group of undergraduates at a neighboring college in a handy classroom, while it is better than nothing at all, is nowhere near what

significant cases require. Use (and pay) strangers who owe you no emotional or pecuniary allegiance. Use a courtroom and a [simulated] robed judge . . . in order to impress your jurors with the importance of their tasks. Use people who are jury-eligible. Question them carefully before they are employed, and test them before they participate. Give them a good deal of time to deliberate—that's where you get your best trial hunches.[23]

Second, the Trial Analysis Group urges attorneys to ". . . make sure you present the strongest possible version of your opponent's case. That's your insurance. If you can make significant inroads against the very strongest version of the opposition, you can sure do well when the opposition falters."[24] Consultants from another firm, San Francisco–based Trial Behavior Consulting, Inc., echo the concern about underplaying the hand of the opposition. They note that "one mistake often made in mock trials is that the less experienced attorney plays the role of opposing counsel. Presentations for both sides must be of equal quality to achieve the desired results. Further, having the lead attorney take the role of opposing counsel forces him or her to reevaluate the case."[25]

All trial consultants suggest that a well-designed mock trial can provide insights that improve an attorney's preparation for a case. In addition to testing themes, theories, and competing strategies, mock trials can address several important questions: (1) How are key witnesses perceived? (2) Is the testimony by expert witnesses understood? (3) Do the pictures, graphs, and videotapes work? (4) Which evidence is most and least convincing? (5) Is certain language or metaphor particularly effective? (6) How do jurors rate attorney performance?

By exposing unexpected juror reactions, mock trials enable lawyers to alter arguments that don't work, clarify matters that remain foggy, and avoid stylistic flourishes that are counterproductive.

TELLING THE JURY A STORY

One of the most highly touted uses of jury research, especially during the past few years, has been to help a lawyer to frame the story he or she wishes to tell the jury. This application grows out of a recent theory of jury decisionmaking called the "story model," but it also has roots in old-fashioned showmanship. In the motion picture *Amistad*, former president and attorney John Quincy Adams will not represent the defendants until their advocates can answer one vital question: "What is the story?" His point is that he cannot win a case unless he can present it as a compelling story.[26]

Many lawyers, before and since, have highlighted the importance of a good tale in gripping the hearts and minds of jurors. The well-known litigator Gerry Spence, who has represented many famous and infamous defendants, including Karen Silkwood and Randy Weaver, advises that "every argument, in court or out, whether delivered over the supper table or made at a coffee break, can be reduced to a story. An argument, like a house, yes, like the houses of the three little pigs, has structure. Whether it will fall, whether it can be blown down when the wolf huffs and puffs, depends upon how the house has been built. The strongest structure for any argument is *story*."[27]

In the academic world, researchers have given formal expression to a fairly complex model wherein ". . . jurors use episode schemata—generic knowledge structures abstracted from prior experience—to remember and organize trial evidence into a plausible story. Jurors then attempt to match the story to available verdict categories, selecting the verdict that provides the best fit."[28] According to one leading analyst of jury research, "The story model is a psychologically plausible account of juror decision making, and it is the only model in which serious consideration is given to the role of memory processes during the trial, but more research is needed to establish its predictive validity and heuristic value for generating testable hypotheses."[29] Researchers, especially psychologists Nancy Pennington and Reid Hastie, have elaborated the tenets of the story model with considerable precision, and they have supported some of these principles with well-designed experiments.[30] But trial consultants, understandably, do not utilize Hastie and Pennington's theory in full academic regalia.[31]

DecisionQuest's consultants convey the essence of their approach to prospective clients by asking them to think about their last visit to the movies:

You probably sat through five or six previews of upcoming features, each of which was approximately 1½ to 2 minutes in length and was comprised of two to three second sound bursts. . . . You probably had a pretty good idea about the movie's story line, yet you viewed only about two to three minutes of the film. How does this happen? Well, the anticipated "story" you formulated was based on experiences with that particular genre, producer, and actors, as well as familiarity with similar story lines. In the same way, jurors begin to develop a story about the entire case based on the previews given in the opening statement. Jurors fill out the story using their own experiences, attitudes and perceptions as a framework. As in the movie example, jurors fill in the gray areas in the dispute at hand and "connect the dots" based on related experiences and their overall views of the world. Jurors then selectively filter information presented to them to maintain a coherent story. While the story is elaborated upon throughout the trial, there is a strong tendency for jurors to discard information inconsistent with the main story line.[32]

Storytelling is a time-honored craft. However, the needs of the master storyteller are not easily met in the context of the jury trial. Rick Fuentes and his colleagues from DecisionQuest explain: "The traditional trial structure is one that calls for inductive information processing. That is, the lawyer presents fact one plus fact two plus fact three, perhaps through a series of witnesses. The presumption is that at the end of the day the jurors will assimilate the information and reach your desired conclusion. This is simply not how jurors listen."[33] Professor Solomon Fulero agrees, noting that "it's all about information processing. . . . A juror is not being presented with a coherent story. It's not like someone is telling them a narrative that has a beginning, a middle and an end. What they get is in snatches. They get the beginning of the story near the end and the end of the story in the beginning. And they have to piece together some kind of coherent narrative from the pieces they get from the trial."[34] Thus, the challenge for consultants is to determine which story to tell and how best to tell it within the rules established by the court. Often, this involves creating a strong framework within the juror's mind during the opening statement, reinforcing that framework as often as possible throughout the trial, and finally hammering it home during the closing argument.

Very frequently, it is no simple matter to determine which theme or themes to emphasize in a story. One consultant maintains that most cases can be expressed through a few themes that recur throughout human history. According to Michigan-based consultant Eric Oliver,

> It is wise to rely on classic themes rather than arcane originals. For example, almost all medical malpractice cases can be—and usually are—framed as David versus Goliath by the plaintiffs. Good versus evil is always nice, and there are great frameworks in the deadly sins and cardinal virtues. Job or Sisyphus striving against overwhelming odds; Prometheus or Thomas Paine paying the price for doing the right thing; Ebeneezer Scrooge or Christ's tax collector undergoing their conversions of spirit; star-crossed or unrequited love; long, hard work deserving reward; or anything lifted from Mother Goose or Aesop will do.[35]

For Oliver, the lawyer generally should not refer to a theme specifically by its literary or historical manifestation. He explains that "... the familiar story line can be presented while leaving observers multiple paths to fill in details, characters, and feelings, reinforcing their own beliefs in them, often in defiance of more rational arguments against them. The very fact that these associations are formed less specifically, out of reach of much conscious scrutiny, gives them the *feeling* of greater veracity to those who opt to internalize them."[36]

Trial advocacy guides offer endless advice on how to select a good theme. For example, two attorneys suggest the following: "A good theme ... has a certain rhythm to it. Its memorable quality comes from its rhyme or parallelism. The case theme may be constructed from an alliteration ..., analogy (a good carpenter measures thrice before he cuts once), or a famous proverb or epigram (a little learning is a dangerous thing)."[37] They also maintain that "the most powerful affective themes [for plaintiffs] involve the betrayal of trust, the arrogance of power, or the impetus of the profit motive. ... An affective theme might be, 'They wouldn't listen to Robert, but maybe they'll listen to you' or 'These defendants have refused to answer this family's question. Today, you can give them the answer they deserve.'"[38]

To create a story, jurors need to answer several questions. What was done? Who did it? How? Why? What were the circumstances? According to Rick Fuentes and his colleagues, motive is most frequently the missing—and missed—element. They explain: "Even if the law does not require a showing of motive, jurors are *always* looking for it and if they do not find it, the story falls apart."[39] Despite this advice, and the apparent confidence with which trial consultants offer it, they and their clients cannot know in advance whether jurors will buy the theme, adopt the story, or for that matter understand where the lawyer is headed. And this creates a strong market for mock juries and focus groups.

California litigator Gary Gwilliam tells of an occasion where jury research helped identify a central weakness in the story that opposing counsel was telling the jury.[40] Gwilliam, who has tried more than 150 cases, is a big fan of the trial consulting industry. In this case, an inebriated driver had rear-ended a 1984 General Motors (GM) Corvette driven by a twenty-nine-year-old California man. The roof collapsed in the roll-over accident, and as a result of the accident, the Corvette driver suffered quadriplegia. He hired Gwilliam and sued GM, alleging that the car manufacturer had poorly designed the roof of the vehicle and thereby made his injuries more likely.

Gwilliam knew of a similar case in Seattle in which General Motors had prevailed. Among other things in that case, the car manufacturer had claimed that the defective roof was essentially irrelevant; this was because the driver would hit the roof so hard that—just before it crushed—his or her neck would break anyway. Gwilliam suspected that this point, whatever its truth, would not play well before a jury. But it had been part of the winning case in Seattle, so he wanted to test his belief.

In focus groups, he learned that jurors indeed treated the argument with ridicule, especially when Gwilliam dubbed it the "diving theory." He explains: "The more we used the word 'theory,' the less the jury liked it." This led to a successful courtroom strategy. Gwilliam recalls: "We kept pushing against the diving theory. [The defense] pushed back. And the jury started to roll their eyes. The jurors saw the diving theory as B.S." Gwilliam's team knew this from their focus groups and, consequently, belittled the theory, never treating it with the seriousness it was given in the Seattle case. The plaintiff won a $6.1 million verdict, 80 percent of which was apportioned to General Motors. It was—according to Gwilliam—the largest single personal injury verdict in the county to date, and the award was upheld on appeal. He assigns a good portion of the credit to the pretrial research, claiming that "our focus groups put us ahead of the other side."

DecisionQuest offers another example of pretrial research at work, this time helping defense attorneys to craft a persuasive story.[41] A fairly young mail-order firm had sued a manufacturer from which it had purchased sophisticated telephone equipment. The amiable entrepreneurs claimed that the manufacturing company had provided them with defective equipment unable to process a sufficiently large number of telephone calls and that as a result they were losing a fortune in business. By their calculations, they deserved an award reaching into the tens of millions. They filed the case in their hometown. Prior to conducting any research, the defense had planned to answer attacks on their equipment and to challenge the way the entrepreneurs had arrived at their damage figures. In addition, they would call into question the credibility of the owners of the mail-order firm and charge them with mismanaging their operation. To test this approach and to fine-tune it, the manufacturer retained DecisionQuest and authorized pretrial studies.

As a result of these studies, the consulting firm recommended a substantial change, one that aimed to elicit in the jurors' minds a story based on the entrepreneurs' portrayal of themselves as the embodiment of American success. The consultants explain:

Completely different in tone and substance from the original story, the new story placed very little emphasis on the equipment and its function, and a great deal of emphasis on how the plaintiffs had become an overnight success. Embedded in our story was a key theme: "They got too big, too fast." . . . We painted a picture of the entrepreneurs as people who were not bad managers so much as they were just unprepared for their sudden success. The story was no longer technical or negative; it allowed the jury to like and admire the plaintiffs yet still find against them.[42]

Although this approach had a certain intuitive appeal, DecisionQuest's consultants pretested it with a new batch of mock jurors to confirm their impressions. They concluded that the story would ultimately become ". . . the filter jurors used to decide the case," a view that they believe was supported by the verdict and posttrial interviews. The jury found for the manufacturer, and the jury foreman later reported that "these were good guys who had good ideas; they simply got too big, too fast." The consultants confidently maintained that "the jurors had embraced our story and made it their own."[43]

The most skeptical of social scientists would not be so sure that pretrial research, even in specific cases, contributes decisively to outcome. One cannot readily gauge the impact of focus groups and trial simulations because one cannot determine how a case would have turned out had they not been used.

Most attorneys seek to identify effective themes and case theories even when they do not retain a trial consultant. As in the advertising industry, talented and experienced practitioners may be very adept at identifying and presenting highly persuasive approaches. And when an attorney abandons a previously favored strategy in deference to one supported by research, one remains forever in the dark about how the original version would have fared.

Thus, Gary Gwilliam's repeated focus on the diving theory may have contributed to his success in the GM Corvette case, or it may have been differences between his California jury and the earlier Seattle one that proved decisive. And his intuitions may have led him to a similar approach, even without the benefits of pretrial research. Alternatively, the diving theory may not have been what turned the jury toward his client's side; it may have been something else entirely. Even in the DecisionQuest example, one remains uncertain about the outcome of the case had the original strategy been retained.

Still, these skeptical quibbles seem a bit curmudgeonly. After all, trial consultants can pretest different arguments with the same mock jurors, noting their responses to each. They can also try out ideas developed during one phase of the research with different participants later on. When an attorney sharply redirects strategy on the basis of study results, it is hard to maintain that he or she would have settled on the new approach anyway.

When trial consultants take all the required steps to ensure verisimilitude, when they present a case faithfully to participants who are in most ways reflective of the anticipated jury, their studies have a high probability of producing realistic results. Whether these findings translate into surprising, useful, or decisive insights depends greatly on the particulars of the case. The value of results that emerge from research where courtroom realities are less faithfully re-created is more open to question. Although some high-end consultants regard inexpensive efforts as essentially useless, most argue that some pretrial research is better than none at all. At least, they maintain, the attorney receives feedback from a sample of people less likely to share his or her biases.

PREPPING WITNESSES

Trained as a clinical psychologist and still in private practice in Palo Alto, California, Florence Keller consults frequently on trial strategy and witness preparation for big intellectual property cases.[44] In her view, trial consulting can also be viewed as providing a helpful service to the public. She notes that her job is often to assist in presenting a case in a meaningful way and claims that ". . . in posttrial interviews [from cases she has worked on], the jurors frequently see the trial as a positive experience and that wouldn't have happened without us." Although not denying the partisan nature of her task, Keller generally sees her contribution to a trial as largely one of clarification. She notes, "In what we do, both sides have so many resources that they can get their own jury consultant. It's not as if one side only is going to have it."

Keller tells how her firm once contributed a very small but critical piece to a major patent infringement case by helping to prepare a key witness.

A tremendous amount of money was at stake. The involved corporations had been to the mat previously, and the opposition had prevailed. But an appeals court had remanded the case back to the trial court for another go. Thus, Keller was not starting at ground zero, and she could learn from errors made during the first trial. Those who had interviewed the original jury after trial reported some disturbing news about how jurors perceived one man, who was supposed to be her client's star witness. The jury hated him so much that he became a central reason why they handed down the unwanted verdict.

Keller met the man (whom she dubs "Leo" to protect his identity) and set about determining what had gone wrong. She reports that he "... turned out to be a charming, ethical man with a lovely sense of humor. But not well versed—as none of us are—in the ways of testifying." She continues: "This particular attorney boxed Leo into answers. . . . [Leo] kept saying, 'It's not that simple.' This went on and on. And when a witness starts battling with a lawyer, it looks like they're trying not to tell the truth. Leo got more and more upset. He looked cantankerous. Argumentative."

For Keller, the solution was simple. Leo needed some training in the art of delivering testimony, and her task was easier than on other occasions because Leo was a very bright guy. "So," Keller recalls,

> we just talked to Leo and gave him some ways to deal with this very aggressive cross-examination. And he was wonderful. We suggested that just when he's boxing you in, give him an answer and say, "May I explain?" It seems so obvious. The attorney was left with the question each time. And if he says no, then fine. You'll get your chance when we do redirect. The approach left the attorney in the impossible situation of having to say, "No, you can't explain." After the seventh time [Leo asked the question], the attorney relented. He said, "Go on and explain," at which time Leo did, and he told a very credible story.

Posttrial interviews showed that this go-round, Leo was her client's best witness. "They were all charmed by Leo. It was a 180-degree turnaround," Keller proudly explains, then adds one last tip that in her view proved useful: "One of the problems with Leo is that he was bald and his head started to sweat (as we all do) and he looked greasy. And 'greasy' was one of the words used about him. [One of the consultants in the firm] . . . approached Leo and told him he had to put powder on his head and very happily he did."

According to Keller and many other trial consultants, preparing witnesses means helping them to become comfortable with the idea of testifying and getting them to understand what the case is really about.[45] Far from putting words in the mouths of witnesses, trial consultants see their role as educational. They give witnesses some tricks of the trade that can help them cope with a difficult and highly novel situation. They work with witnesses, advise them, and videotape them so they can see themselves perhaps a bit more the way members of a jury will perceive them. Sometimes trial consultants offer little more than good judgment. Keller recalls a case where much rested on the testimony of the CEO of a large company, an intelligent man who ". . . looked a little bit like a player." The firm's advice was ". . . to put on a wedding ring—he was married—and to change his hair. . . . And to take off his ten million dollar Rolex watch!"[46]

Another example shows how witness preparation can bear centrally on the outcome of a case. A professional man had been accused of date rape; after the district attorney had decided not to prosecute, the alleged victim sued for battery and intentional infliction of emotional distress.[47] Predictably, the defendant maintained that the sex had been consensual, while the woman claimed that she had been forced. They had both been drunk and, indeed, the defendant typically drank heavily.

Howard Varinsky had been retained by the defense as a trial consultant. In this he-said/she-said case, everything was riding on the testimony of the defendant—and he did not come across well. In an early focus group, participants heard his testimony and voted overwhelmingly against him. After all, he was married, and what he had done was—in their eyes—sleazy at the very least. The focus-group members viewed him as a "sex addict" and disliked his attitudes toward women, describing him as very sexist and a sexual chauvinist. In his testimony before the focus group, when asked how he knew that the plaintiff had been flirting with him, he replied, "It's like when you're fishing and you get a bite." The participants rolled their eyes and looked at each other. In Varinsky's view, the defendant (whom Varinsky believed to be innocent) would cook his own goose.

The remedy was simple. Show the defendant his behavior on videotape and allow him to hear feedback—not from his lawyer or friends—but from a group of about twenty people with whom he had no connection. The defendant heard that focus-group participants didn't like his failure to apologize for his alcoholism. They thought he was in denial. They also wanted him to acknowledge that he had done a sleazy thing. Varinsky reports that the feedback from the focus group managed to pierce the man's psychological defenses and to convince him that he had to change his approach. He also realized that he had to modify his sexist manner, at least for the duration of his testimony.

The next step called for new testimony before new focus groups. This time, the defendant apologized for his alcoholism, indicated it was a problem, and noted that he had joined Alcoholics Anonymous. He declared that it was a sleazy thing he had done to his wife and that he would never do it again. And he adopted a less sexist style. The new research revealed that the tactic worked well, with most jurors reporting that they liked the defendant.[48] Varinsky believes that his witness preparation work, coupled with his insights into jury selection, played a major part in winning the case for the acquittal of his client.

When a key witness capsizes before one set of mock jurors, and then—after receiving advice from a trial consultant—sails smoothly before another, lawyers and their clients would certainly seem to be getting their money's worth. But one might ask what type of preparation is most useful and who is best equipped to offer it. As experts on the science of attitude change and persuasion, social psychologists sometimes claim to know best. Those with advanced training in communications or speech also claim expertise. Many say that since no one can tell what aspects of a witness or his or her testimony will sway a jury, the only reasonable place to start is by measuring the reactions of mock jurors in a focus group or simulation.

But when witnesses require guidance on matters of style or appearance, trial consultants may have little edge over anyone else. Jury psychologist and consultant Gary Moran notes, "Psychologists don't know one damn thing about attire or clothing. They're never taught any such thing at all. There's no reason why as a psychologist I would have more insight than my daughter who is a designer and decorator."[49] Others see the acting coach or drama expert as most appropriately prepared to guide witnesses.

Many lawyers who do not rely on trial consultants are by no means ignorant of the importance of witness preparation, and some can carry it out effectively. Attorneys often provide witnesses with guidelines on how to testify. Litigator Daniel Small has offered ten rules for witnesses, including: (1) take your time; (2) remember you are making a record; (3) tell the truth; (4) be relentlessly polite; (5) don't answer a question you don't understand; (6) if you don't remember, say so; (7) don't guess; (8) keep it simple; (9) be careful with documents and prior statements; and (10) use your counsel.[50] A lawyer who imparted similar tips to his witnesses would go some distance toward avoiding common pitfalls. But the service provided by trial consultants can go beyond these suggestions, mainly by pretesting witnesses before mock jurors.[51]

Elaine Lewis is a trial consultant who specializes in preparing "witnesses from hell," difficult witnesses who "no matter what . . . [their own side's] attorney does or says . . . can't or won't follow instructions."[52] She notes five ways an attorney might err in preparing a witness. First, the lawyer might not have provided enough basic information about the trial or deposition process. Such information would include tips about how to dress, where to look, what to take to the witness stand, how to address the judge, and—most notably—how to respond to questions appropriately by listening carefully, answering only the question asked, seeming helpful, and providing no additional information.

A lawyer might also err by providing the witness with too much preparatory information. She advises, "Someone who has never been a witness before will only be confused and overwhelmed by reading about trick questions, rules of evidence, and types of objections. . . . Too much concentration on too many details breeds fear resulting in the inability to think intelligently. Instead, clients [when they testify] should understand the theory of the case and be familiar with the information to be presented."[53] Lewis also believes that attorneys frequently fail in their efforts to prepare a witness by offering too little praise, by failing to set aside sufficient time for "drill and practice," and by lacking sympathy for the predicament of the witness. On this last point, she comments: "Medical schools have begun teaching doctors to develop a sympathetic bedside manner because it has been found that patients get better faster when the doctor takes time to listen and express how he cares. In much the same sense, legal clients will do better as witnesses if they feel they have their attorney's emotional as well as his intellectual support."[54]

The practices endorsed by Lewis seem sound enough and hard to question. The skills she urges attorneys to acquire and, by implication, claims to possess are, in fact, the skills of a good teacher. Someone who specializes in witness preparation may well have developed patience, techniques, and insights that a typical attorney lacks. Lewis reasonably concludes, "The value of using a witness consultant is that preparing witnesses is what we do on a daily basis. Attorneys rarely prepare witnesses with the same regularity. And when an attorney does prepare a witness for trial, there tends to be more emphasis on the issues in the case than on the communication skills of the witness."[55]

Trial consultants flatly deny that they put words into the mouths of witnesses or encourage them to change the content of their testimony. But the line between legitimate witness preparation and subornation of perjury can sometimes be a fine one. Even in cases where a consultant does not cross the line, one wonders how juries would react if they knew what happened behind the scenes. Would they still believe that the defendant in the date-rape case discussed above had changed if they knew that the impetus for his apologies came not from within but from his trial consultant's notebook?

Still, when a witness owes a poor performance not to the content of his or her testimony or the position taken but to quirks of personality, the stress of testifying, or an inadequate stage presence, a witness preparation consultant may well be serving justice.

TRAINING THE MASTERS

According to trial consultant Eric Oliver, "God's lack of fairness is a matter of record. Likewise the fact that some attorneys are better able to present themselves in a compelling and memorable fashion." A small percentage of lawyers, he says, have sought training to improve their innate abilities, but most have relied on ". . . random reinforcement during their early development." Oliver objects to those who ask ". . . whether successful interpersonal communication can really be taught."[56] In his view, this question is ill-informed because in communications—as in most endeavors—quality instruction can improve skills. The many trial consultants who offer training seminars and individualized guidance to attorneys would undoubtedly agree.

Researchers in communication and the various social sciences offer access to seemingly limitless information bearing on the lawyer's predicament. Social psychologists, for example, have conducted thousands of experiments on how people form impressions, process information, change beliefs, and persuade others. Their findings on these matters and others relevant to the lawyer's task could fill, and indeed have filled, many textbooks. Other social scientists have conducted voluminous research specifically examining the psychology of jury decisionmaking and the legal system. Thus, trial consultants could—in theory—familiarize themselves with a vast body of knowledge and, more important, could serve as conduits between the world of academia and perennially busy legal practitioners. The question these experts must address is whether studies in the social sciences and communication have implications that go beyond theory and whether they can be translated meaningfully and practically into an edge for attorneys who try cases.

The psychology of law is now a maturing discipline that is the focus of numerous texts and professional organizations.[57] It covers dozens of topics including the impact on juries of different types of evidence, the effectiveness of judicial instructions to jurors, and the utility of various trial tactics. One study, for example, found jurors in personal injury cases most impressed by well-organized lawyers who presented themselves professionally and showed moderation in their emotional appeals. According to this study, attorneys were best received when they calibrated the emotionality and enthusiasm of their presentation to the severity of their client's injuries.[58] Another study demonstrated the effectiveness of tricks used by lawyers to cross-examine expert witnesses. In simulated trials, researchers showed that attorneys could successfully impugn the reputation of an expert by asking questions implying that the witness had a poor professional reputation. Whether the expert denied the accusation, admitted it, or objected to the question, he or she typically ended up appearing less competent, less believable, and less persuasive than if the question had never been posed in the first place.[59] Another study found that a lawyer could greatly increase the persuasiveness of DNA evidence by slightly modifying the way experts explained such evidence to a jury. In cases involving DNA testimony, the crucial issue is whether the DNA at a crime scene matches the DNA of the suspect, and jurors must consider whether an apparent match might be the result of pure chance. In the experiment, one group heard the odds of a coincidence expressed as a percentage, being told that the suspect had a 0.1 percent chance of a match purely by chance. The second group of subjects heard the odds as a frequency, learning that one in a thousand other people also matched the DNA. The two statements are mathematically identical. But jurors in the first group—the ones who heard the odds as a percentage—were much more likely to be convinced that the DNA came from the suspect. They were also substantially more confident about their judgment.[60] These few findings from the psychology of law suggest that the field might offer attorneys considerable guidance concerning what to say and how to say it.

DecisionQuest consultant Reiko Hasuike has focused on the social-scientific study of gender. She lists a number of conclusions, drawn from academic studies, that she deems relevant to female lawyers in the courtroom. According to her list,

People (both men and women) think that men generally are more competent than women. . . . When a woman shows competence in areas of expertise considered to be masculine, people may believe that her high performance is caused by luck, not skill. . . . Women who show competence in "masculine" areas are often seen as being more competent than men who perform at the same level. . . . Women benefit tremendously when they perform competently in "masculine" ways, so long as these ways are seen as being positive and so long as the women do not challenge traditionally female values such as motherhood. . . . Women jurors do not necessarily like women advocates more than male advocates. . . . Women jurors with more progressive views on women's role in society tend to like women advocates who deviate from traditional roles; but male jurors with progressive views do not share this view.[61]

Hasuike reasonably considers these findings bad news for the female attorney. But she also maintains that ". . . exposing and describing . . . [the] challenge is the first step toward meeting it."[62]

Unfortunately, the few subsequent steps she recommends, although perhaps sensible, do not go very far. For example, she advises female litigators during voir dire to communicate genuine interest in the family lives and religious activities of jurors. Similarly, she advises women lawyers throughout a trial to take care not to express opinions counter to the traditional values of motherhood and family. Hasuike also counsels that women must work hard to establish their competence early in the trial, perhaps by tackling a seemingly difficult concept and explaining it simply. Additionally, female lawyers should do whatever they can to get a judge or expert witness to signal their approval to the jury.[63]

Still other insights into the trial lawyer's task might be culled from the large discipline of social psychology. Consultant and psychologist Jeffrey Frederick has mined the huge literature on persuasion and attitude change, seeking principles useful to the litigator. According to Frederick, the attorney faces an extraordinarily complex "persuasion situation" in the courtroom. Using the jargon of the academic social psychologist, he notes:

> *Sources* of communication—attorneys, judges, and witnesses—present a *message*—evidence, comments, and arguments—conveyed by some *medium* (including *modality*) to affect a *receiver*—the jurors. For a communication to be persuasive, the audience must attend to it, understand it (process it), store it in memory (encode it), yield to the position advanced, and recall

the message in some form (retrieve it). Each of the major components of persuasion—*source, message, medium* and *receiver*—has special features which affect persuasion.[64]

From the standpoint of the social psychologist, it is no simple matter to understand why one lawyer succeeds in convincing a jury while another does not. Frederick does his best to sift through and filter decades of experimental research, shielding readers from needless lingo while trying to ensure that they do not receive watered down insights. He refers to dozens of technical studies and, in the end, arrives at a lengthy list of trial recommendations regarding opening statements, direct examination, cross-examination, nontestimonial evidence, and closing arguments.

Although Frederick's advice is carefully derived from research on persuasion and attitude change, it may strike many attorneys as little more than common sense. Consider some typical suggestions regarding opening statements. He tells lawyers:

> Where possible, bring into question the credibility of opposing witnesses through such avenues as statements made on depositions or other appropriate sources. . . . Provide a detailed, powerful, but realistic view of the evidence in your case. However, be careful not to overstate the case. . . . Be sure to start your opening in a strong manner and end it in a strong fashion also. . . . Use repetition to facilitate comprehension of complex cases. . . . . Use words which promote the desired impact . . . . vary speech characteristics (e.g. tone) to avoid monotonous effects. . . . With few exceptions, do not waive the opportunity to give an opening statement.[65]

Regarding choice of witnesses, he advises: "Credibility is preferable to attractiveness in considering a witness. However, attractiveness should not be ignored in considering equally credible witnesses. . . . Use higher status witnesses when possible. They tend to be more persuasive, provided the jury does not see them as threatening their freedom to decide the case."[66] The problem with this sort of guidance is not that it is untrue, that it conflicts with what social scientists know, or that it neglects more useful principles. The problem is that most attorneys would already be able to articulate the guidelines without knowing a shred of social psychology. Where difficulties arise is in the skillful implementation of general notions in particular cases. Attorneys know that they should use "words which promote the desired impact," but this does not mean that they can do it. Similarly, female attorneys probably know that it would be useful to have a judge or expert witness indicate their approval of the attorney in the courtroom; the trick is making it happen.

Although nobody would argue that consultant familiarity with the social psychology of persuasion and attitude change is useless, one might argue that the intellectual investment required to master the intricate debates of the discipline might not be repaid with a rich harvest of important insights. Further research is also unlikely to correct this problem. In part, this is because the specific calls an attorney must make in preparing for a trial almost always depend on the particularities of the case and the jury. Moreover, consultants must translate abstract principles into efficacious training and—if this can be done at all—it is certainly more an art than a science. Lastly, when an experienced professional attempts to modify his or her style, one cannot neglect the possibility that the consequences will be unnatural and deleterious rather than beneficial. After all, there is no evidence that social psychologists are any more successful in their social interactions than the average person.

Perhaps those consultants who come to the field from the world of drama will have better results. Acting and speech coaches might help lawyers to smooth out the rough edges of their courtroom performance.[67] Personal image consultants also might offer some tips that occasionally aid a litigator. Teachers often benefit from observing themselves on videotape, and attorneys, too, might learn from this practice. But just how much they will change and with what consequence is difficult to say.

WHEN ALL IS SAID AND DONE: POSTTRIAL INTERVIEWING

Once jurors have returned their verdict and left the courthouse, they understandably believe that they may now get on with their lives, having discharged their civic duty. But from the vantage point of trial consultants

and litigators, these jurors may yet have something important to offer—
if not regarding the case at hand, then perhaps concerning another similar to it. Those seeking to interview panel members usually have one of
two objectives in mind: (1) to assess where the presentation of their case
worked and where it did not, or (2) to gather evidence of juror misconduct that might be useful in an appeal.

In the summer of 1996, posttrial interviews yielded critical information concerning Stevie Manzanares's successful lawsuit against Salt Lake
County, Utah.[68] Four years earlier, Manzanares had been the getaway driver in a beer heist gone awry. In a dimly lit parking lot outside a Smith's
Food and Drug in Salt Lake City, sheriff's deputy Vaughn Allen thought
he saw Manzanares—who was seated behind the steering wheel of the
car—reaching for a gun. The officer discharged his weapon. A bullet entered the right side of the eighteen-year-old's head, ricocheted off the
lower part of his brain, and exited the left side of his face. Permanent
brain damage ensued, although Manzanares was able to father children
and hold down a job.

During the trial, Allen testified that the youth had disobeyed a command to freeze. When the deputy saw a shiny metallic object—which
later turned out to be a beer can—he feared for the safety of his partner,
who had been approaching the car from the other side. Manzanares contended that he had placed the beer can under his seat and that his hands
had been on the steering wheel when he was shot. His lawyer claimed
that deputy Allen overreacted in the parking lot and concocted the phan-
tom gun story as a "postevent rationalization." A federal jury sided with
the plaintiff, ruling that the deputy had used deadly force without justification and violated Manzanares's civil rights. The jury awarded
Manzanares $555,770.

Then, posttrial interviews revealed a startling fact: Two years earlier, the
son of Tulaire Foreman—one of the jurors—had been shot to death while
breaking the law in a Smith's Food and Drug parking lot. Circumstances
differed considerably, as Foreman's son had been attempting to gun down
a gang rival. But there were enough similarities to raise the suspicion of
inappropriate sympathy for the plaintiff. According to the posttrial interviews, Foreman had told one juror that she did not disclose her son's

shooting death because she feared removal from the panel by the judge. Foreman's neighbor told the county's investigators that Foreman had tearfully described how she "kind of adopted Stevie as my own" during the trial.[69] Posttrial interviews also revealed that she had insisted on a fat award, including a large amount for pain and suffering. One juror explained, "She wanted to go all the way with it . . . the whole amount they [the plaintiff] wanted."[70] Foreman apparently wanted to award Manzanares enough money for college and a new start in life, something the county attorney alleged was improper.

The defense claimed that they were denied a fair trial. U.S. District Court Judge Dee Benson, who had presided over the trial, agreed; he vacated the verdict and ordered a new trial. The main difference between the two trials was the jury, and this proved decisive. After eleven hours of deliberation, the second jury found for the defense, concluding that deputy Allen was justified in firing his weapon and that no violation of civil rights had occurred. But this strange case was not yet over.

Manzanares's lawyers appealed Judge Benson's decision to vacate the first verdict. A three-judge panel of the U.S. Tenth Circuit Court of Appeals in Denver reinstated the $555,770 award, ruling that the trial judge need not have set aside the original verdict. Tulaire Foreman, the purportedly biased juror, had never been asked directly about her son's death during voir dire. The closest Judge Benson had come to asking the question was when he inquired of potential jurors whether it would be ". . . difficult for you to sit in judgment of a case that involves a minority youth, Mr. Manzanares, his Hispanic origin and the police shooting incident."[71] Foreman had not raised her hand at that time, but the appellate judges did not believe she was under a clear obligation to do so. Senior Judge Robert H. McWilliams, who penned the ruling, said: "To invalidate the result of a 3-week trial on the basis of a juror's mistaken, though honest, response to a question is to insist on something closer to perfection . . . [than] our judicial system can be expected to give."[72]

The Manzanares case illustrates some of the strengths and weaknesses of using posttrial interviews to challenge a verdict. They may indeed unearth evidence suggestive of inappropriate juror conduct, but judges are reluctant to sanction posttrial fishing expeditions and very unlikely to set aside jury verdicts absent the most blatant bias. Moreover, even in jurisdictions where posttrial interviews are generally permitted, judges often impose restrictions—and sometimes the jurors simply refuse to talk.[73]

It is a basic principle of the American jury system that jurors need not justify their deliberations to anyone. The media, the public, and the courts typically support jurors' rights to be left alone over a litigant's desire to explore the determinants of the verdict.

Thus, some jurisdictions do not permit any posttrial contact with jurors, except under the most circumscribed of conditions. Mainly, such rules aim to preserve the finality of verdicts and to shield jurors from harassment and unreasonable scrutiny. California Supreme Court Justice Ming W. Chin has called for a "juror bill of rights," saying that ". . . there must be a mechanism for redress on those rare occasions when the jury system indeed has gone awry. But fishing expeditions by litigants who lost at trial must not transform the quest for misconduct claims into the witch hunts of the next millennium."[74]

In many jurisdictions, lawyers who want to conduct posttrial interviews for any purpose must apply for the permission of the court, usually by arguing that "extraneous prejudicial information was improperly brought to the jury's attention" or that "outside influence was improperly brought to bear" on a juror. According to some consultants, "Federal courts are loathe to overturn jury verdicts based on post-trial reevaluation of information that should properly be revealed in voir dire. . . . State courts, however, have often reversed when post-verdict interviews revealed personal experiences or biases not revealed in voir dire."[75] In tough jurisdictions, where judges grant permission to conduct interviews only on a demonstration of likely impropriety, trial consultants face a catch-22.[76] How can one document juror impropriety without first questioning the jurors? The matter has never been successfully resolved.

Still, many courts remain very much open to posttrial interviews, especially when conducted primarily for the attorney's self-education—so long as nobody harasses, influences, or embarrasses jurors. Postverdict contact with panel members can shed light on several issues. TBCI, the prominent trial consulting firm, tells potential clients:

After a trial has been completed or terminated, we design and conduct comprehensive telephone, mail, or in-person interviews of the jury. When a case may be retried, or when you are trying a series of cases, all involving similar issues and witnesses, post-trial interviews are extremely helpful. Jurors provide invaluable feedback about: What went on in the jury room; How they understood the major issues in the case; How effective they thought the case themes were in helping them understand and remember the issues; How they perceived different attorney and witness presentation styles; What would have helped them in reaching a verdict.[77]

In effect, the first trial becomes a mock or simulated preview of the second.

Unlike interviews associated with mock trials created by a consultant, however, posttrial interviews give feedback on the actual lawyers and their witnesses, not merely on summaries and stand-ins. Consultant Marjorie Fargo elaborates: "Post-trial interviews allow lawyers to identify specific problems in the evidence that may contribute to the loss of the cases, such as different interpretations of factual issues; attributes that make a witness unconvincing or unintelligible; jury confusion in comprehending case theory or jury instructions; and personal dress or behavior characteristics of lawyers and witnesses that distract or offend jurors."[78] Such insights can be extremely important when attorneys try the same or similar cases again.

Even when a case is closed and all appeals exhausted, attorneys can benefit from feedback on their performance. One trial consultant reports the following assessment of a hapless counsel made by a critical female juror:

Watching the defense was like watching bumbling circus clowns. After [defense counsel] would finish his cross exam he couldn't slam or diffuse anything [plaintiff's counsel] laid out. He would make the hair on the back of your neck stand up. He alienated the jury by his demeanor in the courtroom. And, with all his um, um, uhs. With his questions, you would want to yell at him, "spit it out, what are you trying to say?!" [Defense counsel] didn't have copies of evidence for [plaintiff's counsel]. He did that over and over again. . . . He was objection happy. From the jury's perspective, his objections were annoying and distracting and they interrupted the flow of the trial and 50% of the time, they were unnecessary.[79]

The attorney who commissioned this interview may well have regretted the decision. But this juror's reactions certainly pointed to some ways in which he could improve his future performance.

It has been said that foolish generals are always fighting the last war, crafting tactics for a struggle that has ended while failing to innovate for the crisis at hand. Posttrial interviews are of greatest value only when the jurors, issues, and attorneys in an upcoming case closely resemble those from the earlier trial.

THE PERCEPTION OF INJUSTICE

The behavioral psychologist B.F. Skinner observed that "ways of changing behavior by changing minds are seldom condoned when they are clearly effective. . . . We do not condone the changing of minds when the contestants are unevenly matched; that is 'undue influence.' Nor do we condone the changing of minds surreptitiously. If a person cannot see what the would-be changer of minds is doing, he cannot escape or counterattack; he is being exposed to 'propaganda.'"[80] Although Skinner was not thinking specifically about the American justice system when he wrote these words, his reflection cuts to the heart of why some people feel uneasy about consultants' efforts to sway jurors.

Everyone knows that lawyers try to manipulate the jury. That is their job, part of the system, indeed, part of why the system works. Greater public concern arises from the prospect of consultants manipulating juries, perhaps because of the cloaked aspect of the manipulation, perhaps because of the added ingredient of "science." When one side possesses "scientific methods of persuasion" and the other does not, the basic fairness of the system seems to be undermined.[81] And the fact that consultants often practice the tricks of their trade—running mock trials, crafting stories, prepping witnesses and attorneys—beyond the surveillance of judges, jurors, and opposing counsel compounds the perception that something unjust is afoot.

6

BLACKS AND WHITES IN THE JURY BOX

A LEGACY OF RACIAL INJUSTICE

THE RACIAL ATTITUDES THAT AMERICANS BRING into the jury room at the beginning of the twenty-first century differ sharply from those they brought only a few decades back. After all, the civil rights era altered American society in ways that are difficult to overstate. And although the legal environment is hardly unrecognizable, rules governing juries and their selection have changed dramatically. Black-white relations today are defined by a different set of questions than those dominating the agenda in the 1960s, let alone before then. As a result, it is hard to have much confidence in the contemporary relevance of examples and statistics from more than a decade or so in the past. It makes sense to focus on recent cases.

But we miss a critical part of the story when we speak of the orientations of white or black jurors today without reference to decades of officially sanctioned discrimination against blacks. "Justice" rarely figured into the way the legal system treated African Americans prior to the Civil War, even in states where slavery did not exist. In the century that followed the final surrender of Confederate forces at Appomattox Courthouse, the status of blacks under the law slowly improved, but progress was by no means steady or consistent.

Harvard professor Randall Kennedy, in his book *Race, Crime, and the Law*, documents two strains of discrimination against African Americans:

first, a failure to provide equal protection against crimes, and second, unequal enforcement of laws when dealing with black suspects, defendants, and convicts.[1] Even after the abolition of slavery, no one could reasonably assert that the police or courthouses intended to secure for black Americans the same freedom from crime intended for the white population. Racially motivated assaults, lynchings, and rapes were commonplace, often perpetrated by whites against blacks while law enforcement officials looked the other way or even participated. And when one black committed a crime against another, law enforcement officials frequently viewed the matter as unavoidable, expected, and—in any event—unworthy of their attention.

Similarly, African American suspects and defendants rarely enjoyed protections afforded to whites in similar circumstances. As Kennedy explains, ". . . The white supremacists who authored and administered the criminal laws of the Jim Crow period openly used the machinery of law enforcement to buttress pigmentocracy."[2] Among other objectives, criminal law was used to impose a humiliating etiquette on blacks, to keep them from voting, and to weaken their ability to compete in the labor market. When a white woman charged a black man with rape, the allegation alone often constituted sufficient evidence for conviction.

All-white juries were by no means the sole source of these injustices in the nineteenth and early twentieth centuries, but they did contribute significantly to the problem. Before the Civil War, only Massachusetts, among all U.S. states, permitted blacks to sit on juries. Afterward, blacks began to serve in some jurisdictions; elsewhere, states enacted new statutes formally and unabashedly excluding nonwhites from jury participation. For example, West Virginia passed a law limiting jury service to white males over the age of twenty-one.[3]

Such open and formal prohibitions of black participation in the jury system were denounced in the 1880s with two key decisions rendered by the U.S. Supreme Court: *Strauder v. West Virginia* and *Neal v. Delaware*. The *Strauder* decision held that laws excluding blacks from juries violated the recently passed Fourteenth Amendment, which guarantees equal protection of the laws. The Court explained: "The very fact that colored people are singled out and expressly denied by a statute all right to participate in the administration of the law, as jurors, because of their color, though they are citizens, and may be in other respects fully qualified, is practically a brand upon them, affixed by the law, an assertion of their inferiority, and a stimulant to that race prejudice which is an impediment to securing to individuals of the race that equal justice which the law aims to secure to all others."[4] Additionally, the Court noted: "It is not easy to comprehend how it can be said that while every white man is entitled to a trial by a jury . . . selected without discrimination against his color, and a negro is not, the latter is equally protected by the law with the former."[5]

In *Neal v. Delaware*, state officials had conceded that no blacks had ever served on a jury in Delaware. But they argued this happened not because of an illicit intention to exclude qualified blacks but rather because few, if any, Delaware blacks possessed the qualifications required for jury service. The Delaware Supreme Court agreed, with the chief justice writing: "That none but white men were selected is in nowise remarkable in view of the fact—too notorious to be ignored—that the great body of black men residing in this state are utterly unqualified by want of intelligence, experience, or moral integrity to sit on juries."[6] When the case reached the U.S. Supreme Court, however, the justices deemed Delaware's argument untenable and held that the state had indeed engaged in unlawful discrimination against blacks.

In theory, the *Strauder* and *Neal* decisions should have dispatched the all-white jury to the pages of history. In practice, however, political leaders and bureaucrats in many jurisdictions, especially in the U.S. South, continued to ensure all-white or mostly white panels for nearly a century. Occasionally, when discrimination was extreme and clear-cut, higher courts would intervene. More often, however, local officials managed to circumvent the intent of the *Strauder* and *Neal* decisions through the implementation of discriminatory, byzantine, and otherwise loaded jury selection practices. And when blacks in the Jim Crow South ended up on juries, they often felt pressured to go along with whatever the whites (who were nearly always an overwhelming majority) wanted. When a hapless defendant would seek to challenge jury selection procedures, it was not uncommon for the court to accept the word of a jury commissioner that no unfair discrimination had occurred. This state of affairs persisted well into the twentieth century.

Then, a series of Supreme Court decisions in the 1930s and 1940s ". . . put state courts on notice that the total exclusion of blacks from grand and petit juries would put convictions at risk of reversal."[7] In response, black representation on panels began to increase—slowly. The most substantial reforms did not occur until the civil rights era of the 1960s. It was only then that recalcitrant officials, particularly in the Deep South, received the message, loud and clear, that evasions of constitutional requirements for fair jury selection practices would no longer be tolerated.[8]

Until the 1960s, many courts operated on the assumption that justice would be better served if juries comprised only those individuals assumed to be of above average intelligence, morality, and integrity. Many jury commissioners used a so-called key-man system in which they solicited the names of prospective jurors from notable community members. Whether this method actually raised the moral or intellectual caliber of juries is unknown. However, the approach unquestionably resulted in underrepresentation of blacks and other minorities. In 1968, the U.S. Jury Selection and Service Act eliminated the key-man system in all federal courts, thereby removing that impediment to black representation on juries. The federal law required that jury commissioners choose jurors at random from voter registration lists. When these lists failed to produce proportionate representation of certain constitutionally protected groups in the community, including racial groups, other sources could be added as supplements.[9]

In 1975, the Supreme Court in *Taylor v. Louisiana* redefined the concept of an impartial jury.[10] The case did not center initially on race, but it had important implications for increasing black representation on panels. In this case, a male defendant had been convicted and sentenced to death for the crime of aggravated kidnapping. He challenged his conviction on the grounds that women had been systematically underrepresented on the list from which his jury had been chosen. A majority of the justices agreed, maintaining that no jury could be deemed impartial unless it had been selected from sources representative of all segments of the community.

Professor Jeffrey Abramson notes that this decision reflects a "new theory of impartiality," in which juries are judged impartial not because they are unbiased and fair but because they reflect the range of community attitudes. This redefinition, in itself, amounted to a major change, but the *Taylor* decision stopped short of requiring that *particular* juries be representative of the community. The requirement that jury lists and jury venires reflect a cross-section of the community, according to the Supreme Court, would suffice to prevent the government from tilting jury verdicts through limitation of jury eligibility to favored groups.[11]

A final set of reforms began with the *Batson v. Kentucky* decision in 1986.[12] These reforms set limits on how prosecutors in criminal cases and, later, defense attorneys and litigators in civil suits could use peremptory challenges. The Supreme Court has stated that neither race nor gender can serve as the basis of a peremptory challenge.[13] Lower courts have prohibited the discriminatory elimination of various ethnic groups, including American Indians, Italian Americans, and Hispanics.[14] But certain groups, such as obese or bilingual jurors, are not protected as a class.[15] The limits on the peremptory challenge remain to be worked out. Even for groups clearly protected, however, it has been argued that the legal requirements for establishing a "*Batson* violation" effectively prevent the reforms from having their intended effect, as lawyers can evade *Batson*'s dictates by offering acceptable rationalizations that mask the true racial, ethnic, or gender basis of their challenges.[16]

From the late nineteenth century to the present, reforms have gone a long way toward rectifying racial injustices in the legal system. But in some jurisdictions, African Americans continue to be underrepresented on juries despite the absence of clear racist intent.[17] And many African Americans retain a deep and historically understandable distrust of the law enforcement system in the United States.

A NEW ERA?

A forty-nine-year-old black man had been brutally killed in Jasper, Texas, in June 1998, and three white men stood accused of capital murder, an offense punishable by death. James Byrd Jr. had been walking home from a family gathering when the three defendants offered him a lift. Apparently motivated by racial hatred, they chained Byrd to the back of a pickup and dragged him to his death along several miles of country road.

Each defendant was to face trial separately. Owing to the grisly nature of the crime and the manifest strength of the evidence, most commentators at the time predicted conviction. But it was well known that Southern juries, historically, had a shameful record of freeing whites who attacked blacks, and some observers worried that an all-white or predominantly white jury might disregard evidence pointing to capital murder. Others declared that Southern white jurors would refuse to impose the death penalty in this case. After all, they observed, the defendants were young, physically attractive white men. One had family roots three generations deep in Jasper, where his trial would take place.

Much seemed to depend on the racial composition of the juries that would hear the cases. In each trial, a single racist juror, a single white person who identified too strongly with the defendant, would have the power to thwart a conviction or block imposition of the death penalty.

John William King, the first man to stand trial, faced a jury of eleven whites and one black, despite an initial jury pool containing many African Americans. According to one journalist covering the trial, "When it got down to the final pool, all of the seven potential black jurors . . . [with one exception], exempted themselves by stating that they . . . . [did not] believe in the death penalty," a requirement for serving on a capital jury in Texas.[18] The jurors selected the sole black juror as foreman but denied claims that they intended to send a message with his selection. One white female juror reported that "Joe [the black juror] was just one of us, that's it. . . . We got in there and kind of stumbled around and nobody wanted to do the job, and Joe volunteered to do it."[19]

King was a convicted felon and a virulent racist whose arms and torso were covered with hateful tattoos, one of which depicted a lynching. Although he maintained his innocence throughout the trial, only weak evidence was offered in his defense. Accordingly, the jurors returned a quick conviction on the charge of capital murder. Even after the verdict, King showed no signs of remorse. During the penalty phase of the trial, King's father, sitting in a wheelchair and breathing from an oxygen tank, pleaded for mercy. He testified that prison life had turned his previously decent son, the father of an infant boy, into a racist.[20] Unmoved by these sentiments, the jury sentenced King to death after a mere three hours of deliberation.

Lawrence Brewer, the second defendant, faced a jury in Bryan, Texas, 150 miles from Jasper.[21] Although some blacks appeared in the initial jury pool, twelve non-Hispanic whites and two Hispanics were seated as jurors, two of whom would serve as alternates. One newspaper headline announced, "Jury with No Blacks Will Hear Second Dragging Trial."[22] Still, the prosecutor expressed satisfaction with the jury.[23] The second accused man, like the first, was a white supremacist. At trial, his attorney argued that he had become a racist only after meeting King in prison in 1994. Brewer offered a somewhat stronger defense than King, admitting some involvement in the crime but claiming that his participation fell short of capital murder. On the stand, he cried when he described the killing. He maintained that he never intended to kill Byrd. He testified that he thought Byrd was already dead prior to the dragging, as a result of stab wounds received in a fight with the other defendants.

Based on the evidence, the jury could have returned a conviction for a lesser offense than capital murder, such as noncapital murder, aggravated assault, or assault. But like King's jury, this jury found the defendant guilty of the most serious crime and, subsequently, sentenced him to death. The jurors took fifteen hours to arrive at their sentencing decision.[24]

Shawn Allen Berry, the last defendant to stand trial, seemed the one most likely to escape a capital murder conviction. He would be tried before a hometown jury, where his family had lived for several generations, and—unlike King and Brewer—he sported no racist tattoos. The two convicted men were Berry's friends and roommates, but unlike them, Berry had no verifiably racist past.

Berry claimed that he was guilty only of being in the wrong place at the wrong time. He testified that he had not realized the extent to which prison life had intensified his old buddies' violent and hateful tendencies. Moreover, he claimed, he had no idea that they had intended to harm Byrd, and he even tried to assist Byrd when the attack began. According to Berry's explanation, fear ultimately paralyzed him. He claimed that

King, the mastermind, threatened to turn on him if he persisted in his efforts to help the victim. In this version of events, terror so enveloped Berry that he urinated on himself. Throughout the trial, Berry showed much remorse.

Jury selection had produced an all-white jury, and many suspected that Berry would fare substantially better than the other two defendants. But he, too, was quickly convicted of capital murder. The jury apparently rejected his version of events, concluding that he had played a more central role than claimed. The jurors' sole concession was to spare Berry lethal injection, sentencing him to life in prison with no possibility of parole for forty years.[25]

Some have argued that the sheer horror of James Byrd's murder made it sui generis in its capacity to elicit fair decisionmaking. After the King verdict, a columnist for the *Detroit News* wrote, "Those jurors who brought in a fair and speedy verdict in the James Byrd case didn't have to love blacks—only justice."[26] Often, the system works as intended. We are, however, far more likely to hear in the mass media of cases presumed to teach the opposite lesson—that race matters, often decisively, when jurors assess the evidence, and that panel members frequently "vote their color" in certain types of trials.

No event is mentioned more frequently in discussions of race and the jury system than the O.J. Simpson case. In the 1995 double-murder trial, a jury of nine African Americans, one Latino, and two whites acquitted the former football star, shocking a white public that overwhelmingly believed in his guilt. The verdict, in many circles, was attributed to the skill with which defense attorneys, especially Johnnie Cochran, "played the race card." Then, in the 1997 wrongful death civil suit, a mostly white jury awarded $33.5 million, including $25 million in punitive damages, to the families of the victims.[27]

There are certainly ways to explain the different outcomes of the civil and criminal Simpson trials without reference to the race of the jurors.[28] Nevertheless, many observers have interpreted the verdicts as evidence that the racial mix of the jury, at least in some cases, can matter greatly.

Other prominent trials of the 1990s reinforce this perception. In the California criminal trial of the white officers charged with beating

Rodney King, a jury of ten whites, one Hispanic, and one Asian (but no African Americans) acquitted the officers of nearly all charges. On a single count of excessive force, the jury hung. The verdicts ignited the notorious Los Angeles riots of 1992, partly because many blacks believed that the white jurors had been voting their race in failing to convict the police officers.

As with the Simpson cases, however, nonracial explanations are plausible. After all, surveys conducted at the time revealed that whites as well as blacks overwhelmingly believed in the guilt of Officer Laurence Powell and his codefendants. Many whites were shocked by their acquittal. More important, experts who have studied the evidence offered at trial suggest that the jurors heard a very different set of facts than the public, which relied largely on a highly publicized segment of videotape of the incident.[29] As one noted African American legal scholar concludes: "In the case of [Rodney] King's assailants, the actual (as opposed to reported) facts of the entire (as opposed to merely the videotaped) confrontation provided an arguable predicate for the acquittals."[30]

During the early moments of the Los Angeles riots, several young black men dragged Reginald Denny, a white truck driver, from his vehicle and beat him severely. Damian Williams, one of the assailants, smashed a brick against Denny's head and walked away with what many interpreted as visible pride.[31] The entire event, captured by a TV helicopter on videotape, was broadcast live to viewers across the city.

Williams and several others were arrested, and the case went to trial two weeks after the conclusion of the second trial of the officers charged in the Rodney King beating. This time, charged by federal prosecutors with violating King's civil rights, the officers were convicted. They each received a thirty-month sentence, a punishment substantially less than the ten years' imprisonment and $250,000 fine that might have been imposed. No riots ensued, but many in the black community of Los Angeles remained deeply dissatisfied with the outcome.[32]

The trial of Reginald Denny's attackers took place in this climate. The decision would be rendered by a jury of four African Americans, four Latinos, one Asian, and three whites. Referring to the acquittal in the first trial of the officers charged with brutalizing Rodney King, the defense attorney argued in court that "people caught up in that frenzy were acting out their frustration, their anger, their disappointment. They were so consumed with emotions that they could not have rationally been entertaining the type of reflective thought which gives rise to specific intent to kill or disfigure."[33] The jury apparently accepted this argument, acquitting the attackers on the most serious charges, including those requiring an intent to kill or disfigure. Whatever one thinks of this outcome, it is certainly plausible that a jury of a different racial mix deliberating in a less inflammatory climate would have been less receptive to the defense team's arguments.

There is no shortage of cases in which commentators have pointed to the apparent importance of the racial mix of a particular jury.[34] We have already discussed the New Orleans lawsuit in which the plaintiffs' attorneys argued that several large corporations had neglected to take proper safety precautions precisely because nearby residents were African American. An all-black jury in that case responded with billions of dollars in punitive damages, even though actual damages resulting from the accident appear to have been minimal. And in Steven Pagones's defamation lawsuit against three black activists, a black juror, one of two on the panel, apparently exerted considerable influence in reducing the size of the damage award.

The locally publicized 1998 trial of a white man from Queens, New York, who was charged with the attempted murder of Shane Daniels, a young black man, ended in a hung jury. One juror told the judge, "I think we're just about to go at each other's throats. It has been very, very stressful."[35] The jury included one black, who served as the foreman, and eleven whites. The final vote was nine for acquittal and three for conviction. Roosevelt Price, the black juror, told reporters that race played a definite role in the deliberations. He said, "I went into this with an open mind. It was the evidence that said Offen [the defendant] was guilty, guilty, guilty."[36] He further remarked: "I'm now 57 years old and have seen a lot of things change for blacks, but in this country it's still O.K. for a white person to beat on a black person and still be found innocent."[37] In Pittsburgh several months earlier, a mistrial had occurred when a lone black juror held out for the conviction of two police officers charged with manslaughter in the death of a black motorist, Jonny Gammage. Eleven whites had voted for acquittal.[38]

One can perhaps explain the outcome in all of these cases without reference to race. Most often, that is precisely what jurors, judges, and attorneys do. Very rarely do we hear a juror commenting after a case that his or her own decision (or that of fellow jurors) derived from their racial or ethnic perspective. Nearly always, jurors explain their votes and those of their fellow jurors as logical, necessary, and fair in light of the evidence. Also, as we have seen, juror decisions seldom split entirely along racial lines. White jurors voted for acquittal in the Simpson criminal case. One African American juror strongly opposed the huge verdict in the New Orleans railroad suit. Some whites voted to acquit Damian Williams of serious charges in the Denny beating. Some white jurors agreed with Roosevelt Price regarding the beating of Shane Daniels.

But sooner or later, discussions of the American jury system turn to race. Some argue that white racism, with its long and ugly history in the justice system, continues to sully the decisions of some juries in courtrooms across the United States. Others claim that black jurors tend to be soft on black criminal defendants and to favor plaintiffs in civil suits. Some even construct a moral case for blacks to engage in jury nullification by acquitting black defendants who they believe to be guilty.[39] Lawyers and jury consultants privately assert that race matters greatly in many cases—even while they publicly state that it does not.

FORBIDDEN STEREOTYPES

Since the 1986 Supreme Court prohibition of race-based peremptory challenges, most prosecutors have been tight-lipped about jury selection.[40] At least in public, few have voiced preferences beyond the proverbial "fair and impartial" juror. They might support a "diverse" or "representative" jury, but they rarely reveal their expectations concerning jurors from different ethnic and racial groups. Public discussions of black-white differences in jurors have been especially taboo.

Philadelphia District Attorney Lynne Abraham knew this, and one can only imagine her amazement when, in spring 1997, she first viewed a very frank, ten-year-old training video on jury selection that had been made by her challenger in the upcoming election.[41] In retrospect, prosecutor Jack McMahon's decision to record his comments for eternity seems—from a tactical standpoint—in a league with Richard Nixon's decision to tape discussions of the Watergate cover-up. At the time, however, McMahon was an assistant district attorney trying to train less experienced prosecutors in his office, and perhaps he derived some satisfaction from sharing his insider's know-how.

By 1997, McMahon had switched sides. Now a prominent defense lawyer campaigning for district attorney, he charged that Abraham was "racially insensitive." That, apparently, was the first in a series of events that brought the dust-covered videotape to the public eye. A prosecutor who had worked with McMahon years earlier recalled the videotape as, itself, less than sensitive on racial matters; perhaps incensed by this apparent inconsistency, he unearthed a copy of the tape and delivered it to Abraham. She then felt duty-bound to release it to the defense attorneys representing three dozen defendants whom McMahon had successfully prosecuted for murder. This decision was, she explained, purely a matter of ethics. Had she sought political advantage, she said, she would have waited until just before election day to spring the news.[42]

McMahon's videotaped words speak for themselves:

Let's face it, the blacks from low-income areas are less likely to convict. There's a resentment toward law enforcement. There's a resentment toward authority. You don't want those people on your jury. It may appear as if you're being racist, but you're just being realistic. In selecting blacks, you don't want real educated ones. This goes across the board. All races. If you're going to take blacks, you want older black men and women, particularly men. Older black men are very good. Guys seventy, seventy-five years old [in 1987] are from a different era; they have a different respect for the law. Older black women, on the other hand—when you have a black defendant who is a young boy and they can identify, a motherly type of thing—are a little different. The men don't have that same kind of maternal instinct. Blacks from the South are excellent. Ask where they are from. If they say, I've lived in Philadelphia five years, if they are from South Carolina and places like that, I tell you, I don't think you can ever lose with a jury of blacks from South Carolina. They are dynamite. They have a different philosophy down there. Those people are good. Young black women are very bad. There's an antagonism. I guess maybe because they're downtrodden in two respects: they are women and they're black. So they want to take it out on somebody, and you don't want it to be you.[43]

McMahon also offered advice on factors other than race. For example, he suggested: "If you take middle-class people who are well-dressed, you're going to do well," and "you don't want smart people, because smart people will analyze the hell out of your case." He also suggested that prosecutors avoid people from certain occupational backgrounds: "You don't want social workers. That's obvious. They got intelligence, sensitivity, all this stuff. You don't want them. Teachers are bad, especially the young teachers, teachers who teach grade school. Though sometimes I have had good luck with teachers who teach in the public school system. They may be so fed up with the garbage in their school that they may say, 'I know this kind of kid. He's a pain in the ass.' If you get a white teacher teaching in a black school who's sick of these guys, that may be one you accept."[44]

There is no question that McMahon's comments were impolitic in multiracial Philadelphia. More important, the jury selection strategies that potentially derived from them were arguably illegal under the Supreme Court's *Batson* decision.[45] When the tape was made public, McMahon defended himself, saying, ". . . the best and fairest jury is a racially diverse jury, and I said that on the tape."[46] He asserted that he was not presenting his own legal or ethical preferences but rather what the prosecutorial role demands. On the tape itself he had rationalized his approach as necessary to the job: "Case law says the object of jury selection is to get a competent, fair, and impartial jury. Well, that's ridiculous. You're there to win. The only way you're going to do your best is to get jurors who are unfair and more likely to convict than anybody else in that room. If you go in there, any one of you, and think you are going to be some noble civil libertarian, you'll lose. You'll be out of office."[47] After the video surfaced, he said: "It's done today, it's going to be done tomorrow, and I don't apologize for it . . . I only said what any good jury consultant would charge hundreds of thousands of dollars to tell you: Some people, black or white, help your case, other people hurt it. That's not being racist—that's being realistic. Every lawyer in the world uses these techniques."[48] Indeed, three Philadelphia judges, speaking on condition of anonymity, told the media that prosecutors and defense attorneys regularly employed McMahon's techniques in the city. Edward G. Rendell, then Philadelphia's mayor and a former district attorney, commented at the time: "If you look at the totality of what he's talking about, I think it is a veteran prosecutor lecturing young prosecutors about jury selection."[49] A reporter summed up the reaction nicely: "What finally is extraordinary about McMahon's remarks is not their content, but their wide and unabashed public circulation."[50]

THE JURY HEARD 'ROUND THE WORLD

Law students are warned that bad facts make bad law and that the wise lawyer does not draw far-reaching conclusions from atypical cases.[51] That is surely the case with the O.J. Simpson criminal trial. By the end of the trial, the attorneys, judge, and defendant, as well as the witnesses, victims, their family members, and the entire jury panel, achieved celebrity status. The Simpson criminal case—the so-called trial of the century—teaches us little about the quotidian operations of the American courtroom. Yet in one important respect, the Simpson trial and the reaction to it were emblematic, unearthing racial fault lines that continue to challenge the entire U.S. justice system.

On February 1, 1995, one week into the trial, lead prosecutor Marcia Clark recorded some private doubts about the case: "If it was an ordinary jury I'd just be sitting there laughing because no reasonable mind could possibly buy the garbage they're feeding them. But with a jury where people don't want to believe the evidence, they'll seize on anything."[52] Her assistant, Christopher Darden, recalls similar doubts later in the trial: "No matter how much I wanted these jurors to look beyond race, I don't think they could. . . . We faced a jury looking for the tiniest justification for an acquittal, a jury willing to find reasonable doubt in the slimmest of margins: one in 170 million, one in 6.8 billion."[53] Darden describes how coldly jurors reacted to testimony of domestic violence and to photos of the mutilated victims, calling the jury ". . . the most stone-faced group of people . . . . [he'd] ever seen."[54] He remembers his dismay as one juror raised his fist in a black power salute to Simpson's release and laments that the predominantly black jury had picked a ". . . dreadful time to seek an empty retribution for Rodney King and a meaningless payback for a system of bigotry, segregation, and slavery."[55] In their respective memoirs, Darden and Clark offer many indictments—of Judge Lance Ito, the defense team, uncooperative witnesses, racist cops, and others—but their principal animus erupts toward the jury.

Under ordinary circumstances, one might suspect the motives of prosecutors who blame the jury rather than examine their own conduct in a case. But many others offer similar assessments of the Simpson criminal jury. No one has been more critical of Clark and Darden than Vincent Bugliosi, a former prosecutor in the Los Angeles County District Attorney's office. Bugliosi has scarcely a kind word to say about anyone associated with the Simpson trial, but he argues that the prosecution—above all—mishandled the case from the start. He further maintains that ". . . if the prosecution had given an A+ rather than a D- performance . . . . the verdict most likely would have been different."[56] But Bugliosi also believes that Clark and Darden, even though their performances were lacking, nevertheless proved Simpson's guilt beyond a reasonable doubt. He concludes: ". . . It's hard to imagine how this jury could have been too much worse."[57]

How did it happen? According to Bugliosi, Marcia Clark should have attended more carefully to her jury consultant, Don Vinson, rather than dismissing him on the second day of jury selection. Vinson's firm, DecisionQuest, had already assisted attorneys in more than 3,000 cases, and prior to jury selection in the Simpson case, the firm polled 400 people about the murders. At the time, it was widely believed that blacks had greater sympathy than whites for Simpson and less confidence that he had killed his former wife, Nicole Brown Simpson, and her companion Ron Goldman. The new survey revealed, however, that black men were more than three times as likely as black women to judge Simpson guilty.

Vinson's staff followed up their survey with intensive interviewing designed to probe this gender gap. They learned that black women tended to feel very protective of Simpson; more important, they were disproportionately forgiving and accepting of domestic violence. When provided with evidence that the defendant had beaten his wife, black women typically responded with comments like "every relationship has these kinds of problems."[58]

Asked to reveal their feelings about Marcia Clark, black females in the focus groups weren't reticent. Many admitted their dislike, and more than a few dubbed her a "bitch."[59] According to Bugliosi, they were apt to see her as ". . . a pushy, aggressive white woman who was trying to bring down and emasculate a prominent black man."[60] On the basis of research, Vinson advised Clark to try to minimize the number of black women on the jury and, if possible, to avoid black men as well. (Presumably, she was to do so without violating the law.) If, despite all efforts, the final jury included several black women (as it ultimately did), Vinson suggested downplaying the domestic violence angle and focusing instead on physical evidence. An additional, but tactfully unstated, implication of the research was that Marcia Clark might step aside in favor of someone else more palatable to the jurors.

The prosecution, according to Bugliosi and others, needlessly undermined its position by failing to capitalize on these strategic tips from its jury consultant. Moreover, critics contend, this error compounded an earlier mistake that more than any other had set the stage for a biased jury and an unjust acquittal. Gil Garcetti, the Los Angeles district attorney, could have filed the case in Santa Monica, the judicial district where the crime occurred and where the jury pool would have included a much smaller percentage of blacks thought to be favorably predisposed toward the former football star. According to the prosecution's critics, by transferring the case "downtown"—to downtown Los Angeles—Garcetti lost the battle for jury composition before it began.

Marcia Clark herself had little enthusiasm for the downtown jury pool. She describes her thoughts on reading summary cards about the potential jurors:

It was dismal going. Any way you shuffled the deck, this was far and away the worst pool of jurors either of us had ever seen. Few of these people had ever taken college courses, let alone gotten a degree. Many were out of work. No one had anything good to say about the LAPD. An uncomfortably large percentage of them either knew someone who had been arrested or had been arrested themselves. The Bronco chase seemed to arouse in them nothing but regret for the sufferings of the defendant.[61]

Such concern was justified. Among the prospects who actually made it onto the jury, a few were later dismissed—and the reasons for their dismissal are eye-opening: One had failed to disclose an arrest for kidnapping and assaulting his girlfriend; another did not mention that she had been the victim of spousal abuse; a third apparently imagined court deputies spying on her (after her dismissal, she posed for *Playboy* magazine); finally, a fourth juror was dismissed for physically intimidating and bullying several of the others.

Despite her frustration with the final jury and the pool from which it was drawn, Clark offers a feisty defense of the prosecution's actions. Standard procedure in the district attorney's office, she explains, was to transfer downtown any case that was expected to last a long time. A savvy and crafty attorney might have succeeded in sidestepping this policy to obtain a tactical advantage. But according to Clark, such a strategy would have been "ugly," and she would have considered it a ". . . shameless and inexcusable display of racism."[62] She writes in her memoir that the approach ". . . presupposes that only a white, upscale, West Side jury can deliver justice. Wrong. Dead wrong. I've seen Downtown juries made up of poor blacks and Hispanics do justice time and again."[63] The problem, in her eyes, was not *the* downtown jury pool, but *this* downtown jury pool.

Clark also displays a distaste for jury consultants: "As far as I'm concerned they are creatures of the defense. . . . As a matter of principle, I don't feel that the government should be in the position of market-testing its arguments."[64] But the defense was using highly respected trial consultant Jo-Ellan Dimitrius to assist them, and Clark, who thought she needed all the help she could get, agreed to listen to Vinson's advice. But that advice—to steer clear of nonwhites—turned out to be, in Clark's view, "impractical, unethical, and unconscionable."[65] Blacks, Clark notes, accounted for more than half of the jury pool, and three-quarters of them were women. "Like it or not, black women were going to be a powerful presence" on the jury.[66] Under the circumstances, what Clark wanted from Vinson, and claims he never delivered, was information about *which* African Americans in the jury pool, male and female, were most reachable—along with guidance on how to reach them. "Our biggest frustration [with Vinson] stemmed from the fact that our repeated entreaties for that kind of help fell on deaf ears."[67] The law, after all, strictly forbade challenging jurors on the basis of race.

The final jury included eight black women, one black man, one Latino man, and two white women. On October 3, 1995, after about eight months of testimony and evidence, the jury returned a verdict of not guilty. They had deliberated for less than four hours.

Simpson defense attorney Alan Dershowitz, in his book on the case, *Reasonable Doubts*, defended the verdict, arguing that "different jurors, exposed to the same evidence but with dissimilar life experiences, might have voted to convict. That is the nature of the American jury system. This jury's verdict was well within the tradition of American justice and does not warrant the racist and elitist epithets thrown at it by people who believe the system failed."[68]

But for many others, the acquittal was proof that the justice system had indeed failed. For her part, Clark concluded that a key problem with the Simpson jury was not simply that it included so many black women but that the defendant was a celebrity. "It was not so much that Simpson was a black man; he was a famous black man. And a well-loved famous black man."[69] She further suggests that ". . . if O.J. Simpson had been some black sanitation worker who had killed his white wife in a fit of rage, a jury of twelve middle-aged black women would have convicted the jerk in a heartbeat."[70]

Prosecutor Chris Darden faults, among other things, Judge Ito's decision to permit testimony concerning police officer Mark Fuhrman's use of the "N-word." At trial, Darden argued to the judge that ". . . when you mention that word to this jury or to any African American, it blinds people. It will blind this jury. It will blind them to the truth. It will cause extreme prejudice to the prosecution's case."[71] When the judge permitted jurors to hear the word, Darden felt it would likely result in a miscarriage of justice. "If your blood is tracked all over the scene and the victim's blood is all over your vehicle, if you have motive and opportunity, if there is no way you could have been set up, you are a murderer. All the [racist police officers] in Los Angeles couldn't change that."[72]

Perhaps not. But survey after survey taken before, during, and after the trial established that blacks trust the police far less than whites do. An October 1995 *Los Angeles Times* poll, for example, showed that only 21 percent of blacks (compared with 67 percent of whites) believed that false testimony by the police is uncommon.[73] Thus, race may have influenced the verdict not necessarily because of fondness or sympathy for Simpson, dislike of Clark, relative indifference toward domestic abuse, or a lack of empathy for Simpson's white former wife—but because of racial differences in attitudes toward law enforcement. Black jurors, whether justified or not, may have been more likely than others to accept the notion of a police conspiracy—especially when presented with evidence of officer Fuhrman's use of racist language.

Another, related, possibility is that jurors engaged in jury nullification, conducting a ". . . revolt from the law within the etiquette of resolving issues of fact," as they " . . . yield[ed] to sentiment in the apparent process of resolving doubts as to evidence."[74] The lightning speed with which they deliberated has been cited in support of this thesis. According to prominent jury scholar Jeffrey Abramson, jurors

. . . had heard enough about missing centiliters of blood and the delay in finding blood on socks and gates to suggest that some pieces of evidence could have been planted. From there, the jurors apparently considered it a short jump to the conclusion that no evidence could be trusted. The problem is that this was a large jump, given the mountains of forensic evidence found at the murder scene that implicated Mr. Simpson. At the least, a robust conversation about reasonable doubt required sustained discussion about the chances that all the highly incriminating DNA and hair-fiber evidence could have been planted or mishandled afterward. The fact that the jury cut off deliberations long before it could systematically have reviewed the key evidence suggests that reasonable doubt was not the whole story, and that unspoken anger and defiance primed this jury to find reasons for doubt with breathtaking speed.[75]

One thing is certain: Race was a strong statistical predictor of public attitudes toward the question of Simpson's guilt throughout the trial. Basing its findings on more than a dozen surveys, the Gallup Organization reported in August 1995 (about seven months into the trial) that many people had made up their minds about Simpson shortly after the murders took place and did not change their views as the trial unfolded.[76] In all of these polls, whites were more likely than blacks to believe that Simpson was guilty. In March 1995, for example, 66 percent of white Americans were convinced that he committed the murders, as opposed to 24 percent of African Americans.[77] Immediately after the acquittal, 75 percent of whites, compared with 33 percent of blacks, believed Simpson was guilty.[78]

Some have asked how race-based explanations of the verdict can apply when some of the jurors on the Simpson jury were not black. Jeffrey Abramson explains: "It is true that the three non-blacks on the jury joined with the nine black members to express quick and utter disdain for the prosecution's evidence. But this unanimity does not show that race ceased to matter. More likely, it shows that three is too small a number to resist the pressures that a united group of nine can bring to bear in a jury dealing with a racially sensitive case."[79]

Nonetheless, one can take the race-based explanations too far, regardless of their form. No public opinion poll on the Simpson case has ever shown results approaching racial unanimity on any issue. Some blacks, about one in four, do not agree with the not-guilty verdict or give any weight to Simpson's protestations of innocence. Similarly, some whites, a small percentage, do concur with the verdict in the criminal case and believe that Simpson was framed. And a sophisticated statistical analysis of attitudes toward the Simpson trial confirmed the importance of race, but it also concluded that "older individuals, males, those with higher incomes, and those with more education were less likely to be sympathetic to Simpson and more likely to think he was guilty."[80]

Bugliosi suggests that the Simpson jurors ". . . . did not have too much intellectual firepower."[81] He calls attention, for example, to a seventy-two-year-old woman who had said during jury selection that she never read newspapers, magazines, or books. Indeed, she only subscribed to the racing form, which she could barely decipher. After the verdict, she said: "I didn't understand the DNA stuff at all. To me, it was just a waste of time. It was way out there and carried absolutely no weight with me."[82] Another juror declared the domestic violence evidence utterly irrelevant. When asked whether the fact that O.J. Simpson excelled at football made it unlikely that he could commit murder, three-fourths of the Simpson jury had answered yes.[83]

Columnist Thomas Sowell sees the low intellectual caliber of the jury partly as a consequence of eliminating jurors with prior knowledge and opinions concerning the case. He recounts a joke that made the rounds during jury selection. It goes like this: "'Knock, knock.' 'Who's there?' 'O.J.' If you say, 'O.J. who?' you get put on the jury."[84] The jury included only two college graduates. Clark's view is that "the defense didn't want anyone with an IQ above room temperature. They were kicking jurors [off the panel during voir dire] simply for being too smart."[85] An editorial in *New Republic* commented: "One of the painful lessons of the Simpson verdict is that the representative jury is fatally undermined when jurors in criminal cases are selected by attorneys for their ignorance and credulity and hermetic isolation from civil society. The Simpson jury looked not very much like America."[86]

In any event, Simpson's defense lawyers felt satisfied with the jury. The first person lead defense attorney Johnnie Cochran thanked was his jury consultant, Jo-Ellan Dimitrius. A few weeks after the verdict, Cochran threw a lavish party for the jurors.

A TALE OF TWO VENUES

On the evening of February 4, 1999, four white plain-clothes police officers from New York City's elite Street Crime Unit set out to find a rapist who had been preying on victims in The Bronx. Driving slowly down Wheeler Avenue in the Soundview section, they encountered Amadou

Diallo, a recent black immigrant from the West African nation of Guinea, standing in front of his apartment building. Exactly what happened next remains controversial, but according to the officers, Diallo repeatedly ducked his head in and out of the vestibule, as if he did not want to be seen. The officers suspected that he might be the lookout for a possible robbery and feared that a hostage situation might develop if he managed to enter the building.

Two of the policemen left the car to approach Diallo, and one reportedly said, "Police! Can I have a word?," holding his police shield forward.[87] Again, according to the officers, Diallo turned abruptly toward the entrance of his building and failed to acknowledge the police. One of the officers yelled, "He's got a gun!" Simultaneously, another shouted, "What are you doing?" Gunfire followed, with the officers blasting forty-one shots at Diallo. One of the policemen recalls the moment: "I see Mr. Diallo, he's crouched, I see a gun. I think, 'Oh my God, I'm going to die.' I start firing . . . I was in the line of fire."

Seconds later, they realized that they had made a terrible mistake. The gun turned out to be a wallet. Diallo had committed no crime. He was unarmed. Officer Kenneth Boss approached the bloody body, which had been struck nineteen times. "Where's the f*****g gun? Where's the f*****g gun?" he demanded. Officer Richard Murphy said over and over again, "I can't believe there's no gun. I saw a gun. . . . I can't believe there's no gun."

Immediately, the case grabbed headlines in the city papers and dominated TV and radio broadcasts. Questions were raised about police policy, city governance, and the particulars of the shooting. The case polarized New Yorkers, not entirely along racial lines, for about a year. Why did the officers shoot? Why did they shoot so many times? Would they have been as likely to shoot had Diallo been white or lived in a wealthier neighborhood? What, if anything, did the shooting say about law enforcement procedures? Had they seen a gun because it fit their race-based expectations? Some leaders of the black and Hispanic community urged calm. Dennis Walcott, head of the New York Urban League, said, "I think we have a responsibility as a community to take a balanced look at the whole thing and not to stereotype the police as some police might stereotype the community."[88]

Other leaders were more inflammatory. Reverend Al Sharpton declared: "This is outright slaughter. If he was facing a firing squad, he would not have been shot 41 times."[89] Weeks of protests ensued, sometimes focusing on the specifics of the case, but more often raising general charges of police racism and brutality. The mass demonstrations included huge rallies outside police headquarters; former mayors, celebrities, and more than 1,000 people allowed themselves to be arrested in symbolic protest.[90]

Perhaps most emotionally charged was the question of what should be done with the four officers who had taken Amadou Diallo's life. Were they guilty of murder or some lesser offense? Were they racist cops who acted outside their authority? Were they inept? Or were they competent officers who had behaved in accordance with departmental procedures in an unfortunate situation, with tragic results? These questions would be resolved in a court of law.

On advice of legal counsel, the defendant police officers chose not to provide the media with their side of the story prior to trial. When Bronx District Attorney Robert T. Johnson brought charges of intentional second-degree murder and second-degree murder with depraved indifference to human life, the officers faced possible sentences of twenty-five years to life in prison. Few trials in the city's history had been awaited with greater interest or trepidation; no one had forgotten that the acquittals of the police officers in the first Rodney King case had ignited the Los Angeles riots.

The shooting of Amadou Diallo had occurred in The Bronx, and under ordinary circumstances the officers' fate would be decided there. But on December 16, 1999, a five-member appellate panel surprised most observers by upholding the trial court's grant of a defense motion to relocate the trial from the Bronx to Albany. Change-of-venue motions are often denied. Here, however, the court noted that ". . . this case has been deluged by a tidal wave of prejudicial publicity to such an extent that even an attempt to select an unbiased jury would be fruitless" and that "the few voices reminding the pool of prospective jurors of the sacrosanct right of an accused to the presumption of innocence have been drowned out by this incessant drumbeat of prejudicial publicity."[91] The appellate panel further reasoned: "This is not a simple matter of asking the jurors if they could put aside any opinions that [they] may have formed. Instead, it would also be necessary to ascertain whether they could face their friends and neighbors in the event of an acquittal. The very asking of such questions carries the danger of implanting or reinforcing in the jurors' minds the fear of the consequences of reaching an unpopular verdict."[92]

It should be noted that Albany County is 88 percent white and 9 percent African American, whereas The Bronx is 35 percent white and 38 percent African American.[93] Additionally, 51 percent of The Bronx population is Hispanic (of any race), compared to just 3 percent of the population in Albany County. So, although the appellate court justified its decision in terms of exposure to prejudicial publicity, many critics of the decision viewed the change of venue as an attempt to deliver the case out of the minority community, where it rightly belonged, and into the hands of a whiter and, implicitly, more police-friendly jury.

Sharpton, an unofficial adviser to Amadou Diallo's family, expressed the anger that prevailed among many blacks. Sidestepping the court's arguments, he asked: "If you're a police officer in The Bronx, how come you can't be tried in The Bronx, where you have arrested people and had them tried?" And he voiced the views of those opposed to the court's decision to change venue, indignantly asserting, "They can not disenfranchise a whole county."[94]

More moderate leaders also spoke out against the change of venue, with the editors of the *New York Times* objecting: "It is simply not credible that there are not a dozen people in The Bronx who have the fairness and courage to resist community pressures to render a verdict based on the evidence, when no effort has been made to test the prospective jury pool."[95] H. Carl McCall, the New York State comptroller and an African American, wrote that "the implication that the influence of the media has rendered the people of The Bronx incapable of fair and reasonable judgment is troubling enough. The implication that people of color residing in The Bronx cannot see beyond race is even more disturbing."[96] Bronx District Attorney Robert T. Johnson, an African American and the prosecutor charged with trying the case, reported to the media that he ". . . could not disagree more strongly with the court's decision."[97] Two months later, he went even farther, commenting that the change of venue ". . . is going to go down in history as one of the greatest assaults on confidence in the criminal justice system."[98]

Some community leaders charged that the white male members of the appellate panel, by moving the trial from The Bronx to Albany, had accomplished an additional goal beyond changing the composition of the jury: They had taken the case away from Justice Patricia Anne Williams, an African American female, and handed it to a white male judge. Norman Siegel, the head of the New York Civil Liberties Union, said several days after the decision, "I am hearing in the last 48 hours that at least the result, if not the intention, was to take her out. . . . You don't want to have that as the backdrop to a potentially polarizing and racially charged trial. This gives material to people who don't believe in the legal system or want to undermine the legal system."[99] Eric Adams, a lieutenant in the New York City police department and cofounder of the organization 100 Blacks in Law Enforcement, suggested, "For whatever reason, the decision by these five male judges, who happen to be white, implies that an African-American, female judge cannot be impartial."[100]

Some observers supported the decision to move the trial out of The Bronx but opposed the selection of Albany as the new venue. Professor Alan Dershowitz commented, "Conducting this trial in The Bronx ran the risk of making it a trial of the police for what they have done to the community over a long period of time. But there is only one constitutionally permissible issue in this trial or any other: Are these particular defendants individually guilty, beyond a reasonable doubt, of the specific crime charged?"[101] He further noted that "Bronx jurors might also have feared that an acquittal could spark the kind of incendiary response in their neighborhood that took place in Los Angeles after the initial acquittals of the policemen who beat Rodney King."

Dershowitz also argued that the trial should have gone to a location outside the New York City media market that "more closely mirrored the racial composition of The Bronx. This would have assured that the move would change only the constitutionally relevant variables." *New York Times* columnist Joyce Purnick countered that no such location existed. She explained: "The jury pools in Erie [County] and Monroe

[County] would be about 12 percent black [a bit more than Albany's 9 percent], but Buffalo in Erie and Rochester in Monroe are up to nine hours away from New York City. Syracuse, in Onondaga [County], is only five hours away, but its black population is even smaller than Albany's. Hence, Albany."[102]

The change-of-venue decision was greeted with enthusiasm in some quarters. Mayor Rudolph Guiliani welcomed the move, saying: "When you start marching, demanding that people be indicted—you get out in front of courthouses and demand that people be indicted, that's like the Old West. . . . Five judges unanimously . . . rendered a very, very wise decision."[103] Historian Fred Siegel of Cooper Union College in New York City commented that by trying to use protests to influence judicial proceedings, some civil rights leaders had brought "Southern politics" north. He explained: "If you are looking at the South of 40 years ago, this is the kind of thing that liberals are supposed to be opposed to—that mobs could sway the courts."[104]

Patrick J. Lynch of the Patrolmen's Benevolent Association cited data showing that 81 percent of Bronx residents said there could be no justification for forty-one shots and that 41 percent believed that the officers knew Diallo was unarmed when they fired at him. Lynch reflected, "I can't help seeing poetic justice in the notion that the rabble-rousing strategy employed by Al Sharpton and his ilk has led to this rare granting of the change-of-venue motion. It takes this tragic case out of the Old West, lynch-mob atmosphere that has surrounded it for almost a year and into an environment where it at least has the chance of being tried on the facts, as free as possible of side-show politics and invented racial considerations."[105]

The city-splitting and emotion-laden debate about the change of venue took place at a time when no one knew what facts would come out at trial, much less what the outcome would be. The furor with which the appellate court's decision was met in some circles and the support it received in others tells us something about people's expectations and the confidence with which they held them. All sides said that they desired, simply, a panel of fair jurors. Yet underlying such assertions lay two widely shared, although untested, assumptions: first, that a Bronx jury would be largely nonwhite and would reflect the "community's" desire to rein in the police and hold them accountable, in this instance by returning a conviction on serious charges; and second, that an Albany jury would be all-white, or almost all-white, and would reflect that "community's" support for police, by acquitting on serious charges. Insofar as no one had heard the officers' testimony and that Albany had experienced its own debates over police brutality, the assumptions were particularly bold.[106]

Just as jury selection was beginning, two lawyers who had experience trying police misconduct cases in Albany—one as a prosecutor and the other as a defense attorney—offered their advice in the *New York Post*. John E. Dorfman, who had prosecuted such cases, agreed with the common wisdom that the prosecution might benefit somewhat from the presence of black jurors, although he questioned the appropriateness of attempting to seat them if they seemed hell-bent on a conviction. He wrote: "The color of their skin, political or religious beliefs or financial wherewithal are not controlling. But their biases and prejudices are of great concern—and must be immediately addressed. That the prosecutor would like to seat one or more black jurors goes without saying. Common perception is that, regardless of the proof, a vote of guilty would be expected from such jurors. But while defense attorneys normally have a strong incentive to empanel biased jurors, the district attorney does not have such a luxury."[107]

Steven R. Coffey, who had defended police in misconduct cases, felt that jurors' preexisting biases would be significant. He wrote: "One must also never forget that, despite what they say, most people are guided, and often even motivated by bias, if not outright prejudice. I would not only accept this fact, I would embrace it. You can be certain the prosecution will." But he, too, did not suggest that skin color would be decisive. "I might not want a minority from one of Albany's high-crime areas on the jury—but then, the prosecution isn't going to select a retired cop, either. In between, it's only a guess. Frankly, though, as the defense lawyer I would not be as bothered by the prospect of an African-American on the jury as some might suspect."[108]

During the first day of jury selection, the prosecution wanted to use peremptory challenges to strike ten jurors from the panel of nineteen who remained following challenges for cause. Seven of the ten were white men. The defense wanted to strike six prospects, including three black women. Both sides argued that the other was discriminating on the basis of race—in violation of the law. The prosecution countered that striking white jurors, given the largely white venue, was inevitable. The defense backed its challenges of the black females with nonracial reasons, for example, because two had relatives who had been arrested on drug charges. Justice Joseph Teresi upheld all of the prosecution's challenges but—without explaining his decision—seated two of the three black women.[109] According to local reports, the final panel, one-third black, was ". . . more diverse than any in the county in decades."[110] Amy Waldman, who covered the case for the *New York Times*, wrote: "What . . . seems to drive the judge—along with other Albany officials—is a desire to prove wrong the critics of the change of venue, who had implied that Albany was a homogeneous backwater."[111]

The final jury comprised seven men, all of whom were white, and five women, four of whom were black.[112] The white men included a middle-aged "independent Catholic minister" who stated that he disliked judging people; a veteran of the Korean War who had shot a rifle during the war but had not handled a gun since; a middle-aged former school principal whose daughter had been stabbed a decade earlier but survived; a thirtyish man who said that his parents has grown up in The Bronx but also said that the neighborhood had changed since then; a middle-aged avid newspaper reader who had witnessed the snatching of his wife's purse in Florida; a middle-aged man employed in the financial sector who claimed to be capable of making split-second decisions; and a gay activist in his twenties. All four black women were middle-aged. They included a former Bronx resident whose son, a private investigator, had served in the military police; a self-described churchgoer who had a relative who was convicted on a drug charge; a mother whose initial reaction to the shooting was, "It could have been my daughter"; and a former Bronx resident who sometimes visited relatives in the area but claimed she had never discussed the case during her visits. The remaining juror was an elderly white woman whose husband was an FBI agent and lawyer and whose son was a lawyer.

The trial lasted less than one month. The jurors had to consider what, if anything, Amadou Diallo had done to arouse suspicion or to lead the officers to believe that he was about to fire a gun or flee during a robbery attempt. They had to remember that the officers had the right to approach and question Diallo—but the jurors also had to ask themselves whether it was reasonable for the officers to believe that lives were in danger. Was it reasonable for the police officers to believe that Diallo had a gun? According to the judge's instructions, the jurors could find the officers' actions justified if the jurors concluded that the officers had reasonably believed that Diallo was about to use deadly force. Alternatively, the jurors could find that the defendants had legitimately discharged their weapons to prevent what they believed was a robbery, attempted robbery, or flight from such a crime. The jurors could also acquit if they found that the officers were in the process of trying to make an arrest for a felony. In contrast, if the jurors determined that the officers' actions were not legally justified, they could convict the officers on charges ranging from criminally negligent homicide to intentional second-degree murder.[113]

After three days of deliberation, the jurors voted to acquit. The verdict set in motion another round of intense media scrutiny. Although the jurors had initially declared an intent to remain silent about what went on in the jury room, several soon offered commentaries to the press.

Helen Harder, the white female juror, seemed to capture the sentiment of the other jurors: "I'm not saying it's a happy verdict. I know the cops are happy. None of [the jurors] are very happy. But that's the way it worked out."[114] Harder reported that none of the panel members thought the officers were guilty of murder, and only one or two initially considered conviction on a lesser charge. The relations among jurors were, in her view, amicable. She wondered why the prosecutors brought murder charges against the four men: "The case that was presented by the prosecutors was very lacking. They didn't have anything to work with. . . . . The whole thing happened within seconds. Their actions were justified."[115] Harder suggested that Diallo's family pursue a civil lawsuit. She said: "I think the city is responsible because they're responsible for police procedures. I think the whole unit they belonged to wouldn't have had such a sharp look to the people who lived there if there were some black police officers too."[116]

Ed Powell, a white male juror, said that the jurors believed that the four defendants thought that their lives were in danger. He added, "If I were to pull something out of my pocket, you couldn't identify that quickly whether it was a gun or a wallet."[117] Charise Smith, one of the African American women, explained: "Race was not a factor. Based on the case before us and the instructions given to us, we had no choice. We were told to see the shooting from the officers' point of view, not Mr. Diallo's."[118] Arlene Taylor, the jury's black foreperson, agreed that the verdict had ". . . nothing to do with race."[119]

But many in the community did not accept the verdict. Anticipating this, a number of Bronx clergy organized marches and rallies while the jurors deliberated, during which they appealed for calm in the event of an acquittal. The protests that followed the jury's decision were mostly peaceful—but very angry. Some protesters held signs saying, "Go ahead and shoot. I'm black so it must be justified."[120] A poll conducted immediately after news of the verdict found that about half of the residents of New York State thought the jurors erred. Blacks were much more likely than whites to hold this position, although many whites—especially in New York City—also would have favored conviction on some charge.[121] *New York Times* columnist Bob Herbert, an African American, declared, "The system was twisted this way and that to insure that [the defendants] were treated fairly. More than fairly. The judge, Joseph Teresi, trumpeted his sympathies as soon as the trial was over by hobnobbing at a bed and breakfast with the defense lawyers."[122]

Reverend Calvin O. Butts III, minister at Harlem's influential Abyssinian Baptist Church, announced to his congregation that the juror's verdict reflected entrenched racism similar to that which led once peaceful black leaders in South Africa to pick up weapons in their struggle. He added: "I feel a little like my Lord, I want to kick over some tables."[123] His comments were cheered and applauded. Butts also noted that he had received calls from white officials urging restraint after Diallo's death. "Some of those same leaders called me now to say, 'Let's get together, let's

sit down and talk.' I told them to go to hell."[124] Reverend Sharpton angrily declared: "We are going to boycott in this city. We are afraid to
spend money with certain people because we are considered suspects.
Let's hold our wallets, let's hold our wallets."[125] Many leaders, black and
white, called for prosecution by the federal government on civil rights
charges—although there appeared to be little basis for this request other
than dissatisfaction with the jury verdict. (Approximately one year later,
federal prosecutors decided not to bring federal civil rights charges
against the four officers.)[126]

In certain circles, the Diallo trial was widely denounced as a travesty of
justice and an emblem for racial divisiveness. But few stopped to notice
that the white male judge, far from producing an all-white panel of "good
ol' boys," had interpreted and applied the rules governing peremptory
challenges in a manner that guaranteed a multiracial panel. When the
panel of jurors decided to acquit, they did so aware of the fundamental
tragedy of the situation. One juror suggested, and perhaps others felt,
that the case should now be pursued in a civil court—in order to provide
Diallo's family with some justice. Although the verdict was denounced by
some as racist, the jurors who served in this case carried out their duties
in a manner suggesting that they, if few others, were able to transcend
racial loyalties and decide the case, as constitutionally ordained, on the
basis of the facts. Unfortunately, their fairness and the multiracial make-
up of the panel did little to diminish the anger surrounding the shooting
and stemming from broader social problems in the community.

DISTRUSTING THE JUSTICE SYSTEM

Although the Diallo case was moved to Albany because of pretrial publicity specific to the trial, it spotlighted a phenomenon well known in
New York legal circles—the so-called Bronx jury. One anonymous police
officer explained why he supported moving the Diallo trial to Albany: "It
is known throughout the department that [a police officer] can't get a fair
[jury] trial here. You have to get a change of venue or a judge trial. Either
that, or you go to jail—and then you close the cell door behind you."[127]
Between 1992 and 1998, thirty-six police officers faced criminal charges

in The Bronx; of these, only two chose a jury trial.[128] Attorney Harry Slovis, who successfully defended an officer against police brutality charges in 1996, opined: "I don't think you can really go with a jury in The Bronx. . . . It runs too deep, too much stuff went by, too many incidents with [Abner] Louima and the other kid, [Anthony] Baez, that was killed."[129]

Bronx juries are perceived to be very tough on cops but lenient with regard to most other criminal defendants—especially when they attack police officers. For example, when New York police arrested Amir Tawfiyq Abdullah Aziz for shooting a police captain in the face, they felt they had compiled a formidable case. Among other evidence, there was the testimony from a friend of the defendant that Aziz had, indeed, confessed to the crime. At trial, defense attorney Ron Kuby offered the classic argument that his client—who faced other murder charges at the time—had not been the gunman and, even if he had, the shooting was carried out in self-defense. The jury voted to acquit, apparently with some jurors accepting the first half of Kuby's argument and others accepting the second half. Numerous observers, as well as one of the jurors, claimed that antipolice sentiment played a role in the acquittal. According to that juror, another panel member had said that the captain "got what he deserved."[130]

The Bronx jury also has a reputation for generosity in civil suits. A Bronx jury awarded $76 million in 1998 to Darryl Barnes, who sued New York City after being shot and paralyzed by an off-duty police officer. The officer had seen Barnes carrying a semiautomatic weapon, chased him, ordered him to freeze, then opened fire. The district attorney did not find sufficient wrongdoing on the officer's part for a criminal prosecution.[131] And in 1996, Darel Cabey was awarded $43 million by a Bronx panel. Cabey was the young black man shot and paralyzed by Bernhard Goetz on a subway train during the notorious 1984 incident in which Goetz thought he was being robbed.[132]

But large awards in The Bronx extend to civil cases generally—not only those politicized trials in which public passions run high. In one recent case, a jury awarded $4.2 million to a woman who sued the city after slipping on a snowy sidewalk and damaging her knee; she had been chasing her dog.[133] Juries in the borough find civil defendants liable in 72 percent of cases, compared to 57 percent nationwide. And the average damages award in The Bronx is around $1.2 million, double that in Westchester County, just to the north.[134] Tom Wolfe may not have been far from the mark when he wrote, in *The Bonfire of the Vanities*, "The Bronx jury is a vehicle for redistributing the wealth."[135]

Of course, antipolice and proplaintiff tendencies also exist outside The Bronx. As journalist Arthur Hayes has noted: "The Bronx-jury phenomenon isn't unique. Juries in many other urban areas also tend to favor civil plaintiffs and go easy on criminal defendants. Lawyers think such juries identify with people they perceive as victims, to the detriment of police, prosecutors and deep-pockets civil defendants."[136]

According to Paul Craig Roberts, a columnist for the *Washington Times*, "Inner-city black juries are more suspicious of prosecutors and police and give defendants more benefit of the doubt. Middle-class and white juries, worried about crime, tend to give the benefit of the doubt to prosecutors and police. It comes down to a matter of trust."[137] Roberts continues: "Inner-city blacks understand that the defendant doesn't always get a fair shake from prosecutors and police, who are under career pressures to produce high conviction and arrest rates. Inner-city blacks are not only police smart but also justice-system smart. In contrast, middle-class jurors are naive about the criminal justice system and assume that police and prosecutors are purer than they are."[138]

James M. Kindler, chief assistant district attorney in Manhattan, has a similar view: "There is a trend for jurors to be more inquisitive, more skeptical, asking for more information about the circumstances of a police stop." He continues: "There is little doubt in my mind that when it is generally believed that cops are corrupt and engaged in brutality, that perception will find its way into the jury room. I fear that that, regrettably, may be occurring."[139] For professor Gerald Lynch of Columbia University Law School, this would be an ominous development: "Police testimony is at the very heart of the criminal justice system. If the public does not have the confidence in the police, then acquittals or hung juries will become increasingly routine."[140]

Professor Randall Kennedy, too, regards the distrust of prosecutors and police as a major impediment to the enforcement of fair-minded law and order. He writes,

> Although the precise dimensions of this attitude are unclear, within African-American communities it is certainly appreciable. This attitude causes some black attorneys to eschew joining prosecutors' offices because they feel that doing so will entail 'selling out' and working for 'the Man.'. . . It causes some black citizens to decline to cooperate with police investigations. Even more alarmingly, it prompts some black jurors to be unreasonably skeptical of police testimony from law enforcement authorities or even to refuse to vote for convictions despite proof beyond reasonable doubt of defendants' guilt.[141]

Kennedy concludes that ". . . racially biased miscarriages of justice [which he regards as a reality of the present as well as the past] have strongly influenced American culture, particularly African-American culture. They have helped make many blacks intensely skeptical of police officials, profoundly fearful of the judicial system, and keenly insistent that in the absence of militant, collective demands for justice, white decisionmakers are apt to deal with black defendants with less care than white ones."[142]

REVISITING THE LABORATORY

Different beliefs about the trustworthiness of the criminal justice system apparently lie at the heart of black-white differences in attitudes toward many controversial trials, including the Rodney King, O.J. Simpson, and Amadou Diallo cases. Black Americans may bring to their service as jurors a very different set of experiences—historical and personal—than do white Americans. These experiences can bear on how black and white jurors process different types of evidence, whom they trust, and what level of certainty they require to convict. It is also possible, however, that the experiences, values, and attitudes today *shared* by whites and blacks will generally overwhelm the perspectives that historically have divided the races. We have already seen that for most jurors hearing most cases, background characteristics exert only a small impact on voting tendencies in the jury room. The courtroom situation, so powerful in minimizing other forms of bias, can diminish the effects of race as well.

We might hope to turn to jury researchers and other social scientists to understand the actual behavior of whites and blacks in the jury room. Unfortunately, these experts do not agree among themselves on how to interpret the vast body of research that has been accumulated. Some argue that decades of simulations and other studies prove, beyond reasonable doubt, that white jurors are inherently biased against black defendants and generally cannot put aside their prejudices during deliberations. Others arrive at a sharply contrasting interpretation, concluding that white jurors are not particularly biased against nonwhite defendants and that even though some whites may hold prejudicial beliefs, they typically do not draw on these beliefs to determine guilt or innocence once the judge delivers the jury instructions.[143] The failure to arrive at a consensual interpretation of the empirical findings derives from many sources, including disagreements about (1) the continuing significance of older studies; (2) the realism and generalizability of mock trial research; (3) the relationship between prejudicial attitudes and discriminatory behaviors; and (4) the extent to which discrimination in the justice system can be attributed to juries.[144]

Particular studies can only tell us how subjects behaved in very specific settings; they are best regarded as scattered pieces of a puzzle with many parts missing. In typical studies, white subjects view videotapes or read transcripts summarizing the evidence against a defendant. Sometimes the defendant is white, sometimes black. Everything else is exactly the same. Under various circumstances, especially when the evidence does not clearly point in either direction, white mock jurors tend to rate the probability of guilt higher for black defendants than for white ones.[145] Sometimes acquittal rates for white defendants exceed those for black defendants. When white subjects are told that the defendant is guilty, they occasionally assign more severe sentences to blacks than to whites. White subjects may also be more likely to overlook inadmissible evidence when the defendant is white.[146] But we do not know whether the differences observed in simulations are the result of unfair harshness in judging blacks or undue leniency in judging whites.

Because of a lack of social scientific studies on the subject, we know little about whether black subjects, under similar circumstances, would exhibit the same biases, or how black mock jurors would react to white defendants. Although evidence exists that racial identity between defendant and juror can generally promote greater leniency, some researchers have recently identified a so-called black sheep phenomenon, finding that under some circumstances upwardly mobile, middle-class black jurors can be tougher than white jurors on black defendants accused of violent crimes such as murder and rape.[147]

And still we do not know how often research settings meaningfully resemble real-world cases, or whether biases observed in the laboratory will show up in real jury rooms, or the effect of actual deliberations on the proclivities of blacks and whites.

Put simply, sweeping conclusions about the effects of race on juror verdicts are unwarranted. To even begin to understand what is going on, we must—at a minimum—consider a juror's race along with other aspects of his or her background, including social and economic class. Then, most important, we need to take into account the strength of the evidence, the nature of the crime, the race of the victim and the defendant, and the race of the key witnesses. Notwithstanding the already vast body of jury research, researchers have not truly begun to elucidate the complex relationships among these factors.

JUSTICE, CONSULTANTS, AND RACE

As we have seen, some recent and highly publicized trials suggest that race matters greatly, whereas others imply that jurors have overcome whatever pressures might exist and decided cases solely on the merits. Similarly, social-scientific research suggests that a juror's race sometimes proves important and sometimes not.

So what is a lawyer to do when a consultant's report concludes that the racial composition of the panel is likely to be a key determining factor, yet not because of clear bias on the part of a particular juror or jurors?

And what if an attorney merely suspects (or assumes) that race can be a powerful influence in the case at hand? The U.S. Supreme Court offers a clear answer: The lawyer cannot use a peremptory strike to excuse a juror merely on the basis of race; the juror must be permitted to serve.

As we now know, it is generally not race, in itself, that predisposes a juror to decide one way or another but rather the juror's various experiences and outlooks, which *may* be associated with race. A lawyer who is fulfilling his or her ethical obligation to advocate vigorously for a client will explore the presence of these associated traits in jury prospects and then, perhaps, use them as the basis for peremptory strikes.[148] In that context—theoretically, at least—trial consultants could play a constructive role in the American justice system by providing lawyers with more accurate predictors of what a prospective juror is likely to do during deliberations.

7

SAVING THE JURY

*The process of selecting a jury out of the citizens called for jury service
on a particular day has changed from a necessary safeguard against
potentially biased jurors to a way for highly paid jury consultants to
attempt to ensure a jury favorable to the side paying their fees.*[1]

— *U.S. Supreme Court Justice Sandra Day O'Connor,*
May 1999 speech

AT LEAST A FEW OF THE FOUNDING FATHERS must have winked when
they approved the Sixth Amendment, guaranteeing trial before an "impartial jury." The United States has never provided trials by jurors entirely
devoid of bias or inclination. It could not even if it tried. And the Founding Fathers must have been acutely aware of this fact, having based the
U.S. Constitution on expectations of human fallibility and partisanship.
They never expected the system to produce perfect results in any area.
When the people bear responsibility for a decision, however grave, they
sometimes decide improperly. This is true in electoral politics and in legislative decisionmaking. It is also true for juries.

The Constitution provides no meaningful definition of the impartial
juror, and as a result, it has bequeathed to jurists in every era since the
founding a daunting task: to interpret the concept workably for their
times. Gradually, juries have become more representative of national di-
versity, but the critical question remains: What would a genuinely fair

jury look like?[2] Would it reflect the racial and ethnic make-up of the community? Would it reflect different religious traditions? Different ages? Would half be men and half women? Would it balance jurors sympathetic to one side with those favoring the other, or would it be composed entirely of people with no strong opinions about the crime or matter being litigated? Would it include those with the most prior knowledge or the least, or would it attempt to balance the two? Would it aim to include the brightest citizens, or would it seek a range of intelligences? Should the jury be a random sample? The courts have answered some of these questions in various ways at different times and in different jurisdictions.[3]

Back in 1807, during the treason trial of former Vice President Aaron Burr, Chief Justice John Marshall said that the law did not require the selection of jurors ". . . without any prepossessions whatever respecting the guilt or innocence of the accused," concluding that the attainment of such a goal was hardly possible given the prominence of the defendant.[4] Moreover, Marshall reasoned, it was going too far to disqualify all those "who had formed an opinion on any fact conducive to the final decision of the case" because that would result in the exclusion of ". . . intelligent and observing men, whose minds were really in a situation to decide upon the whole case according to the testimony."[5] In contrast, Marshall wrote, the law required the disqualification of ". . . those who have deliberately formed and delivered an opinion on the guilt of the prisoner as not being in a state of mind fairly to weigh the testimony."[6] Over the years, courts have evolved procedures designed to apply that principle, at the same time struggling to resolve the tension that exists between it and the guarantee of a jury of one's peers. But the basic objective is, and has always been, to obtain jurors who, true to their oath, will decide cases solely upon the evidence developed at trial.

The courts have defined impartiality, in part, to require that a jury be chosen from a fair cross-section of the community.[7] But the U.S. Supreme Court has clearly indicated that individual juries need not be representative in order to be fair. There are sound reasons for this. Any system of quotas or group representation would risk sending the undesirable message to jurors that they are to serve as delegates whose duty is to represent the perspective and interests of their designated group. If this message were communicated to jurors, it would—in effect—substitute interest-group politics for impartial deliberation and destroy the very heart of the system. In any event, nobody has offered a practical plan for achieving group representation on individual juries, and—although the approach has its advocates—it is inherently unworkable.

In practice, the U.S. justice system defines an impartial jury as that which remains after biased jurors have been eliminated through challenges for cause and peremptory challenges. Specific laws, rules, and procedures vary greatly by jurisdiction, but the basic idea is the same: Jurors' answers to voir dire questions provide the judge and the litigants with information needed to determine whether such jurors should be seated; those who survive voir dire and are seated are deemed to be impartial.

The problem is that neither challenges for cause nor peremptory challenges work very well. A judge will remove a juror for cause if he or she concludes that the juror is unlikely to render a decision based solely on the evidence presented at trial. But in so doing, the judge relies heavily on the juror's self-assessment and candor.[8] Although there are exceptions, a juror's declaration that he or she can be fair is generally taken at face value. Liars pass readily though this safety net, and so do those who lack sufficient insight to acknowledge their own biases. Indeed, a willingness to admit the possibility of bias might well constitute evidence of at least a modicum of open-mindedness. Additionally, as has been noted often, one effect of the challenge for cause is to eliminate informed members of the public, who are apt to have developed opinions about a case, in favor of those who do not follow current affairs—and this preference is at least questionable.

In theory, peremptory challenges enable lawyers to remove biased jurors where the level of partiality does not rise to that required for a judge to strike for cause. Evidence suggests, however, that attorneys use peremptories, whenever possible, to seek jurors who are biased in their favor. They sometimes attempt to remove entire classes of jurors—say, those who share some background characteristic with the defendant or litigant—even if there is no basis for presuming unfairness on the part of any particular juror. And the best evidence suggests that no matter how much confidence they manifest or how thoroughly they question prospects, attorneys will frequently fail in their efforts to identify genuinely biased jurors. Thus, it is by no means clear that the exercise of the peremptory challenge results in fairer panels.

When the U.S. Supreme Court in *Batson v. Kentucky* and related decisions placed limits on how peremptories may be exercised, it added a new level of confusion to jury selection procedures.[9] Prior to these changes, the idea was to enable attorneys to dismiss jurors who—for any reason whatsoever, right or wrong, sane or crazy, fair or unfair—were feared the most, thus leaving the litigant with a good opinion of the jury, "the want of which might totally disconcert him."[10] The ability to strike unwanted prospects without explanation was seen to serve a constructive social purpose. As Stanford legal scholar Barbara Allen Babcock explained a decade before the *Batson* decision:

> Common human experience, common sense, psychosociological studies, and public opinion polls tell us that it is likely that certain classes of people statistically have predispositions that would make them inappropriate jurors for particular kinds of cases. But to allow this knowledge to be expressed in the evaluative terms necessary for challenges for cause would undercut our desire for a society in which all people are judged as individuals and in which each is held reasonable and open to compromise.[11]

In short, the peremptory challenge ". . . allows the covert expression of what we dare not say but know is true more often than not."[12]

Very often, however, attorneys' presuppositions were based on race, and as the civil rights movement progressed, legal sanctioning of race-based juror selection grew intolerable. It was difficult to reconcile a nation's march to racial justice with prosecutors deliberately removing all members of a defendant's race from the panel that would hear his or her case.[13] Even if a defendant's right to trial by an impartial jury was not endangered, race-based peremptories challenged the right of the prospective juror to serve. How could the Fourteenth Amendment ensure equal protection of the laws if courtroom practices permitted racist jury selection? Ultimately, the Supreme Court intervened, ruling that some indefensible and offensive rationales—notably, those based on race—were unacceptable while other such rationales were perfectly legal.

Nobody has been satisfied. Professor Leonard Cavise calls the decisions that followed *Batson* a ". . . curiously twisted bundle of cases that leaves nothing more in its wake than a confusing and time-consuming procedural morass . . . that will endure for many years, until trial lawyers and judges make the tacit agreement simply to ignore *Batson*."[14] Others object that, while the Supreme Court and some lower federal courts have extended *Batson*'s protection to women and certain other classes, the courts have not gone far enough. Many legal analysts agree with professor Albert Alschuler that ". . . the Court [in *Batson*] posed issues whose resolution may require the judiciary to draw lines every bit as ugly and invidious as those that the Court condemned."[15] Perhaps the most frequently heard criticism is that the reforms are easily thwarted by attorneys who fabricate neutral explanations to mask their real, discriminatory intentions.[16]

At the time of the *Batson* decision, Justice Thurgood Marshall called for the abolition of the peremptory strike altogether, arguing that "the inherent potential of peremptory challenges to distort the jury process by permitting the exclusion of jurors on racial grounds should ideally lead the Court to ban them entirely from the criminal justice system. . . . [T]his Court has . . . repeatedly stated that the right of peremptory challenge is not of constitutional magnitude and may be withheld altogether without impairing the constitutional guarantee of impartial jury and fair trial."[17] The other justices did not go along. But since that time, the number of observers clamoring for the end of the peremptory challenge has been steadily rising. For example, professor Jeffrey Abramson concludes:

> Given the obvious costs but spotty benefits of peremptory challenges, I believe we can select juries in more democratic and efficient ways. By abolishing peremptory challenges, we end those strategies of jury selection that permit a lawyer's mere hunch (say, that thin people who frown are likely to favor conviction) to defeat a juror's right to serve. I do not hesitate to conclude that the equal protection rights of jurors, as well as the Constitutional

mandate of representative juries, count for more than the litigants' partisan interest in excluding thin people who do not smile.[18]

Legal journalist Stephen Adler agrees, lamenting that peremptory challenges "have been undermining the integrity of . . . [the] jury system for a long time."[19]

Many other analysts of the contemporary jury system—for example, Harvard professor Randall Kennedy, Judge Harold Rothwax, Judge Burton Katz, and jury scholar Thomas Munsterman—have joined the chorus in favor of eliminating peremptory challenges or sharply reducing their number.[20] These critics have arrived at their positions from many different paths, arguing that peremptories are ineffective, inefficient, time-consuming, inherently bigoted, and subject to a wide assortment of abuses.

In this post-*Batson*, post–civil rights era, where all matters are open to public scrutiny and none must be contaminated by stereotypical reasoning, unexplained challenges to jurors might indeed be consigned to the dustbin of history. But if this happens, argue supporters of the peremptory challenge, something of value will be lost. After all, peremptories exist for a reason. They existed long before women or minorities served on juries and, therefore, must have served some purpose other than to mask bigotry. Even the most ardent critics of peremptory challenges admit that there is merit on both sides of this debate. Nearly everyone acknowledges that biased jurors slip through the screen imposed by challenges for cause. Others point out that attorneys can alienate some jurors if they ask tough questions during voir dire, and if the judge then refuses to excuse those jurors, the only recourse is to use peremptories. Trial lawyers have been the most vocal in their defense of the peremptory challenge, wishing to retain as much control as possible over those who have the ultimate control over trial outcome.[21]

Americans face a dilemma. Peremptories can be abused and frequently are. They were created largely to foster confidence in the impartiality of panels, but often they have the opposite effect. Yet their absence sometimes decreases the likelihood of a fair and impartial jury. We believe that there is a solution to this dilemma: A sharp reduction in the allotted number of peremptory challenges, or even their outright elimination, might well make sense, but only as part of a broader plan of jury reform.

One thing is clear: If peremptories were eliminated, the move would devastate the jury selection business. Even a substantial reduction in the number of peremptories would cripple the ability of consultants to shape juries, although perhaps the industry would survive.

We will return to these matters shortly.

THE THREAT TO JUSTICE

When asked, most Americans rate their justice system the finest in the world. As recently as August 1998, 78 percent of Americans affirmed that jury panels offered the fairest means to determine guilt or innocence, and nearly as many (69 percent) deemed juries the most important component of the justice system.[22] In a recent survey, 97 percent of federal judges reported that they concurred with jury verdicts most or all of the time. More telling, by an 8:1 ratio they said that if they were on trial, they would rather have their dispute decided by a jury than a judge.[23]

Yet Americans may prefer the jury system to imagined alternatives without having great faith in how it currently operates. In a 1998 survey, 36 percent of respondents reported "very little" confidence in the way the jury system works in criminal trials.[24] According to another recent opinion poll, more than half of the American people lack confidence that the system treats people equally, without regard to gender, ethnicity, wealth, or race.[25] During the past decade or so many publicized jury verdicts— civil and criminal—have deeply divided the American people, leading to protests, riots, declarations of despair or disgust, and charges of juror bias, manipulation, and incompetence.

Of course, there has never been a guarantee that juries will produce just verdicts in all cases, or even more often than other methods of dispute resolution. However, the institution of the jury traditionally has promised, and provided, a reasonable means of deciding cases that is accepted by the people.

Although the jury system has never worked perfectly, with the advent of televised trials all of its flaws have been magnified and projected into living rooms across the nation.[26] Precisely at the moment when the jury system has been placed under the microscope, a new technology has emerged that breeds suspicion that something is deeply amiss. The U.S. Constitution boldly promises trial before an impartial jury. Nothing flies in the face of this guarantee more directly and powerfully than the image of a team of highly paid experts endeavoring to provide their side of a case with a panel of jurors handpicked for their partiality. Many people first learned of jury selection consultants during the 1992 rape trial of William Kennedy Smith. There, the defense labored for nearly four weeks trying to procure the best possible panel. Then jurors acquitted Smith after deliberating a mere seventy-seven minutes. As usual, nobody could confirm any link between jury selection and the verdict. But many people were left wondering whether jury selection consultants play a constructive role in the American justice system.[27]

When people hear of the hefty price tags associated with jury selection consultants, many understandably conclude that such money does not change hands without the client obtaining something of commensurate value. When only one side can afford such services, jury consultants can seem an assault on the right to trial before an impartial jury. Americans, for better or worse, have grown accustomed to money buying better lawyers, expert witnesses, investigators, and the like. But in those instances, wealth helps one side to polish or perfect the case that they will present to a jury that is presumed to be fair. When money appears to "purchase" the very votes of those who deliberate, the concept of trial before an impartial panel seems more greatly imperiled.

Fortunately, few experts presently believe that jury selection consultants can *consistently* stack juries to deliver a desired verdict. And from the vantage point of those concerned about justice, tentative conclusions offered by social scientists are surprisingly optimistic. Research suggests that most jurors in most cases make their decisions on the basis of evidence and are relatively unaffected by their background affiliations and beliefs. More specifically, social-scientific studies have raised several objections to the claim that selection consultants have a powerful impact on the justice system. First, jury researchers conclude that judges typically agree with jury decisions, and when they do not, the discrepancies can usually be accounted for in terms of reasonable (if incorrect) interpretations on the part of the jury Second, race, ethnicity, gender, and other background characteristics do not—in most cases—play a large role in determining how individual jurors react to the evidence. Third, jurors can sometimes suspend prejudices when asked to do so by a judge. Fourth, jury selection consultants are not very good at identifying jurors' predispositions and inclinations. Fifth, even when bias matters and the consultants are correct, the limitations of the juror pool and the selection process can keep attorneys from seating those jurors perceived as desirable. Finally, a lawyer's intuitions can perform just as well (or as poorly) as consultant techniques in identifying some juror proclivities.[28]

However, it would be a mistake to accept this body of research uncritically, smugly declaring the real story to be the Great Jury Consultant Scam, in which the justice system escapes harm and the only victims are those attorneys (and clients) who pay astronomical retainer fees for quackery. After all, many studies of juror decisionmaking have serious limitations. Consultants, themselves, often boast of high success rates; although these self-interested estimates cannot be taken at face value, they should not be ignored. Many experienced attorneys believe strongly in the efficacy of consultants. Stephen Adler, a prominent legal journalist, concludes: ". . . the market has spoken on this. People pay up to $400 million . . . a year for jury consultants. They're doing it because it works."[29] We think Adler places a bit too much confidence in the judgment of the lawyers who hire consultants. But even the most skeptical researchers do not rule out the ability of scientific jury selection to *sometimes* make a critical difference. As another student of the jury has noted, although "the services of a consultant cannot insure success or be proven in a rigorous sense to have been decisive in any given case, this argument should not receive misplaced weight. The nature of jury decision making and the secrecy of jury deliberations guarantee that the actual impact of consultants, one way or the other, will remain immune to empirical verification."[30]

The most plausible conclusion is that scientific jury selection, even when practiced by the very best consultants, rarely turns a clear losing case into a winner in civil or criminal trials. Where the evidence does not strongly favor either party, the composition of the jury is apt to matter more, and, consequently, selection consultants may have a better shot at affecting a verdict. Similarly, damage awards are more likely to depend on the particular make-up of a panel, and hence they are more subject to the influence of jury consultants.

Attorneys who hire such consultants are investing in a weapon that is infrequently outcome-determinative. However, under certain circumstances—where cases are close, complex, politicized, publicized, racially divisive, or otherwise controversial—the likelihood that jury selection consultants will matter increases. Additionally, selection consultants may have the greatest potential for impact when judges fail to exert sufficient control over courtroom proceedings—especially when they permit trial attorneys to play the race card or engage in other inappropriate appeals to emotion or bias. Finally, the jurisdictions that allow the greatest number of peremptory challenges are more vulnerable to the presence of selection consultants. Thus, although jury selection consultants cannot be described as pervasive in their influence on our system of justice, they do contribute to the outcome of some trials, as they stack the jury—and odds—against the opposing party.

Jury selection expertise is by no means the only ware peddled by consulting firms. As we have seen, the hottest services in recent years have involved focus groups and mock trials designed not to select juries but to pretest theories, tactics, opening statements, and closing arguments. With such approaches, the trial consultant uses the tricks of the market research industry to sell case theories to jurors. Trials have never been simple and straightforward presentations of facts. Attorneys throughout history have used salesmanship and theatrics to increase their probability of success. But the importation of consumer science into the courtroom raises serious concerns.

The market-research industry now directs the management of political campaigns, and many have derided the concept of "selling candidates like soap."[31] We already see marketing science shaping the design and conduct of high-stakes trials. When both sides possess the resources to carry out trial research, it is possible to view such a development as reasonable, with perhaps the positive consequence of ensuring that each side presents its case in terms meaningful and comprehensible to jurors. However, when only one side possesses the resources to retain a litigation consultant, there is not only the appearance of injustice but potentially its reality. Few scientific studies have confirmed the effectiveness of focus groups and mock trials in building a case, but—in contrast to jury selection—these methods are widely believed to be effective.

To date, the use of marketing science to pretest arguments and tactics has not aroused as heated a controversy as has the use of jury selection consultants. Partly, this is because services that do not taint the make-up of the panel are seen to fall more legitimately within the parameters of the adversarial system. Lawyers, after all, are *required* to do all they can to present their client's perspective vigorously and in the best possible light. They have always pretested their inclinations and instincts by running them past associates, family members, cab drivers, and the like. Thus, the new systematization of that process seems less pernicious than the struggle to procure biased souls in the jury box.

Thus far, of course, the image of the scientific jury stacker—while evocative—has not dominated the concerns of most Americans. Even after the O.J. Simpson case, few Americans have a clear sense of what trial consultants do. But with low-cost consulting services becoming more widely available, and high-end consultants offering more refined techniques every day, public awareness—and concern—are sure to increase.

We have reviewed many of the arguments that trial consultants marshal in defense of their jury selection and case preparation services. They argue, for example, that research-based jury profiling lessens the likelihood that lawyers will base their discretionary strikes on illegal and inaccurate stereotypes. They suggest that their efforts contribute to the unmasking of hopelessly biased people who nonetheless wish to be seated on a panel. Those who work for the defense say that their techniques serve to counteract a proprosecution orientation that many Americans bring to jury duty. In certain cases, consultants have argued that their services are essential to an adequate criminal defense. Some who work for civil litigators maintain that selection consultants typically have the effect of producing a more intelligent panel. And consultants who prepare witnesses say that they increase the probability that jurors will hear the *substance* of testimony, rather than be distracted by a witness's quirks and personality traits.

We believe that the United States, on balance, would be better off without scientific jury selection consultants. But this conclusion is by no means the same as saying that jury selection consultants should be banned, or that *all* aspects of the industry are equally harmful.[32] There are practical, legal, and ethical matters to be considered. We turn now to the pressing matter of regulating trial consultants.

TRIAL CONSULTANTS: WHAT IS TO BE DONE?

"Years ago we wanted to be invisible," comments jury consultant Pat McEvoy. "Now we have a visibility committee to increase our profession's reputation."[33] Until the 1990s, trial consultants were the ultimate behind-the-scenes players, content to avoid the public eye as much as possible as long as they could attract the attention of potential clients in the legal profession. As people learn more about trial consulting, sometimes acquiring accurate images, sometimes inaccurate ones, practitioners fear a rising tide of public sentiment that could undermine their livelihoods. Defining the problem as a public relations challenge, McEvoy asks, ". . . How do we undo what has been done by the depictions of trial consultants in the media? . . . And how do we respond to scholarly journal critiques . . . that have criticized the trial consulting field?"[34]

Thus far, despite frequent grumbling, no groundswell of mass sentiment has demanded regulation of trial consultants. But this has not been the case among legal scholars, social scientists, and journalists who have studied scientific jury selection, nearly all of whom—including many consultants—have concluded with proposals for reform or regulation of the industry.[35] The two mildest proposals—and those least likely to affect the industry's status quo—are: (1) to professionalize the field and encourage self-regulation, and (2) to require that trial attorneys disclose the use of a jury selection consultant.[36] These suggestions might well receive the support of those in the industry, as—most certainly—would a requirement that (3) courts appoint jury consultants for those who cannot afford to retain them. The remaining proposals have all been denounced by practitioners, understandably, as they would undermine the economic vitality of the profession. One idea (4) is to make consultants' reports or, at least, their raw data discoverable—that is, available to the opposing side—so as to neutralize any unfair advantage that derives from them. Two plans have called for the banning of jury consultants outright, one (5) through legislative action, and the other (6) by the U.S. Supreme Court declaring jury selection consulting unconstitutional. The final method (7) involves regulating the field as a by-product of more generally reforming the voir dire and jury selection process.

Although the trial consulting field is indeed moving toward professionalization, and perhaps even certification, these developments will—if anything—serve the interests of consultants themselves, most notably by reducing competition and fostering perhaps unfounded confidence in the value of their services. Very little in the move toward professionalization will reduce criticism of systematic or scientific jury selection, as such discontent stems from the fundamental core of what consultants do. The ethics code of the American Society of Trial Consultants includes a provision mandating that trial consultants "[shall] not provide any services with the intent of jeopardizing the integrity of the jury pool."[37] Thus far, the provision has not been interpreted or enforced in a way that has had much impact on practice. Proposals to encourage or require pro bono consulting work would not go far enough toward addressing the perceived inequities that result when one side can afford a consultant and another cannot. In any event, trial consultants have no obligation today to join their professional organization, and many prominent consultants do not. Among themselves, practitioners discuss self-regulation and professionalization as a means of forestalling outside interference. They also see the move toward professionalization as potentially comforting to attorneys who belong to a regulated profession par excellence. But few critics who have expressed concerns about jury selection consultants view self-regulation or professionalization as responsive to the issues they have raised.

The idea that attorneys who retain selection consultants should be required to divulge their use is an idea worth considering, for it would enable the opposing party to make a more informed decision about whether to hire his or her own expert, and it would put that party on notice to pay greater attention to the jury selection process in order to offset any edge the other side might obtain. However, this approach does nothing to address the concern of parties who want to hire a jury consultant but cannot afford one.

Thus, a frequently heard proposal is that courts should appoint and compensate trial consultants for indigent criminal defendants, much as courts appoint legal counsel for such defendants. Although it is unusual for the prosecution to retain a jury expert when the defense does not, an appeal for a court-appointed consultant would gain additional strength on such occasions.

Jurywork, the foremost guide to trial consulting techniques, suggests that a defense attorney might support an application for public funding of a trial consultant by arguing that "equal protection of the law requires that indigent persons be provided with the 'basic tools of an adequate defense when those tools are available for a price to other persons,'" a principle articulated in *Britt v. North Carolina*.[38] However, the authors note that "as a practical matter, the need for jurywork will require a more detailed explanation [than the need for some other court-funded defense services] because the integration of these techniques is a relatively new development in criminal defense work."[39]

In 1991, U.S. District Court Judge William Hoeveler appointed the consulting firm of Rebecca Lynn and Associates to help General Manuel A. Noriega's defense lawyers pick a jury.[40] Two years later, Judge John Ouderkirk of the Los Angeles Superior Court appointed trial consultant Jo-Ellan Dimitrius to aid in the defense of two men charged with the attempted murder of Reginald Denny during the Los Angeles riots.[41] Sheik Omar Abdel Rahman and his associates, charged with committing several terrorist crimes in New York City, also received court-appointed jury experts.[42] But these cases were unusual, extraordinarily publicized, and more likely than most to activate latent juror biases.

Courts generally have ruled against a right to the appointment of a jury consultant.[43] Providing funds for trial consultants remains at the court's discretion, and few judges have deemed them necessary. *Jurywork* lists cases where courts have appointed consultants.[44] Many are California cases drawing on a special fund of state monies designated for services beyond lawyers' fees in death-penalty cases.[45] Professor Franklin Strier notes that "courts disposed to funding requests of indigents for trial consultants will look for authority to *Ake* [*v. Oklahoma*] or the federal Criminal Justice Act of 1964, which allows indigents to request expert services which are 'necessary to an adequate defense.'"[46] The 1985 *Ake* decision established the right of an indigent defendant to an expert psychiatric evaluation when his or her sanity is a substantial factor at trial. Although *Ake* does not directly address jury consultants, one might argue that it has some relevance, especially if it can be demonstrated that the presence or absence of a jury consultant will be a significant factor in the trial. One scholar concludes that ". . . the requirement of providing jury consultants to indigent criminal defendants is coming soon."[47]

Most trial consultants, understandably, think courts should move in this direction. We don't agree. Right now, if a criminal defendant can establish that a prosecutor has hired a consultant, a judge might sensibly rule that the appearance of justice requires the appointment of a jury expert for the defense. In general, however, the law never guarantees lawyers exactly equal resources in building their cases. In light of social scientific research and other evidence presented in this book, we believe that an application for court appointment of a jury expert would not meet *Ake*'s "necessary to an adequate defense" standard—except, perhaps, in the very unusual case. Dennis Stolle and his colleagues remark: "Continuing ambivalence regarding the efficacy of scientific trial consulting among academic commentators . . . will likely prevent the acceptance of arguments that trial consultants are necessary to meet the requirements of effective assistance of counsel. . . . Furthermore, the limited budgets of state court systems will likely further hinder trial judges' receptiveness to such arguments."[48]

The next proposal applies to civil as well as criminal cases. In 1979, just a few years after the birth of scientific jury selection, three scholars—James Herbsleb, Bruce Dennis Sales, and John Berman—suggested that the legal principle of discovery could provide the "least disruptive and most effective remedy" to problems posed by the new profession.[49]

"Discovery" encompasses an assortment of rules and practices that require attorneys to disclose certain information and evidence to adversaries during the pretrial period. The main purpose of discovery is to eliminate surprise and facilitate trial preparation, keeping proceedings focused on the pursuit of truth rather than allowing them to degenerate into the tactical maneuvering of a cat-and-mouse game.[50] Herbsleb and his colleagues argued that when social scientists gather information about prospective jurors through community surveys and other techniques, the raw data from these studies should be discoverable.[51]

One problem with this recommendation is that such information may well be protected under the work-product doctrine. Here, the idea is that attorneys can keep to themselves their mental impressions of the case, their theories, opinions, and conclusions, as well as materials prepared in anticipation of litigation or for trial; they need to disclose relevant and nonprivileged evidence in advance, but not trial strategy. The work-product rule also serves to discourage one lawyer from freeloading off the work of another.[52] To our knowledge, no one to date has been able to use discovery rules to obtain the results of an adversary's pretrial jury research, and those who wish to regulate jury consultants would do well to look elsewhere.[53]

Why not simply ban the consultants, as some critics have advised? To our knowledge, only one legislator has embarked on this path, and he did not get very far. In the immediate aftermath of O.J. Simpson's acquittal, James "Pate" Philip, the president of the Illinois State Senate, introduced a bill that would have made it a crime for nonlawyers to act as jury consultants in civil or criminal trials.[54] Philip's bill prohibited nonlawyers from conducting mock trials, running juror surveys, or helping to select a "sympathetic, favorable, or hostile" jury. Had it been enacted, the measure would have imposed a fine of $1,000 for each day of consultation, plus $1,000 for each juror about whom consulting was done. Lawyers, themselves, would have been able to use the tools of jury science so long as they did not hire nonlawyers to assist them; this loophole, necessary because of the constitutional right to effective assistance of counsel, was not insignificant, as many members of the American Society of Trial Consultants are attorneys.

Quickly and predictably, Philip's bill encountered opposition from trial lawyers and consultants, many of whom argued that the measure was unconstitutional and that it encroached on the authority of the Illinois Supreme Court. The proposal never came close to passing, although it sparked a tremendous amount of debate. Philip's bill appears to have been either a genuine cri de coeur, or perhaps a politician's attempt to make hay from the angst felt by many constituents following the O.J. Simpson trial.[55] It is not clear how one might draft a law banning jury consultants that would be fair, enforceable, and resistant to constitutional challenge. Philip's attempt does not provide a useful model for those who seek to limit the growth of jury selection consulting.[56]

Thus far, no one has mounted a successful constitutional attack on the field. It has been suggested that scientifically based jury selection techniques might be viewed by the U.S. Supreme Court as endangering the right to trial by an impartial jury, but only if convincing evidence were to become available documenting that such techniques are substantially more effective than traditional methods of selection.[57] No such evidence exists, and consequently it seems unlikely that jury selection consulting will be ruled unconstitutional on that ground.

When *Batson* and other Supreme Court decisions placed limitations on how attorneys can exercise their peremptory challenges, another line of constitutional attack opened up. Jury consultants who attempt to predict how prospective panel members will lean in a particular case often draw, directly or indirectly, on race, gender, and other prohibited categories. As case law continues to develop, more of the consultant's statistical predictors may well be ruled out. Professor Jeffrey Rachlinski, trained in both law and psychology, has argued that the more one understands the intricacies of the rules governing peremptory challenges and the complex methods used by social scientists to predict juror proclivities, the more it becomes clear that many aspects of scientific jury selection can be challenged.

His position is reasonable, and we may yet see a case where at least some portion of the consultants' arsenal is found to be in violation of *Batson* and its progeny. Rachlinski is perhaps correct when he advises:

> Although it arises from benign motives, . . . [scientific jury selection's] tra-
> ditional emphasis on immutable demographic characteristics mimics the
> bigotry in jury selection that the Court condemns. Until [recently,] . . . this
> mimicry cast an ethical cloud over SJS, but did not endanger its use. . . .
> [But no] longer is . . . [the advice of consultants] harmless, and possibly
> useful. . . . [Scientific jury selection] now creates the risk of judicial sanction
> and needless appeals . . . SJS can still assist attorneys, but like most trial
> strategies, a litigant must weigh its benefits against its possible liabilities.[58]

Still, despite Rachlinski's caution, current scientific selection practices
have not, to date, been greatly hampered by *Batson* challenges. Consultants have been keenly attentive to developments in the law and have
modified their techniques accordingly.

Barring constitutional challenges, which seem unlikely, scientific jury
selection is likely to remain unregulated—in any meaningful sense—for
the foreseeable future. Much of the difficulty in regulating this industry
stems from the fact that almost everything consultants do can be viewed
as an extension or refinement of what lawyers themselves have always
done. The addition of scientific methodology certainly makes their performance of these tasks seem far more proficient. But it is not at all clear
that it really renders them so. Certainly, there has been no quantum leap
in the effectiveness of jury-picking. Nonetheless, as we have argued, jury
selection consulting certainly creates the perception that something unjust is afoot, and that matters in and of itself.

To some extent, trial consultants have been made the scapegoats for
problems inherent in our jury system. Biased jurors, inept deliberations,
and manipulative lawyering existed long before the consultants appeared
on the scene. The consulting industry has exploited opportunities and irritated wounds. But the challenges faced by our jury system are bigger
than those created by trial consultants. Hence, our preferred solution to
the problem of jury consultants comes as part of a comprehensive plan to
reform the jury system.

We would start by eliminating peremptory challenges, not because we
fail to see their purpose but because we believe they are unworkable in the
post-*Batson* era and because no return to the earlier system is either feasi-

ble or desirable. Peremptory strikes are popular with many trial attorneys, but this is probably because most lawyers overestimate their ability to use them with great effect. Regardless, it is difficult to sustain the argument that the exercise of such challenges generally results in less-biased panels. Peremptories also leave those who have been struck with diminished confidence in the justice system. More than 80 million Americans have been called for jury duty, and because of peremptories, nearly a third have been sent home. According to some studies, many of these "rejects" leave with a negative view of the system.[59]

Peremptory challenges exist because we, as a society, have chosen to credit an attorney's "intuitions not capable of verbalization."[60] If an argument ever could have been made for such an approach, it certainly cannot be made in the current environment, where we outlaw some intuitions (based on race, gender, or ethnicity) but not others (based on body weight, sexual orientation, occupation, etc.). Professor Jeffrey Abramson notes that

> . . . we cannot expect people to take jury service seriously if we excuse them so arbitrarily. Just imagine telling the truth to a juror who is peremptorily removed after having rearranged work and family schedules and driven twenty miles to appear in court. "We thank you for coming. But you see, the defense has a theory about thin people who do not smile. Our system permits discrimination against you for this reason. Do not be offended; we sometimes discriminate against fat people who smile too much."[61]

Still, prejudiced jurors exist, and they are unlikely to be weeded out by the current system of challenges for cause—where so much reliance is placed on a juror's self-assessment and candor. Thus, in addition to doing away with peremptories, we support an expansion of the grounds upon which judges can grant a challenge for cause.

In its current form, the challenge for cause generally requires a showing of inferred or actual bias on the part of the challenged juror and is only infrequently granted in practice. Under that standard, inferred bias is construed narrowly, as when the prospective juror has a business or familial relationship with one of the parties.[62] In contrast, the expanded challenge would broaden the acceptable grounds for striking a juror for cause by focusing on whether the litigant seeking to exercise the challenge has articulated "reasonable, case-specific" grounds to exclude the prospective juror.[63]

Abramson explains that in an expanded for-cause system "lawyers would . . . have an opportunity to challenge would-be jurors on the basis of group bias."[64] Thus, for example, the expanded challenge could be applied to strike a juror having the same occupation as a litigant, particularly where an aspect of the occupation plays a role in the case. In such a situation, "a litigant can articulate reasonable, case-specific grounds for suspecting that a person's occupation would unduly influence him or her. . . . Suspecting persons for bias on these narrow grounds is far different than vague suspicions premised on global intuitions about, say, the anti-establishment attitudes of young people regardless of the case."[65] As Abramson notes, the expanded for-cause system, combined with the elimination of the peremptory challenge, would preserve "most of what is good in peremptory challenges" but "entirely eliminate those challenges premised on arbitrary preferences that resist being put into words."[66]

If we abandon peremptory challenges and expand the grounds for the challenge for cause, we will bring a previously hidden process into the sunlight and add some rationality to a system fraught with irrationality. The new voir dire will require greater scrutiny of prospective jurors in order to determine whether a lawyer has reasonable grounds for suspecting bias. Whether judges or attorneys conduct the voir dire questioning need not be resolved uniformly across jurisdictions. When lawyers ask the questions, the procedure takes longer. But judges may be less effective at rooting out signs of partiality.[67]

Even with expanded strikes for cause, biased people find their way onto juries. When verdicts must be unanimous, idiosyncratic individuals can thwart the will of others, even when they stand alone and cannot marshal arguments in support of their position. If we reject a conviction or acquittal when the vote is 11-1, we are, in effect, wagering that the dissenting juror acts not in error or from bias but because he or she saw matters with greater lucidity or moral vision than the others. This is, of course, possible, but it is also statistically improbable.

The Supreme Court, in its 1972 decision in *Apodaca v. Oregon,* ruled that nonunanimous verdicts in state criminal cases are constitutional.[68] According to the attorney who argued Oregon's case, Jacob Tanzer, very often defense lawyers ". . . try their cases to one juror instead of to 12."[69] He notes,

> In no other decision-making body, even those that make society's most important decisions, do we require 12 people to agree. In every collegial decision-making body, there is some allowance for difference of opinion, whether reasoned, biased or crackpot. Even the Supreme Court, deciding matters of life and death, is seldom unanimous. The important thing for criminal juries is that those who agree do so with a depth of personal belief that is beyond a reasonable doubt. To require that 10 or 11 people hearing conflicting evidence each bear the same opinion is a very high obstacle to injustice.[70]

Professor Akhil Reed Amar has made a similar point: ". . . Other political bodies—legislatures, city councils, even courts—do politics in ways that do not let a single outlier thwart the considered judgment of the rest. Should a single racist juror be able to hang a jury by refusing to convict an obviously guilty white who kills a black, or by refusing to acquit an obviously innocent black charged with killing a white?"[71]

Since 1967, the criminal code in England has allowed 10-2 verdicts, providing that the jury has deliberated for at least two hours. Since 1995, several bills proposed in the U.S. Senate have called for an amendment to the Federal Rules of Criminal Procedure to permit nonunanimous verdicts. Some supporters of the change to nonunanimous verdicts have argued that nowadays defendants enjoy so many safeguards of a fair trial—including a well-designed appellate system—that the additional protection of unanimous verdicts is no longer necessary. They have also noted that adoption of a supermajority rule—permitting, say, 10-2 verdicts—would at times work to the advantage of defendants. Most supporters expect that the change would reduce the number of hung juries, a development widely (although not universally) regarded as desirable.[72]

The strongest counterargument to this proposal is that eliminating the unanimity requirement would alter the character of deliberations, allowing nine, ten, or eleven jurors who share a position to ignore dissenters, giving their views a perfunctory hearing rather than engaging in a systematic, soul-searching inquiry. Reviewing jury simulation research, professors Valerie Hans and Neil Vidmar conclude: "Jurors take a subtle message from the instruction that they need not be unanimous. They deliberate in a different manner, and the influence of jurors trying to argue a minority position is diluted."[73]

However, we can minimize this undesirable effect by requiring, as in England, that jurors deliberate for a set period of time before they are permitted to outvote dissenters. Law professors Akhil Reed Amar and Vikram David Amar propose a plan worth testing. They suggest: "Nonunanimous schemes can be devised to promote serious discussion. Jurors should be told that their job is to communicate with others who have different ideas, views, and backgrounds. Judges could also advise jurors that their early deliberations should focus on the evidence and not jurors' tentative leanings or votes, and that they should take no straw polls until each juror has had a chance to talk about the evidence on both sides."[74] Specifically, the professors favor ". . . a scheme in which a jury must be unanimous to convict on the first day of deliberations, but on day two, 11-1 would suffice; on day three, 10-2; and so on, until we hit our bedrock limit of, say, two-thirds (for conviction) or simple majority (for acquittal)."[75] The plan makes sense.

If peremptories are abolished, challenges for cause expanded, and nonunanimous verdicts adopted, our nation will have taken meaningful steps toward increasing the fairness and logic of jury procedures. At least in our courtrooms, neither the rampant racism of the past nor the disguised prejudice of the post-*Batson* era will endure. Although judges will acquire more discretionary power in ruling on challenges for cause, they will no longer have to engage in the game-playing and sanctioning of pretexts that have resulted from *Batson*. And if one or two jurors are truly biased but the trial lawyers fail to detect such bias or convince the judge that it exists, the parties will be protected by the possibility of a nonunanimous verdict.

The reforms we propose, if adopted in their entirety, would make most of what jury selection consultants do obsolete. If, as others have suggested, attorneys retain the right to exercise a small number of peremptory challenges (say, three), then scientific jury selection will continue, but demand for the services of consultants will decline sharply. A new and more legitimate role might arise for consultants who advise lawyers on how to unearth and document true bias in prospective jurors, in connection with the challenge for cause.

However, trial consulting activities that do not involve jury selection would surely survive, and—as we have suggested—some of these are likely to promote the fair administration of justice. For example, the only way to prove that prejudice has poisoned a venue is to conduct a scientific sample survey. Social-science organizations, including the American Society of Trial Consultants, have developed standards to ensure that such studies are accurately designed and carried out. Courts have often financed change-of-venue research when an indigent party has needed it; this practice should continue. Trial consultants also provide a valuable service when, through mock trial research and focus groups, they calculate the likely value of a civil case or, less often, the expected outcome of a criminal trial. Such estimates promote settlements, which save everyone, including the public, much time and money.

We confess to mixed feelings about most focus groups, mock trials, and simulations, especially when they are used to devise strategies, tactics, story lines, and arguments. We are fairly confident that such techniques enhance the effectiveness of lawyers at trial. Although something about attorneys pretesting their cases with Madison Avenue methods strikes us as unseemly, we recognize that the line is not at all clear between this new approach and the ways attorneys have traditionally tested angles and theories. Mock trials and focus groups provide more effective feedback than less formal approaches to trial preparations, but they do not differ in ways that can be sensibly regulated. Our system of justice accepts the likelihood that attorneys will strive to manipulate jurors, much as our political system concedes that politicians aspire to manipulate the public. The key requirement is that all adversaries must be free to respond to manipulative techniques, to expose them, or to practice their own countermanipulation. In politics, campaign finance laws may to some extent address inequities that stem from the differing financial resources that candidates bring to an election. In court, however, it would seem profoundly unfair to restrict a criminal defendant, or even a party to a civil lawsuit, from using their own money to finance mock trials or focus groups. However, when such methods are used to prepare the testimony of witnesses, we approach a sensitive legal and ethical issue. Consultants generally deny that they ever put words into a witness's mouth. But when a consultant reports to its client, on the basis of research, that one line of testimony will prove more effective than another, the risk of impropriety arises, although it may be difficult to document.

We do not have a solution to all of the problems raised by trial consultants. We believe, however, that our proposals, particularly concerning jury selection, will go a long way toward eradicating bias and injustice while enhancing the integrity of the jury system. We turn now to a series of reforms aimed at providing jurors with the resources they need to deliberate effectively.

SOME FINAL THOUGHTS ON ENABLING THE JURY

Sometimes it seems like the judge and the jury are on different sides. In one recent case, Lonnie Weeks Jr. faced a possible death sentence for his 1993 murder of a Virginia state trooper.[76] During sentencing deliberations, the jurors requested that the judge clarify whether they were required to impose the death penalty if they found that the state had proved either of two aggravating circumstances. The question was entirely reasonable. Instead of providing an answer, however, the judge directed the jurors to re-read the instructions he had already given them on the point. His written reply said simply, "See second paragraph of Instruction #2." The defense attorney asked for clarification, to no avail. Two hours later, the jury returned a death sentence. When polled, most of the jurors were in tears.

When mock jurors read similar instructions, a whopping 41 percent incorrectly deduced that they *were* required to impose a death sentence if the state proved the existence of an aggravating factor.[77] But, in a 5-4 decision, the U.S. Supreme Court ruled that the trial judge had not been required to clear up the jurors' confusion concerning the sentencing instruction. In his opinion, Chief Justice William Rehnquist wrote that "a jury is presumed to understand a judge's answer to its question. . . . To presume otherwise would require reversal every time a jury inquires about a matter of constitutional significance, regardless of the judge's answer."[78] Although the decision was split, the majority sent a loud and clear message: If the jurors don't understand the instructions, well, so be it.

As they begin service, jurors throughout the country are often indoctrinated with a patriotic message along these lines:

> Jury duty is one of the most important responsibilities of . . . an American citizen. It is a privilege enabling us to provide a service to our country, state, community, and fellow citizens. It is a service that should be performed with pride. Trial by a jury of one's peers is a sacred right of every American. It is the cornerstone of our judicial system, and the essence of American freedom. Your participation as a juror guarantees the continuation of this basic democratic process.[79]

Yet almost immediately upon receiving notice of the seriousness of the task they are about to undertake, many start to discern a conflicting message. In many jurisdictions, jurors often spend hours or days in a crowded and unpleasant environment, waiting to be called.[80] The low pay they receive and the automatic exemptions granted in some jurisdictions to those with high status suggest that society perhaps does not value jury service so very much.

More important, jurors soon learn that they must remain passive throughout the trial—seen but not heard. When an intelligent person attends a college lecture, contemplates an expensive purchase, or weighs a career move, he or she nearly always jots down key elements that should not be forgotten. Yet for the juror, note-taking is generally prohibited. Similarly, a sensible person usually asks questions prior to rendering a decision. In most of our courts, the juror cannot.

And when judges carry out the important task of instructing the jury, they do so in impenetrable legal jargon, designed to meet the needs of learned appellate judges. Little or no effort is made to ensure that jurors understand the key points, and even the brightest frequently do not. Several studies have shown that jurors fail to grasp about half of the judge's instructions at the end of the trial. Thus, jurors are given a job but deprived of the tools needed to do it.[81]

Arizona Superior Court Judge B. Michael Dann, a leading proponent of jury reform, recalls a juror's complaint that she had felt "gagged and bound and treated more like a hostage than a responsible adult decision maker."[82] Judge Dann understands her frustration and believes that many jurors experience similar feelings during their jury service. He strongly objects to the traditional notion of jurors as "passive receptacles of information," arguing that this conception

> . . . does not accommodate jurors' need to understand, and it denigrates individual jurors and the institution of trial by jury itself. The "passive juror" notion is an antiquated legal model that is neither educational nor democratic. It flies in the face of what we know about human nature to assume that jurors remain mentally passive, refrain from using preexisting frames of reference, consider and remember all the evidence, and suspend all judgment until they begin formal deliberations.[83]

Many critics from academia, trial practice, and elsewhere have argued, persuasively, that the system's failure to engage jurors more actively has fostered apathy and poor decisionmaking. For the past decade or so, there has been, as one legal reporter notes, "a plethora of problems and remedies swirling around juries," some identifying jurors as the problem but others portraying jurors as victims.[84] Arizona, New York, California, and other states have launched reform programs encompassing a range of modifications, mainly aimed at minimizing automatic exemptions from jury duty, improving the conditions under which jurors serve, and—more generally—encouraging jurors to assume a more active role during the trial.[85]

The simplest, and least controversial, changes involve increasing juror pay, improving creature comforts, and lessening unnecessary time-wasting. One of the most popular proposals calls for allowing jurors to take notes during trial proceedings. Another suggestion is to allow jurors to submit to the judge in writing questions that they would like witnesses to answer. The judge, then, decides whether such questions are appropriate. Some have suggested providing jurors with an independent expert to help them sort out conflicting testimony from partisan experts. Another frequent recommendation is to revamp the content of jury instructions and the method by which they are delivered.

New schemes call for encouraging judges to administer simpler, shorter, and more understandable instructions, often in writing so jurors can bring them into the jury room. But as journalist Stephen Adler points out, revision of judicial instructions to jurors will not occur unless appellate judges ". . . cease demanding that the precise wording of court decisions and statutes be parroted by a trial judge's instructions." Instead, appellate judges should merely ascertain whether instructions remain ". . . faithful to the law in spirit and meaning and whether they [make] sense to the jury."[86] Another idea is for jurors to receive preliminary instructions at the outset of a case and recaps at various points in the trial.

Objections have been raised to most of these proposals. Jurors may, for example, give undue weight to testimony that comes in reply to questions they have submitted. And it is not clear how the court might locate completely "objective" experts to help jurors resolve conflicts among expert witnesses. Moreover, it would be naive to expect the reformers' proposals to revolutionize the way juries deliberate; no reform can completely address such problems as apathy, lack of intelligence, and hidden bias.[87] Still, on balance, the proposals we have mentioned make sense and deserve to be tried, at least on an experimental basis.

But a reform movement based on empowerment of the jury can go too far. For example, one seemingly reasonable suggestion is to permit jurors to discuss evidence when it is presented, instead of prohibiting discussions until the beginning of formal deliberations at the end of the trial. Proponents of this reform note that the current rules violate the natural rules governing human information processing. In addition, they cite several benefits that might result from ending the ban on predeliberation discussions. For example, communication with other jurors might enhance overall comprehension of what is transpiring in the courtroom. Impressions about witnesses and questions about testimony can be raised before they are forgotten. Tentative and unsound judgments might be debunked early by others in the group.[88]

We disagree with this proposal, however. Although it is true that the ban on early discussion is somewhat unnatural, frequently violated, and unpleasant, we believe it serves an important purpose. We cannot prevent jurors from forming early impressions and judgments. But such viewpoints solidify when they are publicly expressed. Thus, allowing jurors to engage in predeliberation discussions can lead to some individual jurors becoming entrenched in their positions before the trial has concluded. Moreover, an early group consensus would essentially shut down receptivity to material presented later in the case, due to a don't-question-the-group mentality.[89] In evaluating reforms, we should remember that juries sometimes work as well as they do, not because jurors control the courtroom situation, but rather because they are controlled by it.

Over the centuries, the justice system has evolved a number of constraints designed to enable jurors to make better decisions than they otherwise might, had they possessed all the facts and complete freedom to process them as they please. The reason for such constraints is not that the public is deemed more base, less intelligent, or less capable than the legal professionals who design and run the system. Rather, juror freedom is curtailed because we know from research as well as long years of experience that human beings, faced with tough decisions, tend to weight certain types of information inappropriately.

Thus, we believe that tighter judicial control of courtroom proceedings can often lead to better decisionmaking. Such control is especially important when lawyers use excessive theatrics or bring prejudicial and irrelevant evidence into the courtroom. Strict application of the rules of evidence can protect jurors from influences that may lead them astray. The O.J. Simpson criminal trial is often cited as an emblem of what happens when a judge fails to exercise sufficient control. The Diallo case, in contrast, shows how a competent judge can prevent a potentially explosive trial from degenerating into jury manipulation. The American Bar Association correctly urges judges, especially in high-profile cases, to ". . . issue detailed rules of conduct from the get-go, putting lawyers and prosecutors on notice that violations will meet swift and severe punishment."[90]

Many jury critics advocate empowering jurors in yet another way—by informing them of their power to nullify the law.[91] In the early days of the American jury, panel members were permitted to render judgment on the law as well as the facts. Gradually, during the nineteenth century, courts limited the role of jurors to that of deciding the facts, requiring that they accept the law as interpreted by the judge. Nothing could be done if jurors chose to disobey; they retained the *power* to nullify but not the legal right. Sometimes, the exercise of that power was inspiring, as when Northern juries prior to the Civil War would often refuse to convict those who had helped runaway slaves get to freedom. Other times, it was despicable, as when Southern juries, after the war, would frequently fail to convict whites who had committed crimes against blacks. More recently, juries have sometimes failed to convict, despite sufficient evidence, defendants charged in a variety of cases ranging from drug possession to mercy killing.

The current debate does not concern the power to nullify; everyone concedes that jurors have that power. Rather, disagreement centers on whether judges should inform panels that they possess the power to reject the law or not apply it in a given instance, and whether lawyers should be permitted to make arguments to the jury urging nullification.

In the middle of the nineteenth century, while the right to nullify was gradually being whittled away, the radical thinker Lysander Spooner offered a classic defense of the practice. He wrote:

> For more than six hundred years—that is, since Magna Carta, in 1215—there has been no clearer principle of English or American constitutional law, than that, in criminal cases, it is not only the right and duty of juries to judge what are the facts, what is the law, and what was the moral intent of the accused; but that it is also their right, and their primary and paramount duty, to judge the justice of the law, and to hold all laws invalid, that are, in their opinion, unjust or oppressive, and all persons guiltless in violating, or resisting the execution of, such law. Unless such be the right and duty of jurors, it is plain that, instead of juries being a 'palladium of liberty'—a barrier against the tyranny and oppression of the government—they are really mere tools in its hands, for carrying into execution any injustice and oppression it may desire to have executed.[92]

More recently, an outspoken advocate of jury nullification has asserted, "Either openly displayed or hidden, nullification remains a timeless strategy for jurors seeking to bring law into line with their conscience. This reconciliation is what the jury system is about, for better or worse. . . . [As] long as we have juries, we will have nullification and verdicts according to conscience. Some of those verdicts will outrage us, others will inspire us. But always nullification will give us the full drama of democracy."[93]

If law professor Paul Butler has his way, part of that drama can verge on a race war. Butler has called on black jurors to use nullification as a means of combating what he perceives as a justice system oppressive to blacks, one that lands too many black males in prison. Thus, he suggests that for crimes such as theft and perjury, ". . . there need be no presumption in favor of nullification, but it ought to be an option the juror considers. A juror might vote for acquittal, for example, when a poor woman steals from Tiffany's but not when the same woman steals from her next-door neighbor."[94] For Butler, "Difficult scenarios would include the drug dealer who operates in the ghetto and the thief who burglarizes the home of a rich white family."[95] Butler's views have generated little enthusiasm among responsible legal scholars.[96]

Indeed, his proposal provides a glimpse of the anarchy that might result if lawyers routinely argued to jurors' broader conceptions of justice rather than to the demands of the law in the particular case at issue. The jury system generally works best and produces the highest consistency of results when jurors render their decisions within traditionally prescribed boundaries and rules. A trial is not a free and open democratic debate over policy, nor should it be; it is a highly constrained, intelligently devised, time-tested procedure for allowing citizen jurors to review appropriate evidence to determine facts.

In the *Federalist Papers*, Alexander Hamilton noted that if the supporters and adversaries of the plan developed at the Constitutional Convention agreed about nothing else, they concurred ". . . at least in the value they set upon the trial by jury; or if there is any difference between them it consists in this: the former regard it as a valuable safeguard to liberty; the latter represent it as the very palladium of free government."[97]

ACKNOWLEDGMENTS

Many trial consultants gave generously of their time, sharing with us count-less stories, opinions, and insights. We would particularly like to thank Philip K. Anthony and Michael Cobo of DecisionQuest; Beth Bonora, for-merly of National Jury Project and now with Bonora D'Andrea; Cynthia R. Cohen of Verdict Success; David Island, formerly of Trial Behavior Consulting Incorporated and Forensic Technologies International and now affiliated with Tsongas Litigation Consulting; Florence Keller of Trial Analysis Group; Judy Rothschild of National Jury Project; Marjorie Sommer of The Litigation Edge; Howard Varinsky, Michael Przekop, and Eleanore Zicherman. We suspect that some, perhaps most, trial consultants will disagree with our central conclusions regarding this fascinating but controversial industry. Nonetheless, we hope that they will recognize in this book an attempt to depict their profession accurately and fairly, even where their final assessments would differ from our own.

Among the jury scholars we interviewed, we owe a particular debt to the colorful and probing perspectives of professors Solomon Fulero, Gary Moran, and Michael Saks. Special thanks are due also to attorneys Mark Baute, Peter Gelblum, J. Gary Gwilliam, John Kidd, and Robert Wallach, who shared with us their experiences in the world of high-stakes litigation.

Several individuals were extraordinarily kind in sharing insights con-cerning cases discussed in Chapter 2: Martha Coakley, now District At-torney of Middlesex County, Massachusetts, and Gerard Leone, now As-sistant Attorney General of Massachusetts, who spoke candidly about their prosecution of the Louise Woodward "nanny" case; defense attorney Andrew Good, who offered a discerning view from the other side; and at-torneys William Stanton and Michael Hardy, who provided essential perspectives from opposing sides of Stephen Pagones's defamation suit against Al Sharpton, Alton Maddox, and C. Vernon Mason.

Michael Liskin's enthusiastic and energetic contributions as our West Coast interviewer were indispensable.

Many colleagues and friends read portions of the manuscript, or otherwise encouraged us and provided support, at various stages of the project. We would like to express our gratitude to attorneys Gage Andretta, Roger Breene, Matt Boxer, Michelle Gerber, Tricia Lawrence, Laurie O'Sullivan, Jerry Ostow, David Samson, Michelle Schaap, Evans Wohlforth, and Joe Zawila; psychologists Tom Haver, Tom Heinzen, and Kate Makarec; Adam Brodsky of the *New York Post*; Mathi Fuchs, Steven Gorelick, Amy Hopper, Robbin Itzler, Albert Lasher, Mary Beth Zeman, Jud Taylor, and Lynn Kressel.

We would also like to thank Justice Gary S. Stein of the New Jersey Supreme Court, whose commitment to judicial excellence is an inspiration and whose warm encouragement was invaluable.

We are deeply indebted to the editors with whom we have worked on this project: Linda Greenspan Regan, who first helped define the topic, and Leo Wiegman, whose light but incisive hand was instrumental in shaping it. The entire team at Perseus/Westview, including David Goehring, Holly Hodder, Trish Goodrich, Meegan Finnegan, Barbara Greer, and Steve Catalano, has been outstanding. We are grateful to Jon Taylor Howard for his diligent and careful copyediting. Our agent, Susan Ann Protter—as always—has been terrific.

The book's merits owe much to the many who have aided us. Perhaps needless to say in a book so filled with controversial judgments, we bear full responsibility for its flaws.

We would, lastly, like to thank our families for their support and encouragement—especially our mothers, Betty Kressel and Sara Fuchs, and the products of our other collaboration, Samuel Warren Kressel and Hannah Yael Kressel, who delight and inspire us every day.

We dedicate this book to the memory of our fathers, Morris Kressel and Warren Fuchs. For honesty, dignity, love, and the pursuit of excellence, we could have hoped for no better role models.

ABOUT THE AUTHORS

NEIL J. KRESSEL is a social psychologist who holds a Ph.D. from Harvard University. Currently Professor of Psychology at William Paterson University of New Jersey, he has taught at Harvard, New York University, and elsewhere. During the past decade, Dr. Kressel has written frequently on psychology and public policy for the popular press, as well as for many leading scholarly journals. His most recent book, *Mass Hate: The Global Rise of Genocide and Terror*, was selected by *Choice Magazine* as an outstanding book of 1996. In a review, the *Washington Post* commented that "Kressel has a jeweler's eye for deflating grandiose conjecture, especially when tainted by ideology. . . . [He] is free of bias. . . . It is easy to develop confidence in the author's discernment."

Dr. Kressel has been interviewed on MSNBC-TV, Fox News Network TV, The History Channel, National Public Radio, the AP radio network, Monitor radio network, Voice of America, and numerous other radio and television programs.

DORIT F. KRESSEL holds a J.D. from Fordham University, where she was Editor-in-Chief of *Fordham Law Review*. Prior to entering private practice, Ms. Kressel served as a law clerk to the New Jersey Supreme Court. She has taught business law and contracts to graduate and undergraduate university students.

NOTES

CHAPTER 1

1. At the time of the rail yard incident, Louisiana law provided that only those companies that handled, stored, or transported the leaky chemicals could be assessed punitive damages. Because Phillips Petroleum did not own the tank car when the butadiene leaked, it could not be held liable for punitive damages. This account of the rail fire case draws primarily on the following sources: John M. Broder, "Stares of Lawyerly Disbelief at a Huge Civil Award," *New York Times*, September 10, 1997, D1; Carol Marie Cropper, "Jury in CSX Case Sent Angry Message with a $3.4 Billion Stamp," *New York Times*, September 15, 1997, D1; Allen R. Myerson, "Supreme Court in Louisiana Blocks Award in CSX Case," *New York Times*, November 1, 1997, D3; Editorial, "Review & Outlook: Louisiana Jackpot," *Wall Street Journal*, September 18, 1997, A14; Associated Press, "Tanker Burns in New Orleans," *New York Times*, September 10, 1987, A29.

2. Pamela Coyle, "Gentilly Tank Car Damages Slashed; State Judge Finds Award Excessive," *[New Orleans] Times-Picayune*, November 6, 1999, A01. Following this reduction in verdict, CSX pursued an appeal, seeking a further reduction of the damages award. At the time of this writing, the appeal was pending. Susan Finch, "Railroad Attorneys Dispute Damages; CSX Tells Appellate Judges Tank Car Spill Not Its Fault," *[New Orleans] The Times-Picayune*, January 13, 2001, Metro 1.

3. Sanjoy Hazarika, "Bhopal Payments by Union Carbide Set at $470 Million," *New York Times*, February 15, 1989, A1.

4. Broder, "Stares of Lawyerly Disbelief," D2.

5. Cropper, "Jury in CSX Case," D2.

6. Broder, "Stares of Lawyerly Disbelief," D2.

7. Cropper, "Jury in CSX Case," D1.

8. Cropper, "Jury in CSX Case," D1, D2.

9. Editorial, "Review & Outlook: Louisiana Jackpot," A14. Notably, the Louisiana legislature enacted legislation in 1996 that greatly limited punitive damages, as part of a comprehensive program of tort reform, but these changes did not affect the CSX case, which had been filed many years earlier. Ibid.

10. Editorial, *[New Orleans] The Times-Picayune*, September 11, 1997, quoted in "Reaction to the New Orleans Judgment," on the CSX Corporation website, accessed May 10, 1999, available from http://www.csx.com/med/reaction.html, Internet.

11. This section is based on interviews conducted by our assistant Michael Liskin with Philip Anthony and John Kidd, as well as on Liskin's observations of the mock trial.

12. John Kidd, interview by Michael Liskin, tape recording, Burlingame, California, June 16, 1998.

13. Ibid. Perhaps Kidd is familiar with DecisonQuest's pamphlet on "Voodoo Jurynomics," warning against "pseudo-clairvoyants," "self-styled panel-pickers," and "jury selection hucksters." See Ross

P. Laguzza, *Voodoo Jurynomics: Self-Styled Panel-Pickers Deceive Lawyers, Media and the Public* (Los Angeles: DecisionQuest brochure), reprinted from *Los Angeles Daily Journal*, April 9, 1997.

14. Philip K. Anthony, interview by Michael Liskin, tape recording, Burlingame, California, June 16, 1998.

15. Christie Davies, "Trial by Jury Should Be Abolished," in *The Jury System*, edited by Mary E. Williams (San Diego: Greenhaven Press, 1997), 20, reprinted from Christie Davis, "Trial by Judges," *National Review*, May 24, 1993.

16. This pithy remark has been attributed repeatedly to Clarence Darrow, but we have been unable to track it to a primary source. It may be apocryphal. Nonetheless, Darrow did write that "selecting a jury is of the utmost importance." Clarence Darrow, "Attorney for the Defense," *Esquire Magazine* (May 1936), reprinted in Clarence Darrow, *Verdicts out of Court*, edited by Arthur Weinberg and Lila Weinberg (Chicago: Ivan R. Dee, 1989), 315.

17. Albert S. Osborn, *The Mind of the Juror as Judge of the Facts or The Layman's View of the Law: A Study of the Contentious Trial* (Albany, New York: Boyd Printing, 1937), 16. Osborn's comments refer primarily to cases requiring unanimous verdicts.

18. Ibid., 22–24.

19. Harold J. Rothwax, *Guilty: The Collapse of Criminal Justice* (New York: Random House, 1996), 200–201.

20. *United States v. Wood*, 299 U.S. 123, 145–146 (1936).

21. Henry Louis Gates Jr., "Marketing Justice: What, Really, Are Juries For?" *New Yorker*, February 24 and March 3, 1997, 11, quoted in "Developments in the Law: The Civil Jury," *Harvard Law Review* 110 (May 1997): 1422, note 7. The *Harvard Law Review* article discusses several defenses of the jury system.

22. Jeffrey Abramson, *We, the Jury: The Jury System and the Ideal of Democracy* (New York: Basic-Books, 1994; paperback ed., 1995), 2.

23. See, for example, Robert S. Erikson, Norman R. Luttbeg, and Kent L. Tedin, *American Public Opinion: Its Origin, Content, and Impact*, 4th ed. (New York: Macmillan, 1991).

24. Ibid., 46.

25. Ibid., 89.

26 W. Russell Neuman, "The Paradox of Mass Politics: Knowledge and Opinion in the American Electorate," in *Political Psychology: Classic and Contemporary Readings*, edited by Neil J. Kressel (New York: Paragon House, 1993), 252–274.

27. *Batson v. Kentucky*, 476 U.S. 79 (1986).

28. See, for example, *J.E.B. v. Alabama*, 511 U.S. 127 (1994) (prohibiting gender-based peremptory challenges); *Georgia v. McCollum*, 505 U.S. 42 (1992) (ruling that the *Batson* prohibition on race-based peremptory challenges applies to the exercise of the challenge by the defense as well as by the prosecution); *Edmondson v. Leesville Concrete Co.*, 500 U.S. 614 (1991) (ruling that the *Batson* prohibition on race-based peremptory challenges applies to private litigants in civil cases); *Powers v. Ohio*, 499 U.S. 400 (1991) (prohibiting race-based peremptory challenges regardless of whether the challenged juror and the defendant are of the same race).

29. Morton Hunt, "Putting Juries on the Couch," *New York Times Magazine*, November 28, 1982, 70; see also, Valerie P. Hans and Neil Vidmar, *Judging the Jury* (New York: Plenum Press, 1986), 79–80.

30. American Society of Trial Consultants, *Membership Directory, 1999–2000* (Towson, Maryland: American Society of Trial Consultants, 1999), 185. See also, Kate Rix, "Jury Consultants Play Meatier Role in Trial Prep: Seeking an Edge, Litigators Run Their Show Past Mock Jurors—and Listen Carefully," *National Law Journal*, August 7, 2000, A13.

31. Hans and Vidmar, *Judging the Jury*, 90. Consultants are less willing now to promote themselves on the basis of win-loss records than they once were. The Code of Professional Standards of the American Society of Trial Consultants, the code of conduct to which its members must subscribe, discourages publication of such ratios, instructing: "The trial consultant may advertise services. Such advertisement avoids material misrepresentation of qualifications, experience, research, or trial outcomes. Client permission is obtained prior to the placement of any advertisement that identifies a client or case. The trial consultant does not publish a claim to a win-loss record." ASTC Code of Professional Standards, Section V, in American Society of Trial Consultants, *Membership Directory 1999–2000*, 11. As one commentator on the code explains in the industry newsletter, "Let us not forget, anxious though we may be to crow over how our brilliant input saved at least a dozen clients from certain ruin within the last year alone, we do not win or lose cases. The attorneys we serve win or lose cases. Or as our clients would claim, the attorneys we serve win cases. Judges lose the others for them. A win-loss record does not belong in an advertisement." Bob Gerchen, "ASTC Code of Professional Standards Commentary," *Court Call* (Summer 1998), 7.

32. Chapter 4 of this book reviews research directly addressing the efficacy of trial consultants. The following sources summarize empirical research on the jury system in general, much of which is relevant to the potential impact of trial consulting: Harry Kalven Jr. and Hans Zeisel, *The American Jury* (Boston: Little, Brown, 1966; Chicago: University of Chicago Press, 1971 [Phoenix ed.]); Rita J. Simon, *The Jury: Its Role in American Society* (Lexington, Massachusetts: D.C. Heath, 1980); Norbert L. Kerr and Robert M. Bray, eds., *The Psychology of the Courtroom* (New York: Academic Press, 1982); Reid Hastie, Steven D. Penrod, and Nancy Pennington, *Inside the Jury* (Cambridge, Massachusetts: Harvard University Press, 1983); Valerie P. Hans and Neil Vidmar, *Judging the Jury* (New York: Plenum Press, 1986); Saul M. Kassin and Lawrence S. Wrightsman, *The American Jury on Trial: Psychological Perspectives* (New York: Hemisphere Publishing Corp., 1988); Reid Hastie, ed., *Inside the Juror: The Psychology of Juror Decision Making*, Cambridge Series on Judgment and Decision Making (New York: Cambridge University Press, 1993; 1st paperback ed., 1994); Neil Vidmar, *Medical Malpractice and the American Jury: Confronting the Myths about Jury Incompetence, Deep Pockets, and Outrageous Damage Awards* (Ann Arbor: University of Michigan Press, 1995; 1st paperback ed., 1997); Irwin A. Horowitz, Thomas E. Willging, and Kenneth S. Bordens, *The Psychology of Law: Integrations and Applications*, 2nd ed. (New York: Addison-Wesley, 1998); Lawrence S. Wrightsman, *Forensic Psychology* (Belmont, California: Wadsworth, 2001); Curt R. Bartol and Anne M. Bartol, *Psychology and Law: Research and Application*, 2nd ed. (Pacific Grove, California: Brooks/Cole Publishing, 1994).

33. National Jury Project (Elissa Krauss and Beth Bonora, eds.), *Jurywork: Systematic Techiques*, 2nd ed. (St. Paul, Minnesota: West Group/Clark Boardman Callaghan, 1999), vol. 2, release no. 20, December 1999, App. A–3.

34. Joseph B. Kadane, "Sausages and the Law: Juror Decisions in the Much Larger Justice System," in Hastie, ed., *Inside the Juror*, 229.

CHAPTER 2

1. Judge David Peeples's comments were made at a panel meeting during the 1998 annual national conference of the American Society of Trial Consultants in San Antonio, Texas, June 5, 1998. The panel, "Jury Selection and Jury Consultants: A View from the Bench," also included Judge Fred Biery of the U.S. District Court for the Western District of Texas, and Judge Charles Gonzalez of the 57th District Court, Bexar County, Texas. Judges Biery and Gonzalez indicated that they, too, rarely know whether a consultant has contributed to a case before their court.

2. Deborah Eappen, October 31, 1997, speaking in court prior to the sentencing of Louise Woodward, as quoted in Carey Goldberg, "Quietly Avowing Innocence, Nanny Is Sentenced to Life," *New York Times*, November 1, 1997, A10.

3. Louise Woodward, October 31, 1997, speaking in court prior to being sentenced, as quoted in Goldberg, "Quietly Avowing Innocence," A10.

4. The foregoing account is based principally on reporting in the *New York Times*, on Court TV, and on the Court TV website.

5. *Commonwealth v. Woodward*, 7 Mass. L. Rptr. 449, 1997 WL 694119, at *3 (Super. Ct. Nov. 10, 1997) (vacating life sentence imposed 10/31/97 and reducing jury's verdict from murder to involuntary manslaughter), *aff'd*, 427 Mass. 659, 694 N.E.2d 1277 (1998).

6. "British Au Pair Chooses 'All or Nothing' Verdict," CNN Interactive [Online], October 27, 1997, accessed February 10, 2001, available from http://www.cnn.com/US/9710/27/au.pair.trial/index.html, Internet.

7. Ibid.

8. Jean McMillan, "Jury Would Have Considered Lesser Charge in Au Pair Trial," *Seattle Times*, November 3, 1997, accessed August 11, 1998, available from http://www.seattletimes.com/extra/browse/html97/nann_110397.html, Internet; Carey Goldberg, "Protesters Back Au Pair in 2 Towns Far Apart," *New York Times*, November 4, 1997, A25.

9. "Juror in Au Pair Trial Explains Murder Verdict," *New York Times*, November 3, 1997, A19.

10. "Juror: Panel Believed Nanny Didn't Intend to Kill," CNN Interactive [Online], November 2, 1997, accessed October 28, 2000, available from http://www.cnn.com/US/9711/02/nanny.britain/index.html, Internet.

11. Ibid.

12. Goldberg, "Protesters Back Au Pair," A25.

13. Michael Bezdek, "Juror in Au Pair Case Says Speculation about How They Reached Verdict Is 'Crazy,'" *Boston Globe*, November 1, 1997, accessed August 11, 1998, available from http://www.boston.com/globe/latest/daily/01/juror.html, Internet.

14. Ibid.; Edward Rothstein, "Technology: The Internet in the Courtroom Results in More Clamor than Consensus," *New York Times*, November 24, 1997, D4; Gallup, CNN, U.S.A. Today Poll, national telephone survey of 1,003 adults conducted November 6–9, 1997, Public Opinion Online (Roper Center at University of Connecticut, 1997), accessed October 28, 2000, available from LEXIS-NEXIS Academic universe, http://wwwlexis-nexis.com/universe, Internet. The Gallup poll revealed that only 38 percent of respondents agreed with the jury that Woodward was responsible for Matthew Eappen's death, and of those respondents, only 30 percent agreed with the murder verdict, while 66 percent believed that Woodward should have been charged with a less serious crime.

15. Goldberg, "Protesters Back Au Pair," A25.

16. Stephen Jakobi, "Nanny Trial Reveals Flaw in U.S. Legal System," *National Law Journal*, November 17, 1997, accessed September 18, 1998, available from http://www.ljx.com/LJXfiles/aupair/nljop.html, Internet.

17. Maggie Scarf, "Lock 'er Up," *New Republic,* March 30, 1998, 14–15.

18. Pamela Ferdinand, "Freed Au Pair Extends Sympathy to Baby's Family," *Washington Post*, November 12, 1997, A3.

19. *Commonwealth v. Woodward*, 427 Mass. 659, 661, 694 N.E.2d 1277, 1281 (1998).

20. Commonwealth of Massachusetts Appeal Petition for Relief Pursuant to GL.C. 211 section 3, in *Commonwealth v. Woodward*, Supreme Judicial Court for Suffolk County, November 25, 1997, available from Court TV [Online], accessed September 23, 1998, http://www.courttv.com/trials/woodward/appeal.html, Internet. Judges in Massachusetts have more power to undo jury verdicts

than judges in many other jurisdictions; in most other states, if a judge concludes that a verdict is unjust, the judge can order a new trial but cannot unilaterally reduce the verdict. Naftali Bendavid, "State Law, Unusual Case Set Stage for Judge's Rare Move," *Chicago Tribune*, November 11, 1997, 10, accessed August 13, 1998, available from http://archives.chicago.tribune.com, Internet.

21. *Commonwealth v. Woodward*, 7 Mass. L. Rptr. 449, 1997 WL 694119, at *7 (Super. Ct. Nov. 10, 1997), *aff'd*, 427 Mass. 659, 694 N.E.2d 1277 (1998).

22. Ibid., *1.

23. Abramson, quoted in Tony Mauro and Richard Willing, "Zobel's Act Overshadows Other Aspects of the Case," *USA Today*, November 11, 1997, 2A.

24. Terry Moran, "In Camera," *New Republic*, December 8, 1997, 18.

25. Abramson, quoted in Mauro and Willing, "Zobel's Act," 2A.

26. "Barry Scheck on Massachusetts v. Woodward," Court TV Library [Online], accessed October 20, 2000, available from http://www.courttv.com/trials/woodward/scheck.html, Internet, quoting from Barry Scheck's November 6, 1997, interview on Court TV's *Cochran and Company*.

27. Bezdek, "Juror in Au Pair Case."

28. Gerard Leone and Martha Coakley were interviewed for this book by Neil J. Kressel, by telephone (Leone on October 14, 1998, and Coakley on October 16, 1998). Unless otherwise indicated, their comments come from these interviews. (Two members of the prosecution team fared rather well politically in the year following the trial. Thomas F. Reilly, the Middlesex County, Massachusetts, district attorney won election as the state attorney general, and Martha Coakley was elected to replace him as district attorney.)

29. Andrew Good, telephone interview by Neil J. Kressel, October 7, 1998. Unless otherwise indicated, this interview is the source of Good's remarks.

30. Another consulting firm, Demonstrative Evidence, Inc., prepared exhibits for the defense.

31. National Jury Project (Elissa Krauss and Beth Bonora, eds.), *Jurywork: Systematic Techiques*, 2nd ed. (St. Paul, Minnesota: West Group/Clark Boardman Callaghan, 1999), vol. 2, release no. 20, December 1999.

32. Leone explicitly denies using consultants to prepare his expert witnesses and claims that he performs this task himself. "I find out as much as I can about the scientifically relevant issues. I go through the data. I ask them to consider counter factual scenarios. [I ask] does that lead them to different conclusions."

33. *Commonwealth v. Woodward*, 7 Mass. L. Rptr. 449, 1997 WL 694119 (Super Ct. Nov. 10, 1997), *aff'd*, 427 Mass. 659, 694 N.E.2d 1277 (1998).

34. Ferdinand, "Freed Au Pair," A3.

35. Gallup Poll, national telephone survey of 623 adults conducted November 10, 1997, *Public Opinion Online* (Roper Center at University of Connecticut, 1997), accessed November 11, 2000, available from LEXIS-NEXIS Academic Universe, http://www.lexis-nexis.com/universe, Internet.

36. Carey Goldberg, "Pediatric Experts Express Doubt on Au Pair's Defense," *New York Times*, November 12, 1997, A14. Other medical experts around the country raised serious questions about the defense's "re-bleeding" theory. An article in the prestigious *New England Journal of Medicine* that did not focus specifically on the Woodward case but addressed more generally the type of injury sustained by Matthew Eappen drew a conclusion that could be read as strongly supportive of the jury verdict. It stated: "There is no evidence that traumatic acute subdural hematoma, particularly that leading to death, occurs in otherwise healthy infants in an occult or subclinical manner" (Ann-Christine Duhaime et al., "Nonaccidental Head Injury in Infants—The 'Shaken-Baby Syndrome,'" *New England Journal of Medicine* 338 [June 1998]: 825). This finding seems to undercut the defense

theory. See also Peter Wehrwein, "Scientific Review on Shaken-Baby Syndrome Undermines Legal Defence," *The [London] Lancet* 351 (June 1998): 1935.

37. *Commonwealth v. Woodward*, 427 Mass. 659, 693, 694 N.E.2d 1277, 1300 (1998) (Greaney, J., dissenting in part) (quoting transcript of sentencing hearing); Carey Goldberg, "In a Startling Turnabout, Judge Sets Au Pair Free," *New York Times*, November 11, 1997, A1.

38. "Martha Coakley on Massachusetts v. Woodward," Court TV Library [Online], accessed October 20, 2000, available from http://www.courttv.com/trials/woodward/coakley.html, Internet, quoting from Martha Coakley's November 10, 1997 interview on Court TV's *Cochran and Company.*

39. Ibid.

40. Ibid.

41. Bruce Fein, "Judge Mocks Jury System," *USA Today*, November 11, 1997, 14A.

42. *Othello*, III.iii.155–160, in *The Complete Works of William Shakespeare* (Feltham, England: Hamlyn Publishing Group Ltd. [Spring Books], 1958), 996.

43. William Glaberson, "The Case That Haunts Sharpton," *New York Times*, October 24, 1997, B4. This account of Steven Pagones's suit against Sharpton, Maddox, and Mason draws heavily on reporting from the *New York Times*, particularly by Frank Bruni and William Glaberson.

44. "The Defaming Statements," *New York Times*, July 14, 1998, B5.

45. Ibid.

46. Ibid.

47. Ibid.

48. *Report of the Grand Jury Concerning the Tawana Brawley Investigation*, Court TV [Online], accessed October 20, 2000, available from http://www.courttv.com/legaldocs/newsmakers/tawana-part4.html, Internet.

49. Ibid.

50. James Barron, "Grand Jury Found Nothing to Back Claim," *New York Times*, December 4, 1997, B12.

51. *New York Times Co. v. Sullivan*, 376 U.S. 254, 279–280 (1964).

52 Frank Bruni, "For Plaintiff in Brawley Suit, a Higher Standard to Win," *New York Times*, December 30, 1997, B1. See also Dareh Gregorian and Rita Delfiner, "Criticizing Officials Is OK— Just Don't Lie," *New York Post*, July 15, 1998, 6.

53. Bruni, "For Plaintiff in Brawley Suit, a Higher Standard to Win," B4.

54. Frank Bruni, "Defendant Becomes an Issue in Slander Case," *New York Times*, December 10, 1997, B5.

55. Jim Yardley, "Brawley Comes to Rally and Repeats Charge of an Attack," *New York Times*, December 3, 1997, B1.

56. Ibid.; Mirta Ojito, "In Brooklyn, Brawley Insists She Was Victim," *New York Times*, August 16, 1998, 34.

57. Richard T. Pienciak, "Suit's Long Journey Began with Brawley," *[New York] Daily News*, July 27, 1997, 2. On October 9, 1998, Judge S. Barrett Hickman decided that Brawley must pay $185,000 for defaming Stephen Pagones. In his decision, he said that she could have been ordered to pay much more inasmuch as she had "literally thumbed her nose" at the court by refusing to testify. He limited the size of the award because he had the sense that she was a woman "caught up in her own fiction" and because she might have been manipulated by her family and advisers. Judge Hickman further commented, "It is probable that in the history of this state, never has a teenager turned the prosecutorial and judicial systems literally upside down with such false claims." "Judge Orders Brawley to Pay $185,000 for Defamation," *New York Times*, October 10, 1998, B7.

58. See, for example, Adam Nagourney, "News Analysis: More Is at Play in Runoff Than Outcome of Vote," *New York Times on the Web*, September 15, 1997, accessed November 13, 1998, available from http://www.nytimes.com, Internet.

59. William Glaberson, "Sharpton Lawyer Says Brawley Case Is Test of Civil Rights," *New York Times*, July 2, 1998, B4.

60. Frank Bruni, "Brawley Adviser Says Checking Claim Was 'Not My Role,'" *New York Times*, December 5, 1997, B6.

61. Clyde Haberman, "3 Defendants Deftly Juggle the Facts," *New York Times*, July 10, 1998, B1.

62. Frank Bruni, "On the Stand in the Brawley Trial, Sharpton Likens Himself to King," *New York Times*, February 10, 1998, B7.

63. Ibid., A1.

64. Ibid., B7.

65. Haberman, "3 Defendants," B1

66. Frank Bruni, "In Brawley Case, Racial Composition of Jury Pool Is Questioned," *New York Times*, November 20, 1997, B6; Frank Bruni, "Delays and Tactics Anger Judge in Brawley Case," *New York Times*, November 21, 1997, B6; Frank Bruni, "Jury and Alternates Selected in Sharpton Defamation Suit," *New York Times*, November 27, 1997, B12. See also Frank Bruni, "A Protest Opens Defamation Trial of Brawley's Advisers," *New York Times*, November 19, 1997, B5.

67. Bruni, "In Brawley Case," B6.

68. Bruni, "Delays and Tactics," B6.

69. Bruni, "Jury and Alternates Selected," B12.

70. Ibid.

71. Frank Bruni, "Juror Subject of Complaint on Behavior," *New York Times*, January 24, 1998, B6; Frank Bruni, "Woman Released from Brawley Trial Jury," *New York Times*, January 29, 1998, B7.

72. Bruni, "Woman Released from Brawley Trial Jury," B7.

73. Frank Bruni, "Arguments, and Tirades, Begin in Brawley Defamation Suit," *New York Times*, December 4, 1997, B1; Frank Bruni, "Defense Team in Brawley Case Calls Lawyer's Remark Racist," *New York Times*, December 18, 1997, B4; William Glaberson, "Plaintiff and Sharpton Lawyer Trade Barbs at Brawley Trial," *New York Times*, April 2, 1998, B4; William Glaberson, "Sharpton's Lawyer Is Given Contempt Threat by Judge," *New York Times*, April 7, 1998, B5.

74. William Glaberson, "$345,000 Damages Awarded in Brawley Defamation Case," *New York Times*, July 30, 1998, A1; Jim Fitzgerald, "Sharpton Calls $65,000 Slander Judgment a Victory," *Bergen [New Jersey] Record*, July 31, 1998, accessed August 10, 1998, available from http://www.bergen.com/region/brawl31199807313.html, Internet; "Sharpton Plans to Appeal Pagones Verdict," MSNBC [Online], July 30, 1998, accessed August 25, 1998, available from http://www.msnbc.com/local/WNBC/108619.asp, Internet; Associated Press, "3 Fined for Defamation in Brawley Case," *Chicago Tribune*, July 30, 1998, 3.

75 Sharpton also repeated his defamatory charges after the grand jury report, in a *Spin* magazine interview, but Pagones discovered the article too late to include it in the suit.

76. David M. Halbfinger, "Jurors Say They Wanted to Teach a Lesson, but Without Rancor," *New York Times*, July 30, 1998, B5. Other juror quotes come from the following articles: William Glaberson, "$345,000 Damages Awarded in Brawley Defamation Case," *New York Times*, July 30, 1998, A1; "Sharpton Plans to Appeal Pagones Verdict," available from http://www.msnbc.com/local/WNBC/108619.asp, Internet; Jim Fitzgerald, "Sharpton Calls $65,000 Slander Judgment a Victory," *Bergen [New Jersey] Record*, July 31, 1998, accessed August 10, 1998, available from http://www..bergen.com/region/brawl31199807313.html, Internet; William Glaberson and David M. Halbfinger, "Race Issue Permeated Brawley Case, Some Jurors Say," *New York Times on*

the Web, July 31, 1998, accessed November 13, 1998, available from http://www.nytimes.com, Internet.

77. Quoted in Glaberson and Halbfinger, "Race Issue Permeated Brawley Case."

78. Halbfinger, "Jurors Say They Wanted to Teach a Lesson," B5.

79. Quoted in Glaberson and Halbfinger, "Race Issue Permeated Brawley Case."

80. Ibid.

81. Ibid.

82. Ibid.

83 Ibid.

84. Ibid.

85. William Glaberson, "Jury Begins Considering Amount to Award Pagones in Damages," *New York Times*, July 15, 1998, B4.

86. Halbfinger, "Jurors Say They Wanted to Teach a Lesson," B5.

87. "Sharpton Plans to Appeal Pagones Verdict," available from http://www.msnbc.com/local/WNBC/108619.asp, Internet; Glaberson and Halbfinger, "Race Issue Permeated Brawley Case."

88. Glaberson, "$345,000 Damages Awarded," B5.

89. "Sharpton Plans to Appeal Pagones Verdict," available from http://www.msnbc.com/local/WNBC/108619.asp, Internet.

90. Jim Yardley, "Rage a Decade Ago, but Now, Alienation," *New York Times*, July 15, 1998, B1.

91. In July 2000, a state appellate court dismissed the appeal filed by Sharpton, Maddox, and Mason two years earlier. However, Tawana Brawley's three advisers continued to seek means of overturning the verdict. See David W. Chen, "Reviving Brawley Case Drama, Defendant Vows to Fight Verdict," *New York Times*, July 15, 2000, B1; Associated Press, "Court Rejects Appeal by an Ex-Brawley Adviser," October 27, 2000, B3.

92. Glaberson, "$345,000 Damages Awarded," B5.

93. Fitzgerald, "Sharpton Calls $65,000 Slander Judgment a Victory."

94. Glaberson, "$345,000 Damages Awarded," B5.

95. Fitzgerald, "Sharpton Calls $65,000 Slander Judgment a Victory." Following the Pagones slander trial, Sharpton's activism resumed with new fury. He orchestrated a series of protests in New York City concerning the police shooting of unarmed African immigrant Amadou Diallo (see our discussion of that case in Chapter 6) and took the lead in organizing civil disobedience in response to the police shooting of four minority men stopped on the New Jersey Turnpike. See, for example, Adam Miller, "Rev. Al Sets Deadline in N.J. Shooting," *New York Post* [Online], accessed April 26, 1999, available from http://www.nypostonline.com/news/8634.html, Internet; Dave Goldiner, "Rev. Al Presses Reno," *[New York] Daily News*, August 26, 2000, 8. More than two years after the verdict, Pagones still had not collected the award. By late October 2000, Sharpton had paid $4,702. Mason had paid $2,660, and Maddox hadn't paid anything. Sharpton announced in December 2000 that he could not afford to pay the judgment entered against him. See Alan Feuer, "Asking How Sharpton Pays for Those Suits: Case Offers a Glimpse of His Finances," *New York Times*, December 21, 2000, B1; Associated Press, "Court Rejects Appeal by an Ex-Brawley Adviser," B3.

96. Fitzgerald, "Sharpton Calls $65,000 Slander Judgment a Victory."

97. The white jurors' admiration for Sharpton, Maddox, and Mason is not shared by a majority of whites and possibly not by most blacks either. In September 1996, the Marist College Institute for Public Opinion polled more than 400 registered Democrats in New York City regarding their impressions of Mayor Rudolph Giuliani's potential Democratic challengers for the 1997 mayoral election. In response to the question, "Please tell me if you have a favorable or unfavorable impression of each [of the following public officials]," 64.8 percent of respondents reported having an unfavorable

impression of Sharpton, whereas only 22.6 percent reported having a favorable impression. Only 2.4 percent of respondents had not heard of Sharpton; 10.2 percent were unsure about their impression of him. Lee M. Miringoff and Barbara L. Carvalho, Marist College Institute for Public Opinion, September 30, 1996, accessed November 13, 1988, available from http://www.mipo.marist.edudocs/nycpolls/960930.html, Internet.

98. William Glaberson, "Sharpton Lawyer Asks Leniency as Jury Weighs Damages," *New York Times*, July 28, 1998, B4. Other quotes from the closing arguments come from this article.

99. Michael Hardy, telephone interview by Neil J. Kressel, October 7, 1998. Unless otherwise indicated, this interview is the source of Hardy's remarks.

100. William E. Stanton, telephone interview by Neil J. Kressel, October 15, 1998. Unless otherwise indicated, this interview is the source of Stanton's remarks.

101. See Chapter 1; see also, Morton Hunt, "Putting Juries on the Couch," *New York Times Magazine*, November 28, 1982, 70.

102. Robert Wallach, interview by Michael Liskin, tape recording, San Francisco, California, April 8, 1998.

103. Quoted in Michele Galen, "The Best Jurors Money Can Pick," *Business Week*, June 15, 1992, 108.

104. Wallach interview, April 8, 1998. Wallach notes that "there is a fair amount of hype in the business." He continues, "The problem is—and it is a problem that works to the benefit of the jury consultants . . . most trial lawyers don't have sufficient jury experience to really evaluate whether their consultant is truly effective so they tend to rely upon surrogate indices—[academic] degrees, resources. . . . Generally speaking, the more expensive [consultants] are, the more they think they are highly qualified." See also, James W. McElhaney, "The Jury Consultant Bazaar," *ABA Journal* (November 1998), 78.

105. Andrew C. Meyer Jr., quoted in Jordan E. Cohn, "Reading the Minds of the Jury," *American Legion*, September 1990, 30.

106. Wallach interview, April 8, 1998.

107. Michael E. Cobo, interview by Michael Liskin, tape recording, Torrance, California, June 2, 1998.

108. Judy Rothschild, interview by Michael Liskin, tape recording, Oakland, California, June 11, 1998.

109. Amy Singer, "Selecting Jurors: What to Do about Bias," *Trial* (April 1996), 28.

110. Eric Oliver, "False Alarm: Can Trial Consultants Ruin Juries?" *Trial Diplomacy Journal* 18, no. 1 (January/February 1995): 14.

111. Gary Moran, interview by Neil J. Kressel, tape recording, Redondo Beach, California, March 6, 1998.

CHAPTER 3

1. A first-hand account of the Harrisburg Seven Trial can be found in J. Schulman, P. Shaver, R. Colman, B. Emrich, and R. Christie, "Recipe for a Jury," *Psychology Today* (May 1973), 37. See also, Stuart Fischoff, "'Recipe for a Jury' Revisited: A Balance Theory Prediction," *Journal of Applied Social Psychology* 9, no. 4 (1979): 335. Several books include useful histories of the early days of systematic jury selection, including: Valerie P. Hans and Neil Vidmar, *Judging the Jury* (New York: Plenum Press, 1986); Jeffrey Abramson, *We, the Jury: The Jury System and the Ideal of Democracy*

(New York: Basic Books, 1994; paperback ed., 1995); Saul M. Kassin and Lawrence S. Wrightsman, *The American Jury on Trial: Psychological Perspectives* (New York: Hemisphere, 1988). For background on the Berrigans, see Murray Polner and Jim O'Grady, *Disarmed and Dangerous: The Radical Life and Times of Daniel and Philip Berrigan, Brothers in Religious Faith and Civil Disobedience* (New York: Westview Press, 1998).

2. John B. McConahay, Courtney J. Mullin, and Jeffrey Frederick, "The Uses of Social Science in Trials with Political and Racial Overtones: The Trial of Joan Little," *Law and Contemporary Problems* 41, no. 1 (1977): 205, is a first-hand account. See also, Jeffrey T. Frederick, "Social Science Involvement in Voir Dire: Preliminary Data on the Effectiveness of 'Scientific Jury Selection,'" *Behavioral Sciences and the Law* 2, no. 4 (1984): 375. Other early uses of jury consultants are described in: Edward Tivnan, "Jury by Trial," *New York Times Magazine*, November 16, 1975, 30; Morton Hunt, "Putting Juries on the Couch," *New York Times Magazine*, November 28, 1982, 70.

3. The use of systematic jury selection in these trials has been well documented. See, for example, Michael J. Saks, "The Limits of Scientific Jury Selection: Ethical and Empirical," *Jurimetrics Journal* 17 (Fall 1976): 3.

4. Robert Wallach, interview by Michael Liskin, tape recording, San Francisco, California, April 8, 1998, offered useful recollections of the early days of trial advocacy education as well as other insights into the early growth of the trial consulting industry.

5. Not someone who defines himself solely by his work, Island described some of his outside interests in a brief biographical statement: "I collect hand-carved wood rabbits and Three Little Pigs stories. (Do the first two pigs escape to the house of their sibs, or are they eaten by the wolf? Is the wolf boiled in a pot of water in the end and eaten by the pigs, or does it escape to lead a better life away from the pigs? From 1890 on, the versions vary remarkably and present interesting moral and ethical dilemmas for the p-c late–1990's.) I'm an avid reader of techno-thriller novels, the author of a book on domestic violence, an accomplished gardener and an active supporter of selected social, environmental, civil rights and political causes. For further fun, rest, relaxation and yard work, I love to spend time at our family cabin at Lake Tahoe." David Island, "Get to Know the Nominees for the ASTC Board of Directors and Board Officers: David Island, Ph.D.," *Court Call* (Spring 1999), 8.

6. David Island, "Voice of Experience Column," *Court Call* (Winter 1998), 9.

7. Island recently left FTI to work on his own and with another prominent firm, Tsongas Litigation Consulting. See his biography on the Tsongas website, accessed February 16, 2001, available from http://www.tsongas.com/people/biographies/david.html, Internet.

8. The posttrial disposition of the case was not unusual. "After the verdict . . . [the supermarket's attorney] and the other side's attorney and the plaintiff . . . sit down. My client says to the plaintiff, 'You know, you may never see this money. We're going to appeal it as hard as we can. It's a wrong verdict. It'll be three, four, five years before you even see a penny, if that. But I'll make you a millionaire today. Do you want a check for a million dollars? There's somebody sitting in the next room and they're going to write it. . . . ' She took it."

9. David Island and Patrick Letellier, *Men Who Beat the Men Who Love Them: Battered Gay Men and Domestic Violence* (Binghamton, New York: Haworth Press, 1991).

10. John Grisham, *The Runaway Jury* (New York: Bantam Doubleday Dell, 1996), 33.

11. Ibid., 5.

12. Ibid., 6–7.

13. Edward M. Bodaken and George R. Speckart, "To Down a Stealth Juror, Strike First," *National Law Journal*, September 23, 1996, B7, accessed January 3, 2001, available from LEXIS-NEXIS Academic Universe, http://www.lexis-nexis.com/universe. Internet.

14. Ibid., p. B7.

15. Amitai Etzioni, "Science: Threatening the Jury Trial," *Washington Post*, May 26, 1974, p C3. This influential essay was reprinted with slight modifications under the title "Creating an Imbalance," *Trial* (November/December 1974), 28. The same issue carried a contrasting opinion by a prominent defense attorney. See Howard A. Moore Jr., "Redressing the Balance," *Trial* (November/December 1974), 29.

16. Amitai Etzioni, quoted in Stephen J. Adler, *The Jury: Disorder in the Court* (New York: Doubleday, 1994), 114.

17. Michele Galen, "The Best Jurors Money Can Pick," *Business Week*, June 15, 1992, 108.

18. Adler, *The Jury*, 113.

19. No author, "Interview: Stephen J. Adler," *American Legion* (June 1995), 58.

20. Abramson, *We, the Jury*, 174.

21. George Cantor, "Jury Tampering Insults Justice," *Detroit News*, October 14, 1995, accessed April 9, 1998, available from http://detnews.com/editpage/sat1014/cantor.html, Internet.

22. Harold J. Rothwax, *Guilty: The Collapse of Criminal Justice* (New York: Random House, 1996), 231–232.

23. Burton S. Katz, *Justice Overruled* (New York: Warner Books, 1997), 109.

24. "Developments in the Law: The Civil Jury," *Harvard Law Review* 110 (May 1997): 1466.

25. See, among others, Irwin A. Horowitz, Thomas E. Willging, and Kenneth S. Bordens, *The Psychology of Law: Integrations and Applications*, 2nd ed. (New York: Longman, 1998), 113.

26. Joseph J. Senna and Larry J. Siegel, *Introduction to Criminal Justice*, 7th ed. (New York: West, 1996), 470.

27. Bureau of Justice Statistics, *Report to the Nation on Crime and Justice*, 2nd ed. (Washington, D.C.: U.S. Government Printing Office, 1988), cited in ibid., 422.

28. Estimates of the number of jury trials vary in part because of differences in the way states define what counts as a jury trial. See Abramson, *We, the Jury*, 265. There are no confidence-inspiring estimates of how many trials use jury consultants, although one reporter sets the number at about 6,000 per year—apparently based on interviews with prominent consultants. See Bernard Gavzer, "Are Trial Consultants Good for Justice?" *Parade Magazine*, January 5, 1997, 20.

29. Abramson, *We, the Jury*, 6.

30. A Florida study showed that 61 percent of trial lawyers had never used a jury consultant, but about 6 percent had contracted their services six or more times. However, these estimates must be taken with a grain of salt due to a low response rate and other limitations. See Albert Gayoso, Brian L. Cutler, and Gary Moran, "Attorney Satisfaction with Trial Consulting Services," unpublished manuscript, Florida International University, Miami, Florida, 1993.

31. Ann Harriet Cole, "Remarks at Meeting of the American Society of Trial Consultants," June 4, 1998, La Mansion del Rio hotel, San Antonio, Texas.

32. Ann Harriet Cole, "From the President," *Court Call* (Spring 1999), 10.

33. Donald Zoeller, quoted in Stephen J. Adler, "Consultants Dope Out the Mysteries of Jurors for Clients Being Sued," *Wall Street Journal*, October 24, 1989, A1.

34. Solomon Fulero, interview by Neil J. Kressel, tape recording, Redondo Beach, California, March 6, 1998.

35. Island, "Voice of Experience," 9.

36. Howard Varinsky, interview by Michael Liskin, tape recording, Emeryville, California, May 14, 1998.

37. Island, "Voice of Experience," 9.

38. Neil J. Kressel attended sessions and conducted interviews at the annual meeting of the American Society of Trial Consultants, held in June 1998 at La Mansion del Rio hotel in San Antonio, Texas. The following section draws in part on observations made at this meeting. See also,

Neil A. Patten and Donna A. Smith, "The Best Justice Money Can Buy? An In-Depth Profile of Litigation Consultants in America," unpublished manuscript, Department of Humanities, Ferris State University, Big Rapids, Michigan, 1998.

39 One hundred-sixteen people, or about 30 percent of the ASTC membership, returned a 1998 survey. The average age of this group was forty-four with about eight years of experience in the field; about 44 percent were male and 56 percent were female. Nearly three in five had a Ph.D., and an additional one in five had a master's degree. Psychology accounted for 51 percent of the graduate degrees, followed by communications with 37 percent. These numbers must be interpreted with care because—among other limitations—many trial consultants do not belong to the ASTC and many of the members did not respond. See Charli Wortz, "1998 Membership Survey Report," *Court Call* (Winter 1999), 15. For another statistical profile of the profession, see Franklin Strier and Donna Shestowsky, "Profiling the Profilers: A Study of the Trial Consulting Profession, Its Impact on Trial Justice, and What, If Anything, to Do About It," *Wisconsin Law Review* 1999 (1999): 441.

40. Judith Jaeger, "Therapy in the Courtroom: Alumnus Uses Psychology to Ensure Fair Trials in High-Profile Court Battles," *ClarkNews*, accessed March 21, 1998, available from Clark University website, http://www.clarku.edu, Internet. (Hirschhorn did not attend the conference; this account is based on published sources.)

41. Ibid.

42. Lynn Bartels, "Consultant's Life Changed by Late Wife," *Rocky Mountain News*, October 19, 1997, accessed March 21, 1998, available from Inside Denver Web Site, http://www.insidedenver.com/extra/bomb/1019okc2s.html, Internet. See also, Kevin Moran, "Consultant Postpones Chemotherapy to Help Kennedy's Nephew at His Trial," *Houston Chronicle*, November 3, 1991, A8; Helen Thompson, "Best-Case Scenario: To Win a High-Profile Trial These Days, You Need to Hire a Jury Consultant," *Texas Monthly* (December 1994), 44.

43. Cynthia R. Cohen, interview by Neil J. Kressel, tape recording, Redondo Beach, California, March 6, 1998.

44. Varinsky interview, May 14, 1998.

45. Florence Keller, interview by Michael Liskin, tape recording, Palo Alto, California, April 1998.

46. Theresa L. Zagnoli, "Getting to Know the Nominees for the ASTC Board of Directors: Theresa L Zagnoli," *Court Call* (Winter 1998), 6.

47. Moe Rouse, "Media Relations," *Court Call* (Spring 1998), 7.

48. Ronald Beaton, quoted in Maura Dolan, "Role of Jury Consultants Controversial and Extensive," *Los Angeles Times*, September 26, 1994, A17.

49. Fulero interview, March 6, 1998.

50. Judy Rothschild, interview by Michael Liskin, tape recording, Oakland, California, June 11, 1998.

51. Varinsky interview, May 14, 1998.

52. Lucy Keele, quoted in Patten and Smith, "The Best Justice Money Can Buy?" 11.

53. Fulero interview, March 6, 1998. See also, *Gideon v. Wainwright*, 372 U. S. 335 (1963).

54. Gavzer, "Are Trial Consultants Good for Justice?" 20.

55. Keller interview, April 1998. See also, Patten and Smith, "The Best Justice Money Can Buy?" 11, who interviewed numerous trial consultants and concluded, "The popular notion that attorneys desire to 'dumb down the jury' was contradicted by many of the consultants we interviewed."

56. Gary Moran, interview by Neil J. Kressel, tape recording, Redondo Beach, California, March 6, 1998.

57. Dolan, "Role of Jury Consultants Controversial and Extensive," A18.

58. Island interview, June 15, 1998.

59. Abramson, *We, the Jury*, 159.

60. Estimates of industry size are notoriously hard to verify and vary considerably based on how one defines a trial consultant. The figures cited here are based on the discussion in Franklin Strier, "Whither Trial Consulting? Issues and Projections," *Law and Human Behavior* 23, no. 1 (February 1999): 94.

61. Ronald J. Matlon, "The History of the American Society of Trial Consultants—A Personal Look," *Court Call* (Winter 1998), 1. See also, Ronald J. Matlon, "ASTC Membership Report," *Court Call* (Summer 1998), 14.

62. Strier, "Whither Trial Consulting?" 94.

63. Philip K. Anthony, interview by Michael Liskin, tape recording, Burlingame, California, June 16, 1998.

64. Michael J. Saks, interview by Neil J. Kressel, tape recording, Redondo Beach, California, March 7, 1998.

65. Fulero interview, March 6, 1998.

66. Varinsky interview, May 14, 1998.

67. Ibid.

68. Anthony interview, June 16, 1998.

69. Keller interview, April 1998.

70. Saks interview, March 7, 1998.

71. Michael E. Cobo, interview by Michael Liskin, tape recording, Torrance, California, June 2, 1998.

72. Fulero interview, March 6, 1998.

73. David Illig, "Position Paper for the ASTC to require 'Trial Consultants' to Fulfill Continuing Education Requirements: 48 Hours of Training Every Two Years," *Court Call* (Summer 1998), 15.

74. Wortz, "1998 Membership Survey Report," *Court Call* (Winter 1999), 17. Many of those who rate the code "very important" are, apparently, only "somewhat" familiar with it. The sample of members who responded to this survey do not agree about the adequacy of the code. Twenty-eight percent judge it "adequate," 30 percent "somewhat adequate," 8 percent "somewhat inadequate," 13 percent "inadequate," and 21 percent are "undecided." Sixty-five percent of respondents agree that the ASTC should develop enforcement provisions as part of the code. These numbers should be interpreted with caution because of the study's methodological limitations.

75. Ellen L. Leggett and Douglas S. Rice, "Ethics: Conflict of Interest," presentation delivered at the annual meeting of the American Society of Trial Consultants, May 17, 1997, St. Petersburg, Florida (photocopy available from the American Society of Trial Consultants, Towson, Maryland). This presentation considered three alternative working definitions of a conflict of interest: (1) "To avoid a conflict of interest, you can't work for both sides of the same case"; (2) "To avoid a conflict of interest, you can't use information from one side of a case to help the other side of the case"; and (3) "To avoid a conflict of interest, you must avoid situations where you could become a conduit for confidential information transferring from one side of a case to the other." Consultants at the meeting were asked to consider various scenarios to determine whether a conflict exists and, if so, how an ethical consultant should resolve the matter. For example, in one scenario, consultants are told: "You work for a firm that does both trial consulting and graphics engagements. You get a call for a new trial consulting project. You do a conflict check and discover that although the firm is not retained on this case, the graphics group is engaged on another case against your client, which is a Fortune 500 company. The graphics group has already billed substantially on this project and believes there will be significant revenues in the future for them on this case. The two cases are headed for trial in different cities and it appears that different lawyers are involved in each case."

76. Moran interview, March 6, 1998.

77. Saks interview, March 7, 1998.

78. Idgi D'Andrea, "Professional Standards Committee—Past and Present," *Court Call* (Summer 1998), 14.

79. The Litigation Edge, "The 999 Focus Group—$999.00," accessed March 21, 1998, from The Litigation Edge website, available from http://acxes.com/The-Litigation-Edge/fees.html; Internet.

80. Marjorie J. Sommer, interview by Neil J. Kressel, telephone, January 9, 2001.

81. The Wilmington Institute Network, "Virtual Jury," accessed January 9, 2001, available from http://www.virtualjury.com/welcome.htm, Internet.

CHAPTER 4

1. Jo-Ellan Dimitrius and Mark Mazzarella, *Reading People: How to Understand People and Predict Their Behavior—Anytime, Anyplace* (New York: Random House, 1998), 33.

2. Mark Miller, "The Road to Panama City," *Newsweek*, October 30, 1995, 84.

3. Marc Davis and Kevin Davis, "Star Rising for Simpson Jury Consultant," *ABA Journal* (December 1995), 14.

4. Miller, "The Road to Panama City," 84.

5. Dimitrius and Mazzarella, *Reading People*, xiii. Although Mark Mazzarella, a San Diego trial attorney, coauthored this book with Jo-Ellan Dimitrius, it is written in the first-person singular and appears to reflect primarily her experience and opinions.

6. Ibid., 215–216.

7. Ibid., xiii.

8. Ibid., 217.

9. Ibid., 217.

10. Ibid., 8.

11. Ibid., 98–99. Dimitrius presents several examples of her people-reading skills in action. In one case, an unfortunate young man had been involved in a car accident. A paramedic arrived on the scene and, apparently after misreading a label, administered some medication inappropriately. When the victim died, his family sued the manufacturer of the drug, arguing that the bottle had not been labeled with sufficient clarity. Dimitrius had been hired to assist the defense in jury selection. She listened attentively as the plaintiff's attorney asked a middle-aged, conservative, white male prospect whether he would limit compensation to a family for the death of a loved one. The man responded, "There is no amount of money that could compensate someone for the death of a loved one" (ibid., 99). Dimitrius recalls: "The plaintiff's lawyer thought he had a great juror, who would award virtually unlimited damages. The man had 'said' the right thing. But the plaintiff's lawyer missed the vocal clues that revealed the juror's true meaning. The man had spoken almost critically, even sarcastically. That tone suggested to me he resented the attorney's asking him to put a price tag on the young man's life. The juror's response was also crisp and to the point, which indicated a certain emotional distance from the case. Given all this, I understood him to mean not that unlimited damages were warranted, but rather that he felt it inappropriate to attach a dollar figure to a human life. We left him on the jury" (ibid., 100).

Another case concerns a defendant charged in a murder-for-hire scheme. None of the answers given by a heavy-set, white, middle-aged woman during voir dire indicated any favorable impulses toward the defendant. Nothing in her background suggested a sympathetic orientation. But something struck Dimitrius as a bit unusual. She recalls that the woman "frequently looked at the defendant almost maternally with warm, kind eyes and smiled gently whenever he looked toward her. Unlike most of the jurors, while walking in and out of the courtroom she did not give the defendant the widest berth possible, but instead seemed almost to try to engage in contact with him by walking close by. This woman's actions told me loud and clear that she somehow connected with the defendant" (ibid., 181).

In both these cases, Dimitrius claims that subsequent events confirmed her judgments. In the suit against the pharmaceutical manufacturer, she recalls that ". . . as it turned out, we were right. [The juror in question] . . . voted with the others, who after only thirty minutes of deliberation found [that] the pharmaceutical company wasn't responsible for the young man's death" (ibid., 100). In the second trial, Dimitrius points out, possibly on the basis of posttrial interviews, that the "friendly" woman turned out to be ". . . an excellent juror for the defense." She also notes that after the trial concluded, the woman befriended the defendant (ibid., 181).

12. Ibid., 226.

13. Ibid., 227.

14. Some of this research is summarized in Susan T. Fiske and Shelley E. Taylor, *Social Cognition*, 2nd ed. (New York: McGraw-Hill, 1991); Sharon S. Brehm, Saul M. Kassin, and Steven Fein, *Social Psychology*, 4th ed. (New York: Houghton Mifflin, 1999); Roger Brown, *Social Psychology: The Second Edition* (New York: Free Press, 1986); David J. Schneider, Albert H. Hastorf, and Phoebe C. Ellsworth, *Person Perception*, 2nd ed. (Reading, Massachusetts: Addison-Wesley, 1979).

15. Miron Zuckerman, Bella M. DePaulo, and Robert Rosenthal, "Verbal and Non-Verbal Communication in Deception," in *Advances in Experimental Social Psychology*, vol. 14, edited by Leonard Berkowitz (New York: Academic Press, 1981), 1.

16. Ibid., 1.

17. Bella M. Depaulo, K. Charlton, H. Cooper, J.J. Lindsay, and L. Muhlenbruck, "The Accuracy-Confidence Correlation in the Detection of Deception," *Personality and Social Psychology Review* 1 (1997): 346.

18. Paul Ekman and M. O'Sullivan, "Who Can Catch a Liar?" *American Psychologist* 46 (1991): 913. Members of the U.S. Secret Service did perform somewhat better than the others in detecting deception.

19 Paul V. Olczak, Martin F. Kaplan, and Steven Penrod, "Attorneys' Lay Psychology and Its Effectiveness in Selecting Jurors: Three Empirical Studies," *Journal of Social Behavior and Personality* 6, no. 3 (1991): 431.

20. Ibid., 443. The researchers report that "within the context of information presented, both groups combined information in a simple, linear manner, and were similarly influenced by attitudes and demographics. Thus attorneys did not use different bases, nor show greater complexity in their reasoning than did college sophomores" (ibid., 442). Unfortunately, from the lawyers' perspective, the simple strategies were not good enough. A second study explored the possibility that attorneys in the first study resembled sophomores in their selection strategies because they had no need for greater sophistication; such simple methods, after all, might have led to accurate decisions. This study compared trial attorneys to law students. Asked to evaluate their favorableness to the defense, both groups judged jurors who had convicted as *more* desirable than those who had acquitted. Combining the results of the series of studies, the researchers conclude that ". . . attorneys seem to use the same strategies as nonexperts, and are as inaccurate in their selections" (ibid., 448).

21. R. Begam, "Voir Dire: The Attorney's Job," *Trial* (1977), 3.

22. See, for example, R.M. Dawes, "Representative Thinking in Clinical Judgment," *Clinical Psychology Review* 6 (1986): 425; R.M. Dawes, D. Faust, and P.E. Meehl, "Clinical Versus Actuarial Judgment," *Science* 243 (1989): 1668; Michael J. Saks, "The Limits of Scientific Jury Selection: Ethical and Empirical," *Jurimetrics Journal* (Fall 1976): 3.

23. Erica Goode, "To Tell the Truth, It's Awfully Hard to Spot a Liar," *New York Times*, May 11, 1999, F1.

24. Saul M. Kassin and Lawrence S. Wrightsman, *The American Jury on Trial: Psychological Perspectives* (New York: Hemisphere Publishing, 1988), 208.

25. Ibid., 61.

26. Victor Villaseñor, *Jury: The People vs. Juan Corona* (New York: Dell, 1977).

27. Ibid., xv.

28. Ibid., xv.

29. A few exceptions are discussed below.

30. In the spring of 1954, Chicago Jury Project researchers hid microphones behind the heating system in a federal jury room in Kansas, and for the first time in American history, actual jury deliberations were recorded. In each of five cases—all civil disputes—the trial judge and counsel for both parties consented to the recording. But the jurors were not informed. Each recording was kept under lock and key until the case ended, and to maintain privacy, juror names and identifying features were altered in transcripts of the tapes.

As planned, the researchers started to comb through and analyze their precious data. Soon after, one tape recording—having been altered to preserve confidentiality—was played at an annual judicial conference. This was when all hell broke loose. In October 1954, a story appeared in the *Los Angeles Times* that started the fury. During the next few days, articles across the country condemned "eavesdropping" and the "invasion into the jury room." Within a few weeks, U.S. Attorney General Herbert Brownell announced that the Justice Department would seek legislation prohibiting any recording of jury deliberations for any reason whatsoever. Warren Burger, the future chief justice of the Supreme Court but then assistant attorney general, also denounced the methodology of the Chicago Jury Project researchers. The Subcommittee on Internal Security of the Senate Judiciary Committee held hearings on whether the "sanctity of the jury room was violated" in Kansas. At the conclusion of these hearings, Senator James Eastland, chairman of the subcommittee, and Senator William Jenner issued a joint statement, charging: "What was done in this .... court constituted, in our separate judgments, flagrant abuse of authority, a violation of the Constitutional guarantee under the Seventh Amendment of the right of trial by jury, and a serious threat to such right for the future so long as there is no guarantee that incidents of this nature will not again take place" (quoted in Seymour Wishman, *Anatomy of a Jury* [New York: Penguin, 1986], 260–261). Most legislators agreed, and a new law made recording federal jury deliberations a criminal offense. Many states passed similar laws.

Why well-intentioned research efforts generated such an angry response remains a matter of speculation and disagreement. Some see the brouhaha as a manifestation of genuine legislative and public concern over invasions of jury privacy. Others perceive darker forces at work, particularly McCarthy-era paranoia about so-called liberal academic types subverting wholesome American institutions. Anti-Semitism has also been cited as a contributing factor, as several of the Chicago researchers were Jewish. Ibid., 259. Wishman's appendix, "The State of Jury Research" (255–262), provides more details on the reaction to the Chicago researchers' jury-recording episode.

31. *CBS Reports*, "Enter the Jury Room," TV program broadcast April 16, 1997 (videotape available from CBS News, New York).

32. Harry Kalven Jr., Hans Zeisel, and others, *The American Jury* (Boston: Little Brown, 1966; paperback, Chicago: University of Chicago Press, 1971).

33. Ibid., 45.

34. Ibid., 58.

35. Many jury scholars have analyzed Kalven and Zeisel's findings and evaluated the merits of their approach. See especially, Valerie P. Hans and Neil Vidmar, *Judging the Jury* (New York: Plenum Press, 1986), 116.

36. Kalven and Zeisel, *The American Jury*, 63.

37. Ibid., 498.

38. Ibid.

39. Ibid. For a more complete and up-to-date consideration of this issue, see Norman J. Finkel, *Commonsense Justice: Jurors' Notions of the Law* (Cambridge, Massachusetts: Harvard University Press, 1995). Moreover, where judge and jury disagreed, the judge often admitted that the case was far from open-and-shut and seldom a consequence of jury ignorance. Kalven and Zeisel concluded: "The judge very often perceives the stimulus that moves the jury, but does not yield to it. Indeed it is interesting how often the judge describes with sensitivity a factor which he then excludes from his own considerations. Somehow the combination of official role, tradition, discipline, and repeated experience with the task make of the judge one kind of decider. The perennial amateur, layman jury cannot be so quickly domesticated to official role and tradition; it remains accessible to stimuli which the judge will exclude" (Kalven and Zeisel, *The American Jury*, 497–498). In any event, the jury's impact was to increase the protection of the defendant who might be innocent. Kalven and Zeisel's final thought was that the imperfections of the lay deciders constituted only half the answer. They wrote: "We know, of course, that on the side of the judge too, discretion, freedom, and sentiment will be at work, and that the judge too is human" (ibid., 499).

40. Imagine that a researcher wanted to explore the tendency of people with various occupations to convict defendants in felony cases. He or she might initially want to present research subjects with *all* of the evidence and arguments that might emerge in a typical courtroom trial. But most likely, the time and money required by that approach would soon lead to a compromise solution—a summary version of a case. The summary might include live performances by actors or hired attorneys, it might be videotaped, or it might be little more than a one-page, printed synopsis of the central facts and arguments. Well-designed studies typically devote great effort to approximating a real courtroom environment—sometimes obtaining permission to conduct the project in an actual courtroom when court is not in session. Lesser research might take place in an unaltered basement of a psychology department or in a shopping center research facility. Good studies permit subjects to deliberate as jurors would in an actual case. Poorer ones simply ask individuals who have not deliberated how they would cast their votes.

If we want to explore connections between one's job and the tendency to convict, we should include many different members of each occupational group, preferably selected from geographically diverse regions. Otherwise, we cannot know whether the results of the research are associated with the occupation or merely with the particular and idiosyncratic bunch of people who ended up in the study. Similarly, we would want to examine how people with various jobs decide many cases for each type of felony, or else our findings might be attributable to the peculiarities of the test case.

Even if these and other conditions are fulfilled in the research, we can never know about the impact of one crucial factor: *reality*. In a real criminal case, jurors know that their decisions will have consequences—often dire ones—for the defendant. In a study, participants know that the situation is not real. Just how this difference affects behavior remains unknown. Jurors might rise above their biases and predilections when they know that someone's life or freedom is on the line. Alternatively, their true colors might emerge in the anonymity of the jury room. Almost certainly, the unreality of the study setting affects different people differently. The American flag, the judge, even the ambience of the courthouse can be replicated in a well-designed study; the consequences of the verdict cannot.

When researchers are well trained, adequately funded, and conscientious, they can increase the likelihood that results of their research will be meaningful and generalizable to real legal settings. But often, one cannot improve one aspect of a study without worsening another. For example, in order to raise the number of participants or the number of cases each considers, one would, most likely, have to compromise on the length of the synopsis of evidence and attorney arguments. Every such trade-off can detract from the validity and usefulness of the study. When research budgets are low, the compromises become frequent. Similar problems cloud many areas of social psychological research; see Neil J. Kressel, "Systemic Barriers to Progress in Academic Social Psychology," *Journal of Social Psychology* 130, no. 1 (1990): 5.

41. This problem is compounded by the tendency of jury researchers to reuse case summaries and other materials from prior studies. The decision to do so can be justified by a desire to facilitate comparison among experiments, but it further reduces the generalizability of the studies.

42. Recently, jury researcher Brian Bornstein of Louisiana State University attempted to face critics head-on, assessing the frequently expressed charge that too many jury simulations reek of artificiality and lack sufficient validity to be taken seriously. Specifically, he examined more than two dozen previously conducted jury simulations that compared undergraduate student participants to participants drawn from the wider community or from prospective jurors. Contrary to the expectations of critics, Bornstein found that most often the undergraduate students behaved similarly to the "real-world" subjects, offering similar proportions of guilty and not-guilty verdicts. Bornstein also examined whether the medium through which the case was presented made a difference; here, too, he found few meaningful effects. His findings provide comfort to jury researchers and appear to lend support to quicker, easier, and less-expensive forms of research. Still, he himself notes that his approach to assessing the adequacy of jury simulations has substantial limitations. And it would be a mistake for researchers to use Bornstein's tentative conclusions prematurely as a justification for less careful methodology. One might, after all, conclude that even the more careful methods of presenting a case summary to mock jurors are insufficiently realistic or that nonstudent subjects behave as unrealistically as student subjects. Brian H. Bornstein, "The Ecological Validity of Jury Simulations: Is the Jury Still Out?" *Law and Human Behavior* 23, no. 1 (February 1999): 75; see also, Robert J. MacCoun, who concludes: "Experiments comparing mock jurors with subjects who thought they were actually trying a case have been inconclusive; different studies have found mock jurors' verdicts to be more lenient, less lenient, and no different from those of 'actual' jurors. . . . Other studies have examined the effects of the frequent use of college students as mock jurors, finding little or no difference in comparisons of verdicts by student and adult jury-eligible respondents for the same cases. . . . There is some evidence that simulated trial presentations might artificially exaggerate the impact of experimentally manipulated variables, particularly defendant characteristics. . . . But mock jurors do not appear to reach decisions by a fundamentally different process than actual jurors." Robert J. MacCoun, "Experimental Research on Jury Decision-Making," *Science* 244 (June 2, 1989): 1046.

43. David Kairys, Jay Schulman, and Sid Harring, eds., *The Jury System: New Methods for Reducing Prejudice* (Philadelphia: National Lawyers Guild, 1975), 1, quoted in Michael J. Saks and Reid Hastie, *Social Psychology in Court* (New York: Van Nostrand Reinhold, 1978), 48.

44. Saks and Hastie, *Social Psychology in Court*, 70. The authors went even farther, noting, "The studies are unanimous in showing that evidence is a substantially more potent determinant of jurors' verdicts than the individual characteristics of jurors. Indeed, the power of evidence is so well recognized by jury researchers that when studying processes other than evidence, they must calibrate the evidence to be moderate so that it leaves some variance to be influenced by the variables under study. Manipulating the evidence powerfully influences the verdict the group renders" (ibid., 68).

45. See, for example, Shari Seidman Diamond, "Scientific Jury Selection: What Social Scientists Know and Do Not Know," *Judicature* 73, no. 4 (December–January 1990): 180; Reid Hastie, "Is Attorney-Conducted Voir Dire an Effective Procedure for the Selection of Impartial Juries?" *American University Law Review* 40 (1991): 703; Martin F. Kaplan, "Jury Selection from a Social Science Perspective," *Illinois Bar Journal* (July 1990): 364; Kassin and Wrightsman, *The American Jury on Trial;* Vladimir J. Konecni, Ebbe E. Ebbesen, and Roger R. Hock, "Factors Affecting Simulated Jurors' Decisions in Capital Cases," *Psychology Crime and Law* 2 (1996): 269; Steven D. Penrod and Brian L. Cutler, "Assessing the Competence of Juries," in *Handbook of Forensic Psychology*, ed. I. Weiner and A. Hess (New York: Wiley, 1985), 293.

46. In one study conducted by Steven D. Penrod, the best combination of predictors could explain only 16 percent of the variation in verdicts in the rape case, 14 percent in the murder case, 10 percent in the negligence case, and 5 percent in the armed robbery case. In other words, when we use all the information gathered in the study, we are still unable to explain between 84 and 95 percent of the variation in verdict preferences. Another way to think about this is to ask how well we would be able to guess whether jurors would vote guilty or not guilty, knowing only the background of the jurors and how they responded to the attitude questions. On this basis, roughly 70 percent could be correctly classified in the rape case compared to 50 percent by flipping a coin or 61 percent, taking into account knowledge of the overall percentage of participants who voted to convict (39 percent). See Steven D. Penrod, "Predictors of Jury Decision Making in Criminal and Civil Cases: A Field Experiment," *Forensic Reports:* 3 (1990): 261.

Professor Penrod explains: "These results suggest that the regression search for attitudinal or demographic predictor variables is unlikely to produce predictive models that contain variables of general applicability across different types of cases. Furthermore, the variables used in these analyses are of roughly equal quality and, in terms of variance accounted for, are mediocre predictors" (ibid., 272–273). If juror backgrounds and attitudes lead to bias, this study suggests that the patterns of such bias are case-specific and extremely difficult to predict. Moreover, the jurors in this research did not deliberate as a group. Had they done so, such give-and-take with others might have minimized or eliminated the impact of initial predispositions, attitudes, and biases.

47. Martin F. Kaplan, "Psychological Factors in the Behavior of Jurors," unpublished manuscript, Department of Psychology, Northern Illinois University, De Kalb, Illinois (1990). Two important theoretical works that bear on these issues are Icek Ajzen, *Attitudes Personality and Behavior* (Chicago: Dorsey, 1988); and Lee Ross and Richard E. Nisbett, *The Person and the Situation: Perspectives of Social Psychology* (New York: McGraw-Hill, 1991).

48. Saks and Hastie, *Social Psychology in Court*, 71.

49. For a statistical demonstration of this point, see Solomon M. Fulero and Steven D. Penrod, "Attorney Jury Selection Folklore: What Do They Think and How Can Psychologists Help?" *Forensic Reports* 3 (1990): 233. They explain: "Although the obtained estimate of 5%–15% of the variance in verdict explained appears low on its face, consider the possible impact of such information. .. . . An attorney operating on a completely random basis with a 50% favorable and 50% unfavorable jury pool would correctly classify 50% of the jurors. However, if a juror survey detected a reliable relation in which 5% of the variance in verdict was accounted for by attitudinal and personality measures, successful use of that information would increase the attorney's performance to 61% correct classifications. With 15% of the variance accounted for, performance would increase to 69% correct. Clearly, although the percentage of variance explained may be small, the potential improvement in selection performance is not insignificant" (ibid., 251–252). See also, Richard L. Wiener and Dennis P. Stolle, "Trial Consulting: Jurors' and Attorneys' Perceptions of Murder," *California Western Law Review* 34 (Fall 1997): 225.

50. Portions of this trial were broadcast on *CBS Reports*, "Enter the Jury," April 16, 1997. All quotations come from that broadcast.

51. Their one hope in the second trial had been a juror who, reportedly, said hello to one of the defense attorneys. This lawyer conceded that a simple "hi" hadn't been much to bet on. But even this small hope was dashed when the friendly juror was selected as an alternate and excluded from deliberation.

52. Diamond, "Scientific Jury Selection," 181.

53. Kassin and Wrightsman, *The American Jury on Trial*, 35.

54. Virginia Boehm, "Mr. Prejudice, Miss Sympathy, and the Authoritarian Personality: An Application of Psychological Measuring Techniques to the Problem of Jury Bias," *Wisconsin Law Review* 1968 (1968): 734. For a brief, recent review of related evidence, see Bryan Myers and Len Lecci, "Revising the Factor Structure of the Juror Bias Scale: A Method for the Empirical Validation of Theoretical Constructs," *Law and Human Behavior* 22, no. 2 (April 1998): 239.

55. See Craig Haney, Aida Hurtado, and Luis Vega, "'Modern' Death Qualification: New Data on Its Biasing Effects," *Law and Human Behavior* 18, no. 6 (December 1994): 619; Ronald C. Dillehay and Marla R. Sandys, "Life Under *Wainwright v. Witt*: Juror Dispositions and Death Qualification," *Law and Human Behavior* 20, no 2 (April 1996): 147. Those scoring high on a complex psychological dimension called "authoritarianism" also tend to convict slightly more often in some close cases. See Douglas J. Narby, Brian L. Cutler, and Gary Moran, "A Meta-Analysis of the Association Between Authoritarianism and Jurors' Perceptions of Defendant Culpability," *Journal of Applied Psychology* 78 (1993): 34.

56. See, for example, Phoebe C. Ellsworth, "Some Steps Between Attitudes and Verdicts," in *Inside the Juror: The Psychology of Juror Decision Making*, edited by Reid Hastie (New York: Cambridge University Press, 1993; paperback, 1994), 42; Valerie P. Hans and Neil Vidmar, "Jury Selection," in *The Psychology of the Courtroom*, edited by Norbert L. Kerr and Robert M. Bray (New York: Academic Press, 1982), 39; Arthur H. Patterson, "Scientific Jury Selection: The Need for a Case Specific Approach," *Social Action and the Law* 11, no. 4 (1986): 105; Susan Moses-Zirkes, "Does Gender Matter in Choosing Juries?" *APA Monitor* (September 1993): 40.

57. Psychologist Martin Kaplan explains: "Personality, occupation, and personal interests simply do not in themselves predict how a juror will act because behavior is very much driven by the particular situation in combination with personal characteristics. Further, the sorts of characteristics found in [lawyers'] stereotypes (physical appearance, occupation, religion, ethnicity, and many others) are not strong indicators of the personal characteristics important to juror behavior." Kaplan, "Jury Selection from a Social Science Perspective," 364. James Turner, a trial consultant trained as an attorney and a psychologist, makes a related point: "Each case has its own unique set of circumstances. Therefore, generalizations about the interaction between juror characteristics and a particular verdict are dubious at best. The results obtained in one case simply are not directly applicable to other cases. Rather, the results from one case must virtually stand alone for that particular case and no others." James R. Turner, "Jury Selection: A Brief Update and Recommendation," *Oklahoma Bar Journal* 67, no. 22 (June 1, 1996): 1792. Some consultants have denounced colleagues who offer general rules-of-thumb to journalists, accusing them of pandering for publicity even though they know better. C.K. Rowland of the Center for Trial Insights in Texas calls such pontificating "masquerade marketing," or marketing that masquerades as research. The consultant who does this seeks publicity by offering simplistic soundbites to the mass media. Rowland's target is ". . . unqualified and unfounded generalizations about juries void of any jurisdiction-specific considerations," claiming that such pronouncements ". . . reinforce stereotypes and fears about irrational jurors." C. K. Rowland, "Voice of Experience: Masquerade Marketing," *Court Call* (Winter 1999): 10.

58. Patterson, "Scientific Jury Selection," 107–108.

59. Ibid., 108.

60. See, for example, Brian L. Cutler, Gary Moran, and Douglas J. Narby, "Jury Selection in Insanity Defense Cases," *Journal of Research in Personality* 26 (1992): 165; Gary Moran, Brian L. Cutler, and Elizabeth F. Loftus, "Jury Selection in Major Controlled Substance Trials: The Need for Extended Voir Dire," *Forensic Reports* 3 (1990): 331; Gary Moran and J.C. Comfort, "Scientific Juror Selection: Sex as a Moderator of Demographic and Personality Predictors of Impaneled Felony Juror Behavior," *Journal of Personality and Social Psychology* 43 (1982): 1052.

61. Cutler, Moran, and Narby, "Jury Selection in Insanity Defense Cases," 180.

62. Moran, Cutler, and Loftus, "Jury Selection in Major Controlled Substance Trials," 335.

63. Moses-Zirkes, "Does Gender Matter in Choosing Juries?" 40.

64. Research on the attractiveness bias is discussed in K. K. Dion, E. Berscheid, and E. Walster, "What Is Beautiful Is Good," *Journal of Personality and Social Psychology* 24 (1972): 285. A brief discussion of more recent studies can be found in Sharon Brehm, *Intimate Relationships*, 2nd ed. (New York: McGraw-Hill, 1992), 64–72. For consideration of how this research relates to judgment of defendants, see Irwin A. Horowitz, Thomas E. Willging, and Kenneth S. Bordens, *The Psychology of Law: Integrations and Applications*, 2nd ed. (New York: Longman, 1998), 65–67. See also, David Stipp and Alicia Hills Moore, "Mirror Mirror on the Wall, Who's the Fairest of Them All?" *Fortune Magazine* (December 9, 1996), accessed June 14, 1999, available from http://www.fortune.com, Internet. According to some recent research, a special type of attractiveness may stand a criminal defendant in particularly good stead with most jurors: a face with a babyish appearance. See Leslie A. Zebrowitz, *Reading Faces: Window to the Soul?* (Boulder: Westview Press, 1997). Baby-faced people are generally seen to be warmer, more honest, and more sincere than those with more mature faces. But it is not all good news. They are also judged less competent and less assertive; not as much is expected from them. Evidence is by no means exhaustive, but in simulated trials jurors were more likely to find against a baby-faced defendant if the case involved negligence and less likely to find against him if it involved intent. Baby-faced defendants apparently come across as less competent and therefore more likely to forget to take necessary precautions. But they also seem more honest and, consequently, less apt to do something wrong on purpose. Research has not determined whether the maturity of a defendant's face is powerful enough to override other factors at work in a case.

65. See, for example, Ronald Mazzella and Alan Feingold, "The Effects of Physical Atttractiveness, Race, Socioeconomic Status, and Gender of Defendants and Victims on Judgments of Mock Jurors: A Meta-Analysis," *Journal of Applied Social Psychology* 24 (1994): 1315.

66. Brehm, Kassin, and Fein, *Social Psychology*, 307.

67. Mike McCurley, "The Ideal Juror Profile and Mitigating the Effects of a Fault-Based Divorce," accessed June 24, 1999, from the American Academy of Matrimonial Lawyers website, available from http://www.aaml.org/ideal.htm, Internet. Texas, unlike other states, permits jury trials in divorce actions inolving child custody.

68. See Barry Meier, "$51 Million Verdict Awarded to Smoker Is Biggest of Its Kind," *New York Times*, February 11, 1999, A1; Barry Meier, "Cigarette Producers Face a Fresh Threat in Individuals' Suits," *New York Times*, February 12, 1999, A1; Barry Meier, "Jury Awards $81 Million to Oregon Smoker's Family," *New York Times*, March 31, 1999, A4; Associated Press, "Mounting Tobacco Suits Seen," *Boston Globe*, February 12, 1999, A22; Milo Geyelin, "Lawyer Credits Classroom Experience in Winning Case Against Philip Morris," *Wall Street Journal*, February 17, 1999, B11; Milo Geyelin, "Behind Giant Tobacco Verdicts, a Legal Swat Team," *Wall Street Journal*, April 12, 1999, B1.

69. Meier, "Cigarette Producers Face a Fresh Threat in Individuals' Suits," A16.

70. See Barry Meier, "Tobacco Industry Loses First Phase of Broad Lawsuit," *New York Times*, July 8, 1999, A1; Richard Willing, "'Damages Here Could Be Eye-Popping,'" *USA Today*, July 8, 1999,

3A; Rick Bragg, "Tobacco Lawsuit in Florida Yields Record Damages," *New York Times*, July 15, 2000, A1; Barry Meier, "Industry Crosses Troubling Line," *New York Times*, July 15, 2000, A11; Rick Bragg and Sarah Kershaw, "Juror Says a 'Sense of Mission' Led to Huge Tobacco Damages," *New York Times*, July 16, 2000, A1; Barry Meier, "Jury's Action Raises Concerns for Tobacco Industry," *New York Times*, July 16, 2000, A19. For an angry critique of the jury's decision, see Walter Olson, "'The Runaway Jury' Is No Myth," *Wall Street Journal*, July 18, 2000, A22. Among other things, Olson argues that repeated tobacco trials constitute an example of multiple jeopardy, ". . . a firing-squad arrangement in which 90% of juries may choose to fire into the air, believing the defendants are unworthy of punishment, yet find their opinions rendered meaningless when the other 10% aim as they're told" (ibid., A22).

71. Bragg and Kershaw, "Juror Says a 'Sense of Mission' Led to Huge Tobacco Damages," A18.

72. Ibid., A18.

73. See, for example, Associated Press, "Florida Court Reverses $1M Tobacco Verdict, *Chicago Tribune*, August 13, 1998, accessed August 13, 1998, available from http://www.chicagotribune.com, Internet. Most commentators agree that the huge punitive damages award in the Florida class-action suit will be reduced or thrown out on appeal. In addition, few jury awards have been allowed to stand in cases where individual smokers have sued tobacco companies.

74. Juror Laura Barrow, quoted in June D. Bell, "Disapproving Jurors: We Let Reynolds Off the Hook," *Florida Times-Union*, May 8, 1997, accessed July 7, 1998, available from http://www.jacksonville.com/tu-online/stories/050897/2a1juror.html, Internet.

75. No author, "Cigarette Makers Cleared in Suit Over a Death," *New York Times*, July 10, 1999, A11.

76. David W. Chen, "Jury Awards $12.7 Million to a Woman Denied Tenure," *New York Times*, January 19, 1999, B2.

77. Ibid., B2.

78. Benjamin Weiser, "Jury Tells N.B.A. to Pay Female Referee $7.85 Million," *New York Times*, April 10, 1998, C1.

79. Mike Allen, "Anchorwoman Wins $8.3 Million over Sex Bias," *New York Times*, January 29, 1999, B1. Mike Allen, "Judge Turns Trial Witness in Anchorwoman's Lawsuit," *New York Times*, January 26, 1999, B5.

80. Walter Goodman, "Latest Defense: The Sitcom Made Me Do It," *New York Times*, July 3, 1997, C22; Del Jones, "'Seinfeld' Case Fallout Award Creates Catch-22 for Companies," *USA Today*, July 17, 1997, B4, accessed June 28, 1999, available from http://www.proquest.umi.com, Internet. No author, "Ex-Miller Executive Wins Award in 'Seinfeld' Case," *Wall Street Journal*, July 16, 1997, B13, accessed June 28, 1999, available from http://www.proquest.umi.com, Internet.

81. Matkov, Salzman, Madoff & Gunn (law firm), "Jury Awards $26 Million to Executive Fired over Racy 'Seinfeld' Rhyme," accessed September 30, 1999, available from http://www.lawoffice.com, Internet. The decision was reversed by a Wisconsin appeals court, after Miller Brewing lawyers argued, among other things, that testimony about the Seinfeld joke had misled and inflamed the jurors. Mackenzie's attorney said he would appeal the reversal to the Wisconsin Supreme Court. See Court TV, "Wis. Court Reverses $25 Million Judgment in Seinfeld Firing Case," February 22, 2000, accessed January 19, 2001, available from http://www.courttv.com/national/2000/0222/seinfeld_fired_ap.html, Internet.

82. These two cases are discussed in Edith Greene, "On Juries and Damage Awards: The Process of Decisionmaking," *Law and Contemporary Problems* 52, no. 4 (Autumn 1989): 225.

83. For example, Professor Neil Vidmar, a noted expert on jury behavior, conducted an extensive review of jury verdicts in medical malpractice cases and concluded that "on balance, there is no em-

pirical support for the propositions that juries are biased against doctors or that they are prone to ignore legal and medical standards in order to decide in favor of plaintiffs with severe injuries. This evidence in fact indicates that there is reasonable concordance between jury verdicts and doctors' ratings of negligence. On balance, juries may have a slight bias in favor of doctors." Neil Vidmar, *Medical Malpractice and the American Jury* (Ann Arbor: University of Michigan Press, 1995; paperback, 1997), 182. Vidmar's listing of recent awards in North Carolina does not leave one with the sense of juries out of control.

84. See Peter Aronson, David E. Rovella, and Bob Van Voris, "Jurors: A Biased, Independent Lot," *National Law Journal,* November 2, 1998, A1, accessed June 24, 1999, available from http://www.global-intelligence.org/newsand.htm, Internet. Bob Van Voris, "Jurors Do Not Trust Civil Litigants. Period," *National Law Journal,* November 2, 1998, A24, accessed June 24, 1999, available from http://www.global-intelligence.org/newsand.htm, Internet.

85. Ellen L. Leggett, "Identifying Juror Bias in Product Liability Cases," accessed Febraury 4, 1998, from the Jury Research Institute website, available from http://www.jri-inc.com, Internet. Leggett's profile is somewhat similar to one that appears in Rick R. Fuentes, "Tips for Voir Dire," *NBA Magazine* (September–October 1993), reprinted as a brochure by DecisionQuest, Torrance, California. For an alternative perspective, see Thomas J. Vesper, "Seinfeld Syndrome: The Indifference of Otherwise Nice Jurors," *Trial* (October 1998), 39. Vesper believes that age provides an important key to juror proclivities in personal injury cases, arguing that "like the characters in the show, many jurors in their late 20s and early 30s—members of Generation X—often seem indifferent to the plight of all but the most horrifically injured plaintiffs."

86. Leggett, "Identifying Juror Bias in Product Liability Cases." All subsequent references to Leggett's theory come from this article.

87. Craig L. White, "Jury De-Selection: Keep It Simple and Open-Ended," accessed June 24, 1999, from the Craig L. White, P.C., website, available from http://www. craiglwhite.com/jury.htm, Internet.

88. Greene, "On Juries and Damage Awards," 246.

89. Reid Hastie, David A. Schkade, and John W. Payne, "A Study of Juror and Jury Judgments in Civil Cases: Deciding Liability for Punitive Damages," *Law and Human Behavior* 22, no. 3 (June 1998): 289.

90. Maximum damage limits similarly can influence juror thinking, sometimes paradoxically, by raising award sizes. See Reid Hastie, David A. Schkade, and John W. Payne, "Juror Judgments in Civil Cases: Effects of Plaintiff's Requests and Plaintiff's Identity on Punitive Damage Awards," *Law and Human Behavior* 23, no. 4 (August 1999): 445; Jennifer K. Robbennolt and Christina A. Studebaker, "Anchoring in the Courtroom: The Effects of Caps on Punitive Damages," *Law and Human Behavior* 23, no. 3 (June 1999): 353; Michelle Chernikoff Anderson and Robert J MacCoun, "Goal Conflict in Juror Assessments of Compensatory and Punitive Damages," *Law and Human Behavior* 23, no. 3 (June 1999): 313.

91. Edith Greene and Elizabeth F. Loftus, "Psycholegal Research on Jury Damage Awards," *Current Directions in Psychological Science* 7, no. 2 (1998): 50; Neal Feigenson, Jaihyun Park, and Peter Salovey, "Effect of Blameworthiness and Outcome Severity on Attributions of Responsibility and Damage Awards in Comparative Negligence Cases," *Law and Human Behavior* 21, no. 6 (1997): 597; Greene, "On Juries and Damage Awards," 225. See also the summary in Horowitz, Willging, and Bordens, *The Psychology of Law,* 307.

92. See Daniel Kahneman, David Schkade, and Cass R. Sunstein, "Shared Outrage and Erratic Awards: The Psychology of Punitive Damages," *Journal of Risk and Uncertainty* 16 (1998): 49; Cass R. Sunstein, Daniel Kahneman, and David Schkade, "Assessing Punitive Damages (with Notes on

Cognition and Valuation in Law)," *Yale Law Journal* 107, no. 7 (1998): 2071; Roselle L. Wissler, Allen J. Hart, and Michael J. Saks, "Deciding Compensation for Non-Economic Damages," unpublished manuscript, presented at the annual meeting of the American Psychology-Law Society, Redondo Beach, California, March 1998; Neil Vidmar and J.J. Rice, "Assessment of Non-Economic Damage Awards in Medical Malpractice Negligence: A Comparison of Jurors with Legal Professionals," *Iowa Law Review* 78, no. 4 (1993): 883; S. Daniels and J. Martin, *Civil Juries and the Politics of Reform* (Evanston, Illinois: Northwestern University Press, 1995).

    93. Ronald J. Matlon, "Selecting the Jury: Factors Affecting the Selection Process," chapter 6A in *Courtroom Communication Strategies: January 1998 Cumulative Supplement*, ed. Lawrence J. Smith and Loretta A. Malandro (New York: Kluwer Law Book Publishers, 1988), 109.

    94. Ibid., 109.

    95. Ibid., 105.

    96. Ibid., 106.

    97. Research includes: Stanley L. Brodsky, Ralph I. Knowles, Patrick R. Cotter, and George H. Herring, "Jury Selection in Malpractice Suits," *International Journal of Law and Psychiatry* 14: (1991): 215, which surveyed adults in one county in the South, finding that ". . . respondents who were most critical of doctors and least reluctant to consider high awards, were more likely to be poor, black, less educated, and living in urban rather than rural areas" (ibid., 220). In another study, Wissler, Hart, and Saks ("Deciding Compensation for Non-Economic Damages") examine decisions in several simulated personal injury cases, finding that men and jurors from wealthier households awarded larger noneconomic damages than women and those from less wealthy homes. Interestingly, the researchers note that the degree of physical disfigurement suffered by a plaintiff affects the awards of urban jurors more than those of rural ones. Finally, Hastie, Schkade, and Payne ("A Study of Juror and Jury Judgements in Civil Cases," 294) conclude that mock jurors with higher incomes are somewhat more likely to say, prior to deliberations, that a defendant is not liable for punitive damages. So are white mock jurors, slightly—although it should be noted that in this study they were compared to the not very meaningful category of "minority" jurors.

    98. Elissa Krauss and Beth Bonora, eds., *Jurywork: Systematic Techniques*, 2nd ed. (New York: West Group, 1997), modified by release no. 18, sections 19–6 to 19–7.

    99. Ibid., section 19–10.

    100. Ibid., section 19–11.

    101. William Glaberson, "Some Plaintiffs Losing Out in Texas' War on Lawsuits," *New York Times*, June 7, 1999, A1.

    102. William Glaberson, "State Courts Sweeping away Laws Curbing Suits for Injury," *New York Times*, July 16, 1999; William Glaberson, "Ohio Supreme Court Voids Legal Limits on Damage Suits," *New York Times*, August 17, 1999, A10.

    103. Krauss and Bonora, *Jurywork*, section 19–28. See also, Lois Heaney, "Jury Selection in the Era of 'Tort Reform," *Trial* (November 1995), 72.

    104. Amy Singer, "Selecting Jurors: What to Do about Bias," *Trial* (April 1996), 28.

    105. Jane Goodman, Elizabeth F. Loftus, and Edith Greene, "Matters of Money: Voir Dire in Civil Cases," *Forensic Reports* 3, (1990): 303.

    106. Gary Moran, Brian L. Cutler, and Anthony De Lisa, "Attitudes Towards Tort Reform, Scientific Jury Selection, and Juror Bias: Verdict Inclination in Criminal and Civil Trials," *Law and Psychology Review* 18 (1994): 327.

    107. Ibid., 324.

    108 See, for example, Craig L. White, "Jury De-Selection: Keep It Simple and Open-Ended."

    109. See Olczak, Kaplan, and Penrod, "Attorneys' Lay Psychology and Its Effectiveness in Selecting Jurors," 431.

110. Lauren E. Handler and Morna L. Sweeney, "Jury Selection: A Primer," *New Jersey Lawyer* (December 1998), 13.

111. F. Bailey and H. Rothblatt (1974), quoted in Jeffrey T. Frederick, "Social Science Involvement in Voir Dire: Preliminary Data on the Effectiveness of 'Scientific Jury Selection,'" *Behavioral Sciences and the Law* 2, no. 4 (1984): 376.

112. Sams (1969), quoted in ibid., 376.

113. Fulero and Penrod, "Attorney Jury Selection Folklore," 240.

114. Hastie, "Is Attorney-Conducted Voir Dire an Effective Procedure for the Selection of Impartial Juries?" 722.

115. See Jeffrey Abramson, *We, the Jury: The Jury System and the Ideal of Democracy* (New York: Basic Books, 1994; paperback, 1995), 143–176. Abramson considers several early "successes" of jury consultants in detail, concluding that although their side often prevailed it was not because their theories about the jurors were on target.

116. See, for example, Franklin Strier, "Whither Trial Consulting? Issues and Projections," *Law and Human Behavior* 23, no. 1 (February 1999): 102; see also, Dennis P. Stolle, Jennifer K. Robbennolt, and Richard L. Wiener, "The Perceived Fairness of the Psychologist Trial Consultant: An Empirical Investigation," *Law and Psychology Review* 20 (1996): 146.

117. Samuel McCracken, "The New Snake Oil: A Field Guide," *Commentary* (June 1999), 27.

118. Saks and Hastie, *Social Psychology in Court*, 62.

119. Diamond, "Scientific Jury Selection," 179. A similar point was made some years earlier by Saks, "The Limits of Scientific Jury Selection," 13–14.

120. Melissa A. Pigott and Linda A. Foley, "Social Influence in Jury Decision Making," *Trial Diplomacy Journal* 18, no. 2 (1995): 102.

121. Hans Zeisel and Shari Seidman Diamond, "The Effect of Peremptory Challenges on Jury and Verdict: An Experiment in a Federal District Court," *Stanford Law Review* 30 (1978): 491. Some try to get at the matter indirectly. For example, when law students are trained to apply scientific jury selection methods as opposed to more traditional approaches, their performance improves for some cases, stays the same for others, and even deteriorates on occasion. Of course, law students with a little consultant training might differ substantially—for better or worse—from real consultants. See Irwin Horowitz, "Juror Selection: A Comparison of Two Methods in Several Criminal Cases," *Journal of Applied Psychology* 10 (1980): 86.

122. Strier, "Whither Trial Consulting," 101.

123. Diamond, "Scientific Jury Selection," 183.

124. Brian L. Cutler, "Introduction: The Status of Scientific Jury Selection in Psychology and Law," *Forensic Reports* 3 (1990): 230.

125. Hastie, "Is Attorney-Conducted Voir Dire an Effective Procedure for the Selection of Impartial Juries?" 723.

126. Saks, "The Limits of Scientific Jury Selection," 15.

127. Diamond, "Scientific Jury Selection, 183.

CHAPTER 5

1. Paul Abercrombie, "Trial Consultants: Juries Are Us," *Tampa Bay Business Journal*, November 29, 1996, accessed December 20, 2000, available from http://www.bizjournals.com/tampabay/stories/1996/12/02/focus1.html, Internet. All of Harvey A. Moore's comments come from this article.

2. Ibid.

3. Sharon S. Brehm, Saul M. Kassin, and Steven Fein, *Social Psychology*, 4th ed. (New York: Houghton Mifflin, 1999), 104.

4. David H. Fauss and Melissa Pigott, "Attorneys and Jurors: Do They Have *Anything* in Common?" *Trial Diplomacy Journal* 20 (1997): 184.

5. Kathryn E. Barnett, "Letting Focus Groups Work for You," *Trial* (April 1999), 74.

6. Michael Tigar, *Examining Witnesses* (Chicago: Section of Litigation/American Bar Association, 1993), accessed March 20, 1998, available from http://www.abanet.org/litigation/pubs/ewchapt1.html, Internet.

7. Ibid.

8. Shari Seidman Diamond, "Scientific Jury Selection: What Social Scientists Know and Do Not Know," *Judicature* 73, no. 4 (December–January, 1990): 183.

9. Abercrombie, "Trial Consultants." See also, Harvey A. Moore and Jennifer Friedman, "Courtroom Observation and Applied Litigation Research: A Case History of Jury Decision Making," *Clinical Sociology Review* 11 (1993): 123, in which the authors suggest that jury researchers might make greater use of nonquantitative methodologies.

10. Ross Laguzza, a principal at DecisionQuest, criticizes trial consultants who ". . . believe they can help you win your case by running focus groups for you [the attorney] at your direction," suggesting that "they know and you know (or come to find out) that the burden of sorting out the strategic implications for any findings rests with you, not them." Ross P. Laguzza, "In the Land of Gurus and Data Dumpers: How to Choose the Right Jury Specialist," *Texas Lawyer*, May 20, 1996, reprinted as a brochure under the same title and available from DecisionQuest, Torrance, California. He further objects to those who ". . . rely on simple, canned methodologies and data analysis programs. Their reports are big, thick, colorful productions of mostly boilerplate nonsense which an unhappy lawyer once referred to as 'form vomit'. They are often very attractive to the lawyer who confuses the means for the end" (ibid.).

11. Robert D. Minick, "Using Pretrial Surrogate Jury Research as a Strategic Tool in Preparing for Trial," *TIPS Newsletter* (American Bar Association) (Spring/Summer 1994), reprinted as a brochure under the same title and available from DecisionQuest, Torrance, California.

12. This list is not meant to be exhaustive. For a comprehensive discussion of current trial consulting services, see the regularly updated, two-volume tome produced by National Jury Project, *Jurywork: Systematic Techniques*, 2nd ed., edited by Elissa Krauss and Beth Bonora (St. Paul, Minnesota: West Group/Clark Boardman Callaghan, 1999). Some firms provide mediation and alternative dispute resolution services. Other firms refine demonstrative evidence, preparing an ever-changing array of enhanced exhibits, graphics, videos, and animation. One writer reports: "Even virtual reality in the courtroom is no longer science fiction. Several years ago, in an apparent first, lawyers for Honda Motors actually took jurors on a three-dimensional, virtual reality motorcycle ride." Robert J. Bingle, "Winning the Verdict with Videos and Virtual Reality," *National Law Journal*, June 15, 1998, B7. Bingle writes: "Animation, such as flight-path reconstructions, has become an almost routine demonstrative tool in airline crash litigation. Jurors in other cases have seen vivid, accurate medical animation of hypoxic brain injuries of babies in utero, closed-head injuries and ruptured disks. As technology continues to evolve, making such presentations easier and cheaper to produce, some trial consultants predict that conventional photographs, diagrams, models and charts may take their places next to 45-rpm records. .. . . Others, however, believe that traditional demonstrative evidence methods, including day-in-the-life videos and other forms of videos that have become common in personal injury trial litigation, are unlikely to disappear anytime soon" (ibid., B7).

13. Amy Singer, "How to Prove Jurors Will Be on Your Side," *Trial* (June 1997) 48. See also, Kate Rix, "Jury Consultants Play Meatier Role in Trial Prep: Seeking an Edge, Litigators Run Their Show Past Mock Jurors—and Listen Carefully," *National Law Journal*, August 7, 2000, A13.

14. Singer, "How to Prove Jurors Will Be on Your Side," 49.

15. Ibid., 49.

16. The three cases discussed in this section are reported in Jeffrey R. Boyll, Alan Walker, and Charles Miller, "A Claims Manager's Guide to Using Jury Research," *Claims Magazine* (November 1998), accessed August 18, 1999, available from http://www..claimsmag.com/issues/November/feature_juryresearch.html, Internet.

17. Ibid.

18. Ibid.

19. This case is reported in Jordan E. Cohn, "Reading the Minds of the Jury," *American Legion* (September 1990), 30.

20. Peter Gelblum, interview by Michael Liskin, tape recording, Brentwood, California, June 4, 1998.

21. For Gelblum, the composition of the civil jury was very important. "If you look at the numbers," he says, "they were knocking off white people and we were knocking off black people. You just can't avoid that fact. Except that we weren't knocking off all black people and they were not knocking off all white people. It was a factor but it was not, 'Oh, they're black, they're off' by any means. . . . What we wanted were rational, logical people who'd look at the evidence because it was so clear" (Gelblum interview, June 4, 1998). For the most part, the law firm got a jury with which they could work.

22. "Focusing Issues," accessed May 29, 1997, from the Trial Analysis Group website, available from http://www.trialanalysis.com/fociss.html, Internet.

23. "Trial Simulations," accessed May 29, 1997, from the Trial Analysis Group website, available from http://www.trialanalysis.com/sim.html, Internet.

24. Ibid.

25. "The Mock Jury Is In," accessed March 31, 1998, from the Trial Behavior Consulting, Inc., website, available from http://www.lawinfo.com/biz/tbci/mockjury.html, Internet.

26. See Jim M. Perdue Sr. and Jim M. Perdue Jr., "Trial Themes: Winning Jurors' Minds and Hearts," *Trial* (April 1998), 42, accessed April 23, 1999, available from http://www.proquest.umi.com, Internet. It is the fictional John Quincy Adams who asks the question; we do not know what the real one said.

27. Gerry Spence, *How to Argue and Win Every Time* (New York: St. Martin's Griffin, 1995), 113.

28. Robert J. MacCoun, "Experimental Research on Jury Decision-Making," *Science* 244 (June 2, 1989): 1047.

29. Ibid.

30. Nancy Pennington and Reid Hastie, "The Story Model for Juror Decision Making," in *Inside the Juror: The Psychology of Juror Decision Making*, edited by Reid Hastie (New York: Cambridge University Press, 1993), 192.

31. See, for example, Edward Bodaken and William Slusser, "Want to Win Complex IP Trials? Simplify, Simplify," *National Law Journal*, July 26, 1999, C11. Nonetheless, academic social scientists seem favorably inclined toward this line of pretrial research. Thus, Professor Solomon Fulero reveals his excitement: "The most cutting edge stuff nowadays . . . we refer to as social cognition goes to court—it's straight out of social psych. . . . In my view, now it's *real* psychology." Solomon Fulero, interview by Neil J. Kressel, tape recording, Redondo Beach, California, March 6, 1998.

32. Rick Fuentes, Robert D. Minick, and Galina Zeigarnik, "Using Story Telling Techniques to Craft a Persuasive Legal Story," *Criminal Practice Report* 11, no. 18, reprinted as a brochure under the same title and available from DecisionQuest, Torrance, California.

33. Ibid.

34. Fulero interview, March 6, 1998.

35. Eric Oliver, "Embodying the Story," *Trial Diplomacy Journal* 17, no. 4 (July/August 1994): 179.

36. Ibid.

37. Perdue and Perdue, "Trial Themes."

38. Ibid.

39. Fuentes, Minick, and Zeigarnik, "Using Story Telling Techniques to Craft a Persuasive Legal Story."

40. Gary Gwilliam, interview by Michael Liskin, tape recording, Oakland, California, May 6, 1998. Information from this interview has been supplemented by details appearing in a brochure distributed by the Oakland law firm of Gwilliam, Ivary, Chiosso, Cavalli & Brewer, entitled *Summary of Major Cases*.

41. This case is described in the DecisionQuest firm brochure, entitled *DecisionQuest*. Available from DecisionQuest in Torrance, California.

42. Ibid.

43. Ibid.

44. Florence Keller, interview by Michael Liskin, tape recording, Palo Alto, California, April 1998. This section is based largely on that interview.

45. For a recent guide, see V. Hale Starr and Paul D. Beechen, *Witness Preparation* (New York: Aspen Law and Business, 1998).

46. Keller interview, April 1998.

47. This section is based largely on an interview with Howard Varinsky. Interview by Michael Liskin, tape recording, Emeryville, California, May 14, 1998.

48. Additionally, the new focus groups suggested that the few holdouts against Varinsky's client tended to be women who saw themselves as victims, possessed low self-esteem, and exhibited observable anger; they also were apt to be overweight and not very attractive. In contrast, women supporters were likely to be professionals who were "out there" and felt good about themselves. Thus, at trial, Varinsky sought jurors with good self-images and struck those who fit his antidefendant profile, including ". . . anybody my ex-therapist eyes said was depressed" (ibid.).

49. Gary Moran, interview by Neil J. Kressel, tape recording, Redondo Beach, California, March 6, 1998.

50. Daniel I. Small, *Preparing Witnesses: A Practical Guide for Lawyers and Their Clients* (Chicago: American Bar Association, 1998). See also, "Instructions for Witnesses," included in Thomas A. Mauet, *Fundamentals of Trial Techniques*, 3rd ed. (Boston: Little Brown, 1992), 391.

51. It is worth noting that the lip-service lawyers pay to careful witness preparation may not be followed consistently. Also, one way consultants can earn their pay is by doing something attorneys could do with equal effectiveness had they the inclination or time. Indeed, consultants sometimes apply principles that have been extracted from years of legal practice. Thus, attorney Steven Lubet's advice on how expert witnesses can avoid attorney tricks during cross-examination was reprinted as the lead article in *Court Call*, the newsletter of the trial consultants' professional organization. In this manner, witness preparation consultants can serve as a vehicle for redistributing and applying the guidelines of particularly insightful attorneys. See Steven Lubet, "Expert Testimony: A Survivor's Guide to Cross-Examination," *Court Call* (Winter 1999), 1, reprinted from Steven Lubet, *Expert Testimony: A Guide for Expert Witnesses and the Lawyers Who Examine Them* (Notre Dame, Indiana: National Institute of Trial Advocacy, 1998).

52. Elaine Lewis, "The Witness from Hell: Causes to Consider," *Fair$hare: The Matrimonial Law Monthly* 16, no. 12 (December 1996): 2.

53. Ibid., 3.

54. Ibid., 4.

55. Elaine Lewis, quoted in Shannon Pratt, "Guest Interview: How to Be an Expert Witness," *Shannon Pratt's Business Valuation Update* 2, no. 11 (November 1996): 1. Interview by Gerald Nissenbaum.

56. Eric Oliver, "More than Meets the Ear: Balancing Verbal and Nonverbal Messages," *Trial Diplomacy Journal* 19 (1996): 221.

57. See, for example, Irwin A. Horowitz, Thomas E. Willging, and Kenneth S. Bordens, *The Psychology of Law: Integrations and Applications*, 2nd ed. (New York: Longman, 1998); Lawrence S. Wrightsman, Michael T. Nietzel, and William H. Fortune, *Psychology and the Legal System*, 4th ed. (New York: Brooks/Cole, 1998); Lawrence S. Wrightsman, *Forensic Psychology* (Belmont, California: Wadsworth/Thomson Learning, 2001); Curt R. Bartol and Anne M. Bartol, *Psychology and Law: Research and Application*, 2nd ed. (Pacific Grove, California: Brooks/Cole, 1994).

58. Valerie P. Hans and Krista A. Sweigart, "Jurors' Views of Civil Lawyers: Implications for Courtroom Communication," *Indiana Law Journal* 68, no. 4 (Fall 1993): 1310.

59. Saul M. Kassin, Lorri N. Williams, and Courtney L. Saunders, "Dirty Tricks of Cross Examination: The Influence of Conjectural Evidence on the Jury," *Law and Human Behavior* 14, no. 4 (August 1990): 373.

60. C.W. [no name], "Numbers Can Confuse Jurors," *Science News* 153, no. 9 (February 1998): 137. The study was conducted by Jonathan J. Koehler at the University of Texas–Austin.

61. Reiko Hasuike, "Credibility and Gender in the Courtroom: What Jurors Think," in *The Woman Advocate: Excelling in the 90's*, ed. J.M. Snyder and A.B. Greene (Chicago: American Bar Association, 1995), reprinted as a brochure entitled *Credibility and Gender in the Courtroom* and available from DecisionQuest, Torrance, California.

62. Ibid.

63. Ibid.

64. Jeffrey T. Frederick, *The Psychology of the American Jury* (Charlottesville, Virginia: Michie [Lexis Law Publishing], 1987), accessed July 10, 1997, available from http://www.michie.com/Bookstore/Reading/fred/fred6.html, Internet. See also, Lawrence J. Smith and Loretta A. Malandro, *Courtroom Communication Strategies* (New York: Kluwer, 1985); and Don Vinson, *Jury Persuasion* (Englewood Cliffs, New Jersey: Prentice Hall Law and Business, 1993).

65. Frederick, *The Psychology of the American Jury*.

66. Ibid.

67. David Ball, *Theater Tips and Strategies for Jury Trials* (Notre Dame, Indiana: National Institute for Trial Advocacy, 1994).

68. The account that follows is drawn from news coverage in the *Salt Lake Tribune*. See Brian Maffly, "Jury Empaneled in Shooting Case Was Tainted, County Says," *Salt Lake Tribune*, August 17, 1996, B1; Ted Cilwick, "County Claims Juror Misconduct," *Salt Lake Tribune*, September 6, 1996, B2; Sheila R. McCann, "Jury: From Silent Body to Seeker of Truth," *Salt Lake Tribune*, September 8, 1996, B1; Ted Cilwick and Sheila R. McCann, "2nd Trial Begins in Shooting by Deputy," *Salt Lake Tribune*, May 2, 1997, C3; Sheila R. McCann, "Jurors Side With Deputy," *Salt Lake Tribune*, May 9, 1997, C1; Editorial, "Case of Contradictions," *Salt Lake Tribune*, May 12, 1997, A6; Sheila R. McCann, "No Third Trial for Manzanares," *Salt Lake Tribune*, June 12, 1997, C2; Michael Vigh, "Appeals Court Rewards Victim Shot by Deputy," *Salt Lake Tribune*, December 16, 1998, D1. All of the foregoing articles were accessed on October 1, 1999, from http://www.tribaccess.com, Internet.

69. This neighbor is quoted in Maffly, "Jury Empaneled in Shooting Case Was Tainted, County Says."

70. This juror is quoted in ibid.

71. Judge Benson, quoted in Vigh, "Appeals Court Rewards Victim Shot by Deputy."

72. Judge McWilliams, quoted in ibid.

73. Another trial (coincidentally also in Salt Lake City) raises important questions about the practice of contacting jurors after a trial has ended. Back in 1981, while driving his car, Curtis Campbell accidentally killed one man and seriously injured another. Campbell's automotive insurer, State Farm, rejected an offer to settle the matter for $50,000, the policy limit, opting instead to face a trial. (The discussion of the State Farm case is drawn primarily from coverage in the *Salt Lake Tribune*. See Sheila R. McCann, "State Farm Attacks Verdict—and Jurors," *Salt Lake Tribune*, January 12, 1997, E1; Sheila R. McCann, "Lawyers Are Seeking $58 Million in Fees," *Salt Lake Tribune*, January 12, 1997, E5; Associated Press, "A Case of Generous Juries," *Salt Lake Tribune*, January 19, 1997, A1; Sheila R. McCann, "Judge Says Damages Excessive," *Salt Lake Tribune*, December 21, 1997, B1. All of the foregoing articles were accessed on October 7, 1999, from http://www.tribaccess.com, Internet. See also Leslie Scism, "Utah Judge Reduces a Jury Award Against Insurer State Farm Mutual," *Wall Street Journal*, December 23, 1997, accessed October 7, 1999, available from http://www.gemhound.com/neighbor.html, Internet.)

According to Campbell, by rejecting the offer to settle, the insurer gambled with Campbell's financial future—and lost. State Farm did this, alleged Campbell, despite significant damaging expert and eyewitness evidence against him. When the jury found Campbell completely at fault and hit him with more than $250,000 in damages, his home and assets were placed at risk. Consequently, Campbell and his wife sued State Farm, charging that the insurer had acted in bad faith by refusing to accept a reasonable settlement offer. Their attorneys argued that the couple had suffered severe emotional distress and, more important, that State Farm's handling of their claim had been fraudulent. The Campbells' lawyers also succeeded in introducing into the trial substantial evidence of a national plan by State Farm to cheat policyholders. They argued that the large corporation typically treated valid claims with a calculated and calloused attitude.

The jury hearing the Campbells' case found for the couple, ruling that State Farm had indeed acted in bad faith. Then, a second jury shocked observers by awarding the couple more than $145 million, nearly all of it in punitive damages. The amount exceeded any punitive damages award ever sustained by an appellate court in Utah. And after returning this verdict in July 1997, the eight-member jury panel told Judge William Bohling that they didn't want to discuss the case with anyone. He subsequently informed both sides.

Defense lawyers nevertheless hired trial consultant Joseph Rice, director of the California-based Jury Research Institute. He contacted several jurors, seeking—among other objectives—to uncover evidence of juror misconduct or anything else that might prove useful in challenging the award or obtaining a new trial.

Feeling that their clearly expressed wishes had been ignored, some of the jurors reacted with dismay. Several hired a lawyer and complained of harassment to the trial judge. One juror complained that investigators had even gotten hold of his unlisted telephone number. Judge Bohling summoned lawyers for both sides, declaring that he was "frankly considerably disappointed" that State Farm had neglected the jurors' wishes to remain silent. He further noted that he regarded the affair as ". . . a matter of some seriousness." (Quoted in McCann, "State Farm Attacks Verdict—and Jurors.")

But the State Farm lawyers countered by explaining that they had not understood that contact with the panel members was officially prohibited. They further maintained that their interviewers had not harassed anyone and that they ceased asking questions as soon as someone informed them that he or she did not want to talk. The judge apparently did not accept the explanation. He then issued a specific order forbidding contact.

The defense lawyers used the jurors' refusal to speak with them as support for an argument that the panel had been biased all along. Joseph Rice, the trial consultant, said in an affidavit: "I have interviewed hundreds of jurors and have not been met with the animosity that was exhibited by those contacted" (ibid.). Defense lawyer Paul Belnap contended that jurors' attitudes toward the posttrial interviews ". . . reflects that the jury abandoned dispassionate debate for emotion" (ibid.). His colleague, Glenn Hanni, said that in nearly fifty years of legal practice this was the first case in which he had been involved ". . . where the jury all said, 'We are not going to talk to you'" (ibid.). But the attorney hired by the jurors suggested that State Farm's advocates had misinterpreted the panel's reluctance to speak after the trial. "They simply want their privacy rights respected," said lawyer David Olsen. "It has nothing to do with animosity or anything else"(ibid.).

Soon the public joined the debate. An editorial in the *Salt Lake Tribune* weighed in on the side of the jurors, arguing that the defense had other ways to challenge the verdict and that the attorneys should abandon their efforts to prove juror misconduct:

"The eight jurors in the State Farm case devoted much of their summer to the trial; surely, they would rather have spent the time doing something else. It is understandable that they would consider their civic duty completed after the trial and would rather not revisit the case through phone calls from attorneys. To suggest that such behavior is unusual or even indicative of possible misconduct is repugnant. More than that, if unwelcome juror contact by the losing side were to become commonplace after civil trials, it could have an erosive effect on the jury system. Americans do not need another disincentive to serve on a jury or to treat that duty responsibly." (Editorial, "Respect Jurors' Privacy," *Salt Lake Tribune*, January 19, 1997, AA1, accessed October 7, 1999, available from http://www.tribaccess.com, Internet.)

In the same spirit, one reader sent a letter to the editor suggesting that "the only new trial needed in this case is one in which State Farm attorney Paul Belnap and jury consultant Joseph Rice can defend why they disregarded the judge's instruction and violated the civil rights of these private citizens." (Arlen T. Einertson [Letter to the Editor], "Leave Jurors Alone," *Salt Lake Tribune*, January 31, 1997, A18, accessed October 7, 1999, available from http://www.tribaccess.com, Internet.)

Nearly a year later, Judge Bohling sliced the award to $25 million. Although the reduction was substantial, the remainder was nothing to sneeze at. But the reduction in the award hardly implied any acceptance of the charge that the jury was biased. To the contrary, the judge wrote, ". . . it became a matter of plain evidence that State Farm has sold as its product 'peace of mind' and has used as its advertising slogan, 'Like a Good Neighbor.' . . . State Farm's actions amount to betrayal of the trust it invites its policyholders to place in it and the trust it has a fiduciary duty to uphold." (Quoted in McCann, "Judge Says Damages Excessive.") He even indicated that State Farm's policies had been so successful that $25 million might not be enough to make the corporation take notice. But Judge Bohling apparently felt constrained by his belief that a higher award would not withstand subsequent appeals.

74. Justice Chin, quoted in "Quizzing of Jurors Irks Calif. Justice," *National Law Journal*, May 24, 1999, A6, accessed September 28, 1999, available from http://www.ljextra.com, Internet.

75. See National Jury Project, *Jurywork: Systematic Techniques*, sections 13–17, 13–18.

76. Ibid., section 13–21.

77. "Trial Consulting and Jury Consulting Services Provided," accessed September 30, 1999, from the Trial Behavior Consulting, Inc., website, available from http://www.lawinfo.com/biz/tbci/services.html, Internet.

78. Marjorie Fargo, "Make the Post-Trial Interview Work for You," *Criminal Justice* (Summer 1988): 4.

79. Patrice Truman, "Jurors' Advice for Attorney Etiquette and Conduct at Trial," *In Jurors' Own Words* (Spring 1999), accessed September 30, 1999 from the Truman Associates website, available from http://www.trumanassocoiates.com/newsltr99w.html, Internet.

80. B. F. Skinner, *Beyond Freedom and Dignity* (New York: Knopf, 1971; paperback, Bantam/Vintage, 1971), 91.

81. A preliminary empirical study has suggested that ". . . the perceptions of trial consulting techniques as being unfair are largely a function of an imbalance of trial consultant assistance among the parties." Dennis P. Stolle, Jennifer K. Robbennolt, and Richard L. Wiener, "The Perceived Fairness of the Psychological Trial Consultant: An Empirical Investigation," *Law and Psychology Review* 20 (1996): 169. The authors further suggest that "the perceived fairness of trial consulting services may vary as a function of the cost of the services, the techniques used by the consultant, the consultant's qualifications, or the degree to which the consultant actively participates in courtroom proceedings" (ibid., 172).

CHAPTER 6

1. Randall Kennedy, *Race, Crime, and the Law* (New York: Pantheon, 1997), 29.
2 Ibid., 87.
3. Ibid., 169.
4. Ibid., 170, quoting *Strauder v. West Virginia*, 100 U.S. 303, 304 (1879).
5. Ibid., 170, quoting *Strauder*, 100 U.S. at 309.
6. *Neal v. Delaware*, 103 U.S. 370, 393–94 (1880).
7. Kennedy, *Race, Crime, and the Law*, 178.
8. Ibid., 179.
9. See discussion in Jeffrey Abramson, *We, the Jury: The Jury System and the Ideal of Democracy* (New York: BasicBooks, 1994; paperback ed., 1995), 99.
10. *Taylor v. Louisiana*, 419 U.S. 522 (1975).
11. Abramson, *We, the Jury*, 118.
12. *Batson v. Kentucky*, 476 U.S. 79, 108 (1986).
13. See *J.E.B. v. Alabama*, 511 U.S. 127 (1994) (prohibiting gender-based peremptory challenges); *Georgia v. McCollum*, 505 U.S. 42 (1992) (ruling that the *Batson* prohibition on race-based peremptory challenges applies to the exercise of the challenge by the defense as well as by the prosecution); *Edmondson v. Leesville Concrete Co.*, 500 U.S. 614 (1991) (ruling that the *Batson* prohibition on race-based peremptory challenges applies to private litigants in civil cases); *Powers v. Ohio*, 499 U.S. 400 (1991) (prohibiting race-based peremptory challenges regardless of whether the challenged juror and the defendant are of the same race).
14. See, for example, *United States v. Chalan*, 812 F.2d 1302 (10th Cir. 1987) (American Indians); *United States v. Biaggi*, 909 F.2d 662 (2nd Cir. 1990) (Italian-Americans); *United States v. Chinchilla*, 874 F.2d 695 (9th Cir. 1989) (Hispanics).
15. *Hernandez v. New York*, 111 S.Ct. 1859 (1991); *United States v. Santiago-Martinez*, 58 F. 3rd 422 (9th Cir. (1995).
16. See, for example, Beth Bonora, "Bias in Jury Selection Continues," *National Law Journal*, February 27, 1995, B8, accessed February 1, 2001, available from http://www.ljextra, Internet.
17. To explain this problem, sociologist Hiroshi Fukurai and his colleagues have developed a complex model of the jury selection process and called attention to procedural anomalies in jury selection, socioeconomic structural barriers to inclusion, gerrymandered jury districts, and other factors. See Hiroshi Fukurai, Edgar W. Butler, and Richard Krooth, *Race and the Jury: Racial Disenfranchisement and the Search for Justice* (New York: Plenum Press, 1993), 13.
18. Faulkner Fox, "Justice in Jasper," Salon.com, February 26, 1999, accessed February 4, 2000, available from http://www.salon.com/news/1999/02/cov_26news.html, Internet. See also, Terri Langford, "Jury Selection in Dragging Death Trial Proving a Slow Process," *Abilene Reporter-News*,

January 28, 1999, accessed February 4, 2000, available from http://www.reporternews. com/1999/texas/drag0128.html, Internet.

19. Rick Lyman, "Texas Jury Picks Death Sentence in Fatal Dragging of a Black Man," *New York Times*, February 26, 1999, A17; Michael Graczyk, "Jury Sentences a Defiant King to Death for Black Man's Dragging," *Abilene Reporter-News*, February 26, 1999, accessed February 4, 2000, available from http://www.reporternews.com/1999/texas/jasper0226.html, Internet.

20. Richard Stewart, "Killer's Father Pleads for Son's Life," *Houston Chronicle*, February 25, 1999, A1 accessed May 31, 2001, available from LEXIS-NEXIS Academic Universe, http://www.lexis-nexis.com/universe, Internet.

21. This change in venue came not, as one might expect, at the request of the defense but because the prosecution wanted to weaken any appeal that might follow a conviction.

22. C. Bryson Hull, "Jury with No Blacks Will Hear Second Dragging Trial," *Abilene Reporter-News*, September 11, 1999, accessed January 28, 2000, available from http://www.reporternews. com/1999/texas/jury0911.html, Internet. See also, Kelly Brown, "No Blacks Picked for Jasper Jury," *Dallas Morning News*, September 11, 1999, accessed February 4, 2000, available from http://www.dallasnews.com, Internet.

23. Hull, "Jury with No Blacks Will Hear Second Dragging Trial;" Brown, "No Blacks Picked for Jasper Jury."

24. Claudia Kolker, "2nd Guilty Verdict Reached in Dragging Murder," *Los Angeles Times*, September 21, 1999, A16, accessed January 26, 2001, available from LEXIS-NEXIS Academic universe, http://www.lexis-nexis.com/universe, Internet. See also, "Second Texas Dragging Defendant Gets the Death Penalty," Court TV [Online], September 23, 1999, accessed January 28, 2000, available from http://www.courttv.com, Internet.

25. C. Bryson Hull, "Last Defendant: Third Dragging Death Defendant Heads to Trial," ABCNEWS.Com, October 4, 1999, accessed January 28, 2000, available from http://www.abc-news.go.com/sections/us/dailynews/jaspertrial991024.html, Internet; "Third Dragging Death Trial Delayed as Judge Considers Change of Venue Motion," Court TV [Online], November 9, 1999, accessed January 28, 2000, available from http://www.courttv.com/trials/berry/110999_ap.html, Internet; C. Bryson Hull, "Jury Selection Begins Today in 3rd Dragging-Death Trial," *Seattle Times*, October 25, 1999, accessed January 28, 2000, available from http://www.seattletimes.com/news/ nation-world/html98/drag_19991025.html, Internet; Associated Press, "Dragging Suspect Says Fear Kept Him from Helping Black Man," *Dallas Morning News*, November 16, 1999, accessed January 28, 2000, available from http://www.dallasnews.com/specials/jasper/1116jasper2trial.html, Internet; "Berry Says Fear Paralyzed Him," *Dallas Morning News*, November 17, 1999, accessed February 4, 2000, available from http://www.dallasnews.com/specials/jasper/1117jasper1jasper.html, Internet; Terry Langford,"JasperJury Gives Berry Life Sentence," *Dallas Morning News*, November 19, 1999, accessed February 4, 2000, available from http://www.dallasnews.com/specials/jasper/ 1119tsw9jasper.html, Internet; Terry Langford, "Berry Begins Serving Life Sentence in Isolation," *Dallas Morning News*, November 20, 1999, accessed January 28, 2000, available from http://www.dallasnews.com, Internet.

26. Betty DeRamus, "Justice, Not Racism, Prevails," *Detroit News*, February 26, 1999, accessed February 4, 2000, available from http://www.detnews.com/voices/deramus/990226/990226.html, Internet. See also, Fox, "Justice in Jasper." Faulkner Fox wrote: "It was King's venomous bigotry, and the horrendous way in which he and two ex-convict friends . . . killed Byrd . . . that seems to have unified the races" (ibid.). No white person in Texas had ever been sentenced to death for killing a black person until the King and Brewer trials.

27. William Booth and William Claiborne, "Simpson Plaintiffs Awarded $25 Million," *Washington Post*, February 11, 1997, A1, accessed January 26, 2001, available from LEXIS-NEXIS Academic universe, http://www.lexis-nexis.com/universe, Internet.

28. One civil juror made this point herself, stating: "This [civil verdict] in no way invalidates the earlier jury's decision. . . . They had a different burden of proof, they had different evidence, they had different forms of presentation." "Jurors Detail the Thinking That Went into Their Ruling," *USA Today*, February 11, 1997, accessed August 11, 1998, available from http://www.usatoday.com/news/index/nns219.html, Internet.

29. See, for example, Laurence H. Geller and Peter Hemenway, *Last Chance for Justice: The Juror's Lonely Quest* (Dallas: NCDS Press, 1997); Kennedy, *Race, Crime, and the Law*. Neither of these books agrees with the verdict in *People v. Powell*, but both suggest how jurors might plausibly have arrived at their decision.

30. Kennedy, *Race, Crime, and the Law*, 119.

31. See, for example, Paul Harris, *Black Rage Confronts the Law* (New York: New York University Press, 1997), 186.

32. Ibid.

33. Ibid., 187.

34. To the list of prominent cases where the racial composition of the jury was presumed by many to be crucial, we might add the Bernhard Goetz trials, the Lemrick Nelson trials, the Central Park jogger case, and police brutality trials in many cities across the country.

35. John T. McQuiston, "Mistrial Called in Beating of Black Man," *New York Times*, April 9, 1998, B1.

36. John T. McQuiston, "Foreman Says Race Split Jurors in L.I. Beating Trial," *New York Times*, April 10, 1998, B1.

37. Ibid

38. Editorial, "No Verdict, No Peace," *Pittsburgh Post-Gazette*, December 16, 1997, A26, accessed January 26, 2001, available from LEXIS-NEXIS Academic universe, http://www.lexis-nexis.com/universe, Internet.

39. See, for example, Paul Butler, "Black Jurors: Right to Acquit," *Harper's Magazine* (December 1995), 11, accessed November 9, 1999, available from http://www.infotrac.com, Internet (adapted from Paul Butler, "Racially Based Jury Nullification: Black Power in the Criminal Justice System," *Yale Law Journal* 105 [December 1995]: 677).

40. *Batson v. Kentucky*, 476 U.S. 79 (1986).

41. Barry Siegel, "Politics: Storm Still Lingers over Defense Attorney's Training Video," *Los Angeles Times*, April 29, 1997, A5, accessed February 14, 2000, available from http://www.proquest.umi.com, Internet; Tony Mauro, "Videotape Upends DA Campaign," *USA Today*, April 4, 1997, A3, accessed February 14, 2000, available from http://www.proquest.umi.com, Internet; "Judge Declares a Mistrial over Tape Made by Lawyer," *New York Times*, April 4, 1997, A12.

42. It is hard to imagine that McMahon could win an election for district attorney in a major city with a large African American population after such a videotape became public, even after *Philadelphia Magazine* published an article charging his opponent, Lynne Abraham, with similarly "racist" jury-picking. See Loren Feldman, "I, the Jury," *Philadelphia Magazine* (June 1997), 21. McMahon did, in fact, lose the election. However, we cannot be sure that the outcome of the election stemmed from the release of the videotape; the local Republicans blamed their candidate for a lackluster campaign, and he in turn blamed them for a lack of financial support. See Associated Press, "Racism Allegations Stir Philadelphia DA Campaign," *Boston Globe*, November 2, 1997, A20, accessed February 14, 2000, available from http://www.proquest.umi.com, Internet. See also, Mary Frangipanni,

"Mary Frangipanni's Political Notebook: The Year in Review," *City Paper Interactive*, January 1, 1998, accessed January 20, 2000, available from http://www.citypaper.net, Internet; Siegel, "Politics: Storm Still Lingers Over Defense Attorney's Training Video." Some black leaders sided with McMahon, and Abraham also found herself on the defensive regarding the racial sensitivity issue.

43. McMahon, quoted in "Jury Rigging Laid Bare," *Harper's Magazine* (June 1997), 21, accessed November 8, 1999, available from www.infotrac.com, Internet. This article includes a partial transcript of prosecutor Jack McMahon's training video.

44. Ibid.

45. But McMahon's approach at the time was probably not unusual. And it is important to note that even though his perspective on jury selection used broad generalizations—older black women identify with young black defendants, for example—and he bought into unfavorable stereotypes, he did not advise prosecutorial avoidance of African American jurors as a monolithic category. The Dallas District Attorney's Office, in those days, gave similar advice: "You are not looking for any members of minority groups which may subject him to oppression—they almost always empathize with the accused." See Dallas District Attorney's Office guidelines, quoted in Billy M. Turner, Rickie D. Lovell, John C. Young, and William F. Denny, "Race and Peremptory Challenges During Voir Dire: Do Prosecution and Defense Agree?," *Journal of Criminal Justice* 14 (1986): 63.

46. McMahon, quoted in Stuart L. Ditzen and Linda Loyd, "Review of Murder Case Is Ordered," *[Philadelphia] Inquirer*, January 26, 2000, accessed February 14, 2000, available from www.philly. com, Internet.

47. McMahon, quoted in "Jury Rigging Laid Bare."

48. McMahon, quoted in Siegel, "Politics: Storm Still Lingers over Defense Attorney's Training Video."

49. Rendell, quoted in ibid.

50. Ibid. Although the release of the old videotapes has not resulted in dozens of convicted criminals being set free, as was predicted at the time, there have been legal ramifications. See, for example, Ditzen and Loyd, "Review of Murder Case Is Ordered."

51. Justice Oliver Wendell Holmes Jr. first offered the advice, saying ". . . great cases, like hard cases, make bad law. For great cases are called great, not by reason of their real importance in shaping the law of the future, but because of some accident of immediate overwhelming interest which appeals to the feelings and distorts the judgment." *Northern Securities Co. v. United States*, 193 U.S. 197, 400 (1904), quoted by Alan M. Dershowitz, *Reasonable Doubts: The O.J. Simpson Case and the Criminal Justice System* (New York: Simon and Schuster, 1996), 196.

52. Marcia Clark and Teresa Carpenter, *Without a Doubt* (New York: Viking, 1997), 279.

53. Christopher A. Darden and Jess Walter, *In Contempt* (New York: ReganBooks, 1996; Harper-Paperbacks, 1997), 381.

54. Ibid., 373.

55. Ibid., 12.

56. Vincent Bugliosi, *Outrage: The Five Reasons Why O.J. Simpson Got Away with Murder* (New York: Island Books/Dell Publishing, 1996), 6.

57. Ibid., 60.

58. Ibid., 115.

59. Clark and Carpenter, *Without a Doubt*, 145.

60. Bugliosi, *Outrage*, 117.

61. Clark and Carpenter, *Without a Doubt*, 190.

62. Ibid., 184.

63. Ibid., 184–185.

64. Ibid., 138.

65. Ibid., 185. Five years after opposing one another in the Simpson criminal trial, Donald Vinson and Jo-Ellan Dimitrius teamed up to form the trial consulting firm of Vinson & Dimitrius.

66. Ibid.

67. Ibid., 196.

68 Dershowitz, *Reasonable Doubts*, 98. See also, Editorial, "Not Guilty, Not Innocent," *World Press Review* (December 1995), 32, reprinted from *The Economist*, October 7, 1995. It is worth noting that three years after publishing *Reasonable Doubts*, even Dershowitz remarked, "Had I been on the jury in the civil case, based on the evidence submitted in that case, I probably would have voted the way the jury voted," *i.e*, to support a $33.5 million award and a wrongful death verdict against Simpson. Dershowitz, quoted in Kristin Savarese, "Dershowitz No Longer Defends Former Client O.J. Simpson," Court TV [Online], June 10, 1999, accessed June 14, 1999, available from http://www.courttv.com/people/1999/0610/oj_ctv.html, Internet.

69. Clark and Carpenter, *Without a Doubt*, 186.

70. Ibid.

71. Darden, quoted in Clark and Carpenter, *Without a Doubt*, 261.

72. Darden and Walter, *In Contempt*, 234. In light of the considerable evidence of guilt, journalist Christopher Caldwell asserted that "there is . . . no intellectually serious argument to be made for Simpson's innocence, nor is anyone likely to try to make such an argument any time soon; this trial will never divide elite opinion as did, say, the Sacco and Vanzetti [trial] or the Alger Hiss case. More hotly contested is the question of why the system failed so badly." Christopher Caldwell, "Johnnie Cochran's Secret," *Commentary* (March 1997), 39. Supporting this contention, Caldwell cites evidence contained in the following sources: M.L. Rantala, *O.J. Unmasked* (Chicago: Catfleet Press/Open Court, 1996); Lawrence Schiller and James Willwerth, *American Tragedy: The Uncensored Story of the Simpson Defense* (New York: Random House, 1996); and Jeffrey Toobin, *The Run of His Life* (New York: Random House, 1996).

73. Poll cited in Dershowitz, *Reasonable Doubts*, 125.

74. Jeffrey Abramson, "After the O.J. Trial: The Quest to Create a Color-Blind Jury," *Chronicle of Higher Education*, November 3, 1995, B1, accessed November 27, 1998, available from http://www.proquest.umi.com, Internet, quoting Harry Kalven Jr. and Hans Zeisel, *The American Jury* (Boston: Little, Brown, 1966; Chicago: University of Chicago Press, 1971 [Phoenix ed.]).

75. Abramson, "After the O.J. Trial."

76. Lydia Saad and Frank Newport, "Majority of Americans Still Believe Simpson Is Guilty," *Gallup Poll Monthly* (August 1995): 15. See also, Victoria Kuhl, "Disparities in Judgments of the O.J. Simpson Case: A Social Identity Perspective," *Journal of Social Issues* 53, no. 3 (1997): 531.

77. Lydia Saad and Leslie McAneny, "Black Americans See Little Justice for Themselves and Most Believe Simpson Not Guilty," *Gallup Poll Monthly* (March 1995): 32.

78. Frank Newport, "Wrapping Up the O.J. Simpson Case," *Gallup Poll Monthly* (November 1995): 24. See also, Frank Newport, "Americans Still Think O.J. Simpson Guilty," *Gallup Poll Monthly* (May 1996): 16.

79. Abramson, "After the O. J Trial."

80. Carl E. Enomoto, "Public Sympathy for O.J. Simpson: The Roles of Race, Age, Gender, Income, and Education," *American Journal of Economics and Sociology* 58, no. 1 (January 1999): 145. Researchers Paul Skolnick and Jerry I. Shaw initially suspected that it was Simpson's "high status" as a celebrity rather than his race that may have helped him with the jury. To explore this hypothesis, they conducted a simulation where mock jurors heard a case with facts modeled closely on the Simpson case.

Their results ". . . suggest that race may have been a more important explanation than status for the acquittal verdict the Simpson jury delivered. . . . The significant interaction of juror race with defendant race on all four dependent measures strongly supports the Black racism explanation, because the extralegal factor of defendant race influenced Black mock jurors' judgments but not those of White mock jurors. Black jurors found the Black defendant guilty less often than the White defendant, but White jurors did not distinguish between Black and White defendants with regard to their verdicts." Paul Skolnick and Jerry I. Shaw, "The O.J. Simpson Criminal Trial Verdict: Racism or Status Shield?" *Journal of Social Issues* 53, no. 3 (1997): 514. Still, one should exercise extreme caution in generalizing from mock jury studies, and as the researchers note, there are special problems raised when one tries to draw confident conclusions about the Simpson trial on the basis of this simulation. The authors also caution that "the Black racism explanation of the Simpson verdict must be understood within. . . . [the context of] the long history of White bias against Black defendants" (ibid., 515).

81. Bugliosi, *Outrage*, 7.

82. Ibid., 60.

83. Albert W. Alschuler, "Our Faltering Jury," *Public Interest* (Winter 1996): 28, accessed November 9, 1999, available from http://www.infotrac.com, Internet.

84. Thomas Sowell, "Courtroom Circuses," *Forbes*, November 7, 1994, 90.

85. Clark and Carpenter, *Without a Doubt*, 199. Clark continues: "This happened to one of the alternates, a chemistry student from UCLA. This guy was absolutely brilliant. I knew that he sure as hell was going to understand our scientific evidence, and you could see that he gave the Dream team *agita*. Sure enough, they struck him with a peremptory" (ibid., 199–200).

86. Editorial, "Unreasonable Doubt," *New Republic*, October 23, 1995, 7, accessed June 3, 1997, available from http://www.infotrac.com, Internet. This editorial cited a CBS poll showing that the more education one possessed, the more likely he or she was to believe in Simpson's guilt.

87. Bryan Robinson, "Remaining Defendants in Diallo Shooting Say They Thought Victim Pointed Gun at Them," Court TV [Online], November 15, 2000, accessed February 16, 2000, available from http://www.courttv.com/national/diallo/021500_ctv.html, Internet. Unless otherwise indicated, quotations from participants in the Diallo case have been drawn from the Court TV website.

88. Walcott, quoted in Gary Tuchman, "Bronx Grand Jury and Protesters Take up Police Shooting," CNN.com, February 16, 1999, accessed December 20, 1999, available from http://www.cnn.com/US/9902/16/police.killing, Internet.

89. Sharpton, quoted in ibid.

90. Amy Waldman, "4 Officers' Trial in Diallo's Killing Moved to Albany," *New York Times*, December 17, 1999, A1.

91. "Excerpts from Ruling," *New York Times*, December 17, 1999, B12.

92. Ibid

93. "At a Glance: Comparing Two Counties," *New York Times*, December 17, 1999, B12.

94. Sharpton, quoted in Waldman, "4 Officers' Trial in Diallo's Killing Moved to Albany," B12. See also, C.J. Chivers, "Near the Bullet Holes, Bewilderment and Anger," *New York Times*, December 17, 1999, B12.

95. Editorial, "The Wrong Venue," *New York Times*, December 18, 1999, A22.

96. H. Carl McCall, "A Just Verdict? I'm Confident," *New York Post*, January 31, 2000, 37.

97. Johnson, quoted in Waldman, "4 Officers' Trial in Diallo's Killing Moved to Albany," A1.

98. Johnson, quoted in Amy Waldman, "District Attorney Defends Handling of the Diallo Case," *New York Times*, February 29, 2000, B5.

99. Siegel, quoted in Amy Waldman, "Protest and Justice: Diallo Trial Move at Issue," *New York Times*, December 20, 1999, B8.

100. Eric Adams, "Casting Doubt on the Entire Justice System," *New York Post*, December 22, 1999, accessed January 31, 2001, available from http://www.nypost.com/12221999/20194.html, Internet.

101. Alan M Dershowitz, "Why Justice Had to Get out of Town," *New York Times*, December 18, 1999, A23.

102. Joyce Purnick, "In Diallo Trial, Best Option Is Albany," *New York Times*, December 23, 1999, B1.

103. Amy Waldman, "Protest and Justice: Diallo Trial Move at Issue," B1.

104. Ibid., B8.

105. Patrick J. Lynch, "An Escape from Mob Justice," *New York Post*, December 22, 1999, accessed January 31, 2001, available from http://www.nypost.com/12221999/20192.html, Internet.

106. See Matthew Purdy, "The Debate on Diallo Goes North," *New York Times*, December 22, 1999, B5, for a discussion of concerns in the minority community over police conduct in Albany.

107. John E. Dorfman, "How I'd Pick the Diallo Jury," *New York Post*, January 31, 2000, 37.

108. Steven R. Coffey, "How I'd Pick the Diallo Jury," *New York Post*, January 31, 2000, 37.

109. Jane Fritsch, "Race Issue Raised as 5 Jurors Are Chosen for Diallo Trial," *New York Times*, February 1, 2000, B5.

110. Amy Waldman, "On Path to Speedy Trial, a Judge with a Firm Hand," *New York Times*, February 24, 2000, B5.

111. Ibid.

112. "Profiles of Diallo Jurors," Court TV [Online], February 22, 2000, accessed February 28, 2000, available from http://www.courttv.com/national/diallo/jury_profile.html, Internet. Juror descriptions come from this article. One of the originally selected jurors was replaced by an alternate when it became known that she had talked about the case to somebody outside the courthouse.

113. See discussion in Bryan Robinson, "Deliberations Begin in Diallo Shooting Trial," Court TV [Online], February 23, 2000, accessed February 24, 2000, available from http://www.courttv.com/national/diallo/022300_ctv.html, Internet.

114. Bryan Robinson, "Diallo Jurors Say They Had No Choice but to Acquit," Court TV [Online], February 28, 2000, accessed February 28, 2000, available from http://www.courttv.com/national/diallo/022800_aftermath_ctv.html, Internet.

115. Ibid.

116. Winnie Hu, "When Case Was Weighed, Prosecution Was Wanting, Juror Says," *New York Times*, February 28, 2000, B5.

117. Robinson, "Diallo Jurors Say They Had No Choice but to Acquit."

118. Ibid.

119. Tom Hays, "Juror: Diallo Verdict Was Clear," *Washington Post*, February 27, 2000, accessed February 28, 2000, available from http://www.washingtonpost.com, Internet.

120. "Diallo's Mother Reacts to Jurors," MSNBC [Online], February 28, 2000, accessed February 28, 2000, available from http://www.msnbc.com, Internet.

121. Marjorie Connelly, "Poll Finds That Half in State Disagree with Diallo Verdict," *New York Times*, February 29, 2000, B5. It is, of course, a mistake to interpret answers to a pollster as predictors of how the respondent would be likely to vote if they actually heard testimony and participated in deliberations.

122. Bob Herbert, "At the Heart of the Diallo Case," *New York Times*, February 28, 2000, A19.

123. Butts, quoted in Eric Lipton, "From Pulpits to Politics, Angry Voices on Diallo," *New York Times*, February 28, 2000, A1.

124. Ibid., B5.

125. Sharpton, quoted in ibid.

126. Frankie Edozien, "Feds Won't Prosecute Diallo Cops," NYPOST.com, January 31, 2001, accessed January 31, 2001, available from http://www.nypost.com/news/regionalnews/diallo 013101.html, Internet.

127. C.J. Chivers, "Near the Bullet Holes, Bewilderment and Anger," B12.

128. Magan A. Crane and Jonathan S. Hershberg, "Charged Cops Prefer to Tell It to the Judge," *Bronx Beat Online*, April 20, 1998, accessed January 28, 2000, available from http://www.bronx-beat.jrn.columbia.edu/indices/042098/cop.html, Internet.

129. Ibid.

130. Michael Cooper, "Jurors Acquit Bronx Man in Shooting Police Officer," *New York Times*, October 29, 1999, B4.

131. "Man Shot by Police Awarded $76 Million by Bronx Jury," *NandoTimes* [Online], April 8, 1998, accessed January 28, 2000, available from http://www.nando.net, Internet.

132. Associated Press, "Judge Rules Bankrupt Goetz Liable for $43 Million Judgment," *[Connecticut] News Times*, August 2, 1996, accessed January 28, 2000, available from http://www.new-stimes.com/archive96/aug0296/nac.html, Internet.

133. "An Accident and a Dream," Public Policy Institute of New York State [Online], accessed January 28, 2000, available from http://www.bcnys.org/new/ppi/accintro.html, Internet.

134. Arthur S. Hayes, "Bronx Cheer: Inner-City Jurors Tend to Rebuff Prosecutors and to Back Plaintiffs," *Wall Street Journal*, March 24, 1992, A1, accessed January 29, 2001, available from http://www.proquestdirect.com, Internet.

135. Ibid., quoting Tom Wolfe, *Bonfire of the Vanities* (New York: Farrar Straus and Giroux, 1987).

136. Hayes, "Bronx Cheer."

137. Paul Craig Roberts, "Savvy Jurors Are Skeptics, Too," *Denver Rocky Mountain News*, February 22, 1997, 48A, accessed January 30, 2001, available from LEXIS-NEXIS Academic Universe, http://www.lexis-nexis.com/universe, Internet.

138. Ibid.

139. David Rohde, "Jurors' Trust in Police Erodes in Light of Diallo and Louima," *New York Times*, March 9, 2000, B1.

140. Ibid.

141. Kennedy, *Race, Crime, and the Law*, 4.

142. Ibid., 128.

143. Jeffrey E. Pfeifer, "Reviewing the Empirical Evidence on Jury Racism: Findings of Discrimination or Discriminatory Findings?," *Nebraska Law Review* 69 (1990): 230, takes the latter position and provides a good review of the dispute. Sheri Lynn Johnson, "Black Innocence and the White Jury," *Michigan Law Review* 83 (1985): 1611, summarizes evidence prior to 1985 suggesting that there is ". . . a widespread tendency among whites to convict black defendants in instances in which white defendants would be acquitted."

144. See, for example, Pfeifer, "Reviewing the Empirical Evidence on Jury Racism"; Johnson, "Black Innocence and the White Jury."

145. Valerie P. Hans and Neil Vidmar, *Judging the Jury* (New York: Plenum Press, 1986), 138.

146. See Johnson, "Black Innocence and the White Jury," 1625, for a comprehensive, although somewhat biased, summary of these studies.

147. M.T. Nietzel and R.C. Dillehay, *Psychological Consultation in the Courtroom* (New York: Pergamon Press, 1986); N.L. Kerr, R.W. Hymes, A.B. Anderson, and J.E. Weathers, "Defendant-Juror Similarity and Mock Juror Judgments," *Law and Human Behavior* 19 (1995): 545.

148. See Abbe Smith, "'Nice Work If You Can Get It': 'Ethical' Jury Selection in Criminal Defense," *Fordham Law Review* 62 (November 1998): 523. Smith concludes that the "new ethics" of expanded prohibitions against using peremptory challenges to strike members of certain cognizable groups "is at odds with other long standing and controlling ethical obligations of criminal defense lawyers" (ibid., 531).

CHAPTER 7

1. Sandra Day O'Connor, "Room for Improvement," *Dialogue* vol. 3, no. 4 (Fall 1999), accessed January 10, 2001, available from http://www.abanet.org/legalservices, Internet. Adapted from a speech delivered at the National Conference on Public Trust and Confidence in the Justice System, Washington, D.C., May 1999.In May 1999, 500 leaders in the American justice system—including Supreme Court justices, state chief justices, and representatives of the federal judiciary—gathered together to ". . . identify the issues affecting public trust in the justice system and to enhance and support state court strategies addressing these issues." See draft document entitled, "National Conference on Public Trust and Confidence in the Justice System: National Action Plan," National Center for State Courts [Online], accessed June 9, 2000, available from http://www.ncsc.dni.us, Internet.

2. "Developments in the Law: The Civil Jury," *Harvard Law Review* 110, no. 7 (May 1997): 1451. See also, Hiroshi Fukurai, Edgar W. Butler, and Richard Krooth, *Race and the Jury: Racial Disenfranchisement and the Search for Justice* (New York: Plenum, 1993).

3. See generally, Jeffrey Abramson, *We, the Jury: The Jury System and the Ideal of Democracy* (New York: Basic Books, 1994; paperback ed., 1995).

4. *United States v. Burr*, 25 F. Cas. 49, 50–51 (C.C.D. Va. 1807).

5. Ibid. at 51.

6. Ibid. The Marshall Court set forth a rule to test the impartiality of a juror: "The opinion which has been avowed by the court is, that light impressions which may fairly be supposed to yield to the testimony that may be offered, which may leave the mind open to a fair consideration of that testimony, constitute no sufficient objection to a juror; but that those strong and deep impressions which will close the mind against the testimony that may be offered in opposition to them, which will combat that testimony, and resist its force, do constitute a sufficient objection to him. Those who try the impartiality of a juror ought to test him by this rule" (ibid.).

7. See Abramson, *We, the Jury*, 99.

8. For example, in the 1986 *Turner v. Murray* decision (476 U.S. 28), the Supreme Court ruled that a trial judge should inquire about jurors' possible racial prejudice in the penalty phase of a capital trial, and if the judge fails to do so, the failure constitutes reversible error. During voir dire, the trial judge had asked prospects whether they knew of any reason why they could not render a fair and impartial verdict, but he did not inquire specifically about racial prejudice. Legal scholar Albert Alschuler comments poignantly on this decision: "The Supreme Court did not require an extended examination of prospective jurors to discover hidden or unrecognized biases. The defendant apparently was entitled only to a single question propounded to the entire jury panel. . . . Although the Supreme Court described this procedure as 'minimally intrusive,' . . . it also seems minimally useful. One doubts that Lester Maddox, Orville Faubus, George Wallace, Theodore Bilbo or anyone else would have responded to the proposed question by confessing a bias likely to affect his or her resolution of a capital murder case." Albert W. Alschuler, "The Supreme Court and the Jury: Voir Dire, Peremptory Challenges, and the Review of Jury Verdicts," *University of Chicago Law Review* 56 (Winter 1989): 160.

9. *Batson v. Kentucky*, 476 U.S. 79 (1986); *Edmonson v. Leesville Concrete Co.*, 500 U.S. 614 (1991); *Georgia v. McCollum*, 505 U.S. 42 (1992); *J.E.B. v. Alabama*, 114 S.Ct. 1419 (1994); *Purkett v. Elem*, 115 S.Ct. 1769 (1995).

10. William Blackstone, *Commentaries on the Laws of England*, vol. 4, quoted in Barbara Allen Babcock, "Jury Service and Community Representation," in *Verdict: Assessing the Civil Jury System*, edited by Robert E. Litan (Washington, D.C.: Brookings Institution, 1993), 464.

11. Barbara Allen Babcock, "Voir Dire: Preserving 'Its Wonderful Power,'" *Stanford Law Review* 27 (February 1975): 533, cited in Babcock, "Jury Service and Community Representation," 464.

12. Ibid., 465. In subsequent years, Babcock modified her thinking on these matters, concluding that the costs of some peremptory challenges, especially those based on race, were too high. She conceded: "What I failed to recognize was that, even though no words were spoken, the same tides of racial passion swept through the courtroom when the peremptory challenges were exercised." Babcock, "Jury Service and Community Representation," 465.

13. Professor Alschuler explains that prior to *Batson* a prosecutor might have justified exclusion of blacks from a panel on tactical grounds, perhaps arguing: "I do not doubt that black jurors can fairly try a case against a black defendant. My goal, however, is to secure a jury that will prove as receptive to the state's case as possible. I must exercise my peremptory challenges on the basis of limited information; and my experience has been that, although both blacks and whites are generally fair-minded and conscientious, whites tend to be more favorable to the state's position in this sort of case than blacks." Alschuler, "The Supreme Court and the Jury," 168. *Batson* has rendered this approach illegitimate.

14. Leonard L. Cavise, "The *Batson* Doctrine: The Supreme Court's Utter Failure to Meet the Challenge of Discrimination in Jury Selection," *Wisconsin Law Review* 1999 (1999): 505.

15. Alschuler, "The Supreme Court and the Jury," 169. See also, Amy B. Gendleman, "The Equal Protection Clause, the Free Exercise Clause, and Religion-Based Peremptory Challenges," *University of Chicago Law Review* 63, no. 4 (Fall 1996): 1639.

16. See Randall Kennedy, *Race, Crime, and the Law* (New York: Pantheon, 1997), 210; Charles J. Ogletree, "Just Say No! A Proposal to Eliminate Racially Discriminatory Uses of Peremptory Challenges," *American Criminal Law Review* 31, no. 4 (1994): 1099.

17. *Batson v. Kentucky*, 476 U.S. 79, (1986) (Marshall, J., concurring).

18. Abramson, *We, the Jury*, 261–262.

19. Stephen J. Adler, *The Jury: Disorder in the Courts* (New York: Times Books, 1994; paperback ed., New York: Doubleday, 1994), 221.

20. See, for example, Kennedy, *Race, Crime, and the Law*, 229; Harold J. Rothwax, *Guilty: The Collapse of Criminal Justice* (New York: Random House, 1996), 207; Burton S. Katz, *Justice Overruled: Unmasking the Criminal Justice System* (New York: Warner, 1997), 108; H. Lee Sarokin and G. Thomas Munsterman, "Recent Innovations in Civil Jury Trial Procedures," in *Verdict: Assessing the Civil Jury System*, 384. See also, Brent J. Gurney, "The Case for Abolishing Peremptory Challenges in Criminal Trials," *Harvard Civil Rights–Civil Liberties Law Review* 21 (Winter 1986): 221; Karen M. Bray, "Reaching the Final Chapter in the Story of Peremptory Challenges," *UCLA Law Review* 40, no. 2 (December 1992): 517. A committee of prominent judges, lawyers, and others recently examined the judicial system at a conference in Washington, D.C., concluding—among other things—that peremptories should be abolished or drastically reduced in number. See Thomas F. Hogan, Gregory E. Mize, and Kathleen Clark, "How to Improve the Jury System," *World and I* 13 (July 1998): 64.

21. See, for example, Raymond Brown, "Peremptory Challenges as a Shield for the Pariah," *American Criminal Law Review* 31, no. 4 (Summer 1994): 1203; Babcock, "Jury Service and Community

Representation," 478. See also, John C. Blattner, "Review of *The Jury: Trial and Error in the American Courtroom*. By Stephen J. Adler," *Michigan Law Review* 93 (May 1995): 1370. Attorney John Blattner explains how peremptory challenges can help legitimize verdicts in the eyes of the parties, suggesting that a person should place oneself ". . . in the position of a civil defendant being sued for an enormous sum of money, or a criminal defendant facing the possibility of a jail sentence. The six or twelve individuals who will decide your case are the most important people in the world to you at that moment. Let us now suppose that a particular potential juror takes the stand during voir dire, and you believe that this particular juror is unfavorably disposed towards you. It may be because she is young, or middle-aged, or elderly, or married, or unmarried, or childless, or nonartistic, or a union activist. . . . It may be simply because of the way she looks at you, or simply because you don't like her looks. You may not even know why you feel as you do. What you do know is that you will not be able to accept an unfavorable verdict so long as this individual, whom you are convinced 'has it in for you,' is on the jury. The use of peremptory challenges makes sense in precisely this kind of situation." Not only the parties but also observers can take comfort in the knowledge that a verdict could not have rested on the views of those who might have prejudged the facts and participants.

22. American Bar Association, "Perceptions of the U.S. Justice System: Executive Summary," ABAnet [Online], February 24, 1999, accessed June 10, 2000, available from http://www.abanet.org/media/perception/perceptexec.html, Internet.

23. Mark Curriden, "Putting the Squeeze on Juries," *ABA Journal* (August 2000), 54.

24. An additional 31 percent said they had "only some" confidence. See Pew Research Center Poll, national telephone survey of 1,218 adults conducted January 1998, *Public Opinion Online* (Roper Center at University of Connecticut, 1998), accessed October 28, 2000, avbailable from LEXIS-NEXIS Academic Universe, http://www.lexis-nexis.com/universe, Internet.

25. American Bar Association, "Perceptions of the U.S. Justice System: Executive Summary."

26. According to one recent survey, 59 percent of lawyers say that televised trials have a negative impact on the legal system; only 14 percent see the impact as positive. Heather Brewer, "Snap Judgments," *Business Law Today* 9, no. 4 (March/April 2000): 4. See also, Christo Lassiter, "The Appearance of Justice: TV or Not TV—That Is the Question," *Journal of Criminal Law and Criminology* 86 (Spring 1996): 928.

27. Lawrence S. Wrightsman, Michael T. Nietzel, and William H. Fortune, *Psychology and the Legal System*, 4th ed. (New York: Brooks/Cole, 1998), 362.

28. This body of evidence is summarized in numerous works, including: Reid Hastie, Steven D. Penrod, and Nancy Pennington, *Inside the Jury* (Cambridge, Massachusetts: Harvard University Press, 1983); Valerie Hans and Neil Vidmar, *Judging the Jury* (New York: Plenum, 1986); Saul M. Kassin and Lawrence S. Wrightsman, *The American Jury on Trial: Psychological Perspectives* (New York: Hemisphere, 1988); Reid Hastie, ed., *Inside the Juror: The Psychology of Juror Decision Making* (New York: Cambridge University Press, 1993); Neil Vidmar, *Medical Malpractice and the American Jury* (Ann Arbor: University of Michigan Press, 1995); Irwin A. Horowitz, Thomas E. Willging, and Kenneth S. Bordens, *The Psychology of Law: Integrations and Applications*, 2nd ed.(New York: Longman, 1998); Wrightsman, Nietzel, and Fortune, *Psychology and the Legal System*.

29. Adler, quoted in Moe Rouse, "Media Relations," *Court Call* (Fall 1998): 9. Adler originally made the comments on the ABC News program *Nightline* in autumn 1994.

30. Franklin Strier, "Whither Trial Consulting? Issues and Projections," *Law and Human Behavior* 23, no. 1 (February 1999): 101.

31. See Larry J. Sabato, *The Rise of the Political Consultants: New Ways of Winning Elections* (New York: Basic Books, 1981); Dan Nimmo, *The Political Persuaders: The Techniques of Modern Election Campaigns* (Englewood Cliffs, New Jersey: Prentice-Hall, 1970); Sidney Blumenthal, *The Permanent*

Campaign (New York: Simon and Schuster, 1980; revised ed., 1982); Joe McGinniss, *The Selling of the President, 1968* (New York: Trident, 1969).

32. We also believe that the nation would be better off without thirty-second political advertisements, but that doesn't mean that we would advise a candidate not to use them or that we would vote to make them illegal.

33. Pat McEvoy, "Trial Consultants Visibility," *Court Call* (Spring 2000), 14. McEvoy is chair of the Professional Visibility Committee of the American Society of Trial Consultants and a partner in the Chicago firm of Zagnoli McEvoy Foley Ltd.

34. Ibid., 14.

35. For scholarly discussions of how to regulate trial consultants, see Franklin Strier, "Paying the Piper: Proposed Reforms of the Increasingly Bountiful but Controversial Profession of Trial Consulting," *South Dakota Law Review* 44 (1998–1999): 699; Franklin Strier and Donna Shestowsky, "Profiling the Profilers: A Study of the Trial Consulting Profession, Its Impact on Trial Justice, and What, If Anything, to Do About It," *Wisconsin Law Review* 1999 (1999): 441; Strier, "Whither Trial Consulting?"; Jeremy W. Barber, "The Jury Is Still Out: The Role of Jury Science in the Modern American Courtroom," *American Criminal Law Review* 31 (Summer 1994): 1225; Jeffrey J. Rachlinski, "Scientific Jury Selection and the Equal Protection Rights of Venire Persons," *Pacific Law Journal* 24 (1993): 1497; James D. Herbsleb, Bruce Dennis Sales, and John J. Berman, "When Psychologists Aid in the Voir Dire: Legal and Ethical Considerations," in *Social Psychology and Discretionary Law,* ed. L.E. Abt and Irving R. Stuart (New York: Van Nostrand Reinhold, 1979); Debra Sahler, "Comment: Scientifically Selecting Jurors while Maintaining Professional Responsibility: A Proposed Model Rule," *Albany Law Journal of Science and Technology* 6 (1996): 383; Dennis P. Stolle, Jennifer K. Robbennolt, and Richard L. Wiener, "The Perceived Fairness of the Psychologist Trial Consultant: An Empirical Investigation," *Law and Psychology Review* 20 (1996): 139; John Charles S. Pierce, "Selecting the Perfect Jury: Use of Jury Consultants in Voir Dire," *Law and Psychology Review* 14 (1990): 167; John B. McConahay, Courtney J. Mullin, and Jeffrey Frederick, "The Uses of Social Science in Trials with Political and Racial Overtones: The Trial of Joan Little," *Law and Contemporary Problems* 41 (1977): 205.

36. Some have proposed regulating trial consultants via the ethical standards of the American Psychological Association (APA). (See, among others, Herbsleb, Sales, and Berman, "When Psychologists Aid in the Voir Dire," 208.) This approach can work only to extent that jury consultants belong to the APA and value their membership in that organization. At present, few of the minority who do belong would suffer substantial professional consequences were they to terminate membership in the APA. Debra Sahler has suggested incorporating a new rule into the American Bar Association's Model Rules of Professional Conduct. Her rule would read: "A lawyer shall not use jury selection information in a manner that is inconsistent with the responsibilities of a lawyer or in a manner that undermines faith in the jury system." Sahler, "Comment: Scientifically Selecting Jurors while Maintaining Professional Responsibility," 404. The articulation of this principle would probably not change the consulting industry's status quo much, but according to Sahler's commentary on her proposed rule, attorneys would be required to disclose the use of a jury consultant at the outset of a trial.

37. Daniel Wolfe, "ASTC Code of Professional Standards Commentary," *Court Call* (Spring 1999), 11. Robert Gordon, director of the Wilmington Institute of Trial and Settlement Sciences, has proposed a list of ten ethical principles designed to ". . . prevent a useful and burgeoning profession from drowning in its own success." Robert Gordon, "Setting Parameters for Trial Science," *Legal Times,* February 6, 1995, 34, accessed November 11, 2000, available from LEXIS-NEXIS Academic universe, http://www.lexis-nexis.com/universe, Internet. Although his guidelines are well-intentioned, it is hard to envision how they might be adopted by consultants and, if they were, how they might be

enforced. For example, principle number four maintains, "It is the responsibility of the trial consultant to assist in the seating of fair and impartial juries. Trial consultants must be committed to applying their skills and techniques to help seat juries that are not biased toward their client or their cause" (ibid.). If enforced, this rule would seem to strike at the very heart of the jury selection business.

38. National Jury Project (Elissa Krauss and Beth Bonora, eds.), *Jurywork: Systematic Techiques*, 2nd ed. (St. Paul, Minnesota: West Group/Clark Boardman Callaghan, 1999), vol. 2, release no. 2, October 1985, App. A–1; *Britt v. North Carolina*, 404 U.S. 226 (1971).

39. Ibid.

40. Ibid.

41. Gail Diane Cox, "King Trial: The Real Story," *National Law Journal*, May 3, 1993, 1.

42. Deborah Pines, "Terrorism Trial Will Use Questionnaires, Consultants for Jury," *New York Law Journal*, November 9, 1994, 1.

43. See, for example, Pierce, "Selecting the Perfect Jury," 179; Stolle, Robbennolt, and Wiener, "The Perceived Fairness of the Psychologist Trial Consultant," 170; Strier, "Whither Trial Consulting?" 112. The authors of *Jurywork* imply that under certain circumstances failure to appoint a jury consultant might, in theory, constitute reversible error if it could be established that the absence of the service was pivotal to the trial. Bonora and Krause, *Jurywork*, Appendix A–2. We know of no cases where this has occurred.

44. National Jury Project, *Jurywork: Systematic Techniques*, release no. 19, September 1998, App. A. This list includes court appointments for a variety of services provided by trial consultants, including venue evaluation surveys. We believe that the case for venue evaluation surveys is stronger than the case for voir dire preparation and jury selection assistance. Sample surveys are widely recognized as the gold standard for assessing bias in a venue, and a defense attorney would be hard-pressed to argue for a change of venue without such data.

45. Ibid.

46. Strier, "Whither Trial Consulting?" 112. See *Ake v. Oklahoma*, 470 U.S. 68 (1985).

47. Pierce, "Selecting the Perfect Jury," 184.

48. Stolle, Robbennolt, and Wiener, "The Perceived Fairness of the Psychologist Trial Consultant," 170.

49. Herbsleb, Sales, and Berman, "When Psychologists Aid in the Voir Dire," 200.

50. *McCormick on Evidence*, 4th ed. (West) at section 96, 354.

51. The proposal continues to receive support in discussions of trial consulting. See, for example, Strier, "Whither Trial Consulting?" 109; Barber, "The Jury Is Still Out," 1247.

52. *McCormick on Evidence*, at section 96, 356–367.

53. In a recent case, a prosecutor sought information about a community survey that he learned was being conducted for the defense by National Jury Project. Prosecutor Julius Finkelstein charged that the jury consultants were, in reality, attempting to taint the jury pool under the guise of standard jury research. Superior Court Judge Kevin Murphy, sensibly, rejected the prosecutor's argument, siding with the defense—for no evidence even suggested that the consultants had any ulterior motives. In opposing the prosecutor's motion, the defense noted that very little case law deals with discovery of materials associated with jury research but that "courts are accustomed to applying the work product doctrine to the appraisals, opinions and reports of a wide variety of experts who are employed as consultants, yet not designated as trial witnesses." "Points and Authorities in Support of Motion to Quash Subpoena Duces Tecum," in *California v. Avant! Corporation*, Superior Court for the State of California, County of Santa Clara, August 9, 1999, available from archives of the American Society of Trial Consultants, Towson, Maryland. The defense further maintained that "all of the lawyer's input into a community attitude survey, from whether to conduct one to how it is to be con-

structed, is subject to . . . absolute privilege [under California law] . . . because it reflects the lawyer's impression as to what is important and what the strengths and weaknesses of the case are. In one sense or another, all of this is bound up with the 'conclusions, opinions or legal research or theories' that are within the ambit of the statute. . . . Since it is impossible to separate out the lawyer's contribution to the design of the questionnaire from what the trial consultant does with this information, the product of the close collaboration between the lawyer and trial consultant—the questionnaire in its entirety—is work product protected. Likewise are the results of the questionnaire, which cannot be 'cleansed,' in effect, of the lawyer's input" (ibid.). See also, Craig Anderson, "'Opinion Survey' Target of Avant Prosecutor," *San Francisco Daily Journal*, August 9, 1999, 1; Craig Anderson, "Judge Rejects Prosecutor's Claims About Avant Poll," *San Francisco Daily Journal*, August 10, 1999, 1. Although states differ in their rules of discovery and work-product protection, this argument is a strong one, stronger in our view than the contention that ". . . the data seem to be 'scientific' or 'experts' reports' rather than the opinion of lawyers." Herbsleb, Sales, and Berman, "When Psychologists Aid in the Voir Dire," 205.

54. Janan Hanna and John O'Brien, "O.J. Leads Philip to Make Case Against Consultants," *Chicago Tribune*, October 31, 1995, C3; Andrew Blum, "Jury Consultants Targeted," *National Law Journal*, November 20, 1995, A6.

55. Eric C. Johnson, *Proposed Reforms to the Criminal Justice System as a Reaction to the Simpson Verdict* (San Francisco: Hastings College of Law, Public Law Research Institute Report, 1994), accessed July 22, 2000, available from http://www.uchastings.edu/plri, Internet.

56. Strier makes the point that "unless advocates of this proposal could demonstrate something singularly pernicious about consulting, they would leave themselves open to a *reductio ad absurdum* attack. That is, if consultants are banned on grounds of unfair advantage, why not also expert witnesses, investigators, and all the other professions in the proliferating field of litigation support?" Strier, "Whither Trial Consulting?" 108. In any event, outright legislative bans on jury selection consulting are unlikely to withstand constitutional challenge, and there appears to be little public will to build a legislative movement around the issue.

57. Herbsleb, Sales, and Berman, "When Psychologists Aid in the Voir Dire," 200.

58. Rachlinski, "Scientific Jury Selection and the Equal Protection Rights of Venire Persons," 1566.

59. Patricia Henley, *Improving the Jury System: Peremptory Challenges* (San Francisco: Hastings College of Law, Public Law Research Institute Report, 1996), accessed July 22, 2000, available from http://www.uchastings.edu/plri, Internet.

60. Alschuler, "The Supreme Court and the Jury," 207.

61. Abramson, *We, the Jury*, 263.

62. See discussion in Jeffrey T. Frederick, *Mastering Voir Dire and Jury Selection: Gaining an Edge in Questioning and Selecting a Jury* (Chicago: American Bar Association, 1995), 172–173. The U.S. Court of Appeals for the Second Circuit recently articulated a somewhat broader interpretation of the for-cause standard, finding that "inferable bias" existed where a juror was engaged in an activity closely akin to the conduct charged in the case. See Donald C. Dilworth, "Second Circuit Broadens Standards for Dismissing Prospective Jurors," *Trial* (January 1998), 92.

63. See Abramson, *We, the Jury*, 262.

64. Ibid.

65. Ibid.

66. Ibid.

67. Without peremptories, lawyers might ask less invasive questions for fear that they would create animosity in a prospective juror who might yet end up on the final panel. If, however, a lawyer

asks a legitimate question, and a juror responds with signs of annoyance or anger, the judge would—of course—have the option of dismissing the juror. If the juror remained, the abandonment of the unanimity requirement (discussed below) would afford some protection.Some have suggested that jurors dismissed by a judge for cause might be angrier at the system than those dismissed by peremptory strike in a procedure that is admittedly and quite apparently irrational. Expanded challenges for cause might result in more dissatisfied jurors, especially when such strikes are based on the reasonableness of suspecting bias rather than the prospect's self-admission. Alschuler notes, however, that methods can be devised to shield a juror from anger or embarrassment. He explains that: ". . . following the voir dire examination of a somewhat larger number of prospective jurors than the number to be empaneled, a trial judge might be permitted to select on a discretionary basis those jurors who appeared best qualified to decide the case impartially. If the judge saw no reason to doubt any prospective juror's ability or fairness, the judge might use a random selection process instead, and someone not included on the jury might be left unaware whether chance or judgment had led to his or her exclusion" (Alschuler, "The Supreme Court and the Jury," 207).

68. See *Apodaca v. Oregon*, 406 U.S. 404 (1972).

69. Jacob Tanzer, "Unanimity Isn't Human Nature," *Los Angeles Times*, August 18, 1995, B9. At present, three states employ nonunanimous decision rules in some criminal trials, although all require unanimity in murder cases. See Margo Hunter, *Improving the Jury System: Nonunanimous Verdicts* (San Francisco: Hastings College of Law, Public Law Research Institute Report, 1996), accessed July 22, 2000, available from http://www.uchastings.edu/plri, Internet.

70. Tanzer, "Unanimity Isn't Human Nature," B9.

71. Akhil Reed Amar, "The Common Touch," review of *Getting Away with Murder* by Susan Estrich, *New York Times [Book Review]*, March 29, 1998, 24.

72. A recent bill calling for nonunanimous criminal verdicts is S.32, introduced in the U.S. Senate by Strom Thurmond (Republican–South Carolina) in the 106th Congress (1999). Judge Eugene Sullivan and professor Akhil Reed Amar report on a debate held in Washington, D.C., in which an audience of notables heard arguments for and against various jury reforms based on the English legal system. Members of the audience voted on each proposed reform. The results have no political significance, but for the record, the audience preferred the English system of majority verdicts over the unanimous verdict requirement by a vote of 55-34. Eugene R. Sullivan and Akhil Reed Amar, "Jury Reform in America—A Return to the Old Country," *American Criminal Law Review* 33, no. 4 (Summer 1996):1141. See also, Akhil Reed Amar, "Reinventing Juries: Ten Suggested Reforms," *University of California at Davis Law Review* vol 28 (1995): 1178. Another line of support for nonunanimous verdicts is offered in Timothy Feddersen and Wolfgang Pesendorfer, "Convicting the Innocent: The Inferiority of Unanimous Jury Verdicts Under Strategic Voting," *American Political Science Review* 92, no. 1 (March 1998): 23.

73. Hans and Vidmar, *Judging the Jury*, 175.

74. Akhil Reed Amar and Vikram David Amar, "Unlocking the Jury Box," *Policy Review* (May–June 1996): 38, accessed November 9, 1999, available from http://www.infrotrac.com, Internet.

75. Ibid.

76. Linda Greenhouse, "Justices Narrowly Resolve Dispute on Jury Instruction," *New York Times*, January 20, 2000, A14.

77. Ibid.

78. *Weeks v. Angelone*, 528 U.S. 225, 234 (2000). Relevant scholarly studies include J. Alexander Tanford, "The Law and Psychology of Jury Instructions," in *Law and Psychology: The Broadening of the Discipline*, edited by James R.P. Ogloff (Durham, North Carolina: Carolina Academic Press, 1992), 305; Amiram Elwork and Bruce D. Sales, "Jury Instructions," in *The Psychology of Evidence*

and Trial Procedure, ed. Saul M. Kassin and Lawrence S. Wrightsman (Beverly Hills, California: Sage, 1985), 280.

79. *You, the Jury: Kentucky Juror Handbook* [Online] accessed July 25, 2000, available from http://www.aoc.state.ky.us/publications/youtheju.htm, Internet. Similar messages are delivered to jurors in most state and federal courts.

80. In several jurisdictions, reforms have been implemented during the past decade, and in many more, changes are under consideration. In this section, we describe the predicament of jurors in locales operating under traditional procedures.

81. Judge B. Michael Dann, quoted in Barbara Bradley, "Juries and Justice: Is the System Obsolete?" *Insight on the News*, April 24, 1995, accessed September 13, 1999, available from http://www.infotrac.com, Internet. Professors Akhil Reed Amar and Vikram David Amar suggest that "juries today are often criticized for reaching foolish decisions. But it's not all their fault. . . . Over the years, the court professionals have conspired to strip jurors of their ability to evaluate the facts. Running the courtroom to maximize their own convenience, they often have slighted the jury's legitimate needs to understand its role, the law, and the facts." Amar and Amar, "Unlocking the Jury Box."

82. Judge B. Michael Dann, quoted in Donald C. Dilworth, "Waking up Jurors, Shaking up Courts," *Trial* (July 1997), 20, accessed November 9, 1999, available from http//:www.infotrac.com, Internet.

83. Ibid.

84. Andrew Blum, "Jury System Undergoes Patchwork Remodeling," *National Law Journal*, January 23, 1996, A1. See also, Douglas G. Smith, "The Historical and Constitutional Contexts of Jury Reform," *Hofstra Law Review* 25, no. 2 (1996): 377.

85. See, for example, Paula L. Hannaford and G. Thomas Munsterman, "Beyond Note Taking: Innovations in Jury Reform," *Trial* (July 1997), 48; Donald C. Dilworth, "Arizona Commission Proposes Far-reaching Changes to Jury Procedures," *Trial* (February 1995), 17; Donald C. Dilworth, "California Jury Commission Calls for Smaller Panels, More Involved Jurors," *Trial* (August 1996), 72; Julie Gannon Shoop, "ABA Section Says Jury Reforms Should Be Standard Practice; ATLA Criticizes Proposals," *Trial* (February 1998), 86. The preceding articles were accessed on November 9, 1999, available from http://www.infotrac.com, Internet. See also David Rohde, "Jury Duty Loses Some Sting in Manhattan," *New York Times*, August 27, 1998, B1; David Rohde, "Do Diplomas Make Jurors Any Better? Maybe Not," *New York Times*, April 10, 2000, B1; Julia Vitullo-Martin and Michael Rothenberg, "Arizona Leads the Way in Jury Reform," *Bridge News*, February 17, 1997, accessed December 19, 1999, available from http://www.vera.org, Internet; Jeff Herman, "Ending the U.S. Jury System Circus," *USA Today* magazine (September 1997), 26; Jeff Herman, "Justice Gone Awry? How to Get the U.S. Jury System Back on Track," *Vital Speeches*, December 1, 1996, 110; Hope Viner Samborn, "Changing the Jury Tool Box," *ABA Journal* (December 1977), 22–23; Henry Gottlieb, "The Day the Jurors Took Over," *New Jersey Law Journal*, February 5, 2001, 1.

86. Adler, *The Jury*, 231–232.

87. See Richard Posner, "Juries on Trial," *Commentary* (March 1995), 49, accessed November 9, 1999, available from http://www.infotrac.com, Internet. Responding to some proposals for reform, Posner explains: "Sensible as they are, I do not think these reforms would have seismic effects. The reason is that they have been made, to a great extent, in the federal courts already. Though practice differs from judge to judge, I have always permitted jurors to take notes and ask questions; I have tried to tell them about the case as it proceeds; I have rewritten the instructions they receive about the law, to eliminate all jargon; I have given them copies of the instructions to take into the jury room for their deliberations, rather than just reading the instructions to them aloud . . . Other fed-

eral trial judges do even more than I do to facilitate the jury's performance of its task. That performance, nevertheless, too often remains problematic." See also, Paula L. Hannaford, Valerie P. Hans, and G. Thomas Munsterman, "Permitting Jury Discussions During Trial: Impact of the Arizona Reform," *Law and Human Behavior* 24, no. 3 (June 2000): 359. They conclude: "The results of the field experiment fulfill neither the fondest hopes nor the worst nightmares of supporters and critics" of the Arizona reforms (ibid., 377).

88. Ellen Chilton and Patricia Henley, *Improving the Jury System—Jury Instructions: Helping Jurors Understand the Evidence and the Law* (San Francisco: Hastings College of Law, Public Law Research Institute Report, 1996), accessed July 22, 2000, available from http://www.uchastings.edu/plri,Internet. This report summarizes advantages and disadvantages associated with three proposed reforms: juror questions, predeliberation discussions, and improvement of judicial instructions. See also, Hope Viner Samborn, "Can We Talk? Preliminary Study Shows Jurors Favor New Rule Allowing Discussion of Evidence During Trials," *ABA Journal* (December 1997), 23.

89. See Irving L. Janis, "Groupthink," in *Political Psychology*, edited by Neil J. Kressel (New York: Paragon, 1993), 360; Irving L. Janis, *Victims of Groupthink* (Hopewell, New Jersey: Houghton Mifflin, 1972).

90. Jan Hoffman, "Disorder in the Court, and How to Avoid It," *New York Times*, December 21, 1997, sec. 4, 5.

91. The literature on jury nullification is large. For brief summaries, see Larry Dodge, "Juries Should Be Informed of Their Right to Nullify the Law," in *The Jury System*, edited by M.E. Williams (San Diego: Greenhaven Press, 1997), 51; Mark S. Pullam, "Jury Nullification Should Not Be Allowed," in *The Jury System*, 59; I.A. Horowitz and T.E. Willging, "Changing Views of Jury Power: The Nullification Debate," *Law and Human Behavior* 15, no. 2 (1991): 165; Andrew D. Leipold, "Jury Nullification: A Perversion of Justice?" *USA Today* (Magazine) 126 (September 1997): 30, accessed November 9, 1999, available from http://www.infotrac.com, Internet.

92. Lysander Spooner, *An Essay on the Trial by Jury* (1852), section 1, accessed June 12, 2000, available from http://www.geocities.com/Heartland/7394/lysander.html, Internet.

93. Abramson, *We, the Jury*, 95.

94. Paul Butler, "Black Jurors: Right to Acquit," *Harper's Magazine* (December 1995), 11, accessed November 9, 1999, available from http://www.infotrac.com, Internet (article adapted from Paul Butler, "Racially Based Jury Nullification: Black Power in the Criminal Justice System," *Yale Law Journal* 105 [December 1995]: 677).

95. Butler, "Black Jurors."

96. See Randall Kennedy, *Race, Crime, and the Law*, 295.

97. Alexander Hamilton, "Federalist No. 83," in *The Federalist Papers*, 2nd ed., edited by Roy P. Fairfield (Baltimore: Johns Hopkins University Press, 1981, originally published in 1788), 257–258.

INDEX

Keller, Florence, 78, 81, 87, 155–157
Kennedy, Patrick, 70
Kennedy, Randall, 171–172, 204, 214
Kennedy, Ted, 70
Key-man system, 174
Kidd, John, 4–5, 7, 14
Kindler, James M., 203
King, John William, 176–177, 178, 276n26
King, Rodney, 9, 93, 178–180, 185, 193, 195, 204
Kissinger, Henry, 61
K-Mart, 119–120
Krauss, Elissa, 31, 125–127, 286n43
Krooth, Richard, 275n17
Kuby, Ron, 202

Ladmirault, Lula, 3, 4
Laguzza, Ross, 85, 268n10
Lawyer. *See* Attorney(s)
Legal Attitudes Questionnaire, 111
Leggett, Ellen L., 121–122, 123, 265n85
Leone, Gerard, 29–30, 33, 38, 56
Lewis, Elaine, 159–160
Lies, detection of, 96–98, 211, 257n20
The Litigation Edge, 91, 92
Litigation Sciences, 77, 84–85
Little, Joan, 62–63, 82–83
Loan Little trial, 62–63, 82–83
Locke, John, 100
Los Angeles Times, poll by, 189
Louima, Abner, 202
Lubet, Steven, 271n51
Lynch, Gerald, 203
Lynch, Patrick J., 196

MacCoun, Robert J., 260n42
Mackenzie, Jerold, 119, 264–265n81
Maddox, Alton, 17, 40, 43, 44, 46, 47, 49, 51, 52, 55, 250–251n97
  Steven Pagones's lawsuit against. *See* Pagones defamation suit
Maddox, Lester, 283n8
Maddox, Roland, 116
Magna Carta, 237

Malice, actual, 42
Manzanares, Stevie, 166–167
Marist College Institute for Public Opinion poll, 250–251n97
Marshall, John, 210, 283n6
Marshall, Thurgood, 213
Mason, C. Vernon, 17, 40, 41, 43, 44, 46, 47, 49, 52, 55, 250–251n97
  Steven Pagones's lawsuit against. *See* Pagones defamation suit
Matlon, Ronald, 124–125
Matthew Eappen murder trial, 9, 17, 23–38
  defense gamble in, 24–26, 28–29, 35
  judge's controversial action following, 27–28, 34–38
  posttrial comments by jurors and, 25–26, 28, 35–36
  sentence in, 27, 36, 38
  trial consultants and, 22–23, 31–33, 56
  verdict in, 24–26, 27, 36, 38
McCall, H. Carl, 194
McConahay, John, 63–64
McCracken, Samuel, 130–131
McCurley, Mike, 114
McDonalds's hot coffee case, 9
McEvoy, Pat, 220, 285n33
MCI antitrust lawsuit, 14–15, 54
McMahon, Jack, 182–184, 277n42, 277n43, 277n45
McMartin preschool cases, 93
McWilliams, Robert H., 167
Men Who Beat the Men Who Love Them (Island), 69
Menendez brothers, 9
Miller Brewing Company, 119
Minick, Robert, 140
Mitchell, John, 64
Mock juror. *See* Focus groups; Mock trial
Mock trial, 5–6, 31–32, 55, 56, 58, 65, 82, 103–104, 145–146, 147–148, 154, 158, 218, 219, 231–232, 259–260n40
Money, prospective jurors' thinking about, 124